DATE DUE

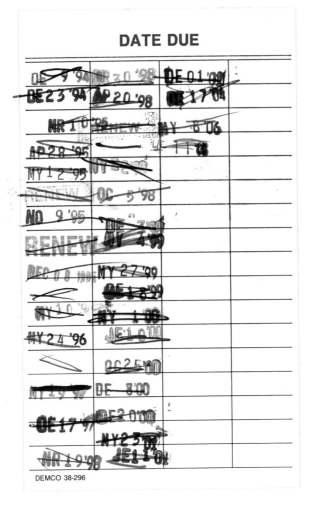

The Politics of Virtue

......

The Politics
of Virtue

Is Abortion Debatable?

. . . .

Elizabeth Mensch & Alan Freeman

Duke University Press

Durham and London

1993

Printed in the United States of America on acid-free paper ∞

Typeset in Joanna by Tseng Information Systems

Library of Congress Cataloging-in-Publication Data

appear on the last printed page of this book.

Originally published as a special supplement,

"The Politics of Virtue: Animals, Theology, and Abortion,"

Georgia Law Review 25, no. 4 (1991).

Contents

......

It is easy also to understand why *protest* becomes a distinctive moral feature of the modern age and why *indignation* is a predominant modern emotion. . . . [P]rotest is . . . that negative phenomenon which characteristically occurs as a reaction to the alleged invasion of someone's *rights* in the name of someone else's utility. The self-assertive shrillness of protest arises because the facts of incommensurability ensure that protestors can never win an *argument*; the indignant self-righteousness of protest arises because the facts of incommensurability ensure equally that the protestors can never lose an argument either. Hence the *utterance* of protest is characteristically addressed to those who already share the protestors' premises. The effects of incommensurability ensure that protestors rarely have anyone else to talk to but themselves. This is not to say that protest cannot be effective; it is to say that it cannot be *rationally* effective and that its dominant modes of expression give evidence of a certain perhaps unconscious awareness of this.

—Alasdair MacIntyre, *After Virtue*

Preface

......

We are extremely grateful to the many friends and colleagues who have taken the time to read our lengthy manuscript. For reactions ranging from detailed critical evaluations to warm words of encouragement, thanks to Gregory Alexander, Michael Ariens, Milner Ball, Guyora Binder, Beth Buckley, Ruth Colker, Walter Dellinger, Tom Disare, Lucinda Finley, Peter Gabel, Marjorie Girth, Mary Ann Glendon, Trina Grillo, George Hezel, Christopher Lasch, Howard Lesnick, Isabel Marcus, Michael McConnell, William McLoughlin, Andrew McThenia, Gary Peller, Michael Perry, Stephanie Phillips, Richard Posner, Jack Schlegel, Bill Simon, William Van Alstyne, Howard Vogel, Elizabeth Warren, Gerald Wetlaufer, Joan Williams, and Steven Winter.

From this long list we must single out two names—Ruth Colker, whose invitation to us to speak at Tulane Law School on the abortion issue marked the origin of this project, and Jack Schlegel, whose detailed, careful, and accurate editorial review of the entire manuscript, both before and after revision for this book, went far beyond the usual norms of collegiality.

We are also grateful to the editors and staff of the *Georgia Law Review*, who published an earlier version of this book as their entire Spring 1991 issue (vol. 25, no. 4) and provided us with patience and support during the long initial phase of this project.

As the project evolved, we were fortunate to have opportunities for presentation and discussion with colleagues and students at a SUNY/Buffalo Faculty Forum in October 1989, at Tulane Law School in November 1989, at Duke Law School in January 1991, and at the Fourth Annual Symposium on Law, Religion, and Ethics at Hamline Law School in October 1991. We are especially grateful to Tulane, Duke, and Hamline for supporting our travel on those occasions.

Locally, we have benefited from the services of our hardworking research assistants, Leslie Darman and Oren Zeve, without whose efforts the revisions for this book would never have been achieved on schedule. Similarly central to this enterprise is Lois Stutzman, whose word processor skills are no less than magical.

We should also note that we have received no extraordinary financial support for this project in the form of leaves, grants, or the like, from either our own or any other institution.

Finally, we are most grateful to our parents, Florence Freeman, Julius Freeman, and Nancy Schofield, and our children, Jonathan Mensch, Jennifer Freeman, Joshua Mensch, James Freeman, and Jeremy Freeman. The costs of these endeavors are inevitably absorbed by those we love the most.

Introduction

......

I f protest, so aptly characterized by Alasdair MacIntyre, has become our characteristic form of moral discourse, abortion is its paradigmatic subject. As we began this book, in the fall of 1990, a new Supreme Court justice faced review by the U.S. Senate; media coverage suggested that the abortion issue counted above all in assessing the fitness of the nominee.[1] More recently, in the summer of 1992 that same Supreme Court justice, David Souter, cast a decisive vote reaffirming the Court's landmark abortion decision, *Roe v. Wade*,[2] while simultaneously upholding restrictions on access to the procedure. When that decision, *Casey v. Planned Parenthood of Southeastern Pennsylvania*,[3] was announced, neither pro-choicers nor pro-lifers were satisfied. Within minutes, both sides appeared on television to denounce the outcome.

The *Wall Street Journal* has called abortion "an issue that has disconnected itself from the normal workings of the U.S. political system. . . . The combatants on both sides have gone off like the fighter ships in 'Star Wars' to wage a death struggle out among the asteroids."[4] The rhetoric is accordingly extreme. Those who are "pro-life," who probably number no more than one-fourth of the population, regard their opponents as actual or potential murderers; those who are "pro-choice," who also probably number no more than one-fourth of the population, regard their opponents as violating the fundamental human rights of women.[5] In between lies a confused and ambivalent middle. For sociologists Peter and Brigitte Berger, "the abortion issue reveals a highly significant rupture in the moral fabric."[6] In the absence of consensus, one finds a "moral pluralism" that is mutually and contemptuously intolerant.

Abortion has been called the "nation's most divisive cultural issue since

Prohibition."[7] For sociologist James Hunter, it serves to confirm, as does no other issue, the existence of a "culture war."[8] Lacking any common moral ground, American antagonists typically move to seize the coercive force of the law. As the Bergers observe:

> [T]his moral difference touches directly on an important area of actual conduct in social life, therefore demands legal regulation, and therefore makes it very difficult for people amicably to "agree to disagree." . . . It is only logical, then, that each side seeks the coercive support of state power—the "pro-choice" side no less than the "pro-life" side. . . . The law . . . may continue to uphold abortion against those who consider it murder, deepening their alienation from the society; or the law may reverse itself and proscribe abortion once again, thereby creating a new explosion of "crime" for which the prohibition era provides a good preview. A sociologist must believe that "victory" would be Pyrrhic in either case.[9]

That the abortion issue has become intractable, as observed by the Bergers, is not to say that it must be so, or that it has always been so. Some seem to have an investment in proclaiming and perpetuating its intractability, as does Laurence Tribe in his book, *Abortion: The Clash of Absolutes*,[10] which serves to advance his implicit agenda in favor of the pro-choice status quo exemplified by *Roe v. Wade*. In contrast, others claim that *Roe v. Wade* is itself a compromise between the extremes,[11] or that despite rhetorical excess, practical compromise is already existent and widespread, belying the bleakness of the debate.[12] We are not persuaded on this issue by either the characterization "inevitable intractability" or "*Roe* as successful compromise." Watching the battles among the asteroids, we find it hard to believe that this is the best result we could have hoped for.

Most people who write about this subject do so to shore up agendas that are strongly pro-choice[13] or strongly pro-life.[14] We therefore feel obliged to disclose our own somewhat odd agenda. In teaching a course in environmental ethics, including issues of human/animal relationship, we were forced to confront the limits of our conventional sources of moral discourse, like utilitarianism or Kantian individualism. We gradually concluded that discussion of our relationship to animals and nature could be enriched through appeal to theological sources.[15] While the hard questions of environmental ethics are not resolved by recourse to theology, they do become more amenable to nuanced and sensitive treatment, especially given the theological commitment to humility. When asked by a colleague to apply those accumulated insights to the abortion question, our immediate reaction was dismay. ("Not *that* subject. Never!") Despite our reluctance, however, we could not forever pretend that the two issues were unrelated. Hence, this book.

Given the potential relevance of personal experience to narrative point of view,[16] we should admit that our own history in relation to abortion is one of almost perfect irresponsibility, of the kind that absolutely precludes self-righteousness. We have both had more than one firsthand experience of abortion, including illegal abortion, although in Alan's case the experience was, necessarily, only that of the "responsible other." We also have, between us, five children (outrageous, from an environmental perspective), and we have never had reason to consider the especially difficult choice of late abortion. We have also been identified with the left/liberal side of law and politics, a setting in which unquestioning adherence to the pro-choice position has seemed obligatory. For that reason we may have tried especially hard to understand the pro-life side of this debate.

Both of us grew up in cultural settings that were starkly secular, where religion played a role that was formal and conventional at most. Also, we were teenagers in the late 1950s and early 1960s, a time when the stifling conventions of 1950s morality (including gender roles) were being rejected, a rejection in which we participated with enthusiasm. We understand our history may seem alien to those who experience life as regularly mediated by religious tradition. Although we are not affiliated with any particular religious tradition, we have for some time been questioning the adequacy of a wholly secular understanding of the world, and rethinking as well the priority assigned by the culture of the 1960s to freedom of lifestyle. Admittedly, that is a reevaluation more comfortably undertaken in middle age, when the appeal of the unconventional begins to wane.

Our goal is not to advance one side or the other in the abortion debate, but rather to explore whether we are necessarily stuck with the grim and destructive fact of moral incommensurability.[17] There is some urgency to this question. We cannot, of course, revise two decades of ugly and hostile abortion politics; yet we might prefer to avoid its repetition as we confront other increasingly difficult moral problems. Perhaps, for example, we can do better than simply running to our respective barricades to show whether we choose owls or people. With that possibility of "better" in mind, we move back in time, to the period before *Roe*, in an effort to recapture the context in which the moral/theological debate about abortion was unfolding. That examination leaves us with the conviction that it might have been otherwise—although we hasten to emphasize the "might." In the midst of a confused period for American churches, especially acute in the 1960s, serious theologians were nevertheless, on *ethical grounds*, moving toward a position of compromise as to the particular moral (as well as legal) obligation to be associated with the sanctity of fetal life.

The effect of *Roe*'s "rights" formulation of the issue was to render that moral dialogue abruptly irrelevant for lawmaking purposes. Whatever the benefits of *Roe*, in lifting out of the legislative arena a divisive moral problem deeply affecting women's lives, its costs became all too quickly apparent. People who were deeply troubled by the moral/religious implications of an absolute right to abortion—even throughout the second trimester of pregnancy—became hardened absolutists in their opposition to all abortion; any compromise became more, not less, unthinkable. Moreover, so long as *Roe* seemed securely in place, that absolutism too easily took on the character of moral highground at no political cost, with the fanciful Republican call, for example, for a "human life amendment" to the Constitution. Undeniably, some Republican politicians learned to channel the outrage sparked by *Roe* into religious support for their own agendas. The pro-choice side, meanwhile, could too easily employ a close-out "rights" and "choice" rhetoric in an aggressive refusal to engage in moral discourse altogether. The result was an ever-deepening cultural divide.

Since we are investigating the possibility of genuine public moral debate on this issue, we refuse to consider either the pro-choice or pro-life position as categorically correct. With respect to the former, we do not think that the only acceptable feminist position is unswerving support for *Roe v. Wade*. There are many women, some of whom identify themselves as feminists, who are nevertheless on the pro-life side.[18] Moreover, in saying that there is a debatable moral issue with respect to abortion, we are acknowledging that there is an issue about fetal life that cannot be dismissed by simply invoking "reproductive freedom."[19] Women, even more than men, do take seriously moral and theological issues. Three-fourths of American women report that they consider religious faith the most important influence on their lives.[20] Moreover, even apart from moral/theological issues, the particular rhetoric of "privacy" and "choice" may represent an effort to universalize a particular and class-based instance of feminism.[21]

With respect to the pro-life side, we reject the persuasive power of the theological close-out. If theological discourse has a place in public moral debate, it cannot be of the variety, "This is what God says, so shut up and don't question me about it." That position, too, is no more than a renewed invitation to the barricaded scene of the protest. By claiming a privileged access to absolute moral truth, such close-outs show a prideful disdain for the complexity of ethical judgment and for the genuine moral concerns of those who may disagree but who are still open to dialogue. If theological argument is to play a valuable role in public debate, it must appeal not to privileged authority but to some version of the common good, as Catholic tradition has in fact recognized.[22] Moreover, even while seeking to be universal rather than sectarian, it must do so in the face of a pluralist reality that may render universalism impossible, a problem that lies at the heart of the church/state dilemma.

We are, of course, a long way from being able to publicly discuss the common good. Consensus on some issues is no substitute for substantive moral dialogue, for when consensus breaks down we have nothing to appeal to but rampant and incommensurable subjectivity. Such is the case with abortion. The alchemical fantasy of liberalism—that process can turn itself into substance[23]—is belied by the reality of conflict. The larger question is whether we can recover a meaningful public moral vocabulary. Thus, the issue of abortion quickly becomes one of substantive morality in post-Enlightenment Western culture: is there any substantive space between the incoherence of Kantian formalism and the grim reality of Nietzschean nihilism?[24] Can a revival of theological traditions, which, after all, serve to mediate our relationship with death itself and are at once seemingly moribund and surprisingly vital,[25] serve such an enterprise?

Since much of the pro-life side of the abortion debate is couched in theological terms, we have tried to understand abortion as a theological issue, principally a Christian one[26] (given the public rhetoric). Our focus .is historical: we sought to situate the particular abortion issue in the larger setting of the substantive and institutional role of theology in fashioning or influencing American public morality, especially in the period since World War II. We have made every effort to comprehend these theological issues in their own terms; the result is a discourse that may well be alien and forbidding to many readers. We hope you will bear with us in the service of replacing stark incommensurability with something closer to mutually respectful dialogue.

We believe that the abortion controversy in the United States can best be understood as emerging from a historical context in which there had been moral consensus, even certainty, about the evil of Nazism and the virtue of the civil rights movement. Our opening chapter employs that context to offer a frame and point of reference for the historical chapters that follow. Both abortion and animals/nature are instances of confusion about the very meaning of membership in moral community—who is in and who is out. The discomfort induced by these issues is a measure of their distance from the two idealized historical models, as is the frequent rhetorical appeal to those models by both sides of both issues. Similar in their seeming intractability, both issues lead quickly to hard questions of theology and the meaning of the "natural."

The remainder of the book will focus primarily on abortion, since the narrative account of animals/nature as a moral/political issue is a tale of the future. Our history begins with a close look at two important moral traditions that were concerned with their own relationship to the potential or actual threat of Nazism. The first of these is the natural law tradition, associated primarily with Catholicism, which saw a period of vigorous revival in the post-World War II American legal culture (especially in a journal called *Natural Law Forum*). The second is the Protestant ethical tradition associated with Karl Barth and Dietrich Bonhoeffer, who were, respectively, expelled and executed by the Nazis for espousing a theology that formed the only institutional religious challenge to the Third Reich. We also take into account the implications of both moral traditions with respect to the abortion issue.

Succeeding chapters detail the institutional setting of religion and morality in the United States in the 1960s, focusing on the powerful impact of the civil rights movement, which drew on the legacy of both the natural law tradition and the Bonhoeffer example of responsible ethical action in the political sphere. The same period saw the rise of conservative Protestant evangelicalism, which became an important source of pro-life support, and the decline of mainline Protestantism, which had once played a significant moral/institutional role in the United States but was becoming increasingly "secularized" to the point of losing its distinctive theological voice.

A pair of strikingly different public conferences on abortion held in 1967 and 1968 illustrate the rapid transformation of the abortion debate. A secular version of the issue triumphed, leading to the constitutionalization of abortion rights under the rubric of privacy. Our final chapter reflects on possibilities for compromise that were lost in that process and asks whether such possibilities still exist.

1

Evil, Good, and Beyond

......

Once we knew the difference between evil and good. The period spanning the 1950s was framed by dramatic instances of each: Nazism as it began, and the civil rights movement as it closed. We have, at least in retrospect, unequivocally named those two cultural images as perfect examples of villainy, on the one hand, and virtue on the other. Their evocative power is with us still.

Each, in its extremity, worked a convergence of law, theology, and politics, creating a sense of moral appropriateness that challenged all inconsistent premises and practices. In law, nothing short of an unprecedented and retroactively applied accountability for "crimes against humanity" was sufficient as a response to Nazism, despite overwhelming victory at war.[1] Similarly, the moral force of the civil rights movement altered the American federal judiciary and, arguably, the structure of American federalism.[2] Theologians, meanwhile, were haunted by the fear that their church's doctrine and practice had not been sufficient to resist the Nazis and would not be able to counter the next cultural example of unambiguous evil. Civil rights then became the limiting case against inaction in the worldly sphere, challenging the doctrinal basis of all compelled otherworldliness.[3]

The abortion debate emerged during a period when images of both Nazism and early civil rights activists still preoccupied moral and political thought. That context shaped the way in which the abortion debate unfolded, and it helps to explain why the debate has assumed such overriding importance in American life. A brief, evocative look at the significance of Nazism and the early civil rights movement may suggest their persistent power.[4]

Nazis were the ultimate affront to the presumptuous complacency of Western culture, an affront that was political, moral, and ultimately theological. How could the highest and most refined of cultures endorse grotesque barbarism and participate with emotional fervor in apparently premodern ritualistic evil?[5] Nazi symbols—giant swastikas, black uniforms, death's head insignias, book burnings, Adolf Hitler as revered supreme leader—all stand as terrifying reminders. The Nazis not only appealed to an irrational, fanatic, premodern sensibility, but they also, ironically, inverted legality, rationality, and science itself in pursuit of their agendas. Thus, legality became a finely tuned engine of bureaucratic oppression, while science supplied military might, gas chambers and ovens, and experiments on human beings so unspeakable that serious moral opposition still remains to studying the results for humane purposes. Even a long and respected tradition of Christian theology in Germany found itself yielding institutionally, almost without exception, to political idolatry in subservience to the German state.[6]

Having met Nazi evil, we remain forever culturally (and personally) unsettled. When are we responsible? When must we take a stand? One might try to pretend that the Nazis were sui generis, a unique case of tribalism run rampant, produced by the intersection of peculiarly decadent German sensibilities and post-World War I frustrations. Whatever truth lies in that account, the appeal to utter specificity is never adequate. Genocide in Western history is not uniquely German. European Americans must reckon with their own history in relation to Native Americans; so too must the English in relation to their history with the Irish, the French in relation to the Algerians, etc. The point is not to induce self-loathing, but to remind us of our own cultural capacity for evil, not easily distinguished, categorically, from that of the Nazis. Meanwhile, Freudianism, at its most cautionary, had alerted Americans to dark impulses lurking within the human psyche. Lest we think it could never happen here, the Milgram experiments of the 1960s only confirmed the worst of earlier fears.[7]

Despite those troubling but more ambiguous parallels, to students of evil the Nazis offer a kind of "naked singularity" not unlike that envisioned by cosmologists to describe occasions when otherwise applicable laws of nature do not apply. The civil rights movement does the same for students of good. We speak here not of the later discordant times of the Black Muslims and Malcolm X, black power, urban disorder, or affirmative action, but of the time of moral clarity, of *Brown v. Board of Education*, Rosa Parks, the young Martin Luther King, Jr., the Great March on Washington, D.C., of 1963, and the subsequent Birmingham bombing deaths.

Americans in the very process of defeating Nazism were reminded in 1944 by Swedish economist Gunnar Myrdal of their own national shame—the pervasive structure of legal and social apartheid directed at black Americans.[8] In fact, most Soviet propaganda in the early cold war period was directed to exposing America's domestic racial oppression to the world.[9] The civil rights movement, especially after 1954, offered an occasion for national redemption from that shame, as the Civil War, in Lincoln's biblical imagery, had offered redemption from the sin of slavery. Myrdal had taught us of a critical gap between the (fundamentally good) American creed and our (bad but alterable) racist behaviors. Thus, the nightly news, as it depicted the arduous struggles of the early civil rights movement in the South, offered an ongoing morality play. Bull Connor and Sheriff Jim Clark, with their dogs and fire hoses and cattle prods, were pitted against decent, peaceful, God-fearing Americans—including children—who were vindicating their basic constitutional rights, and thereby vindicating our own belief in human dignity.

Nazism and civil rights triggered historical responses, intellectual and institutional, that converged in the divisive contemporary issue of abortion. For the moment, however, our focus is on the peculiar political power of the two images. To name one's opponent a Nazi, with any credibility, is to suspend the usual rules of discursive engagement. The Nazi is denied respect, subjected to name-calling, vulnerable to extralegal tactics, and must be opposed by all persons of conscience and good will. Even the usual legal protections may be unavailable to those who take Nazi positions, as many argued in the famous case of the American Nazis' planned parade in Skokie, Illinois, in 1977, and others continue to argue with respect to "hate" speech.[10] Similarly, if inversely, to appropriate to one's cause the aura of the civil rights movement is to demand the unquestioning allegiance of people of goodwill and conscience, to call for a vigorous and singular activism. That activism may include civil disobedience or other extralegal activity, for even formally legitimate legal obstacles are rendered fundamentally illegal. The net effect is to elevate one's cause to a politics of virtue rather than just self-interest.

However powerful these images remain, the moral certainty that once permitted us to assign virtue or villainy to their respective realities has surely unraveled. Today, the characteristic form of public moral dialogue is the protest, with each side ready to display placards, deploy angry, close-out rhetoric, and luxuriate in complacent ownership of moral truth. In that divisive process, the imagery of Nazis and the civil rights movement often informs the content of debate, as if we long to recapture the moral certainty that allows us to name evil or good when it appears.

The abortion debate provides a dramatic illustration. Notably, by way of comparison, so does the issue of animal rights, which is true despite the usual opposition of pro-life activists and animal (and, often, environmental) activists. The abortion and animal issues are, in fact, strikingly similar, for each raises troubling questions about the reach of community and human responsibility.

Similarities of rhetoric and image abound. In fact, one discovers that proponents of both sides of both issues (abortion and animals) regularly resort to civil rights and Nazi images to affirm the virtue of their own side and reveal the villainy of the other. Thus, for pro-life activists, "[T]oday's medical abortionists are doing the same thing to the unwanted unborn as the Nazis did to their victims. . . ."[11] If the doctors are Nazi executioners, then unborn victims can be identified with Holocaust victims, especially children. Thus, in pro-life literature, photographs of discarded fetuses are shown next to photographs of bodies from concentration camps.[12] This graphic portrayal of innocent sacrificial victims, of course, also plays on deeply imbedded Christian cultural themes, made more explicit when, as some demonstrators have done, infant dolls are carried on huge wooden crosses.[13] The Nazi Holocaust inevitably represented for Christians a dramatic and troubling reversal of complacent Christian imagery. Accustomed to describing an innocent Christ handed over by Jews for crucifixion, Christians instead witnessed innocent Jews slaughtered in a supposedly Christian culture, with little Christian resistance. From within their own tradition, American Christians could not doubt that Christ's presence would have been with and among his fellow Jews in Germany, not with the indifferent or murderous Christians. That recognition creates an imperative to identify the true sacrificial victim and to respond with loving and even self-sacrificial, culture-defying concern rather than with the indifference of the "good German." For the pro-life side, fetuses are not just victims, but also persons awaiting legal recognition of their true personhood, like slaves before the Civil War: "[T]his is not the first time our country has been divided by a Supreme Court decision that denied the value of human lives. The Dred Scott decision of 1857 was not overturned in a day, or a year, or even a decade."[14] Pro-life extremists (e.g., Operation Rescue) explicitly analogize themselves to civil rights demonstrators of the 1950s and 60s, adopting the tactics of their predecessors (including the use of child demonstrators), and legitimizing their willingness to test the bounds of legality. Even some members of the U.S. Supreme Court analogize Roe v. Wade to the infamous decision in Plessy v. Ferguson (which upheld compulsory segregation) to justify the immediate overruling of Roe as illegitimate precedent.[15]

In parallel fashion, the pro-choice side also employs Nazi imagery to characterize opponents. Thus, religious fundamentalists who are pro-life activists are considered instances of the "authoritarian" personality, a category developed by post-World War II psychologists to recast adherence to Nazism as a social (even medical) pathology.[16] Pro-life protest tactics are then implicitly likened to those of Hitler's SA (Brown Shirts) and not to those of Martin Luther King, Jr. James Hunter describes the irony of an Orthodox rabbi being accused of standing with Nazis because he demonstrated with pro-life evangelicals and Catholics; and recently pro-life literature has been likened to that of neo-Nazis.[17] The pro-choice civil rights claim is that *Roe v. Wade* is not analogous to *Plessy v. Ferguson*, but instead of equal stature to the most ethically legitimate of all Supreme Court cases, *Brown v. Board of Education*. To invoke *Brown* is to assert invulnerable moral truth; to discard it on account of faltering consensus or political expediency is implicitly obscene. Just as *Brown* relieved black Americans from oppression rooted in (racial) prejudice, so *Roe* relieved American women from oppression rooted in (sexist) religious prejudice (especially Catholic, but later Protestant fundamentalist as well). *Roe* thus represents the legal recognition of female personhood, as against a sexism that attempts women's systematic subordination. Those seeking entry to abortion clinics are recast by this imagery as the students seeking to vindicate their personhood rights by gaining attendance at previously all-white schools in the South in the 50s and 60s. A *New York Times* story on the Operation Rescue activities in Kansas is headlined, "Little Rock, 1957. Wichita, 1991,"[18] with the story devoted to the explicit analogy. Even a federal district judge analogized the use of cameras and videotaping equipment by pro-life protestors to the use of clubs and attack dogs by segregationists.[19] While conceding the difference in degree of physical threat, he nevertheless deemed the "camera, like the attack dog," as a "tool used by defendants to intimidate women from exercising their constitutional rights."

Animal rights activists, as do their pro-life counterparts on abortion, liken their opponents to Nazis. Philosopher (and guru of the animal rights movement) Peter Singer explicitly analogizes animal experimentation to the grotesque practices in Nazi concentration camps. Singer finds "striking" the parallels between the attitude of the Nazi doctors experimenting on prisoners and that of "experimenters toward animals."[20] The analogy goes beyond experiments. When we sponsored for our seminar a showing of the Frederick Wiseman documentary film *Meat*, a seemingly matter-of-fact account of procedures in a modern slaughterhouse, an animal rights activist who attended at our invitation left angrily, proclaiming the slaughterhouse workers to be "just like Nazis; they should be killed." Similarly, we have heard militant environmentalists ask derisively, when denouncing loggers for killing old-growth forests and their resident spotted owls: "Don't they have Nuremburg laws for that sort of thing?" Even Vice President Albert Gore repeatedly invokes the Nazi analogy to support his environmental agenda ("an environmental holocaust"—"an ecological Kristallnacht").[21]

Paralleling the use of pro-life fetal imagery, animal rights groups graphically depict the plight of helpless, innocent creatures sacrificed solely for the sake of commercial gain and human self-indulgence. Pictures show baby seals being clubbed to death, struggling, penned veal calves, and rabbits blinded by the Draize test (a grotesque procedure once routinely used by cosmetics companies). The cover of the December 1990 issue of The Animal's Voice is a large color photograph of an apparently still-alive monkey staring helplessly at us with a metal hoop circling its skull through which, at frequent intervals, screws have been driven directly into the monkey's flesh.[22] Inside, with appropriate warnings, are similarly gruesome pictures. The civil rights analogy is no less explicitly drawn in the case of animals. First, there was racism, then sexism, and now "speciesism,"[23] with the implicit call for an appropriately militant political response. One finds the famous proclamation by abolitionist William Lloyd Garrison, which appeared in the first issue of The Liberator, invoked as a demand for action on behalf of animal rights: "I will not equivocate, I will not excuse, I will not retreat a single inch. And I will be heard."[24]

As with pro-life activists, animal activists are viewed by their opponents as "ignorant fanatics, fascist in their sweeping demands," and "driven by fundamentalist visions."[25] They are described retreating to an absolutist fundamentalism as an antidote to moral ambiguity and relativism, thereby "reifying their own principles as ultimate Truth."[26] University researchers, given their experience as representatives of reason and scientific inquiry as against sometimes terroristic fanatics, will quickly remind us that the actual Nazis were also animal rights proponents.[27] We learn that Hitler was a vegetarian, Himmler believed in animal rights, and even that Hermann Göring in 1933 issued an order prohibiting vivisection of animals in Prussian territory, because, "To the Germans [as to animal rights activists] . . . animals are not merely creatures in the organic sense, but creatures who lead their own lives and who are endowed with perceptive faculties, who feel pain and experience joy. . . ."[28]

A common charge of opponents is that animal rightists are indifferent at best to questions of human rights and employ arguments that inevitably undercut the claim of universal human dignity that lies at the heart of the civil rights movement. Animal rights activists, for example, are easily caricatured as "one-issue" people: middle-class white women who deviate from class interest only for the sake of animals.[29] That assumed combination of fervent concern for the suffering of helpless animals with an apparent indifference to the suffering of, for example, people with serious illnesses who might be helped by animal experimentation is captured by Gordon Gekko's quip in the movie *Wall Street* that "the thing about WASPs is that they love animals, but they hate people."[30]

That both sides on both of these issues can invoke the Nazi and civil rights images is surely testament to our state of moral confusion. Both abortion and animals might be presented as case studies of MacIntyre's notion of "incommensurability." It is also the case, however, that each side, in presenting these powerful images, is grasping a partial truth in response to equally extreme opponents. Important moral issues are at stake that are not fully answered by the extreme positions on either side of either issue. Serious debate on those issues, unfortunately, is hampered by political rhetoric.

Philosopher Rosalind Hursthouse asks: "Would not one expect someone arguing against the way we slaughter animals to be rather 'pro-life' in general, and hence against abortion and infanticide?"[31] The typical answer, with few exceptions, seems to be that it is politically implausible to be both pro-animals and pro-life on the abortion question. We are speaking here not of the great muddle of people who are confused and ambivalent, but of visible activists on behalf of one or the other issue. Thus, for feminist animal rights activists, abortion is an easy issue, for rights belong to individuals, and the only relevant individuals are women and animals.[32] The fetus is just a physical appendage, defined as "a human being to be created and grown by a woman if she chooses to do so." Even cows and sows, who are individuals and have rights, should "not be forced to be pregnant against their will." The predictable response of the equally intransigent other side is that equating animals and people is nothing less than moral insanity.

Nevertheless, we believe that the two issues share much more common ground than is usually supposed. First, both pro-lifers and animal rightists deploy their imagery of the slaughter of the helpless and innocent to show that they are clearly on the side of life as against the side of death. To be sure, by graphically isolating these issues in their purity and simplicity, advocates avoid the ethically troubling fact of human responsibility for both life and death. One suspects that the real opponent is death itself—

as if by building a wall of absolute protection around fetal or animal life, one could pretend away the reality that the life of some will inevitably carry with it the death of others, that "choice" over questions of life and death is part of the human condition.

Nevertheless, those graphic images do serve as an effective antidote to a similar ploy of death avoidance by the other side on both issues. Pictures remind us that the forlorn dog in the testing laboratory does not become a "thing" merely by being called the "subject of the test" or assigned a number rather than a name. So too we are properly reminded by pro-life graphics that a fetus or embryo is in fact a developing child. We do violence to that reality (however complex its ethical implications) by denial through objectifying labels like "mere tissue" or "products of conception." Some will insist that the images appeal to "irrational" fears and anxieties; yet even philosophers concede that the line between "emotional" and "logical" arguments, elusive at best, simply cannot be drawn on borderline issues of membership in a moral community.[33]

A second similarity lies at the level of substantive moral argument. Both pro-life and animal rights positions are characterized by their appeal to a priori absolutist categories as constituting the necessary limit to our power over others. As applied, however, the categories invoked by each side have troubling implications for the other. Two leading animal rights theorists, Tom Regan and Peter Singer, have taken positions consistent with permitting not only late abortions but infanticide. For Regan, a neo-Kantian, moral rights attach to any being who fits the category "subject-of-a-life," which in turn depends on whether it has "beliefs, desires, and the like."[34] While many (but not all) adult animals are included in the category, he regards inclusion of "newly born or the soon-to-be-born" humans as "an open and much debated question."[35] Singer has gone even further. With his utilitarian emphasis on "capacity to suffer" as defining the primary relevant category, he has argued for the moral legitimacy and logical consistency of both abortion *and* infanticide.[36]

Utterly predictable is pro-lifers' outraged reaction to those who advocate respect for animal life but would deny protection to fetal and infant life. A leading pro-life philosopher and natural law theorist, John Finnis, observes that "[t]he animal rights publicists, who are generally the same people who defend abortion and infanticide, are denying humane quality when they accuse 'prolifers' of 'speciesism.' They are laying foundations of a new range of discrimination and denial of rights more devastating than racism."[37]

In contrast, pro-life advocates support their position by reliance on the single category "person" with rights, security, and protection attaching by virtue of membership in that category. This approach draws on a basically theological tradition associated with Aquinas, Descartes, and even Kant, all of whom categorically distinguished (rational) human beings from (irrational) animals, largely on the assumption that only the former have souls.[38] Novelist Milan Kundera sarcastically sums up our Cartesian heritage: "Man is master and proprietor, says Descartes, whereas the beast is merely an automaton, an animate machine, a *machina animata*. When an animal laments, it is not a lament; it is merely the rasp of a poorly functioning mechanism."[39] John Finnis insists on preserving precisely that rigid human/animal dichotomy for the sake of recognizing and protecting the distinct worth of all humans:

> [T]he injunction "Treat like cases alike" must be taken in a more than merely formal sense; it must, for example, implicitly treat all human beings as alike in their humanity and in their basic entitlement to be treated differently from animals. . . . Those who propose that animals have rights have a deficient appreciation of the basic forms of human good. . . . The basic human goods are not abstract forms, such as "life" or "conscious life": they are good as aspects of the flourishing of a person. And if the proponents of animal rights point to very young babies, or very old and decayed or mentally defective persons (or to some asleep?), and ask how their state differs empirically from that of a flourishing, friendly, and clever dog, and demand to know why the former are accorded the respect due to rights-holders while the latter is not, we must reply that respect for human good reasonably extends as far as human being, and is not to be extinguished by the circumstance that the incidents or "accidents" of affairs have deprived a particular human being of the opportunity of a full flourishing.[40]

Although both sides of both issues would have us resolve everything by reference to universally applicable categories ("sentience," "capacity to suffer," "personhood," "viability") that lead to "in" or "out" conclusions, the experiential reality seems to be more of degree, of varying levels of affinity, rather than clear lines of demarcation. We respond differently to the suffering of puppies or kittens than we do to that of baby snakes or insects. Similarly, photographs taken of nineteen-week fetuses are more compelling than those taken at eight weeks, which are in turn more compelling than those of two-week-old embryos. Most of us would save our children from fire before saving our dogs, and we might save our children before saving the children of strangers, or care more about our immediate neighbors than those at some distance. As philosopher Richard Rorty puts it with specific emphasis on the animals' issue, the facts needed to make such difficult moral judgments are "not discoverable independently of sentiment."[41] And it may be that issues requiring the guidance of sentiment are better understood as theological.[42] That is not because theology's peculiar (and implicitly trivial) concern is with the sentimental, but because questions about life and death, and human responsibility in the face of those mysteries, are difficult to address in our culture except by reference to theology. This difficulty becomes especially apparent at those points where the boundaries of conventional categories are tested, as with both animals and the unborn. Philosopher John Rawls is acutely aware of this difficulty. Toward the end of his massive *A Theory of Justice*, he acknowledges the "limits of a theory of justice," among which are that it gives no account of "right conduct in regard to animals and the rest of nature." Rawls goes on to concede that a correct conception of our relation to animals and nature would "seem to depend upon a theory of the natural order and our place in it."[43]

Lurking within the abortion and environmental debates, then, are hard questions about the relation between theology and the natural. For example, both sides of the abortion debate implicitly adopt Martin Luther King, Jr.'s assertion that laws antithetical to human equality are both immoral and unnatural ("an unjust law is a human law that is not rooted in eternal and natural law. . . . All segregation laws are unjust because segregation distorts the soul and damages the personality.").[44] Pro-choice activists are less apt than their opponents to adopt King's explicitly theological language and the natural law tradition that he invoked, but they do make vague assumptions about the relation between the moral and the natural. Like King, they assume that laws destructive of the fundamental rights of their personhood (as they take abortion restrictions to be) are "unjust" in a clearly moral sense. In turn, that "injustice" is taken to be part of a systematic subordination of women, which is viewed as resulting from the socially constructed exercise of patriarchal power, not from any "natural" difference. Most pro-life activists, of course, are explicit in their appeal to religion, while also viewing abortion as a deeply "unnatural" violence, sanctioned by a hedonistic modernism that has substituted the artificial values of a secularized culture for the more traditional values rooted in both religion and nature. For some, this includes assumptions about a woman's natural role as wife and mother.[45]

Environmentalists, of course, routinely appeal to "nature" as a "good," but they just as routinely fail to articulate the supposed connection between the two. The result may be an unreflective ecological fundamental-ism. Meanwhile, their opponents confidently assert human domination of nature, and the priority that humans assign to their own needs, to be both "natural" and theologically justified.

To label a question "theological," however, is not to supply a quick answer. And to ask, "What is natural," may be to ask an unanswerable question. Jewish and Christian scripture, for example, is notoriously am-biguous on the question of abortion, despite attempts by both sides to appropriate it. Consider an example often cited by pro-lifers: Deuter-onomy 30:15 ("I call heaven and earth to witness against you this day, that I have set before you life and death, blessing and curse; therefore choose life, that you and your descendants may live, loving the Lord your God. . . ."). We think this passage does show why a believer might not see the abortion issue (or environmentalism either) as one of private rights alone. Nevertheless, the generalized "public" choice for life that God re-quires does not have to be translated into absolutist prohibition in every single case, since the concern is actually for the public character of the people and is metaphorical. This passage equates obedience with blessing and life, disobedience with curse and death. Obedience is to be taken not as "wooden legalism" but as "obedience on the level of proper love." The metaphorical biblical use of "death" is one that contrasts "life" with a "psychological, sociological, and spiritual 'death,' which holds the world in its grip."[46]

It is often assumed that the Judeo-Christian religious tradition, invoked most explicitly by the pro-life side of the abortion debate, is unambiguous in justifying a Western history of domination of nature. In 1968 historian Lynn White blamed the entire Judeo-Christian tradition for our environ-mental crisis, insomuch as that tradition had served to validate categorical, hierarchical human self-importance in relation to nature.[47] Even there, however, the message is in fact more ambiguous. The unchecked domi-nation of nature denounced by White may derive more from the secular Enlightenment descendants of Christianity than from religious tradition itself, which seems simultaneously to validate human freedom with re-spect to nature, but also to impose responsibilities that limit human freedom.[48]

The same Jewish tradition, for example, that makes abortion a mat-ter of grave concern[49] can be read as imposing an ethic of stewardship with respect to nature.[50] The notion of "domination" ("Let him [Adam] have dominion over the fish of the sea, and over the fowl of the air, and over the cattle, and over all the earth, and over every creeping thing that creepeth upon the earth.")[51] definitely served to separate Judaism from more totemistic religions that deified or mythologized animals. Jews were obliged to serve a God who transcended nature, not nature itself. That primary obligation, however, did not render the world a mere instrumentality for the satisfaction of every human whim. Ancient Jews included in their notion of dominion an obligation of respect and care, growing from the recognition that the world had been created by God. While Jewish scripture does not lay down a blueprint for environmental regulation, it does suggest a kinship between the human and the natural that binds both to God's covenant.[52]

The Christian half of the Judeo-Christian tradition is also far from unproblematic with respect to animals and nature. St. Paul dismissed the idea that God's providence extends toward animals in the same way that it extends toward persons.[53] Later, Thomas Aquinas said that "by divine providence [animals] are intended for man's use in the natural order,"[54] and the long Thomist natural law tradition still treats the human/nonhuman category distinction as critical, for example, in distinguishing unborn humans (to be protected) from animals. John Calvin, despite all his differences with the Catholic church and Thomist thought, readily agreed that God "created all things for man's sake."[55] Yet there is another side.

Even Aquinas conceded that irrational creatures might be loved out of charity.[56] Meanwhile, his contemporary in thirteenth-century Italy, St. Francis of Assisi, drew on the tradition of the Celtic saints and desert monasticism, characterized by reciprocity and harmony among all creatures, to exemplify a love for nonhumans as well as human creatures. His teachings gave rise to a still-living tradition of rich Christian piety.[57] David Tracy, a Catholic and one of our most respected academic theologians, in fact suggests that Francis of Assisi might

> be allowed to speak anew to all Christians concerned to establish new relationships to all creatures (not only humans) and thereby to the whole earth. This may seem a strange claim, for Francis of Assisi is the one Christian saint whom all Westerners profess to love even if most quietly continue to view him as a kind of holy fool who somehow wandered off the pages of Dostoyevsky. . . . [He was] a Christian of such excess and challenge to ordinary, even good, Christian ways of understanding all of God's creation as beloved that we still cannot see him clearly.[58]

America's greatest Protestant theologian, Jonathan Edwards, with an extraordinary understanding of the limits of Enlightenment rationalism, rejected both the strict spirit/nature dualism and the separation of human society from the rest of nature. He explicitly saw in our abusive treatment of animals and the natural world (already apparent to him in eighteenth-century New England) evidence of sin for which we would be held accountable.[59]

Anglican scholar Andrew Linzey, drawing on the work of Paul Tillich, argues that the doctrines of creation, incarnation, reconciliation, and redemption, taken together, cannot be limited to human beings.[60] When Christ became "flesh," he became part of what, in the Old Testament vocabulary, humans share with the animals; furthermore, reconciliation must logically include all that was previously unreconciled, a state that humans have shared, according to scripture, with nature. As Tillich writes, "Man cannot claim . . . that the infinite has entered the finite to overcome its existential estrangement in mankind alone."[61] James Gustafson, a preeminent American Protestant ethicist, specifically argues against the assumption that the human species is "the moral measure of all things."[62] Humility before an unknowable God also implies a humility within a natural order whose reason for being is not exhausted by the bestowal of benefits upon us.

Nevertheless, as with abortion, no gospel text lays out for Christians a precise definition of human obligation. The gospel does not speak in terms of rules and categories. Thus, philosopher Stephen Clark, himself a Christian, repudiates the Cartesian duality that justifies human instrumentalism, but he also concludes with respect to "the Christian attitude to the non-human" that, "There isn't one."[63] His summary: "All educated Christians should agree that they [animals] do not belong to us. All should agree that there are limits on what we may properly do with God's creatures. But all do not agree on the nature or extent of those limits; nor do all agree on what office God has designed for us."[64]

It is this theme of limits, however hard to define, that ties the question of abortion most closely to the question of animals and of environmental ethics generally.[65] Even committed pro-choice activists usually sense limits of appropriateness with respect to abortion (for example, sex selection), even while insisting that the choice must ultimately rest with the woman. So too, the Catholic tradition, theologically committed to the human/nonhuman category distinction, is also recognizing limits of appropriateness in our relation to nature. In a recently published collection of essays, Catholic theologian James Burtchaell, author of *Rachel Weeping: The Case Against Abortion*, describes precisely that growing awareness of human limits:

The ecological movement, now well underway, is the first effectively persuasive rebuke to a belief that had grown apace with modern science and technology since the Enlightenment. The doctrine held that human purpose and choice would encounter no limits in its dominion over nature. Or, to put a finer point on the doctrine: it held that there was no nature, no creation with an ingiven character and requirements quite beyond what we could choose to infuse in things or bleach out of them.

But the environmental disillusionment was all to do with the elements and with plants and animals. We have yet to be persuaded that there are given, natural forces and needs in humanity ourselves that may be as aloof from our willful preferences and choices as are the tides of the ocean that make sport of our retaining walls and waterways.[66]

Similarly, a series of advertisements placed in the regional edition of *Newsweek* by the Catholic Archdiocese of Buffalo depict a mother and infant and ask, "What do I believe in?" The ads answer, in part, "I believe in marigolds, when they're only a few dry seeds. In butterflies, when they are still grey cocoons. In the song of birds before their eggs begin to hatch."[67] Thus, advertising intended to elicit attitudes of reverence, humility, and wonderment for the sake of opposing abortion does so by suggesting the unity of life rather than the Catholic tradition of human/animal duality.

Burtchaell takes for granted that both natural forces and needs in humanity are given, that there is a "nature" with an "ingiven character and requirements" that remains aloof from our "willful preferences and choices." To speak of our subservience to, or responsibility for, "nature," however, may obscure the contingency of what we choose to label "natural," a contingency made all too apparent when so many sides on so many issues rhetorically appropriate "the natural" as their own.

Animal rights activists, for example, often celebrate the naturalness of the human-animal bond, yet an ecologist would wonder whether there is anything natural about our millions of pampered pet dogs and cats, or the unwanted thousands dying daily to support our collective pet-loving affections. Unlike animal rights advocates, ecologists are concerned primarily with habitats, ecosystems, or species survival, and they may be (like nature itself) indifferent to the suffering or death of individual animals.[68] Yet even ecologists find the natural difficult to define, as with the status of marauding suburban deer (aptly characterized as "hoofed rodents"); or endangered species preserved in zoos; or grizzly bears in Yellowstone; or animals in wildlife preserves (where hunters are allowed to "manage" the resident animal populations). It may be "natural" for people to eat meat, but it is more ecologically sound to be vegetarian. Technology is easily defined as "unnatural," but rapid technological advances may be necessary if nature is to be preserved. Ravaging diseases and famines may be a fact of nature, and even useful in controlling excess human population, yet most of us find in ourselves a sympathy for our fellow humans that we cannot dismiss because it is ecologically unsound. Some now argue that we have reached the point where the natural world has been so transformed by humanity as to be rendered, finally, a mere human artifact.

The question of what is natural becomes especially acute with respect to gender difference, as the rhetoric of the abortion debate has illustrated. Men and women may be the same, except for culturally contingent role definitions easily transformed, with childbearing capacity only a gender-specific controllable variable (controllable by way of birth control and abortion, so long as a repressive social system does not intervene). Or there may be intractable, essential differences in role, attitude, perception, or behavior attributable to some mix (that cannot be sorted out) of culture, tradition, and biology.[69] One source of supposed difference derives from the fact that women in our culture have been identified, and have identified themselves, with nature. The result has been a distinctly feminist approach.

While most animal rights activists are women and many are feminists, there has traditionally been no well-articulated correspondence between animal rights activism and feminist activism as such. One significant exception occurred in turn-of-the-century England, where for a time feminists and antivivisectionists formed a strong alliance.[70] Women at the time could easily identify their own domination and victimization with cruelty to animals, an identification that accounted for the enormous popularity of the novel *Black Beauty*[71]. This association was particularly acute given the cruel gynecological procedures of charity hospitals—justified explicitly by the stereotype of women as animal-like. (A woman doctor, horrified by the medical treatment of poor women, explained that "[p]aupers are thus classed with animals as fitting subjects for painful experiments, and no regard is shown to the feelings of either.")[72]

While poor men also experienced the lower-class fear of charity hospitals, for women that fear was intensified by the element of lewd sexual domination. Indeed, Victorian pornography was closely related to gynecological practices, and both in turn were associated with the treatment of animals. (Women were "put in stirrups," "broken to the bit," made to "show their paces" and "present themselves.")[73] Thus, women came to see their own condition "hideously and accurately embodied in the figure of an animal bound to a table by straps with the vivisector's knife at work on its flesh."[74] Given that legacy, it is not surprising that some feminists otherwise committed to reproductive choice are nevertheless hesitant to endorse the rapid advance of objectifying reproductive technologies; and even simple, painless abortions can be experienced as technological violence.

A growing body of scholarship has, in fact, been exploring the ideological connection between the domination of women and the scientific objectification of nature. Carolyn Merchant, for example, has traced the emergence of the dualistic imagery which described nature as a dark, mysterious, feminine force to be subdued by aggressive rationalist scientific "penetration."[75] As she quotes Bacon: "For you have but to follow and as it were hound nature in her wanderings, and you will be able when you like to lead and drive her afterward. . . . Neither ought a man to make scruple of entering and penetrating into these holes and corners."[76] Bacon insisted that direct experimentation should replace the abstract theorizing of the Scholastics, for nature is a force that must be "bound into service" and made a "slave," put in "constraint," to be "molded" by the mechanical arts. "Nature must be taken by the forelock," and any science that does not include experimentation will "permit one only to clutch at nature, never to lay hold of her and capture her."[77]

Merchant is careful not to take an essentialist position on the relationship between women and nature. While male scientific discourse has historically linked the objectification of nature with domination of women, that male history does not mean that women, as a matter of inescapable essentialist reality, are in fact somehow more "natural" than men. On the other hand, the history of identification has provided feminists with a valuable vantage point from which to assess Baconian dualism, with its inflated claims to universal, ahistoric validity, as well as Bacon's (now scientifically outdated)[78] legacy for modern attitudes toward nature.

Feminists try to make critical use of that historic identification, without allowing it to set the terms of self-identification. The line between the two is not always easy to draw. By reference to reproduction, women have been traditionally associated with their "natural" capacity for nurturance. At times this has offered an alternative to a mainstream masculine culture of selfish acquisitiveness. Faye Ginsburg has described, with much sensitivity, the fear among pro-life women that pro-choice activists have simply adopted the values of the mainstream masculine culture.[79] Similarly, Sidney Callahan has described the pro-life feminist position:

> Faced with a choice between men and women, prolife feminists choose women, and faced with a conflict between women and the fetus, the choice is made for the fetus, by analogous reasoning. In tragic conflicts and choices, one must give the benefit of the doubt to the more powerless and renounce solutions that do harm to human life. Thus, most feminist prolife advocates are, like myself, not only for the ERA, but also against capital punishment, against nuclear arms, against the draft, and for redistribution of income. Perhaps the most important feminist prolife demand is for family allowances, health care, day care, and the end of society's virtual abandonment of women and children, which increases pressure for abortion as the quick, less expensive solution. To be consistently prolife, we must challenge the status quo and all the expedient utilitarian values so embedded in a world indifferent to suffering.[80]

The pro-life movement, suggests Ginsburg, exists in some historical continuity with a long line of women's movements—including the temperance movement, the women's suffrage campaign, and progressive era women's reform groups—which, despite some differences, shared similar assumptions about women's natural and distinct nurturant role.[81] Such movements drew on the values associated with motherhood and domesticity to tame and "domesticate" some of the worst aspects of a male-dominated culture. Jane Addams, for example, talked of extending "household" values into the broader social/economic arena.[82] The Women's Christian Temperance Union (WCTU), now ridiculed for its appeal to a ("feminizing") Victorian moral righteousness, did raise real concerns, not just about the family abuse and dislocation that came with excessive male drinking, but with male domination and economic exploitation generally.[83]

Especially as women join the work force in greater numbers, the distinct sphere of female domesticity becomes constricted, confined to the "natural," physical process of reproduction itself. It is hardly surprising that reproduction then becomes an arena of social conflict. Some women find it painful to surrender this last source of distinct gender identity to the dominant culture's rhetoric of privatism and self-interested choice: that surrender seems to entail losing the one remaining source of values at odds with a selfish, commercialized American culture. For that reason, Joan Williams asks whether the pro-choice movement might appeal to the values of domesticity, rather than repudiating them so thoroughly with the rhetoric of private choice.[84] Women do, after all, often choose abortions for ethical reasons, out of concern for others, and rarely as pure assertion of self-interest.

Nevertheless, as Williams has also argued,[85] an appeal to domesticity is doubled-edged, for the language of domesticity repeats a culturally contrived vocabulary that has particularized and trivialized women's lives,[86] even while the language of private individuals' rights used to defend abortion rights replicates acquisitive male culture. What seems needed is a vocabulary that somehow transcends that linguistic divide, making possible a real moral discourse about abortion—about life and death, and human responsibility in the face of those mysteries.

Ecofeminists claim a privileged access to those mysteries, not through the social contrivance of domesticity, but through a holistic appreciation of natural life processes. They celebrate a special feminist sense of connectedness to nature, unshackled by the dualistic structures that have characterized masculine rationalized thought.[87] In our culture the male ego defines itself, some say, by separating itself simultaneously from nature and woman, a dualistic subject/object split that women do not require for a mature sense of identity. Therefore, women (at least in our culture) may be better able than men to look to nature itself for an understanding of the human role in the natural order and our responsibility toward it.

Any special feminist appeal to nature, however, must be tempered with humility. As the great British biologist, J. S. Haldane, is reported to have observed, if nature reveals anything at all to us, it is that "God has an inordinate fondness for beetles."[88] Less ironic are the tragic observations of those who wanted to celebrate the beneficence of nature, but discovered instead that nature has a "more hideous face, blighted and polluted by its own forces," that it may be "bleak, depraved, and hostile, at least by human standards," a reality of "extinction, conflict, depravity, terror."[89] Even Thoreau was aware of the "maniacal hooting" of owls.[90] The danger lies in forgetting that we live, after all, in a "fallen world."[91]

Annie Dillard's opening chapter of *Pilgrim at Tinker Creek* describes a frog grimacing in terror while being sucked alive, from below, by a large brown beetle called a giant water bug.[92] True to Haldane's observation, most of our fellow creatures are insects, and Dillard tells us that they do "one horrible thing after another."[93] Consider the female mantis, systematically gnawing the male to death even during the act of mating. Ten percent of the world's species are parasites,[94] born to suck the blood or guts of others, or to chew away at their skin. A sensible human editor, presented with the design of creation, would blue-pencil most of it.[95] By any human standard, architectural or ethical, the world is simply unacceptable—pointlessly intricate, elaborate, and abundant beyond all apparent requirements of function, rampantly pluralist, profligate, anarchic, obscene, violent, inegalitarian, with no regard for anyone's rights whatsoever. Nature's terrifying fecundity means that the children of most species are routinely discarded, lost, or eaten. Life is cheap. The "awesome pressures to eat and breed"[96] mean that nature requires death as surely as it gives life.[97]

Excessive celebration and romanticization of nature may have serious moral and political consequences.[98] We might perhaps be wary of seemingly contemporary ecological observations:

> [T]his planet once moved through the ether for millions of years without human beings and it can do so again some day if men forget they owe their highest existence, not to the ideas of a few crazy ideologists, but to the knowledge and ruthless application of Nature's stern and rigid laws. . . . At the end of the last century the progress of science and technique led liberalism astray into proclaiming man's mastery of nature and announcing that he would soon have dominion over space. But a simple storm is enough—and everything collapses like a pack of cards.

The author? Adolf Hitler.[99]

Nazi ideology was premised on views about nature that were very much in the mainstream of Western thought at the time, views that are regaining currency with the modern sense of environmental crisis.[100] We noted earlier that Hitler was a vegetarian and that top Nazi officials, like Himmler and Göring, recognized the rights of animals. More significantly, Nazi ideology represented an attempt to transcend the dualities of body and spirit, man and nature, which pervaded traditional Western science and theology. The new man brought into being by National Socialism would see himself in and of nature, not over and above it, finding infinity not in a transcendent God, but in life itself. He could achieve this connectedness in part by reaching inward to redevelop that special affinity of the pagan Aryan volk for the life spirit.

Jews, of course, were said to have no such affinity. Their religious traditions and their history as city dwellers closed them off from nature and made them parasites within the natural order—as were the disabled and the otherwise unfit. And so these Nazi celebrators of life, paradoxically employing technical and instrumental rationality, became

> purveyors of death, and the most idealistic of them wore the death's head as a sort of absolving talisman. Finite beings can never, of course, "embrace life"; but, they can fetishise death. . . . Justifiably, the ultimate expression of that negativity which was the core of National Socialist "life-bound" nationalism, is viewed as policies of extermination. Yet, at all times, it would seem that the most important of the "life-affirming" bearers of National Socialist religious principles were always at their best in the valley of the shadow.[101]

Which of us can claim to celebrate life without being a purveyor of death? When pro-life literature shows photographs of the discarded bodies of concentration camp victims and then, next to those pictures, photographs of fetuses stuffed into plastic garbage bags for disposal, some of us who have had abortions have troubled doubts. Questions have been raised, of course, about the illegitimate appropriation of Jewish experience for Christianizing purposes.[102] Equating routine early abortions with the horror of the Holocaust seems to deprive Nazism of moral significance and debase Jewish history by exploiting it for sectarian Christian goals.

Yet the West German Constitutional Court drew the same parallel in its 1975 decision overturning a 1974 provision for complete decriminalization of first-trimester abortions: "The priority given to the value of life in the West German constitutional order is . . . a reaction to the taking of innocent life in the years of the 'final solution.' Not only the protection of life . . . but also the express prohibition of the death penalty . . . have to be read, against the background of Germany's experience with a regime which classified certain forms of human life as worthless."[103] All categorical objectification is frightening, in part because of that Nazi history. When, then, *are* we entitled to treat the other as a disposable object? Before birth? When the other is part of a statistically necessary risk? (When B>PL?)[104] When the other is a murderer? Disabled? Comatose? Severely retarded? A member of a different class, race, gender or species? An enemy soldier? An "enemy" civilian? Which of these categories is appropriate, which obviously illegitimate, and on what grounds?

Jonathan Kozol, who has studied the problem of homeless families and is careful not to indulge in rhetorical excess, draws tentative parallels to Nazi policies of extermination.[105] When is the parallel legitimate, when not? When does it merely trivialize, and when does it make us confront a moral reality we would rather ignore? In living, we *all* cause death. Vegetarians, if they consume dairy products, contribute to the production of veal, the cruelest of mass meat-producing practices. Even growing grain destroys animal habitats. Yet we are not all Nazis, and we cannot be ethically immobilized, refusing, for example, to be concerned about destruction of the environment because the Nazis preached an ethics of the natural. Ours is a world in which death is bound up with life, not an idealized world, cleansed of darker realities. The challenge, both social and individual, is to confront rather than avoid those realities and to make the life-and-death decisions we must make in a morally responsible way.

2

Natural Law and Catholic Tradition

......

Philosophy 101, at a prestigious (not Catholic) liberal arts college, circa 1960: The professor probes the class as to whether euthanasia is wrong, calling on a number of students whose ambivalent, uncertain responses are obviously not what he is looking for. Finally, a frumpy female student raises her hand, and answers timidly but with felt conviction that euthanasia is wrong because "it is against the will of God." The teacher's eyes light up; he's got just what he wants. We then learn through the humiliation of the only person in the room willing (publicly) to affirm a belief in God that her response illustrates an "authoritarian ethic," one whose moral truth is rooted not in the rationality of its substance, but only in its source. Such an ethic, of course, is derided as running counter to our own presumed individual moral freedom (although later, as parents, many of us would appreciate the soundness of locating virtue and authority in one place, with no requirement of rationality).

In the same course we students learned to be ever wary of committing the "naturalistic fallacy," that is, presuming that one could infer a moralistic "ought" from an empirical "is." No natural ordering of the world, we discovered, supplied categories to guide our sense of moral appropriateness. Since there was no "natural" law, matters moral were largely relegated to the realm of individual subjectivity, and ethical values were understood not as rational or objective, but as a form of "emotivism" disconnected from the factually verifiable, scientifically apprehensible world around us.[1]

Implicit in Philosophy 101, however, was the assumption that we would exercise our moral freedom by sensibly maximizing our "utilities," while also respecting each other's individual rights. This vaguely conceived blend of utilitarianism and Kantianism, which Jeffrey Stout has called our modern secular "moral Esperanto,"[2] was taken to be rational virtually by definition. Most of us adopted it without further reflection. Nevertheless, our cultural reality, more than we recognized, was still informed by moral "survivals," leftover moral capital rapidly being dissipated by the force of its unverifiability. Thus we (middle-class secular college students) still believed we should show compassion for the suffering and the marginalized, a belief that came to the fore in the civil rights and antiwar movements. And most of us still found abortion to be at least a source of moral queasiness, although sometimes necessary to solve a frightening and embarrassing problem. If pressed, we would not have been able to define the source of that queasiness—some combination of concern with taking life and disquiet over our otherwise cheerful abandonment of conventional sexual mores.

By the 1970s, Philosophy 101 would seem to take over American law, morality, and politics. This book will describe the process of takeover, and also the failure of its worldview to secure a firm cultural grip on a diverse and restive populace. Nevertheless, despite the premises of Philosophy 101, other, less secular alternatives had once compelled the attention even of liberal intellectuals in the post-World War II era. Times of moral challenge or despair, especially, heighten the appeal of one of those alternatives—natural law. Natural law's claim is that a timeless and universal justice is rooted by God in the essential reality of an objective natural order and reveals itself to our careful human reason. The power of that claim led those who opposed slavery, like Frederick Douglass and Abraham Lincoln, to bypass the ambiguous positivism of the U.S. Constitution and to invoke instead the natural law premises of the Declaration of Independence ("We hold these truths to be self-evident, that all men are created equal. . . .").[3] Following that example, Martin Luther King, Jr., explicitly invoked natural law to justify civil disobedience in the face of segregation laws.[4]

The natural law tradition to which Douglass, Lincoln, and King appealed derived from the yet older Catholic natural law tradition of Thomas Aquinas. In the anxious years following Nazi defeat, American legalists sought refuge quite specifically in the Thomist natural law tradition, which offered the security of universal norms of human decency. When Nazis loaded people into railroad cars for slaughter and made lampshades of human skin, those were not just crimes against a proper balancing of utilities. Rather, they were moral abominations, a notion that comes into play when some crucial category of our cosmological ordering of reality has been violated. Nazi acts were "crimes against humanity" because, by treating humans like animals, Nazis debased the meaning of "humanity" itself, a category experienced in our culture as both deeply rooted in nature and sanctioned by God—hence, a category rooted in natural law.

In the face of Nazism's moral abominations, many American intellectuals sought to reestablish those categories, and those norms of decency, that could be located in the "laws of nature and nature's God." No less seemed required in order to insulate Western culture from the threat that human lives might once again be deemed categorically expendable. Moreover, if the Nazis had rooted their barbarism in a pre-rational and grotesque romanticism of nature, what better antidote than a long tradition in which that same nature had been more wisely understood through the mediation of deliberate human reason.

This reaction of American liberal intellectuals was exemplified by Walter Lippmann, who in 1941 told a group of Catholic theologians that the American people were doomed to be unsatisfied because they had lost sight of a higher moral order and had "accepted the secular image of man."[5] Lippmann considered joining the Catholic church because it offered communion in a "moral order above the whims of transient majorities and the dictates of tyrants;"[6] and in *Essays in the Public Philosophy* in 1955 he argued that the "decline of the West" could be countered only by adherence to that "doctrine of natural law" which held that there was a law "above the ruler and the sovereign people . . . above the whole community of mortals."[7]

For those who wanted assurance from the prevailing legal culture itself that "it can't happen here," American jurisprudence had little to offer. The tradition of legal positivism, dominant in both English and American jurisprudence, defined law in Hobbesian terms as no more than sovereign command.[8] Nothing in legal positivism repudiated Hitler's version of legalism as "illegal." Meanwhile, the American legal realists had just finished demolishing the elaborate conceptual categories of American constitutionalism (like "freedom of contract"), exposing them as situational by-products of ongoing legal decision-making. Legal reasoning was thus basically circular and self-referencing. According to the realists, judges described as reasons only their own conclusions, not an independent reality "out there" available for judicial discovery and protection. A contract right, for example, did not come into being by force of one's natural expectations following a promise, but only because of an ongoing legal process of decision-making that awarded remedies in case of breach. Similarly, property had no "natural" definition, but was only a bundle of legal rights and, in effect, a delegation of sovereign (political) power. Sociology, psychology, and political science might be usefully employed, said the realists, to understand why and how legal decisions were made, but after the realist assault on traditional legal thinking, it was difficult to believe that the conceptual language employed by judges was about anything other than the culture of judging.[9]

As against an American jurisprudence that offered nothing better than the bleakness of the realists' cultural relativism, in 1947 a group of scholars undertook to shore up traditional Western values. Their project, which we will review in some depth, was most fully realized in the *Natural Law Forum*, a journal published from 1956 until 1968. By the 1950s natural law had become so much a mainstream agenda that the *Forum* could, with some confidence, herald itself as the standard-bearer of a rising tide. Its stated mission was no less than to rescue jurisprudence from the "positivist conclusion that the ideology of one person or nation is as valid as that of any other," a conclusion, the *Forum* said, that led all too quickly to "totalitarian excesses." [10]

Published by Notre Dame Law School, the *Forum* arrayed a distinguished cast of editors and supporters. Many still-familiar names were among its associate and advisory editors: Lon Fuller, Friedrich Kessler, Jerome Frank, Robert Hutchins, Edward Levi, Leo Strauss, Myres McDougal, F. C. S. Northrup, Edward Corwin, Jacques Ellul, William Curran,[11] Carl Friedrich,[12] and John Noonan (Noonan not among the original editors, but eventually editor-in-chief).[13] However improbable the image of that assemblage of legal scholars poring through Thomas Aquinas, their earnestly stated goal was to explore, "with all the resources of scholarship and modern science, the full extent of the contribution natural law can make to the solution of today's problems." [14] From their perspective, a jurisprudence premised on relativism alone posed an intellectual and political crisis.

We can gain an appreciation of both the persistence of traditional natural law and its problematic basis by taking a close look at what the *Forum* actually offered its post-World War II readers. The scholarship was extensive. The first issue contained a comparative review of natural law and positivism as well as a classical and medieval history of natural law (with many footnotes in German and French).[15] With an ecumenical tilt, the editors also included a review of *The Moral Decision* [16] by Jewish legal scholar Edmond Cahn. No legal positivist himself, Cahn tried to reintroduce moral (and explicitly biblical) discourse into legal decision-making, but the *Forum*'s reviewer faulted his more contextual approach for slighting the natural law tradition of Aquinas and thereby failing to articulate a moral standard extrinsic to legal case analysis.[17]

By way of optimistic counterpoint (or comic relief?), legal realist Myres McDougal, of Yale Law School, rang in with his usual call for a law school curriculum based on an understanding of law as constituted by the "social and power processes of a community."[18] Even McDougal, however, whose "science" had little room for Aquinas, postulated as "enduring" the value of "human dignity in a free and abundant society," which McDougal found wholly realized in the "stream of the rising common demands and expectations of our time."[19] He saw no need for external validation of these values from religion, natural law, or even metaphysics, perceiving instead a "general trend" of moral progress in human history itself. McDougal confidently relegated Nazism's threat to the status of mere historical glitch, reflecting "feudal residues and the counter-currents of totalitarianism."[20]

Serious natural law scholars, however, saw the need for more than either faith in historical progress (McDougal) or contextual intuitionism (Cahn). In that regard, the most serious entrant in the opening volume of the *Forum* was A. P. d'Entrèves of Oxford University, an eminent natural law scholar and émigré from Italian fascism. D'Entrèves's introductory article, based on four lectures he had delivered at the University of Notre Dame, fully represented the spirit and purpose of the new journal.[21] D'Entrèves, moreover, is strikingly contemporary in anticipating the issues that still characterize the debate over the nature and sources of our "fundamental rights" (such as the privacy right enshrined in *Roe v. Wade*). He carefully considers both consensus as a source of legitimacy (through "shared values") and the claim of process (if the process is sufficiently democratic, its results are necessarily just).[22] He concludes, as we shall see, that only the natural law tradition itself, which he presents in its richness and subtlety, can offer a secure ethical basis for law.

For d'Entrèves, the central question is the relationship between law and morality. The relativistic English and American positivists, whose jurisprudence was then dominant, treated this question as a nonissue. Law was simply the command of a particular sovereign in a particular place. Such was the grim purity of Hobbesian extremism.[23] Some positivists, however, were already retreating from the extreme, seeking to define law as more than mere command without going so far as to concede the existence of an objective moral order.

One effort was that of the young H. L. A. Hart, later to be famous with his publication of *The Concept of Law*.[24] In his inaugural address at Oxford University, Hart, adopting a metaphor much in vogue among English philosophers, had suggested that law was best understood as analogous to the "rules of the game."[25] Thus, law could be understood as a shared social practice, an image more benign than the bleak exercise of Hobbesian power. D'Entrèves, however, found the game analogy more whimsical than satisfying, even while conceding that the game of cricket, for example, was indeed more complex than could be captured analytically by the notion of mere command. With a wry remembrance of his own first-hand experience of totalitarianism, he commented that "[i]f we want at all costs to stick to the analogy between law and the rules of the game, let us admit that it is a peculiar game which we are asked to play, and one which has little to do with the placid setting of a sunny English afternoon."[26] The game analogy, he pointed out, leaves "us entirely indifferent to the kind of game that is played. Nor does it tell us why on earth we should choose to play it."[27] While the game analogy, in other words, offers a richer and more experiential account of law than Hobbesianism, it still fails to cross the line from procedure to substance.[28] And if the analogy's underlying goal is simply evocative, to infuse the game (and with it, law) with the moralistic aura of an English public school cricket match, that goal must be dismissed as foolish romanticism.

D'Entrèves next confronts the claim of shared values. His foil is Arthur Goodhart's lectures on *English Law and the Moral Law*.[29] As if picking up on the implicit cultural hint in the cricket analogy, Goodhart saw English culture as offering a happy coincidence of positive law and shared moral obligation, mediated by precedent—thus constituting a self-enclosed social system without any recourse to natural law. While Goodhart had noted the "revival of 'natural law' thinking" as an expression of the legitimate search for law's "moral" underpinnings,[30] harmonious England apparently already provided those underpinnings in its shared culture.[31]

Goodhart's sociology, even if accurate, hardly answers the question. D'Entrèves politely compliments the English on their shared moral norms. Nevertheless, he points out, the real problem arises when law and morality are at odds with one another.[32] Hitler's laws were the extreme case, but in most other countries as well the fit between law and morality is imperfect, and laws will be challenged on moral grounds. That law in the particular instance of England might serve simultaneously as external authority (coercion) and internalized norm (motive) is therefore no solution, for that cultural fact provides no external, objective reference point from which to judge the moral validity of a particular law or, as with Nazism, a whole legal system.

The theoretical distinction between law and morality had arisen most sharply in the seventeenth century and heralded the modern secular state.[33] Unlike the church, d'Entrèves points out, Leviathan demands obedience, but not inner conviction; it requires outward conformity, but leaves conscience to the individual.[34] For a believer in natural law, however, there must be a necessary connection between legal and moral obligation: "Law may or may not be obeyed for the sake of its obligatoriness. But there is only one ground for the obligation of the law, and this is a moral ground."[35]

The question, then, is how to achieve a "good society," one where there is no divorce between legal and moral authority. In Aristotelian terms, that means a society where the " 'good man' is also a 'good citizen.' "[36] So stated, the issue quickly becomes one of politics, of the legitimacy of process.

The modern resolution of this issue, of course, dating back to Rousseau, is democracy.[37] Through democracy, argued Rousseau, legal and moral obligation can be made to coincide. D'Entrèves focuses on two passages from Rousseau. The first shows democracy as resolving the problem of individual freedom in a collectivity, for "each, while uniting himself with all, may still obey himself alone, and remain as free as before."[38] The second passage makes clear that we are not talking about freedom as mere self-interest (to which we have become all too accustomed), but rather "moral liberty, which alone makes him [the citizen] truly master of himself; for the mere impulse of appetite is slavery, while obedience to a law which we prescribe to ourselves is liberty."[39]

D'Entrèves astutely saw the Reformation as a source of these heady notions: to become the citizen of Rousseauian democracy was to experience spiritual rebirth, to have a radical transformation. The new Adam as citizen, obeying only himself, reunites moral and legal obligation.[40] One is reminded of the radical Puritans who inverted hierarchy (and loosed some chaos) in the seventeenth century by proclaiming that "the voice of the People is the voice of God." Such proclamations so frightened Hobbes that he was eager to surrender his freedom to Leviathan in exchange for protection.[41]

Rousseau's similarly stirring version of citizenship may be no less dangerous. D'Entrèves sees a clear path from Rousseau through the Hegelian state to totalitarianism. Totalitarianism works, not by crude coercion or brainwashing, but by fulfillment of the Rousseauian promise: "They claim to be the good society because they maintain that, by belonging to them the individual leads the good life, that, in other words, by finding in the State his 'real self,' his true moral nature, man will cease to obey out of fear, but obey out of conscience and full conviction."[42] Thus, neither culture (Goodhart) nor democracy (Rousseau) serves alone to reconcile moral and legal obligation. Natural law cautions us that politics (even *democratic* politics) is always "a method rather than an end."[43]

How, then, can we speak of ends? For one thing, d'Entrèves insists that we must reject the false dichotomy between "is" and "ought," between "fact" and "value," the dichotomy so central to the worldview of Philosophy 101. Serious natural law, says d'Entrèves, begins with ontology, with a "willingness to seize the bull by the horns":[44] "[t]he ontological approach welds together being and oughtness, and maintains that the very notion of natural law stands and falls on that identification."[45] Natural law is first and foremost a "conception of an order of reality,"[46] established "in its essence by God's wisdom,"[47] in which human beings participate because they are rational creatures. The "real" is the foundation for the "good." It is participation through reason in the "order of reality" that provides a basis for human knowledge, and knowledge of the "order of reality" is the "condition and the source of all laws pertaining" to human beings.[48] As d'Entrèves emphasizes, the whole majestic structure of natural law rests on that ontological position about reality itself, which allows for an intimate connection between nature, reason, and law, premised on the existence of a divine benevolent being.[49] That structure, with its explicit ontology, was, for d'Entrèves, the only antidote to legal positivism, moral relativism, and the threat of fascism.

D'Entrèves's natural law ontology does not require that we look to revelation for the content of the law. While it is true that d'Entrèves's precursors, the natural law theorists of the Middle Ages, had devised an intricate structure of law to mediate the infinite distance between human and divine, that structure, for the most part, did not depend on revelation. Thomistic natural law itself represented a fusion of Christianity with Aristotelian essentialism, and for most affairs of the world, natural reason would suffice; Aquinas had carefully stated that the divine law, revealed through grace, perfects, but does not overturn, the human law that is based on natural reason.[50] The most critical question, therefore, is not whether God exists, but whether there exists in the world any discernible moral order that reveals itself to us through the application of reason to the nature of humanity. For example, while a proper understanding of the Trinity would depend on revelation, as interpreted by the church and accepted in faith, a prohibition against genocide can be, according to natural law theory, rooted in an understanding of the nature and purpose of humanity that is accessible to natural reason alone.[51] Similarly, Catholic doctrine takes abortion to be a violation of natural law, which means that understanding it to be a wrong should not require Christian faith or church authority.[52]

Jacques Maritain, the well-known modern natural law theorist, made the ontological point absolutely clear. Citing Antigone as "the eternal heroine of natural law"[53] (although she was no Christian), he spells out the basically Aristotelian assumption:

> Since I have not time here to discuss nonsense . . . I am taking it for granted that we admit that there is a human nature, and that this human nature is the same in all men. I am taking it for granted that we also admit that man is a being gifted with intelligence, and who, as such, acts with an understanding of what he is doing, and therefore with the power to determine for himself the ends which he pursues. On the other hand, possessed of a nature, or an ontologic structure which is a locus of intelligible necessities, man possesses ends which necessarily correspond to his essential constitution and which are the same for all—as all pianos, for instance, whatever their particular type and in whatever spot they may be, have as their end the production of certain attuned sounds. If they do not produce these sounds they must be tuned, or discarded as worthless. But since man is endowed with intelligence and determines his own ends, it is up to him to put himself in tune with the ends necessarily demanded by his nature. This means that there is, by the very virtue of human nature, an order or a disposition which human reason can discover and according to which the human will must act in order to attune itself to the essential and necessary ends of the human being. The unwritten law, or natural law, is nothing more than that. . . .
>
> When I said a moment ago that the natural law of all beings existing in nature is the proper way in which, by reason of their specific nature and specific ends, they should achieve fullness of being in their behaviour, this very word should has only a metaphysical meaning (as we say that a good or a normal eye "should" be able to read letters on a blackboard from a given distance). The same word should starts to have a moral meaning, that is, to imply moral obligation, when we pass the threshold of the world of free agents. Natural law for man is moral law, because man obeys or disobeys it freely, not necessarily, and because human behaviour pertains to a particular, privileged order which is irreducible to the general order of the cosmos and tends to a final end superior to the immanent common good of the cosmos. . . .
>
> Let us say, then, that in its ontological aspect, natural law is an ideal

order relating to human actions, a *divide* between the suitable and the unsuitable, the proper and the improper, which depends on human nature or essence and the unchangeable necessities rooted in it.[54]

This passage from Maritain highlights the central dilemma of essentialism. The familiar issue implicit here is that of freedom and necessity. As we observe animal cultures, for example, we form judgments about their intrinsic norms. We can study wolves, or baboons, or elephants and infer the way in which such creatures should behave to be successful ones of their kind, to be true to their species nature. While much traditional learning had it that animals behaved as they were supposed to because they merely followed instinct (necessity), recent scholarship assigns more weight to notions such as thinking and problem-solving, even with respect to animals, and pays attention to local differences in species behavior, validating the use of terms like "culture" to describe animals.

The basic claim of natural law is that we can comprehend our own animality in the same way, that there are correct, or appropriate, ways of being human and of perfecting our human virtues. Even allowing for great diversity across historical time and geographical space, the assumption is that there are underlying, even invariant, norms of human behavior, the violation of which amounts to denial of our essential nature.[55]

On the other hand, whatever the norms we articulate, we must confront their widespread disregard. Widespread violation of norms—badness, or sin, as some would have it—is the reality of people in the world. But that is precisely why, for those like Maritain, the subject is *morality*, not just sociobiology. Our burden, our responsibility, which, at least in conventional theory distinguishes us from animals, is our freedom. To discover the norms is not to obey them. We are free to choose and are therefore placed in an endless dialectical engagement between duty (necessity) and desire (freedom).

Against this background of reality, natural law theorists concede that there never can be a perfect fit between legality and morality. For one thing, as even Aquinas admits, some laws *are* merely "penal," which oblige not in conscience, but only in that one must pay a penalty for nonobedience (precisely Oliver Wendell Holmes, Jr.'s "bad man" conception).[56] Conversely, there are *also* limits on the extent to which law can make people virtuous. Even if law, as envisioned by Aquinas, was rooted in natural reason and therefore had moral content, it might fail to enact morality, since "bad" people will, after all, "conform to the law without . . . becoming virtuous."[57]

Even more striking is Aquinas's concession of moral triage:

Now human law is laid down for the multitude the major part of which is composed of men not perfected by virtue. Consequently, all and every vice, from which virtuous men abstain, is not prohibited by human law but only the gravest vicious actions, from which it is possible for the major part of the multitude to abstain, and mainly those— like homicide, theft, etc.—which are harmful to others, and without the prohibition of which human society could not be preserved.[58]

Human law can lead people to virtue, but only "gradually"; if the unvirtuous are required to abstain from every kind of evil, they will only "plunge into worse evils."[59] One telling example, of course, might be abortion. Some would argue that given its frequency (even when illegal), a human law proscribing it represents an unrealistic and, in *Thomistic terms*, a morally counterproductive attempt to legislate "perfect virtue." On the other hand, abortion considered as "homicide" could be argued to be the sort of "vicious action," with victim, which is appropriately made a violation of human law. In other words, simply invoking the Thomist natural law tradition does not necessarily provide quick answers to hard ethical questions, or to the complex relation between law and morality. Rather, it provides an ethical frame of reference within which a rational discussion of these questions can take place.

Thus, the essentialism of natural law is not a surrender to the necessity side of the freedom/necessity duality. It is merely an assertion that we can talk about whether human beings are behaving as such creatures are supposed to behave, and that such conversation is relevant to a particular exercise of our freedom. In that sense, natural law is surely a challenge to the hubristic presumption of human agency associated with existentialism, or, currently, with the postmodern pose of unlimited contingency, the claim that we "can do it all," can "be whatever we want to be." What we can be or do may ultimately be constrained by what *we are*.

Nevertheless, it is not at all clear that the Forum's ostensibly eager American audience was really ready for natural law in its fullness. Revealing in this regard are two points on which d'Entrèves was somewhat evasive, but which had been made clear by Maritain (whose work d'Entrèves knew and cited with respect).[60] One is the question of historical relativism (or multiculturalism?). What do natural law theorists make of cultures that have not yet perceived the universality of natural law principles, or, for that matter, of Christianity? D'Entrèves's brief comment on the issue was a quote from Strauss to the effect that, if natural law is rational, "its discovery presupposes the cultivation of natural reason."[61] One guesses that not every person, or every society, will perform the necessary cultivation. Indeed, traditional natural law had not been just about untutored people as they were, but about people as they would be if they realized their proper end, or telos—and about the rules to be followed and the virtues to be cultivated if people were to flourish, progressing in time from one stage to the next.[62]

Maritain had been more forthright than d'Entrèves on the question of relativism. He argued that the Thomistic notion of natural law is not one of rational knowledge alone, nor of "concepts and conceptual judgments."[63] For that reason, natural law cannot be expected to be uniform through the ages or across cultures. Instead, Maritain insisted that when Aquinas speaks of human reason discovering the regulations of natural law, he does so by reference to "inclination."[64] Knowledge through inclination is "obscure, unsystematic, vital knowledge by connaturality or congeniality in which the intellect in order to bear judgment, consults and listens to the inner melody that the vibrating strings of abiding tendencies make present in the subject."[65]

It was probably wise of d'Entrèves not to lecture his audience of American law scholars on "vibrating strings" and "the inner melody" by which we distinguish the appropriate from the inappropriate response. This was surely an audience more used to categories and "concepts." But Maritain was making a crucial point about relativism. "Inclination," unlike the fixed norms one usually associates with natural law, is in a process of continual refinement. It exists, Maritain said, in only rudimentary form in "primitive" societies (which is why their practices may be so varied), but with the advance of civilization and the increase in moral knowledge, "inclination" becomes ever more capable of discerning the specifics of natural law.[66]

This might be taken as routine Western presumption, but it also goes to the elusive relation between natural law and Christianity. By "civilization," Maritain clearly means Christian civilization. By "inclination," Maritain insists on something that is being refined by the precepts of a culture with a Christian tradition. Maritain's solution to the problem of relativism is, in effect, to Christianize natural law—or, at least, natural law as it is understood by a person in our culture.[67] (Its full understanding awaits, he says, the fulfillment of the gospel.)[68] This is, of course, a good deal more forthright than the more typical post-Enlightenment claim, that one in our culture can do "moral reasoning" in a manner that completely transcends the Christian tradition of reason.[69] But it raises afresh the problem of relativism (and, implicitly, of the social construction of culture), unless one assumes that Western (traditionally Christian) culture is *not* just one more culture among many in a world of utterly relativized difference. But on what basis does one make such an assumption, except by reference to Christian norms?

The second point evaded by d'Entrèves was the place of individual "rights" in the natural law setting. D'Entrèves noted that the Enlightenment version of natural law (with its natural rights, as in the Declaration of Independence) was probably more familiar to moderns than was Scholastic natural law. He commented that "the time was not ripe," in classical antiquity or in the Middle Ages, for a conception of rights. He also reminded his audience that there is no "right" without a legal duty, so that "the very notion of a subjective claim presupposes that of an objective order."[70]

But what do we mean by an objective order, and where do individual rights fit in? In effect, the Enlightenment had tried to universalize the claims of natural reason by taking the natural person as its foundation, leaving behind traditional Aristotelian and Christian notions of virtue and purpose. The result was to remove the notion of virtues and ends from an objective moral order, and to locate it instead in the subjective will and pure preference of the individual. Hence, too, the Enlightenment would remove the Reformation's core claim of "freedom" from its Christian context and locate it in the subjective freedom of the individual, now protected as a matter of natural right.

Maritain conceded that the notion of rights, properly understood as an expression of natural law, represented an advance in political thought.[71] The key phrase here is "properly understood." The understanding associated with the rationalist conceptualism of the Enlightenment Maritain dismissed as "artificial systematization" or prideful "geometrising reason." The true conception of natural law, he insists, can be discovered only "within the being of things as their very essence is, and . . . precedes all formulation."[72]

Inevitably, Maritain argued, the aggressive and self-sufficient Enlightenment conception of reason resulted in a philosophy of rights that ended, as in Kant, "by treating the individual as a god and making all the rights ascribed to him the absolute and unlimited rights of a god."[73] Finally, "human Will or human Freedom . . . was to replace God . . . as supreme source and origin of Natural Law[,] . . . [which] was to be deduced from the so-called autonomy of the Will."[74]

D'Entrèves was, again, probably wise not to raise with his audience any conflict between traditional natural law and "rights" as conceived during the Enlightenment. If American postwar scholars had wanted a rousing call for fixed legal norms rooted in reason, they had already received a far more subtle and complex configuration than they had expected. The appeal of natural law was in its offer of moral security, civility, and a baseline of decency as against the encroachments of anarchy, chaos, and amorality. Yet its acceptance demanded a surrender to commands rooted in Aristotelian essentialism and in pre-Enlightenment epistemology.

In the immediate postwar period, however, complete rejection of natural law implied a bleak and incontestable relativism. Celebrating that relativism by locating it in the subjective freedom of post-Enlightenment selves who exercise autonomy and choice is satisfactory only so long as that freedom is exercised in a manner at least minimally consistent with the demands of traditional, religiously rooted morality. Yet if the very theory of freedom displaces the authority of tradition, the substantive content of tradition will eventually be relegated to irrelevance. Thus, the ultimate irony of the natural law revival: faced with the moral abomination of Nazism, postwar intellectuals, many of whom were no doubt otherwise epistemological agnostics or skeptics, scurried to seek solace in the anticipated moral certainty of the natural law tradition. Soon secular legal scholars would forget their flirtation with natural law, losing themselves in the heady liberalism of the 1960s. They would then look to the courts to articulate what became, in effect, a new morality premised on an individual autonomy that was legally secured by a regime of rights.

In doing so, most legal scholars would forget the extent to which their own methodology so often depended on presuppositions and methods of reasoning borrowed directly from traditional natural law. D'Entrèves described as the actual methodology of natural law a process familiar, in fact, to most legalists. First, one must name and discuss the value or purpose implicit in the development of any given law or set of laws. A law is then applied, not mechanically, but in light of the value to which it gives expression, in light of competing values that may command our acknowledgment and force us to make choices or recognize exceptions, and in light of the objective facts of social and natural life.[75] John Noonan, a master of the methodology described only briefly by d'Entrèves, in 1965 used the *Forum* as a vehicle for demonstrating the extent to which the natural law approach, as applied to particular issues, is what we now recognize as, simply, skilled and sophisticated legal analysis.

Noonan first made the case for the natural law method by selecting two of his own (Catholic) church's most problematic and controversial prohibitions, those directed at usury and contraception.[76] The Catholic position on usury had, of course, already been reversed. Noonan was a leading Catholic advocate for reversal on contraception as well, and he was determined to show that natural law did not require rigid adherence to past rules, but rather careful application of a reasoned methodology. His approach was a legally subtle mediation between generally stated values and the human social condition.

Noonan concedes with respect to both usury and contraception that the very concept of "nature" or "natural" had been manipulated rhetorically and adjusted or reconstructed to suit human conceptions of "function" or "purpose."[77] (In the case of usury, the function of money had been reconceived to include generation of wealth as well as facilitation of exchange; in the case of contraception, the purpose of sexual relations had been revised to include expression of marital love as well as reproduction.) Noonan also concedes that the absolute prohibitions initiated in both cases would and did, in time, yield exceptions in response to changes in culture, technology, or environment. In short, the absolute was sure to be mediated by the contingent.[78]

Nevertheless, Noonan, proceeding in the manner laid out by d'Entrèves, names with passion the underlying values that are themselves ordained, he believes, by divine command and sought to be realized through the once absolute rules: charity and love for usury;[79] and dignity and sanctity of life for contraception.[80] For Noonan, such values are best preserved by prescriptive moral absolutes rooted in an appeal to nature that invites reasoned discourse within, but only within, that particularized rhetorical framework.[81] Noonan rejects the notion that life itself, in any of its instances, might be "purposeless, measureless, uncontrollable, or arbitrary."[82] The best protection against surrender to purposelessness lies in a structure of categorical rules that are expressive of values, with exceptions carved out by rational argument; and rational argument is facilitated by an analysis of the "natural," even though our conception of what is natural may, in any given instance, itself be based on the values or purposes we ascribe to natural processes.[83]

Two years later, in 1967, Noonan again demonstrated the same natural law methodology by including in the Forum an article against abortion.[84] His goal was to engage in reasoned debate on the subject, a debate framed and contained by the rationalism of natural law analysis. The article was a carefully constructed invitation to dialogue. Nazism was a danger to be invoked, but not yet a charge to be leveled at opponents.

Noonan takes the abortion question to be basically a question about when a person should be treated as human. Obscure theological discussions of ensoulment, he says, are simply discussions of that critical question.[85] His reasoning proceeds from a description of a particularized legal history during which rules were developed, not always with consistency or uniformity. He then moves to an elucidation of the value that those rules were instituted to protect—in the case of antiabortion rules, the value is a respect for human life and a "refusal to discriminate among human beings on the basis of their varying potentialities."[86] From that value he derives a uniform rule category designed to give it effect, the rule that there should be no taking of human life after conception. Noonan argues that attempts to limit humanity by denying the status "human" to any creature conceived by humans parallels other forms of invidious exclusion. The fact, for example, that we may not "think of" a month-old embryo as human should not be decisive; social groups have all too often been known not to "think of" some subgroup (for instance, a particular race) as being quite human.[87]

In defending the precise line between conception and preconception, Noonan carefully argues from nature and probabilities. He concedes that the formation of life is a continuous process, without sharp, absolute dividing lines. Nevertheless, as between conceptus and sperm, for example, the line is rationally defensible because only 20 percent of fertilized eggs will spontaneously abort, whereas each spermatozoa must compete with 200 million others to fertilize an egg.[88] Noonan rejects a distinction based on physical viability or nonviability as too variable and arbitrary given the facts of nature, especially, for example, the fact that infants remain "dependent" well after birth, and that some can survive with artificial incubation earlier than others.[89] In other words, alternative formulations to the initial rule-category are carefully considered by reference both to the value being discussed and to the facts of natural life.

On the complex question of preference for the mother's life over the fetus in cases of conflict, he describes the traditional direct/indirect distinction. That traditional distinction allowed for a cancerous uterus, for example, to be removed from a pregnant mother even if removal resulted in the death of a fetus. The doctor's purpose in such a case was not to kill the fetus; rather, the purpose was to remove the cancerous organ, the death of the fetus being only an unintended, indirect consequence.[90] That exception does not destroy the validity of the general rule, Noonan claims. The exception was limited to cases of ectopic pregnancies and cancerous uteruses, so that the widest protection possible for fetal life was still retained.[91] No rule can be absolute—values must be weighed, even the value of innocent life, and the direct/indirect exception is just a spatial metaphor for the careful weighing of values that constitutes the work of rational moral analysis.[92] Only the mother's life should be weighed against the child's, however, not other supposed utilities. The value that ultimately animates this abstract moral analysis, Noonan says, is the scriptural command to "love your neighbor as yourself," which means that the fetus must be treated as having full value as a human life, even in this process that is concededly one of weighing.[93]

Challenging Noonan's moral assumptions, John O'Connor, a philosopher from Case Western Reserve, wrote a response in the *Natural Law Forum* disputing Noonan's insistence that humanity is an objective attribute that must be acquired at some definite time.[94] This assumption, O'Connor argues, tilted Noonan's analysis of alternatives unduly toward the uniform rule of "human being at conception."[95] O'Connor emphasizes the relativist point that an attribute is a function of social decision-making[96] (a point that Noonan had been too sophisticated to try to deny, but had not exactly highlighted either). In fact, in an earlier *Forum* article Margaret Mead had pointed out that while all societies develop criteria for determining humanity, the criteria are quite various—sometimes infants are not included, so that infanticide is allowed.[97] O'Connor reads Noonan as assuming that, even if the attribute "humanity" *is* a function of social decision-making, not a quality "in" a person, some criteria are objectively better than others, even objectively "right" or "wrong," for defining the category.[98]

O'Connor sees no such objective baseline. The correct criteria can never be "discovered," he says, but are themselves a function of social decision-making. For that reason, one can look only to the moral assumptions of the particular culture. In modern societies it would be considered reprehensible to kill a baby, and quite possibly a seven-month-old fetus, but probably not reprehensible to kill a two-month-old fetus—or a tree. Such views can change, however, depending on whether people respond to the fetus (or tree) as a creature very like themselves. All societies draw a circle of "alike" somewhere—including some, excluding others. They may change the degree of inclusiveness based on new information or perception, but they cannot "discover" the proper placement of the circle, the boundary that defines the category. They can only decide where to draw it.[99]

The realist challenge to classical legal conceptualism was, of course, playing itself out. As Noonan conceded in his reply to O'Connor:[100] "After all, one of the principal insights of modern jurisprudence has been that judges do not 'discover' the law. I have always supposed that there was an analogous insight to be followed in moral discourse."[101] Unlike classical legal conceptualism, however, Noonan's natural law approach was more explicitly and honestly rooted in moral values, which he seriously sought to articulate in a final reference to divine injunction—the obligation to love your neighbor.[102] Without that reference, Noonan's categories had no ultimate moral content, despite the rationality and objectivity of his methodology.

The realists, like O'Connor (and Protestants, as we will see), were impatient with fixed categories, eager to sweep them away and demand direct confrontation between the concrete situation and the moral requirement. The content of the moral requirement in law, however, had never been articulated: There had been no realist version of the gospel. With Nazism in the past and abortion on the moral/legal agenda, Noonan had no confidence that legal realism as mere negation could provide moral guidance. To deconstruct the category "humanity," to treat it as having no objective content whatsoever, as just a function of cultural decision-making, meant a world of complete moral relativism. Noonan argued that before claiming, as O'Connor did, that we can look only to the "feelings" of people in a given culture for our membership criteria, we need to recall that "[i]f feelings are the key, many slave owners have felt it perfectly moral to abuse and even kill their slaves . . . many Nazis felt no twinge of guilt in exterminating Jews and Poles whom they believed not to belong to the human species. . . ."[103] Noonan ends with the explicit comparison of the unborn to Jews: "The embryo, too, if he could speak, might say like Shylock, 'If you prick us, do we not bleed?' "[104]

Noonan's arguments against abortion, especially these earlier ones, deserve to be taken seriously by liberals, precisely because they raise the problem with which the *Natural Law Forum* had begun its mission: to articulate a legal methodology that would provide a hedge against totalitarianism, whose worst aspect was the treatment of people as expendable objects. Noonan was too sophisticated to suggest a return to simple classicism in legal thought, and he was more honest than even d'Entrèves in frankly acknowledging that inevitably the source of moral value in Western culture, including legal culture, has been religion. His method was a delicate interweaving of category as premised on value, rational argument about distinctions based on the objective realities of the natural world, and calculated exceptions based on the values that gave rise to the initial category, along with careful consideration of competing values. Legal argument has not offered a more well-considered methodology.

Nor did Noonan dodge moral responsibility for the exceptions he acknowledged, in the way that legalist casuistry often seems to allow—as if a killing is less a killing when it is labeled "indirect." He was willing to use the word "balance" instead—but only on the assumption that nothing could be allowed to outweigh an individual life except another individual life. On that point, however, as Noonan knew, there is a more troubling reality. In a wholly different context Noonan, a good scholar of tort law, had once pointed out that the "whole of automobile tort law" rests on the assumption that human lives will routinely be taken (in automobile accidents) for the sake of "values more highly prized by the society" than human life, values realized through the facilitation of transportation.[105] Noonan's own brilliant essay on *Palsgraf*,[106] a case about passenger injury on a railway station, deals explicitly with the statistical analysis of railway accidents and deaths, tolerated by our society for the sake of the benefits of mass transportation. Noonan, a person of real moral sensibility, is clearly troubled by that reality, and he correctly senses that we have not yet developed a moral vocabulary with which to deal with it. It almost seems, however, as if Noonan seeks to avoid that reality by building a special categorical wall of protection around the fetus. Feminists, of course, are not surprised that women are expected to bear the burden of his need for the comforting category. Yet what does our culture have to offer in its place?

The answer, at least in terms of acceptable public discourse, was rapidly becoming other than traditional and religiously rooted morality.[107] It is perhaps a fitting symbol that in 1969 the *Natural Law Forum* changed its name to the *American Journal of Jurisprudence*, having published in its last *Forum* volume articles by both John Rawls[108] and Robert Nozick.[109] Most of mainstream legal thought had by then turned away from the hard questions of natural law (although there may be a current rerevival—as Maritain once commented, "[e]very fair and every war brings forth a new natural law)."[110] Throughout the 1970s, thoroughly secular and non-Aristotelian legal philosophy achieved its hold on American legal thought—the universe was composed of utilitarians[111] and deontological liberals[112] and the ambitious few who might try to reconcile those two traditions.[113]

The same last issue of the *Forum* also featured a very different kind of essay, "Karl Barth and Moral Natural Law," by Louis Midgley.[114] The essay raised a troubling point that seemed, oddly, not to have occurred to the earlier enthusiastic revivers of natural law, although it is well known to theologians: the only serious Christian institutional opposition to Hitler in

Germany arose, not on the basis of natural law, but rather quite explicitly and emphatically in the context of *rejecting* natural law. That extraordinary irony was not mentioned in the pages of the Forum until the 1968 volume, and then only in a halfhearted effort to claim that the rejection was not so emphatic after all.[115]

3

Protestant Ethics:
The Legacy of Barth
and Bonhoeffer

......

The rejection of natural law was rooted in the Reformation. Legal scholars often find Reformation theology less congenial than the stately principles of natural law, which are still familiar as embodied in such documents as the United Nations Declaration of Human Rights. In that sense the Catholic natural law tradition has been successfully universalized, albeit at the cost, during the Enlightenment, of losing its distinctly Christian character.

In contrast, the ethics of serious Reformation theology can sound stubbornly sectarian, too peculiarly Christian to have any relevance to the world outside the Christian church. Nevertheless, it was an uncompromising reaffirmation of the Reformation that inspired the German Confessing Church to refuse to compromise with Nazism. That refusal was embodied in the Barmen Declaration of 1934, a declaration of opposition to Hitler drafted chiefly by the great Protestant theologian Karl Barth.[1]

In the early 1930s Hitler was seeking, with great success, both loyalty and submission to civil authority from the German Lutheran Church. Many church leaders compliantly accepted the authority of the Nazi Ministry for Church Affairs. In contrast, the dissenters at Barmen openly and unequivocally rejected

> the false doctrine that the Church, as the source of its proclamation, could and should, over and above God's one Word, acknowledge other events, powers, images and truths as divine revelation . . . . the false doctrine that the form of her order and mission can be left to the discretion of the Church or to the ideological and political views

that happen to prevail . . . or that she can set up, or allow herself to be given, special leaders with sovereign powers.[2]

The Barmen Declaration was a theological rather than a political state-ment, but when it proclaimed in 1934 Germany that "[w]e repudiate the false teaching that there are areas of our life in which we belong not to Jesus Christ but another Lord, areas in which we do not need justi-fication and sanctification through him,"[3] its political implications were inescapable. At the end of the Barmen synod, some ten thousand persons gathered for a worship service. As they departed, they sang Luther's hymn, "A Mighty Fortress Is Our God," which became a symbol of resistance throughout the Nazi period.[4]

Karl Barth, a Calvinist theologian, wrote the Barmen Declaration at a time when many of the more "liberal" German Lutherans were using a modernized version of natural law (one considerably more "imprudent," Barth said, than traditional Thomism)[5] to justify embracing Hitler. Catho-lics, meanwhile, often heroic in their individual efforts to thwart Hitler and help Jews, found their church, for the most part, silent on what natural law required.[6] The Confessing Church stood out in frank and utter oppo-sition. Karl Barth was expelled from Germany; he returned to his native Basel.[7] His theological and political ally, Lutheran pastor and theologian Dietrich Bonhoeffer, chose to remain in Germany and eventually joined the secret resistance; he was imprisoned in Berlin in 1943, transferred to Buchenwald following the failed attempt to kill Hitler, and summarily executed on April 9, 1945.[8]

Given that history, which would seem to suggest at least an initial claim to ethical credibility, and also given the profound influence of both theo-logians in modern theology (including Catholic theology), it may be sur-prising that they were ignored by the postwar legal world—even at a time when the legal world was taking theology seriously. In part, the expla-nation is an odd quirk of misinterpretation. When Barth's work was first becoming known in the United States, Reinhold Niebuhr was the leading American Protestant theologian, the one whom legal scholars were most likely to associate with Protestantism. Niebuhr's own powerful work had seemed to reach a dead end at a time when Protestantism generally was also foundering.[9] George Kelly has characterized American Protestantism of the period as a cacophony of frustrations, a motley collection composed of self-contradictory elements: fundamentalism's "defensive suspicion of all treatments of Scripture . . . [except] literal inerrancy; sugar-coated liberal modernism that forsook dogmatics for a soft and safe bourgeois ethic; self-righteous pacifism and quietism; sectarian extravagance; and Social Gospel extremism that reduced Christianity to a kind of idealistic case work."[10] Niebuhr himself apparently failed to understand Barth, sometimes attributing to him positions that were almost precisely the opposite of the ones he actually had taken.[11] Meanwhile, Paul Tillich, the philosophical theologian whose work was receiving considerable attention, read Barth more carefully but objected to his extreme antiessentialism and his strong stand against natural law.[12] That rejection of natural law led many Protestants in the United States to consider Barth's theology irrelevant to the task of formulating an ethical response to Nazism and to the problems posed by legal positivism and moral relativism generally.[13]

By the 1960s, however, Bonhoeffer's Prison Letters were becoming almost faddishly well-known even in the secular United States, and Barth's work had been more thoughtfully interpreted. By then, the law world was shifting its attention away from theology altogether—it had been, at most, a brief flirtation. To the extent that Nazism was remembered as raising metaphysical questions, "these were," as Peter Berger writes, "typically anthropological rather than theological in character: 'How could men act this way?' rather than 'How could God permit this?' "[14] Yet the appearance of Midgley's essay in the Natural Law Forum does remind us—as did, in fact, the best of legal realism in relation to law—that ethics need not rely on normative, essentialist categories to be serious about moral responsibility.

Bonhoeffer, when later popularized, was often treated as a secular existentialist or a utilitarian rather than as a devout Christian.[15] The most serious study of Barth and Bonhoeffer was confined to the realm of academic theology,[16] where once-influential departments had become intellectual backwaters, curiosities in a secular age. The two points are related, for Bonhoeffer was surely an authentic hero, yet secular intellectuals of the 1960s, however impressed by Bonhoeffer, could no longer take his theology seriously on its own terms, as being something that might be real or important, rather than just another cultural or political phenomenon to be studied and dissected for its functional value, like labor unions, television shows, or zoological societies. For secular elite intellectuals, religion was simply not visible, almost too embarrassing to take seriously. As Garry Wills describes them, such intellectuals "have a serene provincialism, dismissive of the ordinary torments of people less optimistic, irreverent, and pragmatic than they."[17]

Karl Barth and Dietrich Bonhoeffer were concerned with those "ordinary torments," basic issues of life and death, of pain and suffering, the realities that serve constantly as antidotes to our pride and arrogance, as reminders of our ignorance and inability to master our own fate. We will therefore offer a survey of their moral landscape, knowing full well that we are inviting most of our readers into a territory that will seem strangely sectarian and therefore alien. Their discourse is starkly theological, with lots of "God-talk," and we will take it seriously as such. Yet the issues within that discourse are familiar to contemporary purveyors of critical theory— freedom and necessity, subject and object, fact and value, contingency and timelessness. In fact, such issues, treated with more sophistication than most of our recent forays, have been the stuff of Reformation thought for more than four hundred years. Perhaps we still have something to learn about morality and the limits of human agency from Martin Luther, John Calvin, or Jonathan Edwards, as well as their latter-day expositors and interpreters—just as we have more to learn from the subtlety of real Thomist natural law thought than we usually suppose.

Many have credited (or blamed) the Reformation for making modern scientific and liberal moral/political thought possible. Its insistence that salvation comes only from faith had the unintended but perhaps inevitable effect of relegating theology to the realm of private, subjective desire. If faith and grace alone led one to God, then reason was "freed," as it were, to master the objective facts of nature or outline rational principles of secular governance and morality.[18] By the time of the Enlightenment, God had become, as Barth said, an "'old Lord,' to whom regard must occasionally be had, but who is not normally considered." [19]

At their best, however, Protestant theologians have a maddening knack for toppling and upending ostensibly comfortable and seemingly stable structures of thought. Scholastic natural law theory, for example, created an elaborate hierarchical structure that seemed to mediate the supposedly infinite distance between human beings and God, and between nature and grace. Thus, it was said, grace "perfects" nature, but does not overturn it. It almost seemed as if, through natural reason, people could ascend the hierarchical ladder of speculation that led from the earthly to the divine.

The Reformation seized on that point of perfecting, but not overturning, as one of infinite distance, beyond the capacity of human mediation. Hence, the elaborate scholastic structure, which exactly at that point had seemed to reconcile Aristotle and Christianity, began to crumble.[20] Perhaps the most easily accessible legal analogy to that critical edge of Protestant theology is to the legal realists, who had a knack for taking the

dilemma of the "hard case" and showing it to be, not peculiar and peripheral to an otherwise intact structure, but rather, at the core of the whole
structure, the problem of legal reasoning itself.[21]

Barth was a master of that critical technique, by which he affirmed the
central Reformation teaching that, as he said often by tautology, "God is
God"—hence, "we humans may not speak of God by speaking of ourselves in a loud voice,"[22] which is what he took natural law theorists to be
doing. Barth was therefore not surprised when natural law theory offered
so little basis for resistance to the idolatry of Nazism.[23]

Given its emphasis on the frailty of overconfident human structures of
thought, Barth's theology depicts a reality that is both paradoxical and dialectical, one that cannot be captured by analytic, conceptual categories.
Thus, the gospel is described as the overcoming of a series of completely
contradictory categories: "nothing new, but the oldest; not particular, but
the most universal; not historical, but the presupposition of all history,"
while simultaneously "not an old acquaintance, but a new one; not universal,
but the most particular; not a mere presupposition, but history itself."[24]
Similarly, being faithful to Kierkegaard's insistence on the " 'infinite quali-
tative distinction' between time and eternity,"[25] Barth described divine
encounter with the world as the "impossible possibility," as "a moment
with no before and no after."[26]

As metaphor for such formulations, Barth drew, not on Aristotle, for
whom our existing reality was self-contained, unfolding within time, but
rather on Plato, for whom the reality we name was never more than provisional.[27] For example, the metaphor for the moment of "no before and
no after" can be found in Plato's description of rest and motion. Rest and
motion, as we conceive them, by definition exclude each other, yet the
reality of the world is constituted by transition from one to the other, by a
moment that can only be defined negatively, the essence that is in no place
or, as Schleiermacher translated it, "this incomprehensible essence, the
moment."[28] With no place and occupying no time, this moment nevertheless constitutes both space and time: "That which cannot be identified
spatially or temporally in this world is that which holds the world together
at its core."[29]

Barth's favorite among his own works was a study of St. Anselm's proof
of the existence of God, which, for Barth, turned an absolute prohibition on thought into an affirmation that made human thought possible.[30]
Anselm's proof was rooted in a formulation, a name, for God: "That than
which nothing greater can be conceived."[31] Notably, states Barth, this

name is not "that which is the greatest of all things," as it had been mis-interpreted.[32] That would be an affirmative claim, which would amount to placing God in the realm of the ontic. Instead, Anselm had located that point of radical and complete disjuncture analogous to the gap between finite number and infinity (Anselm had, in effect, defined infinity many years before mathematicians had done so).[33] By naming God only through prohibition and negation, Anselm affirmed our inability to name God at all, giving us knowledge of our finitude. Again, the perhaps too slick analogy to numbers—we have knowledge of finite numbers as such only with reference to infinity, which we can name but cannot comprehend.[34]

Similarly, in discussing human attempts to formulate scientific laws of nature, Barth zeroed in on the inevitable gap between human prediction and the actual occurrence of events, which he called the gap between the noetic and the ontic—the lack of necessary connection between what is apprehended by mere thought and what actually occurs:

> No high measure of noetic certainty or clarity can give to laws known to us, i.e., discovered and guaranteed by us, the character of ontic laws. . . . Concerning the actuality of the laws known to us we will already think rather more modestly because we will be aware that they cannot in any case originate or effect the event itself and as such, that even presupposing their validity they must still be referred to the fact that the event takes place at all only on the basis of a completely different operation [which, for Barth, was "foreordination"].[35]

Humility, a sense of the finitude and contingency of human thought in the face of what can really be known only from the (impossible) vantage point of infinity, makes, as Barth points out, for better science. We should "leave the laws known to us open to the revision of content and formula-tion which may become necessary as a result of our encounter and their confrontation with new and actual occurrence. These laws are as it were arrows pointing in the direction of real order and form, i.e., of the order and form which are objectively immanent in and proper to actual occur-rence itself. But for this reason they can never become absolute dogmas, nor assume the character of ontic law. . . ."[36]

Barth, in fact, did not reject science, but audaciously reclaimed theology as a science. As against skeptics, he argued that all scientific knowledge is necessarily contingent, with its particular methodology suited to its own specific object of study, and that all science is rooted in a faith that the object of study will reveal itself, at least provisionally, through the

method fashioned by scientists within their traditions.[37] Properly understood, Barth argued, science was actually more akin to theology than
to the presumptuous and complacent nineteenth-century positivism that
had succeeded, for a time, in forcing theology to adopt a defensive and
conciliatory stance.

Barth's description of science is, of course, in accord with our current
understanding of scientific methodology. Modern science does, in fact,
resemble sophisticated theology more than it resembles the elaborate
claims of certainty that are more typical of Newtonian physics, and too
often, ironically, of social science as well. Good scientists now concede
the tentativeness of their conclusions and the dependence of science on
an object too large for its own comprehension. No science is complete,
but depends on a metascience that is itself incomplete.[38] In a criticism of
positivism strikingly similar to that of Barth, physicist Werner Heisenberg
noted that both science and theology are compelled to speak in "images
and parables," that "Truth dwells in the deeps."[39]

For Barth, then, to do theology as a *scientist* meant that one must be "fully
cognizant of his presuppositions, his method, the time-boundedness or
temporality of his thought, and hence the transient and provisional nature
of his own theology."[40] Theology, being "entirely dependent upon God's
decision rather than upon any independent decision of its own," knowing "only the actuality of being bound (*Bindung*) to its object, the object of
its faith," . . . "knows itself to rest on sheer contingency."[41] Thus, Barth,
in taking a "scientific" approach to theology, repudiated not only the
self-deluding claims of Baconian positivism, but also the certainty that
people invented for themselves in the name of religion. In fact, both Barth
and Bonhoeffer were known for advocating "religionless Christianity," for
"[r]eligion forgets that it has a right to exist only when it constantly does
away with itself."[42]

Barth's greatest concern was not simply to expose the fallacies of positivist science, but to combat a Protestant willingness to elevate contingent
human projects to the status of natural or essential reality. The ground-
work for that mistaken direction, Barth thought, had been laid by Friedrich Schleiermacher. Schleiermacher had insisted that Protestantism, to
be taken seriously in the post-Enlightenment world, must make an "eternal covenant" with modern culture. Otherwise, "Christianity becomes
identified with barbarism and science with unbelief."[43] While Barth never
rejected using, eclectically, the contributions of philosophy, science, and
historical criticism, he feared that Schleiermacher's "eternal covenant" inevitably meant a willingness to make theology and the church subservient

to the demands of prevailing political ideologies and scientific or cultural orthodoxies.[44]

This fear was, of course, realized when so many German Christians were willing to make their own covenant with the claims of the German volk culture. In turn, Barth saw that willingness as linked to the renewed interest in natural law which occurred within German Protestantism during the Nazi period. Barth feared that if church and culture were too bound together by the link of a natural law theology, then contingent human projects (politics, science, cultural traditions) could claim the status of ontological reality, not subject to God's revealed word. Natural law too easily became a theological excuse for alliance with Nazism to the extent that it suggested a correspondence between the natural order and the political order of the German state. Thus, when a former friend, Emil Brunner, wrote in support of a doctrine of "orders of creation," by which he meant a return to a form of natural theology,[45] Barth's famous answer was entitled, simply and dramatically, "Nein!"[46]

Brunner had argued that even the Reformers taught that God graciously preserves both natural life and the "ordinances" of historical and cultural life, such as marriage and the state, and the civil and secular functions and offices.[47] These ordinances can be recognized as good and necessary by "rational man" through the exercise of unaided natural reason. It is "peculiar to the preserving grace of God that he does his preserving work both by nature acting unconsciously and by the reason of man."[48] If such notions sound like St. Thomas, Brunner had announced, then so did Calvin, who used the term lex naturae, and also "order of creation."[49] Brunner had conceded that both lex naturae (the will of God implanted on creation) and the ordinances of creation were "somewhat obscured" by sin and must be made known afresh by Christ; but the original order still "clearly shows through," despite sin, and can be recognized by the light of natural reason.[50] Brunner was in effect suggesting the possibility of discovering a self-sufficient rational system, "with which sin 'has . . . nothing to do.'"[51]

Barth answered with scorn. Even St. Thomas, by incorporating Augustine, had rejected so brazen a claim for natural reason. As Barth reminded Brunner, Catholics had a doctrine of prevenient and preparatory grace, which meant that only God, not "natural" human beings, made the correct operation of reason in nature possible: "[R]eason, if left entirely without grace, is incurably sick and incapable of any serious theological activity. Only when it has been illumined, or at least provisionally shone upon by faith," can it produce statements of truth about the human and natural world that can be considered truths of reason rather than revelation.[52] In other words, Barth argued, even within Catholicism "[t]here can be no question of separating nature and grace 'neatly . . . by a horizontal line.'"[53]

Thus, according to Barth, Brunner oversimplified the question of nature and grace and was so confident about the unsullied capacity of reason as to offend any "Roman Catholic theologian who knows his subject at all."[54] But even more offensive was the claim that the ordinances of creation (described by Brunner as representing Reformation thought) were really consistent with the message of God's absolute transcendence. Brunner had blunted and tamed the critical Reformation claim, leaving the way open for Protestants who called themselves "German Christians" to argue a correspondence between God's will, natural law, and the "ordinances" of German nationalism—German culture, the German state, the German race. Barth was unforgiving, saying that Brunner had "gone and calmly claimed Calvin for his own; . . . he has confronted me together with his 'Calvin' and has patted me on the shoulder and told me to be a good boy; he has seen to it that the 'German Christians' can, if they wish . . . quote now not only Luther but also Calvin in their support. It is the fact that he managed to do all these things which I am so far unable to forgive Brunner."[55]

Barth thus insisted that natural law offers no basis for real ethical judgment; instead, it opens the way for oppressive ideology by pretending that what is contingent, provisional, and merely human is really "natural," as part of the divinely sanctioned nature of creation, its essential reality. What then can be the basis for ethical decision if not natural law? Barth and Bonhoeffer forged an answer to that question in the pressing moral and political context of Nazism—ethics was not an abstract question, but one on which a person could be called to stake his or her life, as did Bonhoeffer. Barth's critical methodology had been sharpened by Franz Overbeck, a friend of Nietzsche and an utter religious skeptic; it was Overbeck who had inspired Barth to attack the arrogant pretension of conventional religious thought and, especially, the complacent claims of liberal Protestants.[56] Bonhoeffer, too, viewed the problem of ethics as the problem posed by Nietzsche: after criticism, what remains except the Nietzschian claim that power is its own excuse for being?[57]

Could one reject abstract normative categories, whether derived from natural law or the secularized rationalism of Kant, and nevertheless fashion an ethics that would require responsible action in the world? The answer for both Barth and Bonhoeffer lay not in ethics itself (based on a supposed knowledge of the world and the operation of human reason), but in theology—in the dialectical process of looking first "upward," as it were, to the command of God, which is a divinely initiated and revealed claim, the call to the covenant "I-Thou" relationship, and then downward, to a particular person in a particular context. The content of the command is known only by virtue of another dialectic—that of incarnation and redemption—so that the (impossible) command is always accompanied by the promise of grace, of the "giving" which is its meaning. (Those are, to put it mildly, unfamiliar terms in modern secular thought—sin and redemption have almost dropped out of the vocabulary, but for Barth and Bonhoeffer they were still central.) Hence, the gospel was the core of ethics—the command that is fulfilled by the life lived wholly for the neighbor.[58]

Barth's ethical method always retained a critical edge—a method designed to undercut ethical categories for the purpose of forcing direct confrontation with the "command." Usually, Barth said, the ethicist produces a prescriptive legal text—by drawing from the Bible, or from natural law perceptible to reason, or from "particular norms handed down historically in the tradition of Western Christianity, which then lay claim to universal validity."[59] Then this text, with its carefully defined categories, is applied to particular cases by the method of casuistry, the working out of detailed exceptions and distinctions. This method has much to recommend it, Barth concedes (but only sarcastically), in no small part because it eliminates the "often very oppressive task of making [one's] own orientations and decisions"—for which "everyone will be grateful to the moralist for the superior knowledge" that is thereby brought to the situation.[60]

As always, however, Barth points to the gap that makes this whole elaborate ethical enterprise impossible—here precisely a point that the legal realists made clear to American jurisprudence: There simply is no "method or technique of applying this text to the plenitude of conditions and possibilities."[61] That means the legalist model for ethics as premised on objective categories simply cannot work. Quoting Bonhoeffer, Barth explains that "[a]n ethics cannot be a book in which there is set out how everything in the world actually ought to be but unfortunately is not,"[62] for it is the "unfortunately is not" which is the whole point. It is precisely in the real, creaturely world, the world as it is, a fallen world, that decisions must be made.

Legalist ethics thus makes the "objectively untenable assumption" that command comes in the form of "a universal rule, an empty form, or rather a tissue of such rules and forms."[63] Instead, "[i]t is always an individual command for the conduct of this man, at this moment and in this situation; a prescription for this case of his; a prescription for the choice of a definite possibility of human intention, decision and action."[64] The failure to understand this leads, for example, both Jews and Christians to seek *timeless* commands in the biblical texts, rather than to see biblical injunction as command *within* a particular historical reality, and therefore, in the covenant sense, as a "witness to God's special commanding here and now."[65] Barth concludes: "No wonder, then, that wherever it is treated as a timeless truth, it can only be made applicable and usable with the help of some interpretation which is more or less arbitrary even in relation to the texts, and of all kinds of amplifications and additions drawn from the treasures of natural law and tradition."[66] Those efforts to amplify, explain, and interpret simply reveal the self-contradiction inherent in the ethical method itself.

Legalist ethics are false, Barth argues, not only because they are logically impossible, but because they lead to two paradoxically related problems. First, unwarranted arrogance: the moralist seeks to "set himself on God's throne, to distinguish good and evil" through claims that in a "*summa* of ethical statements compiled by him and his like from the Bible, natural law and tradition, he can know the command of God, see through it and past it, and thus master and handle it . . . like a possession or domain"[67]— the precise opposite of true obedience. At the same time, however, even in this arrogance, casuistical ethics also destroys human freedom. On this point Barth always insists, following Dostoevsky, that the command of God is an appeal to freedom—not a freedom of "choice, preference, or selection" but (again paradoxically) the freedom of obedience.[68]

Thus, casuist ethics calls a person away from real responsibility; it "conceals from him the character of his conduct as his own, direct responsibility."[69] An absolutist, categorical ethics does not encroach too much on people, but "too little."[70] As Bonhoeffer said, "The commandment of God is permission. It . . . commands freedom. It is by overcoming this contradiction that it shows itself to be God's commandment; the impossible becomes possible, and that which lies beyond the range of what can be commanded, liberty, is the true object of this commandment. That is the high price of God's commandment; it is no cheaper than that."[71]

Bonhoeffer is well known for phrases that capture the form of that command—the real "cost of discipleship," which he demonstrated most fully not by words, but by living it, contrasted to the "cheap grace" of the liberal Protestants.[72] Discipleship means being responsible "to and for the neighbor, in his concrete possibility." A given situation is not "material on which to impress an idea or program"; rather, the responsible person may have to prefer what is "relatively better to what is relatively worse, and . . . perceive that the 'absolute good' may sometimes be the very worst."[73] One may, in fact, have to incur guilt in order to act responsibly; the neighbor and the future, for which we are responsible, do not exist in some ideal world, but in a real world of sin.

Confronted with his insistence on notions like "discipleship" or "sin," those of us who are not theologically predisposed are likely to dismiss Bonhoeffer as an anachronism, offering little in the way of contemporary moral guidance. We, after all, are so very modern (or postmodern), complacent in the embrace of secularism and the rejection of foolish "supernatural" worldviews. Bonhoeffer was just a Lutheran pastor, albeit a brave one, who died almost fifty years ago, as did many others who resisted Hitler. Or, out of sheer admiration for his moral courage, we may be tempted, as were many in the 1960s, not to dismiss Bonhoeffer, but to appropriate him to the pantheon of existential heroes, lonely individuals who affirm for the rest of us the very possibility and nobility of human agency. Both of these reactions, however, are simply off the mark.

Bonhoeffer the hero cannot be understood apart from Bonhoeffer the theologian; and Bonhoeffer the theologian was no less the modern for his effort to comprehend the world in theological terms. He grew up in a starkly secular intellectual environment and was the beneficiary of as sophisticated an education as twentieth-century Europe had to offer. When he chose theology, the profession of his grandfather, over the science more prevalent in his immediate family, he did so initially out of intellectual curiosity, not faith.[74] He had thoroughly mastered the legacy of Enlightenment rationalism, and also the critical insights of Kierkegaard, Heidegger, and, especially, Nietzsche. As an intellectual matter, Bonhoeffer saw the necessity of confronting, not evading, both the tradition of Kant and the criticism of Nietzsche.

With respect to ethics, Bonhoeffer set himself "self-consciously and explicitly" against the tradition of Kant. Like Barth, he did not believe that the "ethical formalist," or the "transcendent character of the universal," could reach actual persons in their real historical situations. If Kant sought to rise above time and history through the principle of universalization, Bonhoeffer sought to embrace time and history, insisting on responsible action in concrete times and places.[75]

Bonhoeffer thus responded to Kant's ethics with an insistence on the concrete here-and-now instead of ethereal absolutes or formal categories: "The ethical, in this sense of the formal, the universally valid, and the rational contained no element of concretion, and it therefore inevitably ended in the total atomization of human society and of the life of the individual, in unlimited subjectivism and individualism."[76]

From an intellectual standpoint, Bonhoeffer, like Barth, took the teachings of Nietzsche more seriously than those of Kant, for while Kant might merely be opposed, Nietzsche had to be assimilated. Bonhoeffer's affirmation of "concrete times and concrete places" meant, as it did for Nietzsche, an affirmation of the earthly "this-worldliness" of our existence.[77] In fact, one of Bonhoeffer's favorite stories was the Greek myth of Antaeus, the giant wrestler and son of Mother Earth, who could not be defeated so long as he remained in contact with the earth, from which he gained constant renewal. Only the shrewd and powerful Hercules knew enough to hold the giant in the air, apart from the earth, until the life had been squeezed out of him.[78]

Despite his fascination with Nietzsche, Bonhoeffer did not embrace "life" as an absolute end in itself. Such "vitalism" "cannot but end in nihilism": "Life in itself, in the strict sense of the word, is a void, a plunge into the abyss; it is movement without end and without purpose, movement into nothing. It does not rest until it has involved everything in this movement of destruction.[79] Bonhoeffer saw such vitalism "running wild in the race, blood, and soil ideology of the Nazis."[80]

Nevertheless, Bonhoeffer's descriptions of earthly reality seem, if only on the surface, to resonate with the existential accounts to which we have become accustomed since Nietzsche. Fundamental to our experience in a fallen world is alienation, which Bonhoeffer calls "disunion":

> Man knows good and evil, against God, against his origin, godlessly and of his own choice, understanding himself according to his own contrary possibilities; and he is cut off from the unifying, reconciling life in God, and is delivered over to death. . . . Man's life is now disunion with God, with men, with things, and with himself. . . . The peculiar fact that we lower our eyes when a stranger's eye meets our gaze is not a sign of remorse for a fault, but a sign of that shame which, when it knows that it is seen, is reminded of something that it lacks, namely the lost wholeness of life, its own nakedness. To meet a stranger's gaze directly, as is required, for example, in making a declaration of personal loyalty, is a kind of act of violence, and in love, when the gaze of the other is sought, it is a kind of yearning.[81]

Also fundamental is ambiguity, best captured for Bonhoeffer by a theological account of the simultaneous existence of sin and grace:

Sin is a word that describes the whole creation as distorted and grace is a word that claims this distorted creation as the object of God's redemptive work in Christ. The ambiguity arises in the fact that these two conditions exist at the same time and that both conditions penetrate the total reality. . . . Sin and grace therefore mean that there is no place (church authority, civil law, moral expert) to which to go, no part of one's own person (conscience, intuition, reason) to which to go, to find simple guidance for pure behavior.[82]

One can hardly imagine a more dialectical account than Bonhoeffer's portrayal of the paradox of God in a "world come of age." Conceding that "God as a working hypothesis in morals, politics, or science, has been surmounted and abolished," and that "the same thing has happened in philosophy and religion," Bonhoeffer concludes that, "for the sake of intellectual honesty, that working hypothesis should be dropped, or as far as possible eliminated." Sounds very Nietzschean, so far? Where does one go? Not back, but instead,

> our coming of age leads us to a true recognition of our situation before God. God would have us know that we must live as men who manage our lives without him. The God who is with us is the God who forsakes us (Mark 15:34). The God who lets us live in the world without the working hypothesis of God is the God before whom we stand continually. Before God and with God we live without God. God lets himself be pushed out of the world onto the cross. He is weak and powerless in the world, and that is precisely the way, the only way, in which he is with us and helps us. Matthew 8:17 makes it quite clear that Christ helps us, not by virtue of his omnipotence, but by virtue of his weakness and suffering.[83]

Ethical choice, for Bonhoeffer, is a "venture of responsibility."[84] That responsibility means both freedom and obedience: "In responsibility both obedience and freedom are realized. Responsibility implies tension between obedience and freedom. There would be no more responsibility if either were made independent of the other. Responsible action is subject to obligation, and yet it is creative. To make obedience independent of freedom leads only to the Kantian ethic of duty, and to make freedom independent of obedience leads only to the ethic of irresponsible genius."[85]

Bonhoeffer's own "venture of responsibility" took its final form in the summer of 1939, when he was safely in the United States and had received four different job offers through American friends who wanted him to stay. Fully aware of the implications of his choice, he decided on June 20, 1939, to return to Germany. The reason "was simply his readiness to recognize that he now was and would have to remain a German in full acceptance of guilt and responsibility."[86] As Bonhoeffer later explained in a letter to Reinhold Niehbur:

> I have made a mistake in coming to America. I must live through this difficult period of our national history with the Christian people of Germany. I will have no right to participate in the reconstruction of Christian life in Germany after the war if I do not share the trials of this time with my people. . . . Christians in Germany will face the terrible alternative of either willing the defeat of their nation in order that Christian civilization may survive, or willing the victory of their nation and thereby destroying our civilization. I know which of these alternatives I must choose; but I cannot make that choice in security.[87]

He returned to become an active participant in the secret German resistance, including the conspiracy to kill Adolf Hitler.[88] After the failed attempt in July 1944, when Bonhoeffer had already been in prison for more than a year, he knew that he faced the certainty of death.

Bonhoeffer's death is best understood, from his own perspective, not as the predictable consequence of heroic action against evil, but as a redemptive act of love. For central to the worldview of Bonhoeffer as theologian and Christian was a God who had become flesh, taking on the sufferings of his people and in so doing offered the promise of redemption. Thus, for Bonhoeffer, "[t]o be a Christian does not mean to be religious in a particular way, to make something of oneself (a sinner, a penitent, or a saint) on the basis of some method or other, but to be a man—not a type of man, but the man that Christ creates in us. It is not the religious act that makes the Christian, but participation in the sufferings of God in the secular life."[89] Or, "[i]t is evident that the only appropriate conduct of men before God is the doing of His will. The sermon on the mount is there for the purpose of being done. Only in doing can there be submission to the will of God. In doing God's will, man renounces every right and every justification of his own; he delivers himself humbly into the hands of the merciful judge."[90] From within this starkly Christian context comes the elemental message that "our relation to God is a new life in 'existence for others,' through participation in the being of Jesus. The transcendental is not infinite and unattainable tasks, but the neighbor who is within reach in any given situation."[91]

In its emphasis on "living" and "doing," along with its refusal to seek refuge in the transcendent, absolute, or categorical as guides for action, Bonhoeffer's outlook bears ostensible similarity to existentialism. In fact, both Bonhoeffer and Barth were greatly influenced by Kierkegaard and found the modern existential description of nothingness suggestive of the Christian conception of evil. The Sartrean social world in which people are constantly objectifying others is, after all, a description of a fallen world, a world without grace.[92] Confronting that nothingness, Barth and Bonhoeffer both believed in a theology that was also praxis. Their great quarrel with Sartre lay in Sartre's continued Enlightenment presumption that *ego cogito*, unaided human agency, could successfully confront sin. "Real nothingness," Barth says, "mocks" this "manliness" of spirit.[93] Speaking in the guise of the modern existential person, Barth asks

> Might it not be that in real nothingness I have an adversary who is quite unimpressed by my vaunted sense of responsibility for myself and mankind . . . ? Might it not be that I have to do with a refutation and abolition of the very existence which I boldly assert to precede all essence? This . . . one who refutes and abolishes my existence, this No which strikes and brackets the Yes with which I try to overcome it, might well be real nothingness. And Sartre does not have the slightest inkling of it. . . . [T]he dragon envisaged by him is comparatively innocuous. . . . It may be a subject of literary elegance. It may be continually presented and represented as a spectacle which affords the public enraptured dread or dreadful rapture . . . [but] the sickness unto death, real nothingness, is . . . unknown to him. . . .[94]

Given the subsequent influence of both theologians, especially on post–World War II American culture, one is of course curious to know the positions of Barth and Bonhoeffer on abortion. Neither, however, offered a clear-cut ethical rule. Barth must certainly be read as condemning abortion on demand for whatever reason, but if one takes into account the fact that he was writing on the subject more than forty years ago, he seems to offer a solid basis for serious contextual ethical analysis of the subject.

To be sure, Barth's context is "respect for life," which means "astonishment, humility, awe, modesty, circumspection and carefulness. . . . What matters is that everyone should treat his existence and that of every other human being with respect. For it belongs to God. It is His loan and blessing."[95] Indeed, for Barth this "respect of life" extended to nonhumans as well. In the "Freedom for Life" section of *Church Dogmatics*, he devoted as many pages to the taking of animal life as he did to abortion, insisting that killing an animal is very like "homicide." If there is freedom to take animal life, it is a freedom we exercise only in relation to the "prior command to desist," and that carries with it an enhanced responsibility of stewardship.[96]

When it comes to the difficult subject of abortion (and capital punishment as well), his position is far from absolute. He challenges the Catholic tradition of absolutism, calling it "horribly respectable" and "[n]ever sparing in its extreme demands on women."[97] According to Barth, "even Roman Catholic nuns raped when the Russians invaded Germany in 1945 were not allowed to free themselves from the consequences" with abortions.[98] Yet Barth insists on noting "the wicked violation of the sanctity of human life which is always seriously at issue in abortion, and which is always present when it is carried out thoughtlessly and callously,"[99] even though he is also convinced that the Roman Catholic "abstract prohibition . . . is far too forbidding and sterile to promise any effective help."[100]

For Barth, the ultimate answer must be a "wholly new and radical feeling of awe at the mystery of all human life."[101] Barth sees abortion to be as much a social as an individual problem, and recognizes that "[h]uman life, and therefore the life of the unborn child, is not an absolute."[102] While God's commandment with respect to abortion is, for Barth, a resolute "No," it is a "No" to be engaged dialectically by human freedom and conscience.[103] He reminds us that "there is a forgiveness which can be appropriated even for this sin" and refuses to spell out categorical exceptions to the "No," leaving us with the typically paradoxical message that with respect to a decision to have an abortion, "[t]here is always required the most scrupulous calculation and yet also a resolute venture with a conscience which is bound and therefore free."[104]

For Bonhoeffer as well, the question of abortion was more complex than the simple categorical prohibition. What little he wrote on the subject appears in his *Ethics*,[105] a posthumous work based on fragments he wrote in Berlin from 1940 through 1943. On the blunt side, he offers no relief from the conclusion that an abortion means that a "nascent human being has been deliberately deprived of his life," which is "nothing but murder."[106] Yet the question of guilt is not so quickly resolved: "A great many different motives may lead to an action of this kind; indeed in cases where it is an act of despair, performed in circumstances of extreme human or economic destitution and misery, the guilt may often lie rather with the community than with the individual."[107] He also notes that under legal prohibition, the poor who transgress, however reluctantly, will be more likely to be held accountable, than the wealthy, for "money may conceal many a wanton deed."[108] Despite the "fact of murder," for Bonhoeffer, these other considerations "must no doubt have a quite decisive influence on our personal and pastoral attitude towards the person concerned."[109]

This is not to suggest that had Bonhoeffer appeared in the United States in the 1960s he would have joined the pro-choice movement. One cannot extrapolate with much certainty from his content, especially given his particular historical situation. The more significant point may be that the Protestant tradition of serious contextual theological ethics does offer an alternative to the stark and uncompromising contemporary approach now taken by both sides on this issue.

4

The Fragile Umbrella of
Pluralism: American Religion
in the 1950s

......

Our emphasis in the last two chapters was largely intellectual and theoretical. There is an inevitable gap, however, between theoretical moral discourse and its translation into the lives of people who are making both individual and social ethical decisions. Thus, in this and the following three chapters, we include institutional history along with intellectual history.

In the United States the key institutional setting for the realization of cultural and moral values has been the church (we use "church" generically to describe a diverse range of more or less institutionalized religion). U.S. churches have traditionally served as important "mediating structures" between the privatized self and the public realm of government.[1] The later 1960s marked a seeming triumph of secular liberal morality, with a concomitant repudiation of religious tradition, especially that of mainline churches, as mediating structures. How that triumph of secular morality occurred, and why it was no more than "seeming," is the subject of these four chapters. Inevitably, Roe v. Wade was taken to be a powerful symbol of that triumph—not just because it legalized abortion (a process that was happening anyway, albeit more gradually), but because Roe's "private rights" formulation of the abortion issue effectively secularized it, rendering moral/religious debate irrelevant for purposes of public policy.

First, we will go back to the 1950s to see how an effort to achieve religious unity by emphasizing America's bland and vague "shared values" failed to mediate the ever-present religious tension between universalism and sectarianism—a tension apparent at the intellectual level in the contrast between d'Entrèves's emphasis on a universal human nature and Barth's emphasis on a distinctly Christian revelation. Then we will explore a major fault line of sectarianism, Protestant fundamentalism, to show how its history, persistence, and cultural concerns shaped its adherents to the point where they were poised to take a firm public stand against *Roe v. Wade*.

We also shall show how mainline churches were challenged by the compelling ethical claims of the civil rights movement to become committed political activists (creating an example that their conservative counterparts would follow in the 1980s). In that process, some clergy would be seduced away from theological traditionalism, and become intoxicated by the trendiness and modernity of secular morality. Many Protestant clergy, however, were also grappling with a real dilemma—how to interpret and translate a nonfundamentalist Protestant ethics, especially in light of the haunting example of Dietrich Bonhoeffer. The ultimate result of developments during this period was schism and our current "culture war," with each side cartooning and ridiculing the other, and *Roe v. Wade* the contested prize in the battle zone between them.

In the midst of these current battles it may be hard to recall the seeming religious unity of the immediate postwar period, a unity forged in part by response to Nazism, and to a threatening communist totalitarianism as well. In fact, in the 1950s America's religions quite deliberately sought to minimize sectarian and doctrinal differences. Those efforts of the 1950s, however, reveal some fundamental quandaries faced by religion in a pluralist society premised on church/state separation.

In celebrating ecumenical unity, churches were compelled to yield on the sureness and certainty of their various particular beliefs. In the United States, religious unity has succeeded, paradoxically, only by reaffirming pluralism. People choose their own beliefs or doctrines or practices, but only in the manner of consumer preference, never as "truth." Thus, each religion becomes a fungible package of belief, available for "religious choice," under the common umbrella of "America's faith." In the ironic name of unity, religion then becomes nothing more than a personal preference, to be freely selected like one's favorite color or bird, and thereby ceases to serve as a persuasive and constitutive source of truth.

Simultaneously, as religions, in their zeal not to offend one another, minimize their claims to truth and allow religious faith to be reduced to a matter of personal preference, or mere subjective feeling, they also facilitate their own surrender to physical, and then, social science, as the only acceptable modern sources of objective truth. This process is accompanied by an ethical relativism that hears moral assertions as nothing more than expressions of emotion. To those for whom religion is the basis of a coherent, integrated ethical life, such surrender represents a sellout. The result is an ever-widening gap between religion and science, between the religious and the secular. Efforts during the 1950s to celebrate pluralism as unity masked these underlying differences only for a time, and they may have contributed to the consciousness that saw *Roe v. Wade* as mandated by triumphant secularism.

Put somewhat differently, the centripetal move toward unity in American religion, as in the Americanism of the 1950s, inevitably produces a centrifugal counterforce, operating simultaneously at institutional, epistemological, and normative levels. Postwar efforts to hail a new religious unity obscured this dilemma, creating the impression of a core, conventional American denominationalism that could mediate the conflict between religious freedom and moral authority. That core, vaguely conceived denominational center was inherently unstable, however, and destined to break asunder.

The post-World War II situation of American denominational religion illustrated a peculiar combination of enthusiastic public participation on the one hand, and bland superficiality on the other. American churches thrived in terms of numbers and finances. Many heralded a religious revival. During this period of economic prosperity, growth in church contributions outpaced even consumer expenditures;[2] church construction, long delayed by depression and war, expanded dramatically, while the number of seminary students doubled by 1950.[3] Shortly after the war, 94 percent of Americans believed in God,[4] and for most this was not simply an expression of personal piety, but was linked to association with a church as a social institution.[5] Churches, in turn, were assumed to have an easy "taken-for-granted" alliance with the state,[6] an alliance that transcended denominational boundaries. Despite residual anti-Catholicism and anti-Semitism among Protestants, whose values still dominated the culture, all three major faiths saw themselves as transmitters of values that were simultaneously "religious" and self-consciously "American."

Accordingly, as Will Herberg argued in his much-discussed book of 1955, *Protestant-Catholic-Jew*, to be Catholic, Protestant, or Jewish had become little more than "alternative ways to be American."[7] While sociologist Talcott Parsons saw a unified American religion as functioning positively, to provide an integrating value system,[8] Herberg's depiction of its shallow complacency rang true for many. Subsequent books, like Peter Berger's *The Noise of Solemn Assemblies*[9] and Gibson Winter's *The Suburban Captivity of the Churches*[10] raised similar complaints. Churches seemed content to supply a cosmetic window dressing to the American way of life, without nerve or spirit to do more than "[b]aptize all that was wrong with society." [11]

Well-publicized events during the Eisenhower years symbolized what was worst about a religion that had become only bland Americanism: the postwar religious revival ushered in a time of " 'piety on the Potomac,' of presidential prayer breakfasts, Billy Graham's 'engineering of mass consent,' Norman Vincent Peale's 'Let the churches stand up for capitalism,' Msgr. Fulton J. Sheen's equation of Christianity with Americanism," and the aligning of Christianity with the anticommunist crusades of the McCarthy period.[12] As Eisenhower himself supposedly said in 1954: "Our form of government has no sense unless it is founded on a deeply felt religious faith, and I don't care what it is." [13]

The 1950s, in other words, represented the taming effect that America's "toleration" but "separation" model of church/state relations can have on American religion, as described by Garry Wills:

> Thus is religion trapped, frozen, in its perpetual de facto accommodation of power. It becomes a social ornament and buttress, not changing men's lives, only blessing them; not telling me to do this or omit that, just congratulating them for whatever they do or do not do. Religion is invited in on sufferance, to praise our country, our rulers, our past and present, our goals and pretensions, under the polite fiction of praying for them all. The divine is subordinated to the human—God serves Caesar. This is what Americans quaintly call "freedom of religion," and what the Bible calls idolatry.[14]

In fact, however, beneath this public veneer of shallow complacency were both real institutional strengths and complex inner dilemmas. The war had been a chastening experience for American religious leaders. Neither religious traditionalism, with its emphasis on sin, nor the particular experience of Nazism provided grounds for complacency, and most religious discourse was in fact a mixture of optimism and apprehension,[15] of promise and peril.[16] Jews seriously struggled to find the right mix between despair (the Holocaust) and optimism (Israel);[17] so, too, Christians urged a "sober serenity"[18] in a discourse that linked "threat" with "opportunity."[19] If this reflected some measure of self-importance,[20] it also represented a positive sense of social responsibility. Most secular leaders, in fact, agreed with the clergy. Along with sociologists like Parsons, they saw a decent society as dependent on sound, broadly based cultural values, with religion providing both the capstone[21] and the crucial mediating structures[22] within which those values could be nurtured in a pluralist democracy.

Many clergy were willing to carry out that responsibility even while carefully distinguishing any single worldly social or political accomplishment (including American culture) from divine will. Thus, both liberal Protestants and fundamentalists warned against the tendency to equate particular institutions (even the church) with the true Zion, "which cannot be located in any part of earth."[23] If the churches were critical of communist totalitarianism, many clergy in the 1950s were also critical of America's excessive celebration of material well-being; some recognized that possession and pleasure, when taken as the embodiment of the ultimate good, were no less than totalitarianism, a form of idolatry.[24] The Kingdom of God, after all, existed over and against any concrete human manifestation.[25]

Most church leaders, however, did not question the universality of the basic "values" they taught from the pulpit. They did not see values as relative, as socially constructed or as a function of power, but rather as self-evidently applicable to the whole culture. This was apparently no less so for Protestants than for Catholics,[26] who could in theory draw more confidently on natural law for their tradition of universal values. Nor did church leaders question the direct relationship between good individual values and a decent society. Although there was considerable expansion of social service programs, the basic religious assumption was that if clergy did their job at the local level, instilling sound (internal) values, then overall (external) social decency would prevail.[27] (That assumption was not seriously challenged until the civil rights movement, which issued to clergy a call for action that would inevitably blur the distinction between the personal and the structural, and hence between the pulpit and politics.)

The postwar period saw not only a unity of spirit among American denominations, but an accompanying move toward institutional unity as well. There was much talk about ending petty denominational and interfaith rivalries. Within Protestantism, John D. Rockefeller, Jr., donated more than $1 million to promote the ecumenical spirit of the World Council of Churches,[28] a kind of religious United Nations, and was a strong force behind the National Council of Churches—which in 1950 opened under a banner with ten-foot letters proclaiming, "This Nation Under God," and which scheduled Dean Acheson and Harry Truman as speakers.[29]

Evangelicals, seeking mainstream acceptance and influence, were determined during the postwar period to put old controversies behind them for the sake of theological unity.[30] In 1943 the National Association of Evangelicals (NAE) was formed, not for the purpose of challenging the major denominations, but to promote cooperation. The NAE encouraged continued activity in the mainstream churches,[31] up-to-date scholarship, north-south unity, and a constructive approach to social ethics. For example, Carl Henry, an influential evangelical writer and leader, said evangelicals should cooperate with other groups in opposing war and racial injustice.[32] Interdenominational colleges and seminaries, like Wheaton and Fuller, encouraged sophisticated theology and a concern with social ethics, not just a literalist counting of the biblical days of prophecy;[33] and evangelical groups—centered in northern cities as well as the rural South and Midwest—created important ties to business and community leaders.[34] While some conservative southern groups, like the Missouri Synod Lutherans, were becoming more restrictive in their views toward women and increasingly critical of a "hedonistic" modern culture,[35] evangelicals were not generally more conservative than mainstream churchgoers, and in the 1950s probably moved somewhat to the left, rather than right of center,[36] during a period of steady but not well-publicized growth.

Meanwhile, mainstream churches generally welcomed the vigor of evangelical preachers—Billy Graham was the best-known—and agreed that the churches should move in a more evangelical direction, stressing the individual experience of faith and redemption. This evangelical emphasis meant rejection of the older Social Gospel movement, which had located the fulfillment of the Kingdom of God too optimistically in progressive secular politics.[37] It also was consistent with the emphasis on sound personal values as the key to maintaining a decent society. As testament to the general unanimity on this core centrist theological message, Carl Henry and William Sloane Coffin, later well-known for his left/liberal politics, agreed during this period on the correctness of the Protestant move toward the center.[38]

This ecumenical spirit within Protestantism did not automatically translate into interfaith tolerance. Paul Blanshard published *American Freedom and Catholic Power* in 1949,[39] a book that raised the specter of a Catholic church trying to take over the country; and serious anti-Semitism was often not far from the surface.[40] Nevertheless, Herberg's tripartite "Protestant-Catholic-Jew" did describe at least part of the religious reality. Unity was facilitated by the fact that Catholics were entering the mainstream of American economic and social life—moving toward "average" in terms of both education and attitude.[41] As Garry Wills comments, Blanshard may have described priests as sinister foreign agents, but the everyday Catholic church of the 1950s was thoroughly American, its "spirit more easily aroused by a Father Coughlin or Senator Joe McCarthy than by papal encyclicals."[42]

Indeed, given the combined pressure of no public support for parochial schools on the one hand, and a firm commitment to Catholic education on the other, parish priests were in large part fund-raisers, a role that demanded practicality and a convivial relationship with local business leaders.[43] When Catholics vied with Protestants over which faith did the best job of instilling American values, Protestants would base their claim on the transformative power of personal faith, while Catholics would base theirs on the soundness of a solid Catholic education.[44] Neither, however, doubted the appropriateness of the goal, nor did either seriously doubt that the goal was common to both faiths, despite lingering suspicions.

This greater ecumenicalism, however, was achieved in part by distancing church members from their own denominational histories. Since Schleiermacher, many Protestants have emphasized the universality of the "religious experience," in effect turning it into a logically unassailable premise that could be used to defend, rationally and philosophically, a commitment to religious faith. As this emphasis on personal experience played itself out in the Protestantism of 1950s America, it meant that the most significant feature of religion was located, not in the specific forms and disciplines of a shared tradition, but in the pre-reflective depths of the self. Denominational traditions were then seen as aids to self-realization, available according to personal preference, rather than as bearers of normative realities. Religion so conceived, as the ultimate expression of personal experience, appealed to the humanistic, romantic, and even existentialist strands of the post-Enlightenment preoccupation with the self and the "personal." In that sense, it seemed decidedly modern, and also profoundly ecumenical in its appeal to a universal human experience.[45]

Especially within mainstream Protestantism the tendency, therefore, was to make only passing references to the past, and then in vague, romantic images drawn from more distant times, or from the Bible, without specific denominational content. One Presbyterian pastor explained that dwelling on the past showed a "lack of progress in spiritual things."[46] People were less inclined to identify, for example, with being specifically Methodist or Presbyterian, since theological historical differences among denominations were treated as only minimally important. Thus, church members were, so to speak, culturally severed from their denominational traditions and left more open to other cultural influences.[47]

At the same time, however, differences did continue. Despite the public mainstream stance of basic centrist uniformity, Americans continued to practice widely different religions. As Robert Wuthnow graphically points out, while John D. Rockefeller, Jr., was, with much fanfare, promoting world ecumenicism, a moderate-sized congregation in Dolly Pond, Tennessee, routinely opened services with hymns and poison snakes.[48] Even by the 1980s, 4 percent of the American population still claimed to speak in tongues, a fairly exotic religious practice. By way of comparison, fewer than that number of volunteers worked for any party or candidate in the 1980 election.[49]

America's disestablishment, and the privatized, personalist "choice" model of religion that was thereby mandated, created conditions for rich religious diversity, but a diversity that ultimately could be disciplined only by consumerist preference.[50] The strength of mainstream denominationalism had once served as a counterweight to that unchecked freedom of personal choice: as traditional denominational identity weakened, that counterweight was lifted. Also lessened was the authority of the various denominations to contain controversy, both theological and cultural. And despite the general postwar move toward uniformity, unresolved tensions and potential sources of cleavage remained.

While American religion found new unity in the 1950s by organizing itself around a conception of shared values and personal experience, it left open, most significantly, the nagging question of objective truth—just as the law left unanswered the realist assault on legal objectivity, pretending the problem away by embracing ethical relativism and a more flexible and process-oriented jurisprudence.[51] The greatest potential for religious discord lay not in the simple pluralism of disparate traditions, but rather in the unresolved, underlying challenge to religious "truth" as objective reality, issued by the ascendant realm of secular "science." The tension embodied in that contest over truth itself serves in part to account for the historically rooted and surprisingly persistent appeal of American fundamentalism, an appeal that could not be quite contained by the pervasive call for unity in the 1950s.

5

Protestant Fundamentalism

......

Conventional wisdom tells us that the fundamentalists waged war on science because science challenged the objectivity of religious truth and, in particular, because evolution challenged the biblical account of creation. As modern scholars have shown, however, that history is more complex than once assumed. For most of the eighteenth and nineteenth centuries in the United States, Enlightenment science and Christianity were viewed as utterly compatible. The Reformation had sufficiently severed the old medieval sacral order[1] as to allow for unabashed examination of the natural world, an examination welcomed by Calvinist Puritans and by evangelicals in the United States as heartily as it was by more religiously skeptical (or indifferent) rationalists. The typical American assumption was that the laws of nature "below," discoverable through the methods of Baconian science, would support belief in the existence of a transcendent God "above." This two-tier formulation dominated American thought. At times, of course, the relation between the details of natural science and religious faith might seem somewhat attenuated, but a common way of relating Christianity to science was "doxological": The scientist emerged from an inquiry into nature devoutly praising God for the marvels of creation.[2] Even if some scientists might fail to express sufficient praise, most Christians were nevertheless firmly wedded to a scientific culture.

For that reason, Christian—including evangelical—reaction to Darwin was by no means uniformly negative. Indeed, many of the most committed Bible-believers had already decided that Genesis should be reinterpreted in light of modern geological discoveries. When On the Origin of Species by Means of Natural Selection appeared, a commonplace view among biblicists already was that the six days of creation really represented eons.[3] Thus, initial reaction to Darwin did not break down along lines of religious conservatism/liberalism, or even along lines of evangelical/rationalist.[4] Indeed, the most serious concern voiced by Charles Hodge of Princeton Theological Seminary, the most influential bastion of biblical conservatism, was not with evolution as such, or with natural selection, but rather with Darwin's rejection of design, or final causes.

Harvard's Asa Gray, America's foremost botanist, was both a staunch Darwinian and a committed evangelical. He corresponded at length with Darwin on the question of whether Darwin's evidence necessarily led to rejection of all divine design. Gray thought not, and he also argued that Darwinianism should lead to a new, less prideful, and therefore decidedly evangelical recognition of the interconnection between human life and animal and plant life. Gray asserted that through Darwin's work people could come to understand that other creatures have a moral claim that humans are obliged to respect. Despite Charles Hodge's concerns, conservative evangelicals generally favored Gray's view with respect to the compatibility of Darwin and divine design, thereby allowing for reconciliation between Darwin and the Bible. Even at Princeton, where Hodge and the doctrine of biblical inerrancy reigned, some (including Hodge's son and successor) thought reconciliation possible.[5]

Some defenders of the Christian faith, especially in the South, did hold out against Darwinism, but the real move in the direction of fierce warfare came less from the ranks of the Christians than from an emerging scientific-academic elite at the universities. For example, Andrew Dixon White, the young president of Cornell University, lectured on "The Battle-Fields of Science," an address that became the two-volume *A History of the Warfare of Science with Theology in Christendom.*[6] A favorite spokesman of the scientific cause was T. H. Huxley, who rallied the intellectual "agnostics" proudly to affirm Comte's view that the objectivity of positivist science should replace outmoded religious traditionalism as civilization's single mode for discovering the truth. The perceived need to cleanse science of leftover religious traces led Huxley to declare that "Warfare has been my business and duty."[7] Notably, Huxley, unlike Gray, found in Darwin no new need for humility in relation to animals and nature, but only confirmation of our exalted view of ourselves.[8]

George Marsden has argued that among the educated elite, so-called fundamentalists actually lost their war with science well before they ever quite realized they were fighting it.[9] The triumphant cultural champion of the new secularism was John Dewey, who abandoned his study of

religious philosophy and his Calvinist background to become a spokesman for experimental social science. He urged the intrinsic significance
of experience and the human capacity to uncover meaning by use of
the scientific method, believing that science, freed from outmoded religious suppositions about the supernatural, would progressively increase
human harmony and tranquility.[10] Dewey insisted that, properly understood, ethical judgment required not command issued by a transcendent
God, but a clear sociological knowledge of consequences, combined with
knowledge drawn from psychology as to what it was that people actually
wanted. Morality could thus be verified by experience, through the social
sciences.[11]

Bruce Kuklick has recently shown that Dewey's claims on behalf of
social science cannot be separated from his earlier Calvinism.[12] The "common faith" in democratic values and in science that Dewey thought should
be promoted through the schools could be "viewed as a secular version of the ideals of the New England standing order."[13] If Jonathan
Edwards insisted on the possibility of redemption through grace, Dewey
too preached the possibility of human redemption, although only through
the human and, ostensibly, nonreligious instrumentality of science—science "came to serve, for Dewey, what in the nineteenth century was
plainly a divine purpose."[14]

Rationalist social scientists, following Dewey, could thus claim neutrality because they so confidently believed in an essentially good and
orderly universe—no less than did the "two-tier" thinkers of the nineteenth century. Unconsciously, they assumed certain values, and could
not imagine their rejection.[15] Those values in turn became basic to the
pragmatic managerial politics of the New Deal period—the politics of
professional technicians and efficiency rather than the democratic participation Dewey had urged—and those politics are with us still.

Dewey did not go unchallenged. In fact, the most bracing confrontation between science and religion was not between Clarence Darrow and
William Jennings Bryan,[16] but between John Dewey and Reinhold Niebuhr
in the 1930s and early 1940s. Niebuhr came from within the ranks of liberal modernist theologians, so he could not be dismissed as a premodern
biblical literalist. Nevertheless, he consistently challenged the myopia and
complacency of Dewey's progressive optimism—insisting that Dewey's
secularized faith in unaided human agency ignored the reality of sin, paradox, and tragedy in social life, a reality that theology elucidated far better
than did social science.[17] Niebuhr feared that a politics guided only by
social science, without religion, would degenerate into mere self-interest.

Conceding that religiously motivated politics could become intolerant and absolutist, he affirmed that decency in politics required recognition of a God who judges "not only social injustice but the self-righteousness even of those who [fought] against it."[18] Indeed, sin, pride, and imperfection were part of all human beings, who remained "creatures as well as creators."[19] According to Niebuhr, nothing in Dewey's social science provided access to that reality, a reality no less "true," Niebuhr insisted, than the data of the sciences.

Niebuhr did not, however, challenge the value of science itself, although he tried to discredit its claims to ultimate truth. His brother, H. Richard Niebuhr, who was more Barthian than Reinhold but a strong influence on Reinhold's thought, actually praised the scientific spirit for its capacity for humility and self-criticism and for its recognition of the unrelenting objectivity of existence.[20] Science, both social and natural, revealed the contingency of all human knowledge and the fragile, shifting nature of human perception. That understanding, Niebuhr argued, in fact provided a foundation for recapturing evangelical faith in the sovereignty of God. Science and religion were not at odds, but rather joined in continuous dialectical interplay, having to do with the meaning of ("internal") freedom and ("external") necessity.[21]

Notably, like Asa Gray, H. Richard Niebuhr was critical of religious views that too pridefully elevated the role of human beings, creating an opposition between humanity and the rest of nature symptomatic of a narcissistic selfhood that imposed artificial boundaries on the reach of moral obligation. As Richard Niebuhr wrote, there is an "inversion of faith" when man "puts himself into the center" and "constructs an anthropocentric universe."[22] This especially occurs when "man's dominion over nature is put prior to his dependence on the creator."[23] Thus, he insisted that all being should be included in the sphere of value, and no artificial boundaries should be placed on the community of being.[24]

It is a commonplace of intellectual history that Dewey won the battle. It was a battle between intellectuals known mainly to the intelligentsia.[25] Dewey forced intellectuals to choose between the (admittedly imperfect) notions of social science and what Dewey claimed to be a groundless faith in religion. Niebuhr could not convince an emerging academic and managerial class that its own social-scientific rationality was also something of a fiction or a metaphor, useful in mobilizing support for the intellectual class, but less able than theology to grapple with the paradoxes of existence.[26]

In the face of that defeat, American divinity schools, once central to the educational enterprise, became marginal to the modern university. The great private universities allowed them to survive, relegated, however, to a backwater, where Christians were free to do their own thing without credible academic influence. Meanwhile, Dewey's philosophy dominated the American public school system, a fact that is well-known and still a point of controversy among those Christians who resent the takeover by Deweyan "secular humanists."[27]

Parallel controversies were replicated within Protestantism itself. Disputes at Princeton, whose divinity school had traditionally been a major base of American evangelicalism, illustrated the split, not only between religious "liberals" and "conservatives," which is now a commonly held distinction,[28] but between evangelicalism as rationalist fundamentalism and evangelicalism as personalist born-again "experience." The Princeton disputes affected nonintellectuals more directly than is commonly the case with elite intellectual controversy. The abortion debates have only highlighted the importance of those disputes.[29]

For many years Princeton was dominated by the biblical inerrancy school, which held that the Holy Spirit dictated, or at least suggested, the very words of scripture. Some took this notion more literally than others, but the basic view was that the Bible, as God's word, must be as accurate in its precise accounts of science and history as in its basic theological message.

Despite common misconception, biblical inerrancy, or fundamentalism, does not represent a retreat from science to blind irrationalism. When Charles Hodge at (Presbyterian) Princeton defended biblical inerrancy as against Darwinism in the nineteenth century, he was also defending it against too much emphasis on Edwardian "internal evidences," or personal religious feeling. The goal of theology was to gain the "assent to the truth, or the persuasion of the mind."[30] J. Gresham Machen, the last great Princeton defender of the "Princeton theology" of inerrancy, explained that the problem of allowing any deviation, even a "limited" or "mediated" view of inerrancy, was that it was "logically untenable": one could not simultaneously think that the Bible was "the truth" and think that it contained factual errors. As emphatically as Hodge, Machen objected to religion as personal feeling or experience. The goal was not blind faith, but theology as a science: "Theology . . . is just as much a science as is chemistry . . . the two sciences, it is true, differ widely in their subject matter; they differ widely in the character of the evidence upon which these conclusions are based; in particular they differ widely in the qualifications required of the investigator: but they are both sciences, because they are both concerned with the acquisition and orderly arrangement of a body of truth."[31]

By the 1920s, however, the method of higher criticism was gaining ground in mainstream Presbyterianism and Protestantism generally, undercutting the inerrancy position. Karl Barth's sophisticated hermeneutics managed to affirm the rigorous "truth" of revelation (as against the theological liberals in Germany), while simultaneously rejecting literalism, incorporating critical historical knowledge,[32] and reminding us that "at the moment" when the "Word of God" has "left its source it has become the word of man."[33] That prodigious hermeneutic feat, however, did not necessarily solve the epistemological problem of "knowing" God's word,[34] and at any rate it depended on a surprisingly sophisticated, non-Baconian view of science. The Princetonians were incapable of that sophistication, and the Presbyterian church of the 1920s was, not atypically, in a state of schism. In 1927 the Presbyterian Assembly effectively repudiated Princeton theology.

Machen and his fellow conservative teachers and students left Princeton in protest and formed the Westminster Seminary in Philadelphia; after quarrels about the Presbyterian Missionary Board, Machen was actually removed from the ministry.[35] In retrospect, that Presbyterian move was dramatically significant for the abortion debate, for Francis Schaeffer, who probably more than any other single person inspired fundamentalists to focus on the abortion issue, became a student of Machen, who had continued to teach despite his disaffection. Throughout his life, Schaeffer was a defender of Machen's Princeton theology and of the rational character of Christian belief.

Fundamentalism's appeal lies precisely in this offer of a rational basis for Christianity, replicating the "two-tier" nineteenth-century technique of finding in nature itself evidence of scriptural claims, using Baconian induction as the preferred method. Modern "creation science" represents, in effect, an effort to restore the lost harmony between evidence from nature and evidence from scripture. Both sources of truth, scripture and nature, are approached in a spirit of "common sense" (probably a legacy of Scottish philosophical realism) that fundamentalists find lacking in modern scientific theory as well as in modern biblical interpretation. The symbolic and the metaphorical are rejected; the goal is to be straightforward and factual. This approach has had considerable appeal for engineers. For example, Henry Morris, a widely read creation scientist writing during the 1960s, was an engineer and claimed to apply engineering methods of common sense and reason to his reading of the Bible.[36] If the Bible states

God created the world in six days, then it means exactly what it says, not what some fancy literary scholar claims it "symbolizes."

Biblical inerrancy also functions to provide a single unassailable foundation from which other claims can be derived with confidence, and against which they can be tested. This quest for some foundational assertion, far from being irrational in the modernist Enlightenment sense, has in fact characterized most of post-Enlightenment philosophical rationalism. The difference lies more in the choice of foundational assertions (Cogito ergo sum, for example, rather than scriptural literalism) than in the nature of the quest itself. As noted, more "liberal" Christians often sought an equivalent foundation in the universality of religious experience. Only recently have postmodern philosophers (for example, Richard Rorty) [37] been abandoning the search for rationally unassailable foundational assertions as an unrealizable fantasy project. As they do so, they are closer to those theologians who, unlike the fundamentalists, have also abandoned that philosophical quest. [38] Schaeffer, however, would always insist on the need for a literalist scriptural foundation.

Schaeffer started studying under Machen in 1935. By 1947 he was headed for Europe on an unlikely mission to confront and interpret all of European culture from the fundamentalist perspective. His L'Abri (Switzerland) Fellowship opened in 1955 and, with its loving, communitarian commitment to serious dialogue, rapidly gained a surprisingly large international following, despite fundamentalism's distinctly American character. [39] Meanwhile, Schaeffer was starting to write the books and, later, to make the films that quickly found their way into church groups and the curricula of evangelical colleges throughout the United States. Schaeffer became a powerful influence (on, for example, both Jerry Falwell [40] and Randall Terry) [41] in part because, true to his Machen heritage, he recognized the central dilemma of modern Christianity: if it was not "true" and "real" in some sense that could be taken to be objective, then no amount of talk about values, spirituality, Americanism, love, or human needs would rescue Christian theology.

Barth, like Schaeffer, had also recognized the objective "truth" point, but Schaeffer dismissed Barth and neo-orthodox European Protestants generally with the disdain of the practical, commonsense American. He accused them of "mental gymnastics" and "black magic in logic," so that "contradictions and changes are accepted with complacency, and paradoxes with joy." [42] Like Machen, Schaeffer continued to affirm the literal inerrancy of the Bible as the only grounding for an objective Christian truth. However, under the influence of Reformed Calvinists who taught with Machen, he modified Machen's simplistic Baconianism with a "pre-suppositionalism" which, as with Barth, understood in Kuhnian fashion that nature itself will be viewed differently depending on the presuppositions one brings to its study.[43]

Schaeffer's peculiar gift lay not only in reaffirming the "truth" of Christianity, but in realizing its critical potential as against modern secular culture. During the 1950s evangelical fundamentalism had shed some of its more wooden and divisive literalisms and entered the mainstream of American religious culture. Like other leading evangelicals of the 1950s, Schaeffer understood that a fundamentalism which defensively insulated itself from modern culture, retreating into purist doctrinal squabbling, would dig itself into the ground. During that same period of 1950s unity, of course, mainstream culture did not seem dramatically antithetical to the basic evangelical message, whatever differences might exist within and among denominations over questions of inerrancy. After American culture lurched into the disruptions of the 1960s, however, and flaunted a proud secularism, Schaeffer's insistence on evangelicalism's critical potential was realized.

Schaeffer became emphatically "culture reclaiming" rather than "culture denying," a move that in turn helped induce Falwell's willingness to enter the public arena, despite the traditional Baptist aversion to church involvement in political action. Schaeffer's goal was not to reestablish literal biblical rules as secular law (although more recently his son has moved in that direction). Rather, he wanted to show that a culture without Christianity as the central truth of its worldview was doomed to moral floundering. He demonstrated his cultural thesis in part by long descriptions of the history of Western culture (on film as well as in print) that were accurate enough to seem plausible, but were also oddly skewed; untangling the truth from the falsehoods is a mind-numbing task.[44] Nevertheless, he did succeed in bringing European culture to the brittle world of fundamentalism. As Garry Wills describes the effect on Randall Terry, "[i]t was a heady experience, to be dealing with the world's great thinkers in a confident and urbane way, giving grades to Aristotle and Picasso in terms of their Biblical acceptability. At last American evangelicals had their own C. S. Lewis."[45]

In *Whatever Happened to the Human Race*,[46] a book and movie about biomedical issues that he coauthored with C. Everett Koop in the late 1970s, Schaeffer was to depict abortion as the single most compelling symptom of a modern culture fallen into a non-Christian worldview, and he is well-known for the startling accuracy of his prediction that Christians could be mobilized on the single issue of abortion to start reclaiming a culture of decay, one he likened emphatically to the culture of Nazi Germany. Elsewhere, however, he had also addressed destruction of the environment (actually the first ethical issue he raised specifically), racism, and unbridled economic exploitation as symptomatic of the same cultural malaise. However reductionist his work may be, with its extravagant slippery-slope claims, Schaeffer was nevertheless starting to rouse conservative Christian ethics away from an exclusive preoccupation with sin as personal (usually sexual) immorality—to be remedied as fast as possible by personal conversion—toward a greater understanding of social responsibility and the meaning of culture.[47]

The full force of Schaeffer's influence, and the accuracy of his predictions, would not become apparent until the 1970s. By then, moral issues of concern to many evangelicals were becoming central to national politics. This process was dramatically heightened by the *Roe v. Wade* decision in 1973, which was taken as a message that questions of morality were now going to be decided by public agencies, and in particular that a new and alien morality could be imposed by courts. It was thereby also taken as an invitation for evangelicals to overcome their traditional theological inhibitions and enter the public realm to seek favorable state intercession on abortion and other moral issues. This post-*Roe* political activism came despite the fact that on the eve of *Roe* the Southern Baptist Convention had actually passed a resolution in favor of liberalizing abortion laws and had otherwise not made abortion a public issue.[48]

In 1976, for the first time since 1896, two self-described born-again Christians—Jimmy Carter and Gerald R. Ford—ran against each other for president.[49] Carter's victory was attributable in part to his greater success in mobilizing evangelicals and fundamentalists. Three years later, in 1979, Jerry Falwell, a Separate Baptist, founded the Moral Majority to combat pornography, abortion, and homosexuality; to restore prayer to the public schools; and to elect political conservatives. In 1980 groups making up a "new Christian right" formed part of the coalition that placed Ronald Reagan in the White House. That extraordinary political success raised difficult questions about church/state relations and the dangers of idolatry that Francis Schaeffer seems never to have comprehended—as a somewhat chastened Jerry Falwell was to learn by the end of the 1980s and as some Republicans have learned in the wake of their 1992 convention.

6

The 1960s:
The Secularization of
Mainline Religion

......

From the perspective of the early 1990s, we are accustomed to the deep cultural clash typified, if not identified, by the abortion issue. The pro-choice defenders speak the voice of secular liberalism, while their pro-life opponents speak that of religious conservatism. The two camps have been named by sociologist James Hunter as, respectively, the "progressive" and the "orthodox."[1] However unintentionally, that vocabulary seems pejorative, paralleling the pro-choice version of the dispute that sees feminist modernity (or postmodernity) resisting the patriarchy of outmoded tradition.

What is missing from these characterizations is the reality that the pro-choice side has had much support from institutional American religion. The mainline churches have for the most part taken official positions on the pro-choice side (though not without continuing dissent), and, conversely, where pro-life sentiment prevails officially, as with Catholics, or even Southern Baptists, there is a good deal of dissent from believers. Thus, in many respects the abortion controversy is one between liberal and conservative members of the same denominations.

There is good reason, however, for the perception that secular liberal vs. religious conservative captures the character of the abortion debate. The mainline denominations, insofar as they have unswervingly supported the basic abortion-on-demand reality of *Roe v. Wade*, have been difficult to distinguish from secular liberal adherents of the same position. A distinctively theological voice has been lost that might have questioned the extremism of *Roe* without surrendering to the categorical, close-out anti-abortion arguments of the other side. Thus, many religious people who are neither fundamentalists nor Catholics have found themselves taking pro-life positions in reaction to the seemingly empty secular liberalism of their own churches.

We have focused (chapter 5) on the continuing vitality of fundamentalism. In this chapter we will trace the dramatic secularization of mainline American denominations that crested in the late 1960s. Ironically, two of the most significant features of that process were the undeniable ethical challenge posed by the civil rights movement, which transformed churches into hubs of political activism, and the legacy of Dietrich Bonhoeffer, which seemed to mandate that activism. That legacy was later translated by activist clergy, along with academic theologians, into the basis for an enthusiastic embrace of "socially relevant" secularism.

The vague ecumenical unity achieved by mainline Protestant churches in the 1950s, through alliance with conventional American culture, left many churches without strong denominational or doctrinal identity. Moreover, by the beginning of the 1960s an insistence on sectarian doctrinal tradition might well have been rejected, since the relatively well-educated, eastern population that had formerly constituted the core strength of the mainline churches was quickly becoming the "new class"— the educated, secular, managerial elite.

John Dewey's victory over Niebuhr captures for intellectual history the ascendancy of pragmatic, progressive secularism, whose institutional realization would mature in the 1960s. Although Dewey himself might have been troubled, given his commitment to democracy, social scientists hailed a political takeover by managerial experts. Pragmatism in philosophy translated into pragmatic liberalism in politics. Power in the modern world, intellectuals came to believe, should be exercised "dispassionately, impartially, and objectively,"[2] which would occur only if those who exercised authority were trained in a political morality secured not by religious truth, but by rationality and efficiency.

Membership in that elite, as well as internalization of its norms (e.g., Philosophy 101), came through higher education. And higher education had changed since the nineteenth century in both its content and availability. Nineteenth-century education, so long as it remained largely in clerical hands, sought to preserve both sound learning and religious morality. This spirit was replaced by an emphasis on ethically and religiously neutral standards of technical skill and achievement.[3] Gradually, through expansion and specialization, the universities became the institutions that determined competence in American life by "screening, formalizing, and standardizing, and, above all, by certifying with credentials."[4]

Along with the changing role of universities came vast increases in numbers. In 1870 there were only forty-four students enrolled in graduate schools in the United States; by 1930 there were 47,255; and by 1972 the number had increased to 908,000. In 1876, forty-four Ph.D.s were conferred; in 1970 this number reached 29,872.[5] Increased government aid to higher education during the 1960s meant their vast enlargement, with special emphasis on science and technology in reaction to the former Soviet Union's launching of Sputnik. A primary function of this professionalized university system, B. J. Bledstein has argued, was to render universal scientific standards credible to the public[6] and also to reduce potentially divisive issues to scientific and technical terms, thereby containing controversy.[7] Ideas became the subject matter of academic experts, who managed them with the tools of scientific reason.[8]

These changes, which intensified during the 1960s, contributed to academic theology's marginalization as departments of theology, once the pride of their universities, became academic backwaters. Furthermore, training for the clergy itself, especially within mainline Protestantism, became professionalized and specialized. Study was compartmentalized, with academic expertise required for the mastery of any one of the specialties, in the manner typical of academic disciplines generally.[9] Theology thus became not only marginal to general education and irrelevant to the educated person's basic understanding of the world, but also fragmented within its own already isolated sphere. Abandoning its once powerful integrative function, academic theology was effectively distanced from the laity and was expected to make scant contribution to public discourse. Theologians would continue to produce serious academic work, but the religious voices reaching the public were those of Francis Schaeffer and of radio and television preachers who knew how to manipulate the media instead of surrendering to its secularity.

This same period saw not only the dramatic expansion of the universities, but general economic expansion, development of an increasingly important mass media, increased mobility, and a growing population of young people. Meanwhile, jobs funded directly or indirectly by government provided employment for a larger percentage of the population. In both government bureaucracies and universities, the basic assumptions of (Deweyan) secular pragmatism prevailed and became what has been called the ideology of the new class—an educated elite who spoke authoritatively on behalf of the public interest in schools, government agencies, and the media.[10]

The ideology of knowledge and expertise of the new class served not only to validate that class's own credentials, but carried with it a new emphasis on life-style choices—including toleration for sexual freedom and divorce—not just among 1960s rebels, but among two-career households on the "technological fast lane" [11] whose jobs increasingly depended on government spending.[12] Along with changing attitudes, which clearly tilted toward the secular,[13] came, not surprisingly, a decline in religious involvement. For the first time in 150 years, both contributions and membership began to decline in the 1960s.[14]

Nevertheless, American churches in 1963 received a call and rediscovered a reason for being. That call came, appropriately, from jail, where Martin Luther King, Jr., stung by the rebuke of white liberal clergy urging him to cease his protests in Birmingham, Alabama, wrote a twenty-page letter addressed principally to those same white liberals. First published in its entirety in the ecumenical weekly, Christian Century, King's letter issued a challenge to white churches that had too often "remained silent and secure behind stained glass windows" [15] in the midst of racial injustice. If the church did not "recapture the sacrificial spirit of the early church, it [would] lose its authenticity, . . . and be dismissed as an irrelevant social club with no meaning for the twentieth century." [16] The reference to the early church was telling: jail was the appropriate setting for spiritual judgments. King and his associates understood that "buried within most religious Americans was an inchoate belief in persecuted spirituality as the natural price of their faith. Here was the early church reincarnate, with King rebuking the empire for its hatred, for its fearful defense of worldly attachments." [17]

King challenged not just complacency, but an assumption basic to the American churches of the 1950s—the presumed relation between good personal values and social justice. Churches had assumed that by shaping sound individual values within their congregations, they could insure that decency would prevail in social life. The problem of race highlighted the extent to which social evil was structural, not merely personal—a point that Reinhold Niebuhr (who was the theologian most admired by Martin Luther King) had made in response to Dewey's social science optimism.[18]

Many within the clergy were finally willing to recognize that, with respect to racism, the good values that churches supposedly had been teaching were leading neither to good behavior nor to a just society. No longer convincing was Gunnar Myrdal's optimism in assuming (as a social scientist) that American racism was basically an attitude problem, a gap between America's core creed and its behavior that could be easily corrected. American clergy began to conclude that they needed to put their own values on the line with respect to civil rights, through their own behavior and direct political action. Merely preaching values was no longer sufficient.[19]

There is no reason to suggest that this reaction was sparked simply by the publication of King's letter from the Birmingham jail. While the letter presented the theological challenge faced by white clergy, the well-publicized events of the five months following its writing (from mid-April to mid-September 1963) mark in themselves the singularity of the civil rights movement. Even a short recounting of those times cannot avoid seeming overstatement, for the symbols remind us of the civil rights struggle as a narrative of stark moral purity, of buoyant optimism in the face of terrible tragedy and despair, of a biblical test of American possibility.

In the spring of 1963 the nightly news on television showed protesting children in Birmingham being attacked with powerful firehoses. An Associated Press photograph showed the actual work of police chief Bull Connor's dogs: a "white policeman in dark sunglasses grasping a [fifteen-year old] Negro boy by the front of the shirt as his other hand gave just enough slack in the leash for the dog to spring upward and bury its teeth in the boy's abdomen."[20] Children were demonstrating with adults because, it was said, any child old enough to belong to a church was eligible to march to jail, and the only condition for Baptist church membership was acceptance of the Christian faith. Thus, children, even against the wishes of their parents, could feel called on to bear witness.[21]

During the great March on Washington in August 1963, King invoked the prophet Amos to proclaim, "We will not be satisfied until justice runs down like waters and righteousness like a mighty stream."[22] Exactly three weeks later, on September 18, 1963, King spoke at the funeral for three of the four young girls killed in the bombing of their Birmingham church on Sunday, September 15: "At times, life is hard, as hard as crucible steel." Notably, among the mourners were eight hundred Birmingham pastors of both races, making them "many times over the largest interracial gathering of clergy in the city's history."[23] According to Taylor Branch (King's biographer, who tried to avoid overstatement), the two events, the March on Washington and the Birmingham bombing, "etched a conflict of mythological clarity: purpose and suffering of blinding purity against a monstrous evil. Such extremes of reality were inherently unstable, but they opened new eyes."[24]

For the many American clergy who had read Bonhoeffer's *Letters and Papers from Prison*,[25] the connection seemed obvious. Bonhoeffer put his life on the line in opposition to Hitler; opposition to American racism offered an apparently unambiguous parallel.[26] As King (and Bonhoeffer) understood, however, this meant a direct challenge, not just to the sufficiency of personal values, but to the supposed separation between the sacred and the secular. King's letter stated clearly and forcefully: "In the midst of a mighty struggle to rid our nation of racial and economic injustice I have heard many ministers say, 'Those are social issues with which the gospel has no real concern,' and I have watched many churches commit themselves to a completely otherworldly religion which makes a strange, unbiblical distinction between body and soul, between the sacred and the secular."[27]

That sharp distinction between the sacred and secular spheres, which is stronger in Christian than Jewish theology, had not been made traditionally by black churches in America, given their history of struggle and community-building.[28] It had also been largely rejected earlier in the century by the Social Gospel movement[29] that influenced King.[30] In the context of the 1960s struggle against the unambiguous evil of racism, as well as the compelling spiritual power demonstrated by the black churches, quibbles over the precise "boundary" between the "sacred" and "secular" seemed excessively and inappropriately legalistic. As Reinhold Niebuhr himself commented in a TV appearance with James Baldwin one week after the Birmingham bombing, where the two discussed the "missing face of Christ": "[T]he great ethical divide is between people who want to be pure and those who want to be responsible. And I think King has shown this difference."[31]

American churches responded impressively to King's direct challenge, even before the events of that summer. Many clergy became involved in civil rights demonstrations.[32] Moreover, finally galvanized to take action, the National Council of Churches (NCC) dropped its earlier ban of activity on behalf of specific legislation and formed a Commission on Religion and Race (NCC-CORR), which led an ecumenical drive to enact civil rights legislation. Jewish and Catholic leaders gave full support, but encouraged the (Protestant) NCC to take the lead, a leadership role that was recognized by President John F. Kennedy.[33] The NCC-CORR quickly organized church participation in the March on Washington and then directed extensive lobbying and grass-roots letter-writing campaigns.[34]

Working with the NAACP and the Leadership Conference on Civil Rights, both more experienced lobbyists, the NCC drew on church organizations across the country and used its access to the structures of political and economic power to insure enactment of the 1964 Civil Rights Act. Examples: B'nai B'rith gathered all its lawyer-members in Iowa to pressure Senator Bourke Hickenlooper; Quaker professors from Earlham College lobbied the senators from Indiana; James Hamilton, a leader of the NCC, contacted a businessman in Omaha to ask a Methodist minister to encourage the president of the largest state bank to apply pressure on a reluctant Nebraska senator.[35] Meanwhile, church groups, joined even by some members of conservative congregations such as the Missouri Synod (which was not even an NCC member), orchestrated campaigns that flooded Congress with letters supporting the act.[36]

Such sophisticated politicking was probably not necessary once President Kennedy was killed, but until the powerful moral impact of his assassination, passage of the act was by no means certain, underscoring the significance of those efforts. The same church leaders went on to press for enactment of the Voting Rights Act, and the NCC shortly thereafter became involved in organizing and distributing funds to the Head Start Program.[37]

Suddenly, American religion, once the bastion of 1950s conventionality, found itself on the cutting edge of political action and social change. As Taylor Branch commented, however, extremes of moral reality *are* inherently unstable,[38] as those who try to carry their lessons into the future often come to realize. In 1965, one year after passage of the Civil Rights Act, Harvey Cox celebrated the new political role of the church in his book *The Secular City*.[39] In that book Cox defended the social relevance of religion as symbolized by the success of the act, but offended many with his seemingly extravagant celebration of secularism generally. Drawing specifically on Bonhoeffer's expression, "man's coming of age," and on his questions, "[h]ow do we speak of God without religion [and] . . . [h]ow do we speak in a secular fashion of God,"[40] Cox suggested that the secularization process in American life was a positive one, and that a secular worldview could in fact be traced to biblical origins. The Exodus from Egypt, Cox argued, represented release from a cosmology of nature and place, and also from the idolatry that linked any given political ruler with an overarching sacral order.[41] Thus, modern Christians should not regret the depersonalization and alienated mobility of the modern, bureaucratic, secularized world. Much time was wasted, Cox said, in longing for a lost period that was more religious, while the real freedom of the Judeo-Christian message lay precisely in freedom *from* religion, and in the consequent possibility of human action in a truly "profane" world.[42] This meant a release from ontology to pragmatism, and from a closed (natural law) view of what the world *was* to an open examination of how the world *functions*. That shift allowed for new possibilities of action in the world.[43]

Similarly, Cox insisted that the gospel was not concerned with objective truth, but rather with *doing*.[44] This meant frankly acknowledging that "truth" and "value" were socially constructed, human creations.[45] People are not limited by the natural order, but create, in fact, the meaning of nature itself—a point that the Bible symbolizes with Adam's naming of the animals.[46] People are thus invited to be partners in God's creative work in a secular world. The gospel is the summoning to seize the forever new possibilities of the world.[47] We are, Cox said, always in a "catalytic gap"—that point where the new is suddenly revealed within the old—and are free to act responsibly in the world if we can only wake up to our responsibilities.[48]

For his models of men "come of age" Cox chose both Camus and Kennedy—the latter, of course, had just been killed, a fact that seemed not to dampen Cox's optimism.[49] Cox's description of Kennedy is revealing. He was the "technopolitan man" as pragmatist, which means he "disciple[d] himself to give up certain things."[50] In particular, he wasted little time thinking about "ultimate" or "religious" questions. Instead, he was satisfied with "highly provisional solutions," which were arrived at by "bringing to bear the knowledge of different specialists."[51] "He sees the world not so much as an awesome enigma, evoking a sense of hushed reverence, but as a series of complex and interrelated projects requiring the application of competence. He does not ask religious questions because he fully believes he can handle this world without them."[52]

Some of Cox's phrases were easily perceived as unnecessarily flippant. He enthusiastically borrowed, for example, the description of God's work in the world as a "floating crap game," so that the Christian's obligation is to "know where the [catalytic] action is" and "dig it."[53] Nevertheless, despite such excess, Cox's book was a serious effort to explain the link between the Judeo-Christian tradition and the capacity to think in secular terms. It also captured the heady optimism of the early 1960s, when all of the world's problems seemed solvable by unaided human agency, drawing solely on its own professional competence. If Dewey's secular pragmatism, in its triumph, threatened the relevance of theology, the answer for theology, Cox seemed to suggest, was to claim secular pragmatism as its own—as the true spirit of both Jewish and Christian scripture. In using the vocabulary of Dewey, theology was really speaking its own language after all.

Cox's book was widely read; Cox and discussion of *The Secular City* became a mainstay on the lecture circuits and in the media. Meanwhile, Cox's basic theological optimism was shared by the many Catholics who also read his book with enthusiasm. In a different sense, they, too, had "come of age" in modern American culture. No longer a defensive im-migrant enclave in an alien society, they were now in the mainstream of social, economic, and academic life. For many, Kennedy's presidency represented the full-fledged Americanization of Catholicism.

The background to the Catholic embrace of the "secular city" had been laid in the 1950s by the Jesuit theologian John Courtney Murray, who had argued that Catholicism was in fact consistent with the long American tradition of church/state separation. He had elaborated, in the manner of classical legal thought,[54] a magnificent series of further compartmentalizations: state/society, natural law/revealed law, temporal/spiritual, and others. Within that structure, Catholics had a duty to participate in political life and could do so in a manner that was both conscientiously Catholic and utterly secular. Vatican II later incorporated Murray's formulation, and Kennedy drew on it for his famous Houston statement.[55]

There were, of course, differences between the Cox and the Murray approaches despite the fact that both so fully embraced the pragmatic Kennedy approach to governance. Murray was a natural law theologian, whereas Cox rejected arguments based on ontology. Murray was a careful compartmentalizer, especially of the sacred and secular, whereas Cox was eager to label the secular as the only "true" (gospel) interpretation of the sacred. Murray accommodated himself to pluralism, while Cox embraced it.

Despite those differences, Vatican II and the new secular direction of Protestantism were similar phenomena. Both represented a self-conscious shift from the sacral to the secular. As Murray stated with extraordinary candor, "The notion of the sacral society is dismissed into history, beyond recall. The free society of today is recognized to be secular."[56] Similarly, Robert Cushman, a delegate-observer to the council, stated that "[i]n principle, the era of Constantine—sixteen hundred years of it—passed away."[57] While this did not change the church's claim to be the one true church, it did signify a new openness to the pluralist, secular world.[58] The two main focuses of Vatican II, Sister Marie Augusta Neal wrote, were "openness to the world and . . . recognition of the laity as a partner,"[59] in marked contrast to the view of the church as a spiritual oasis in a sinful world, with the religious life clearly superior to secular life.

Sister Neal even saw Vatican II as embracing an American, Deweyan pragmatism as well as an American separation of church and state. Norms were to be established, not just by a bishop's pronouncement, but by experience and commonsense judgment in a joint effort in which "pursuit of science and the development of political and economic institutions for

the enrichment of mankind are good."[60] Natural law would no longer be
the sole basis for moral theology; instead, new emphasis would be given
to people as viewed from the perspective of the social sciences.[61] Cox was
cited as "the first American theologian [thus] to emphasize the spiritual
potential of the secular city."[62] Actual council documents, of course, not
only treated the question of religious liberty (Murray's chief concern),
but opened an entire range of Catholic subjects to reappraisal, including
creed, liturgy, canon Law, cult, education, institutional hierarchy, laity,
and the role of women (who were given more responsibility and personal
choice).[63]

Not surprisingly, therefore, during this hopeful time, when all things
seemed possible and all change was for the better, liberal, educated Catholics embraced Cox's secular city—symbolized by Washington, still in the
afterglow of its young, pragmatic Catholic president—as eagerly as did
liberal, educated Protestants. Cox appeared on the lecture circuits with
Sister Corita, the artist-nun who celebrated The Secular City by composing
advertisements for big corporations in a happy "Warholism of the super-
market"; her "hymn to the Virgin (as the juiciest tomato of them all)" was
superimposed on a soup can design.[64] Meanwhile, Cox's work was printed
in the Catholic press, used in Catholic schools, and endlessly quoted.[65]
Bonhoeffer, meanwhile, became nothing short of faddish, subject of a
photo essay in Life and an article in Time.[66] He was so popularized that
serious divinity school professors continued to assign his work almost
sheepishly. As one theologian said, "[w]e have to continue studying Bonhoeffer even though he is a fad."[67]

Studying and interpreting Bonhoeffer, however, especially on the dilemma of the church's relation to the secular world, was no easy task. Some
seemed too ready to adopt startling phrases like "religionless Christianity"
while forgetting the more somber ones, such as the "cost of discipleship."
As Cox was later to point out, with more care than was evident in The Secular City, Bonhoeffer was writing within a very particular context[68]—a long
tradition of "two sphere" Lutheranism which so separated the church
from the world, the sacred from the secular, that it was immobilized even
in the face of extraordinary evil. It was this "world-despising" aspect of
Lutheranism that required a new dose of maturity. That is not to suggest,
however, that the right relation between the two spheres is easy to define.
It may be misguided to try to find in Bonhoeffer's thought some particular
correct location for the church on a supposed continuum between the
sacramental and the secular, or to describe the single right "mix" between
religion and politics in Christian life. Bonhoeffer's utterly Christological

perspective can be taken as so completely sectarian as to be irrelevant to politics in a liberal democracy; yet in another sense its Christological message was so all-embracing as, in effect, altogether to collapse the spheres of sacred and secular (and private and public as well), accounting for Cox's reading of the message. That seeming collapse, however, did not occur because Bonhoeffer had a theory of politics and justice that could be applied to the secular political realm, certainly not an agenda that could be identified with a particular American presidency, Cox's celebration of Kennedy notwithstanding. It derived instead from the teaching at the heart of his own tradition—that the discipleship called for by the gospel is about freely serving and freely suffering, about having one's self-involvement challenged by the needs of the neighbor, in whatever context.[69]

Bonhoeffer never believed, therefore, that one could suddenly step forth to confront a God who somehow had nothing to do with the religious tradition that had been interpreting God's word for centuries. Those who found in Bonhoeffer a welcome relief from the heavy learning of Barth's many-volumed *Church Dogmatics* too quickly forgot that Barth's long work was an extended conversation with the same tradition with which Bonhoeffer aligned himself, and to which he gave full expression. As both theologians knew, there is an idolatry that says one can capture and contain God within any single (human) tradition, yet there is also an idolatry that claims any single moment of history, any particular modern insight, to be the new truth taking us to an Archimedean point that transcends history, including the history of religious tradition. Who was the "God" we confronted anew and areligiously in Cox's *The Secular City*, except the God of Jewish and Christian religions? Put in Christian terms, even the gospel does not remove us from history, but rather sets in motion the dialectic that Barth described in paradoxical phrases like "nothing new, but the oldest . . . not an old acquaintance, but a new one."[70]

Like the Enlightenment (including Enlightenment legalism) in relation to religion, and also like many Protestants in relation to Catholics (and many Christians in relation to Jews), those who were part of the Bonhoeffer fad in the 1960s forgot the first part of the paradox. Cox, however, reflecting on his own work, made the point persuasively, both about Bonhoeffer and about an American theology that was prone to adopt the latest novelties of the secular culture at the expense of theology itself:

> Bonhoeffer's vaunted radicalism grew out of a tradition which was so much a part of him he rarely felt the need to affirm it. His genius was that he could deal with frontier issues, but was able to do so

in the light of a theological heritage which he loved and cherished. This is why our American theological enterprise, which often tends to be ahistorical as well as anarchic, can still learn much from him. Too often our traditionalists have no interest in emerging issues and our pioneers feel they must exude a lusty disrespect for anything that happened before 1961. This is why so many new movements in theology end up in old blind alleys. Bonhoeffer knew the revolutionary power of a tradition understood and applied.[71]

Meanwhile, however, other faddish "secular" theologies were gaining as much publicity as Cox, chiefly by asserting, as the new gospel message, that "God is dead." This was argued, ironically, as both a culmination of Barthian dialectics and as the real meaning of Bonhoeffer.

The phrase "God is dead" was reminiscent of Nietzsche, but the argument was actually drawn from Hegel. Like Barth, Hegel had taken the Enlightenment's idolization of the finite subject to be at the root of modern atheism. Unlike Barth, however, Hegel had seen the remedy to lie, not in reaffirming the utter transcendence of an infinite God (Hegel considered such opposing of the Absolute to the finite to be, inevitably, a finitization of the Absolute), but in integrating human subjectivity in a dialectical move that would relativize the God/human opposition. The "atheism of the moral world" was a necessary stage in the process by which absolute freedom (which Hegel thought epitomized Christianity, especially Protestantism) would finally realize itself fully in communion with God.[72]

In the *Gospel of Christian Atheism*,[73] Thomas Altizer returned to that Hegelian argument but described the death of God as simply the final stage of the dialectic,[74] freeing people for authentic selfhood. For this to be accomplished, no less than a "third testament" was required: "The Old Testament knows only the alien, transcendent, externally commanding Father. He became the Son, incarnate and immanent, in the New Testament. It will be left for the third testament to come dialectically to deny the Son's resurrection to transcendence, and along with it the Father who makes this resurrection possible." Thus would the final stage of the dialectic be achieved, revealing the "full and actual presence of the Christ who is a totally incarnate love."[75]

Akin to Altizer was Anglican bishop John A. T. Robinson. In *Honest to God*,[76] which sold over 500,000 copies in the United States, he announced that Christianity was formulated at a time when mythology still dominated human consciousness. On the basis of Bonhoeffer and others, he argued that theologians should give up such relics of the past as transcendence. And Paul Van Buren, in *The Secular Meaning of the Gospel*,[77] argued on the basis of modern linguistic philosophy that the traditional language used to describe God is empirically meaningless; the gospel, to be made meaningful, must be translated into empirical terms—the terms of science and technology. Van Buren took all "faith language" to be merely emotive, as opposed to the objectively "true" world of empirical science.[78]

The God-is-dead theologians were, of course, featured in the media and even on bumper stickers. So catching a phrase could not be resisted. Atheism itself had been successfully appropriated by theology—the ultimate adaptation of theology to a secular world. The dawn of this new secular era was heralded as if the end of history had arrived. As Wills described it: "If the world were to be truly secular, God must die to it, release his claim on it. The God-is-dead theologians even congratulated God on his sacrifice, on his death traded for secularity's life. We should rejoice, not be sad, at his demise, said Thomas Altizer: 'All things will dance when we greet them with affirmation.' "[79] Jesus might still be praised as a moral example, but such emphasis on Jesus operated as a kind of "theological chaser, making it all go down easier."[80]

Cox, despite the optimism of *The Secular City*, was never quite part of the exuberant pride that dared to proclaim the final stage of the dialectic. Chastened as early as the mid-1960s, he acknowledged the limitations of his own book. His enthusiastic emphasis on human possibility, on people as God's pragmatic "partners," had threatened to overwhelm his own (avowedly Barthian) understanding both of God's transcendence and of human sin.[81]

Other serious commentators during the mid-sixties were troubled as well by unresolved dilemmas in the Cox analysis, which in fact reflected unresolved dilemmas in nonfundamentalist Protestant ethics generally. Cox exemplified the Protestant emphasis on "context" in moral reasoning—the rejection, as in both Barth and Bonhoeffer, of universal authoritative norms. As with the legal realist rejection of formal legal categories, this rejection can be taken as suggesting that "context" alone will yield its own normative analysis—as if a deep description of the situation alone, uninformed by value, will supply its own particular ethics as a kind of natural law of the moment.

Catholic ethicist Daniel Callahan pointed out that Cox's pragmatic insistence on context rather than false universals sought to have it both ways. Could the pragmatic Christian be "unreservedly contextual" in ethics, yet still employ categories like "biblical perspective" or "Kingdom of God," which, after all, "cut across time and through history?" Such categories "illuminate the contextual without themselves being wholly contextual." [82] For many people, moreover, the most pressing context, as Callahan pointed out, is not the context of enhanced possibility in a sophisticated urban environment, but the (universal) fact of death, a fact that Cox acknowledged ignoring in the secular city reality. [83] As Callahan also stated: "Some people are going to die tomorrow. That is their context, and they want to know why. This is a very personal question, not something that [Deweyan] history or sociology or politics can throw much light on. A question like this is wretchedly ultimate, direct and noncontextual. It just will not go away." [84]

Neither would other realities that challenged the adequacy of "context" as its own ethical norm. Cox had dismissed the Holocaust, which had taken place only twenty years earlier, as only an atavistic resurgence of premodern tribalism. Yet its grim efficiency also depended on the modern, rational technology that Cox so admired. [85] Hence:

> Cox sees the action of the God of history in technopolis. If there is such a God, He has also manifested himself in Auschwitz. . . . Our problem is not how we shall think of God in a secular way. It is how men can best share the decisive crises of life, given the cold, unfeeling, indifferent cosmos that surrounds us and given the fact that God the Holy Nothingness offers us only dissolution and death as the way out of the dilemmas of earthly existence. [86]

Cox's emphasis on context raised another, but related, normative problem—the nagging one of cultural relativism. Making the point we now associate with Geertzian anthropology, astute commentators bluntly suggested to Cox, in effect, that we are all "natives now," even including sophisticated, proudly secular, and pragmatic WASP Harvard professors like Cox.

The particular urban context of enhanced possibility that Cox celebrated was more available to some than to others: "The *Playboy* bachelor can make the most of urban anonymity; not everyone else can. Mobility is grand if one has brains and a future; not everyone does. And so on. The urban-secular coin has two sides and so does man." [87] In fact, as some argued, the particular world that Cox both described and represented was the intellectual one of a university-trained elite. In the actual U.S. cities, according to Andrew Greeley, ethnic and religious traditionalism was more the rule than the outmoded exception. As Greeley stated: "My problem is not whether religion can live with secular man, but whether he exists; and I will contend that save in senior faculty positions in some universities and in certain places in the communications industry, secular man is not common in the United States and does not seem to be growing more common. On the contrary, secular man is a theologian's romanticized version of mass man—and he doesn't exist either."[88]

As a matter of sociological fact, Greeley's observations were accurate. The particular worldview of The Secular City and the God-is-dead theologians was just that—a very particular worldview, one possibility among many, and one most easily embraced, as Rabbi Rubenstein pointed out, by successful young men (and soon, women) who could delight in their own competence.[89] It was also, as Rubenstein noted, for the most part peculiarly Protestant, despite Vatican II, and best represented those very traditional WASP enclaves of "tribal" power, the corporation and the university—precisely those arenas within the modern secular city that Cox praised for having progressed beyond "earlier," more "immature" tradition and tribalism into the new era of secular pragmatism.[90]

7

Schism

......

ven in the early 1960s, a period of relative religious unanimity supporting civil rights, there was increasing disharmony in response to Supreme Court decisions banning school prayer and school Bible-reading. In 1962 the Court in *Engel v. Vitale*[1] held that reciting a non-denominational prayer ("Almighty God, we acknowledge our dependence upon Thee, and we beg Thy blessings upon us, our parents, our teachers and our country") composed by the New York Board of Regents violated the establishment clause despite provisions allowing nonparticipants to remain silent or leave the room. The prayer was not saved by the excuse provisions, the Court held, because, unlike the free exercise clause, under the establishment clause neither compulsion nor coercion is the basis of the violation. Rather, the mere fact of public (governmental) religious expression triggers the ban. Only Justice Potter Stewart dissented, chiding the Court for its indifference to the "history of the religious traditions of our people" and citing the frequent instances of religious expression in American public life, such as the "under God" in the Pledge of Allegiance.[2]

A year later, in *School District of Abington v. Schempp*,[3] the Court extended the doctrine to prohibit reading of the Bible (without commentary) as part of daily opening exercises in schools, even if student readers could choose the passages to be read. Justice Stewart again dissented, viewing the decision "not as the realization of state neutrality, but rather as the establishment of a religion of secularism, or at the least as government support for the beliefs of those who think that religious exercises should be conducted only in private."[4] While Stewart was the lone dissenter, the view that the Court was imposing a "religion of secularism" on the country was widespread, among both Catholics and Protestants. Billy Graham, as just one example, said *Engel* was "another step towards the secularization of the United States."[5] Consistently, about 75 percent of the American public has favored voluntary organized prayer in the schools.[6] In many areas, of course, these Court decisions were simply ignored. A 1966 study of Tennessee showed that in all but one school district, Bible-reading was continued despite *Schempp*.[7] Polls indicate that no other Court rulings (including *Roe*) have elicited so much criticism.[8]

Already outraged[9] over *Engel* and *Schempp*, Americans were hardly pleased to learn from the media that their supposedly most sophisticated theologians were preaching God-is-dead theology while praising the delights of secularism.[10] Increasingly, the caricatured image of the new class liberal secularists emerged: an educated elite that was contemptuous of the religious beliefs of the majority and was able to use access to the government and to the media to impose a secularist culture on American society. When many old-line Protestant churches (mainly Episcopalian, Presbyterian, and Congregationalist), along with liberal Catholics, seemed to side with the secularists, they too were viewed as having abandoned the faith.

This divisiveness was compounded when the moral/political issues of the late 1960s failed to arouse the relative unanimity that had marked the campaign for the 1964 Civil Rights Act. Moral consensus in the country as a whole broke down across a wide range of issues. In the late 1960s, unlike the brief Camelot period, the correct course of action for churches in the world became increasingly unclear. In the face of that moral uncertainty, the shallowness of the liberal theological presumption that sectarian tradition could be discarded had its most corrosive effect.

It was, after all, the pragmatic experts in Washington, so celebrated by Cox, who had started the Vietnam War, revealing the potentially tragic dimension of action in the world. Sorting out the ethical meaning of a war that was tearing the country apart required more than the categories of Deweyan pragmatism. When action is taken by the powerful, Langdon Gilkey commented, one begins to find relevant "some of the older theological categories descriptive of sin and guilt within all active social involvement, categories expressing the need for communal repentance, forgiveness, reconciliation, and meaning beyond the ambiguity that is consequent to everything that man does."[11] Even the apparently unambiguous morality of racial justice was revealing its own fateful ambiguity, with struggles over the legitimacy of violence rather than nonviolence and black power and separatism rather than integration.[12]

Similar breakdowns were occurring within Catholicism. Murray's carefully formulated legalist categories seemed to collapse in the absence of actual national consensus. Under Vatican II, the church was not supposed to have a particular political agenda, but it did have a responsibility to help shape society's moral culture. As American bishops, following the Vatican II mandate, have explained, public policy decisions necessarily involve moral judgments, and the church must share (indeed, cannot avoid sharing) in the development of a public moral consensus on the basis of which such decisions can be made. In theory, since human rights, to which both the church and the American polity are committed, are the basis of church positions, the church cannot be said to violate the Constitution when addressing specific moral issues.

In that spirit, American bishops in the 1970s would issue statements critically evaluating the morality of the Vietnam War (1971) and the American economy (1975). Later, they would issue their dramatic pastoral letter condemning nuclear weapons (1983), explicitly appealing to that natural law "written on the human heart by God," from which "reason draws moral norms." On the same basis, Joseph Cardinal Bernardin would insist on a consistent pro-life philosophy, a "seamless garment" encompassing the church's position on nuclear armaments, abortion, and the death penalty. The goal was to help define a set of principles that would structure public debate and policy but not enter into detailed disputes over specific proposals.[13]

That Vatican II goal remained uncontroversial only so long as there was some basic public agreement on the meaning of human rights (and natural law). In the mid-1960s, however, consensus over basic American values had dissolved. Was the Vietnam War a "just war" or a violation of natural law? Was the right to economic well-being a fundamental human right, as Vatican II proclaimed, or did it run counter to the priority American constitutionalism gave to "negative," libertarian rights? In other words, as the church tried to play a responsible role in public debate, it found itself unable simply to stake out a high ground of moral guidance. Instead, it was taking a stand on issues that aroused resentment even within the church itself.[14]

The breakdown of moral consensus raised hard questions about the proper role of the Catholic church, questions that were just coming to the fore as the abortion debate began. Conservatives were generally urging the church to draw back from the expansiveness of Vatican II and to retreat into a sacramental role—to facilitate personal salvation, not set the terms for public debate. At the other extreme were the Berrigans, who, in their radical opposition to the war, exemplified an activist ministry of gospel-oriented Christian witness. The Berrigans were part of the long, morally compelling church tradition of prophetic witness, which some now think is the proper role of the church in an increasingly secular world. That tradition, however, was bound to run counter to the church's institutional goal of a broad-based inclusiveness and an ethically constructive cooperation with state power.[15] Many, therefore, continued to strive for the Vatican II ideal of a church that could play a responsible, but not divisive, role in public life without surrendering its special Christian mission and becoming just another player in the secular field.

Those efforts were undercut in 1968 when Pope Paul issued *Humanae Vitae*,[16] the encyclical that announced his decision to continue condemning "artificial" contraception. The pope had assembled a commission to study the question of birth control, and a majority of the commission had actually recommended that the church change its position. John Noonan, who was a member of that commission and a determined advocate of reform, carefully showed, as in his *Natural Law Forum* article, that the church could both adhere to its natural law methodology and change its position on a particular rule. By tracing the subtle dialectic of continuity and change in church teaching on both usury and birth control, Noonan demonstrated that such a reversal was not a surrender to relativism but was in the best tradition of Catholic ethical thought.[17]

The issue of birth control was a charged one, however, and the extremists on both sides of the debate ignored Noonan's careful approach. Commentators on both left and right insisted that the whole tradition somehow depended on this weakest link in the Catholic moral chain. Conservatives argued that if the pope admitted "error" on this point, the church would abandon all claim that its natural law teachings were authoritative. Moreover, despite the peculiar inconsistencies that had developed in the church's earlier arguments, the distinction between "artificial" and "natural" means still held powerful appeal.

Secular liberals, in turn, mockingly adopted the conservative line—if the church pragmatically changed its mind on this point, it would just reveal the emptiness of its claims to principled moral authority and, implicitly, the absurdity of the whole Aristotelian, natural law tradition on which the birth control teachings had been based.[18] The pope's decision to maintain tradition then, of course, convinced skeptics that the church had rejected the spirit of Vatican II, retreating instead into rigid moral absolutism and inordinate preoccupation with channeling sexuality. The church's opposition to abortion would later be dismissed by many outside the church as simply an extension of the rigid Catholic stand on birth control.

In fact, however, by the end of the 1960s, one's position with respect to tradition itself had become the principal measure of one's location in the American religious landscape. Familiar denominational squabbles (even Protestant against Catholic) became displaced, as the recurring and insistent dividing line for American religion became "old" (traditionalist) versus "new" (secularist). To be sure, denominational difference did not disappear, but the old/new line became the sharpest one—and on no issue was that line so starkly evident as with abortion.[19]

There was, of course, caricature in the conservative image of the new secularist Christians: morally loose, compromised by secular humanism, hung up on faddish social issues with a shallow knowledge of the Bible and of what religion is really about, having an "anything goes" attitude with "marshmallow" convictions, etc.[20] Nevertheless, institutional realities exacerbated the tension and fed suspicions produced by the 1960s. After the dramatic success of the effort on behalf of the Civil Rights Act, many national church-affiliated groups began to descend on Washington (and New York City), perfecting the techniques of expertise that seemed to be required for effective deployment of power in the modern secular state.[21] Most of the special-purpose religious groups concerned specifically with influencing government date from no earlier than the 1960s. Some groups were still involved with civil rights, while others arose in response to specific governmental rulings, or in response to the needs of groups about whose welfare there was special religious concern—children, the hungry, gays, women, handicapped, single parents, and others. Having learned from the civil rights era that social evil is a problem of social and legal structure, not just personal morality, the churches' response was also structural, directed to the deployment of government power.

These church groups have dealt with Congress and government agencies, and sometimes they have involved themselves with litigation. They are typically labeled the "National" or the "American," rather than by reference to denomination or to religion at all. This is perhaps a symbol of the extent to which they draw on the modern, secular techniques of politicking rather than on distinct religious heritages.[22] Many have professional staffs and complex budgets; they hire specialists, consultants, researchers, and newswriters. Intricate bureaucratic chains link groups to each other and to church institutional structures.[23]

This "move to Washington,"[24] which occurred in the 1960s chiefly among denominations who were members of the active NCC, was also accompanied by organizational restructuring within the denominations themselves. With the accumulated resources of the 1950s, churches already had extensive bureaucracies, but a newer tendency was for those who were more secular in outlook to exert a more powerful influence. One Presbyterian minister described the process as follows: "[P]erhaps because they are by inclination more alert to the new, open to the secular world, and inclined to respect science in any form—[they] have become the skilled process managers, strategy planners, and agents of change." [25] Denominational representative bodies increasingly fell into the hands of the church bureaucracies—new managers who understood pragmatic politics, knew how to control agendas, control the courses of expert opinion and ultimately to control denominational decisions.[26] Later, of course, conservative Christians, especially evangelicals, would try to reseize the terrain—with marked success in the Southern Baptist church, and also in Washington, under the manipulative guidance of skilled conservative political activists.[27]

The "new-breed" clergy of the 1960s elicited resentment, less for the specific causes they advanced than for their seemingly contemptuous failure to relate those causes to the denominational traditions they were representing. Cox had set the tone by dismissing most churches (not without reason) as so stifling and conventional that they usually failed to represent the "real church," which is, he said, the reconciling act of God in the world, wherever it may be occurring.[28] That "real" work was more likely to occur, it was often claimed, during a civil rights march than during an ordinary church service.

Notably, the freedom of the new-breed clergy to involve themselves in direct social action overtly aimed at challenging existing social structures—which they did in growing numbers during the 1960s and 1970s—arose from their ability to separate themselves, institutionally, from the laity. The so-called managerial revolution in church organization produced a number of well-educated specialist clergy, trained in universities as well as in major divinity schools and serving, not as pastors, but rather as staff persons in church social action bureaucracies or in university ministries.[29] Studies showed that the clergy who were most likely to be involved with direct social action were precisely those who were not working as pastors to congregations and were not directly subject to lay control.[30]

Social action by the clergy, as in the antiwar movement, became more visible and radical exactly when public consensus was breaking down. Often, lay resentment was directed specifically at the most highly visible new-breed "tactics," and did not represent, for example, racist opposition to civil rights. Yet from the vantage point of those involved in direct action, if the problems were structural, only tactics directed at the structure could be effective.[31] Clergy not only took visible part in civil rights and antiwar demonstrations, but also led rent strikes, organized pickets, served in community action projects, financed low-cost housing projects, and organized welfare recipient unions.[32] Some were so determined to break with the church tradition of "charity," as opposed to real empowerment of the poor, that they advocated noncooperation even with the government programs that church organizations were generally supporting unless real provisions were made for power and participation of the poor. Thus, the Presbyterian Division of Church Strategy and Development warned: "There are serious dangers in the way current community action programs are being structured. Lines of control are being drawn tightly to a central bureaucracy. Vital dynamic elements in the city are in danger of being smothered by the kinds of control of the local citizens which are built into . . . the poverty operation."[33] The point was, of course, accurate in its depiction of government bureaucracy, as reassessments of the War on Poverty have shown. The irony was the extent to which the same defects characterized the new breed themselves in relation to their own "communities," the churches.[34] Disdainful of their own frumpy denominational traditions and communities, and not able (or willing) to awaken those communities by reference to theology, they offered no explanation for their actions except an increasingly secular political vocabulary of social justice. Resentment grew, and opposition groups formed, even within the mainline churches, to oppose the most activist stances of the clergy, even as the most conservative evangelical churches grew in numbers.[35]

Saul Alinsky, the political activist who came to the fore in the 1960s, described the special contribution that new-breed clergy were making to radical politics. He had never before seen, he said, the "pure flame of passion for justice you find in these young ministers today."[36] As Cox pointed out, there was good theological basis for that passion in the special gospel status assigned to the poor and also in the notion of the "blessed community" of equal participants.[37] Yet there was also theological reason for caution. Karl Barth, with his own leanings toward socialism, nevertheless warned of the dangers of a too arrogant (and too idolatrous) commitment to political opposition. "The revolutionary Titan," Barth wrote, "is far more godless, far more dangerous, than his reactionary counterpart—because he is so much nearer to the truth."[38] As Barth explains, the biblical message does, indeed, expose the injustice and the arrogance of all worldly authority:

> Rulers! What are rulers but men? What are they but men hypocritically engaged in setting things in order, in order that they may—cowards

that they are—ensure themselves securely against the riddle of their own existence? . . . That men should, as a matter of course, claim to possess a higher right over their fellow men, . . . this whole pseudo-transcendence of an altogether immanent order is the wound that is inflicted by every existing government—even by the best—upon those who are most delicately conscious of what is good and right. . . . Men have no right to possess objective right against other men. And so, the more they surround themselves with objectivity, the greater is the wrong they inflict upon others. . . . Is there anywhere legality which is not fundamentally illegal? Is there anywhere authority which is not ultimately based upon tyranny? There is a certain imperfection in the existing ordinances by which we are enabled to detect that their existence is, as such, evil. . . . There is a certain strange and penetrating perception which sees through the fiction that lies behind our bondage.[39]

The critical impulse is thus born of gospel truth, and of accurate perception—a perception that sees through the "fiction" of ideology, rightly detecting the "imperfection in the existing ordinances." (Hence, for example, critical legal studies.) Too easily, however, the revolutionary, as well, falls into idolatry, forgetting

that he is not the One, that he is not the subject of the freedom which he so earnestly desires, that, for all the strange brightness of his eyes, he is not the Christ who stands before the Grand Inquisitor, but is, contrariwise, the Grand Inquisitor encountered by the Christ. He too is claiming what no man can claim. He too is making of the right a thing. He too confronts other men with his supposed right. He too usurps a position which is not due to him, a legality which is fundamentally illegal, an authority which . . . soon displays its essential tyranny. What man has the right to propound and represent the New, whether it be a new age, or a new world, or even a new spirit? Is not every new thing, in so far as it can be schemed by men, born of what already *exists*? The moment it becomes a human proposition, must it not be numbered among the things that are? What man is there who, having proposed a novelty, has not proposed an evil thing? Far more than the conservative, the revolutionary is *overcome of evil*, because with his "No" he stands so strangely near to God.[40]

The popular disaffection from the "liberal" political action direction of mainstream churches in the 1960s and 1970s can be overstated. Sometimes it is assumed that people left those churches in droves and switched to evangelical churches instead. The story is more complex. Even in what came to be called the liberal denominations, ministers tended to be less politically liberal than staff, although more liberal than their congregations. Moreover, they continued to perform their pastoral functions, concerning themselves with issues such as death, where the ordinary and the ultimate intersect to place our temporal concerns in appropriate perspective.[41] In churches where the education level was highest, the gap between the laity and new-breed church leadership was narrowest, especially in Episcopalian churches[42] that became among the most liberal. And in many ways, those denominations at the forefront of social action were successful, both in bringing American religion out of the complacency of the 1950s and in providing social services whose value few have seriously questioned. During the 1980s, when there was too little American concern in Washington or elsewhere about the ethical dimension of social responsibility, liberal mainline churches helped to keep that concern alive. Those churches still represent a vital tradition in American life, which may regain some of its lost force.

Yet the mainline churches did dramatically decline in numbers, losing members for the most part to the "nonaffiliates." Most affected by the decline were the old-line denominations, once the mainstay of American religion: Episcopalian, Presbyterian, and Congregational. Those denominations, which had always comprised the best-educated, saw their youth, especially, defecting to the secular culture, losing interest in religion altogether.[43] The increasingly secular vocabulary of clergy, while not necessarily offensive, hardly differentiated the church from liberal secular culture generally. Meanwhile, the birthrate among the old-line membership declined, and the population shift away from the U.S. Northeast also drew members away from the old-line churches whose base had been there.

Traditionally, the Presbyterians and Episcopalians had gained members from the upwardly mobile, who "switched" as they achieved higher social status. If one began life as a poor evangelical Baptist, wealth might eventually lead one to become Episcopalian.[44] Such switching did not disappear, but its rate declined as evangelicals entered the mainstream in terms of education and social status. More significantly, evangelicals (whether politically "conservative" or not) were able to keep their younger members committed to their churches—and those members had larger families. By 1976, one-third of Americans said they were "born-again."[45]

With the possible exception of school prayer, no aspect of new-breed secularized theology alienated traditionalists as much as its failure to offer any basis for personal, ethical decision-making.[46] Even as it stood resolute on morally grounded social issues, like racism, the new theology failed to address basic questions of personal and family responsibility. One could conclude that theology, in becoming secularized, had simply surrendered to the "do your own thing" life-style culture of the 1960s. No theologian fulfilled this characterization so much as Joseph Fletcher, an Episcopalian theologian from Cambridge, Massachusetts, whose well-publicized *Situation Ethics: The New Morality*[47] was published in 1966. Given his broad influence, Fletcher was taken by critics to represent the erosion of all traditional, external sources of moral authority.[48]

Fletcher emphatically rejected all legalism, all appeal to scriptural law: *Nothing* remained, he said, but love.[49] Fletcher simply ignored the complex Barthian dialectic of command and moral freedom. On the other hand, he also rejected love as antinomian intuitionism[50] or pietistic sentimentality, a danger of Protestant ethics.[51] Love, he said, represents concern for the other, which can basically be reduced to a utilitarian calculus of consequences.[52] Nothing was wrong "in itself," but only if it led to greater harm than benefit. Ends did, therefore, justify means.[53] He urged a deemphasis on sexual morality[54] and a more utilitarian concern with responsible (pragmatic) decision-making. Absolutist abortion restriction was one of his examples of an outmoded moral authoritarianism.[55]

Fletcher's offensiveness lay in openly and wholeheartedly embracing what others recognized as a second danger of Protestant ethics—its reduction to mere utilitarianism, distinctively Christian only in that its underlying motivation was a vaguely conceived "love." Fletcher was controversial in part because, to avoid the Protestant danger of ungrounded intuitionism, he made the utilitarian calculus so explicit, even quantifiable, while fetishizing technology.[56] Writing at some length about medical ethics, he actually stated, for example, the precise number that a person should score on an I.Q. test before sensibly being treated as "human" for medical policy purposes.[57] Schaeffer's outraged "absolutism" on the question of medical ethics, including abortion (as in the movie and book coauthored by Koop), was in part a response to that "situational" approach to the subject.[58]

Fletcher tried to appropriate both Barth and Bonhoeffer as complete situationalists, in each instance through oversimplification.[59] He regarded abortion as just another means of fertility control, perhaps the least desirable, but nevertheless "good if the good to be gained is great enough to justify the means."[60] He dismissed the "natural-law ethic" as "self-contradictory, problematical, and dead as Queen Anne."[61] On euthanasia, Fletcher suggested that in "this day of existential outlook," we might "think twice on Nietzsche's observation, 'In certain cases it is indecent to go on living.'"[62]

Ironically, in view of the subsequent history of public division over moral issues such as abortion, and probably because Fletcher thought he had history on his side, he proclaimed that "Without a *consensus,* a democratic agreement about what is immoral, there can be no true civil law."[63] In fact, sounding much like his liberal legal counterparts, Fletcher offered his situationist baseline that, "In the end there is nothing but process."[64]

To his credit, however, Fletcher forced modern Christians to face a technological world in which they could not avoid ethical responsibility for calculating life-and-death decisions. Everyday social decision-making involves choosing death. Noonan's own observation about facilitation of transportation is an example. So too is the routine introduction of factory procedures that pose "acceptable" risks to workers. More dramatic examples are, of course, going to war or ending a patient's life. We are all purveyors of death. As Fletcher insisted, that reality does not disappear because we refuse to acknowledge it and pretend to an absolutism we cannot carry off.

But Fletcher represented something other than just an antidote to religious absolutism. To the extent that he sought to fuse Christian "love" with rationalist utilitarianism, he was trying to have it both ways, to seize on the rhetorical power of Christian tradition without having to make concessions to its ethical content. That peculiar relationship to tradition would soon characterize mainline religion in its relation to moral issues such as abortion.

Thus, when we talk about the "secularization" of American religion in the late 1960s and afterward, we are describing specifically what James Hunter has aptly called the "tendency to resymbolize historic faiths according to the prevailing assumptions of contemporary life."[65] Traditional sources of moral authority lose their status as predominant sources of power over peoples' lives; real moral authority becomes located in the prevailing culture, in the personal experiences that the culture offers and in its mode of scientific rationality. Yet tradition continues to be mined for artifacts (e.g., isolated scriptural passages) that will serve, instrumentally, to shore up otherwise established agendas. The Bible thus becomes a useful human document, no different from any other book.

We are therefore assuming that an important (albeit decidedly elusive) distinction can be made between two approaches to tradition. One is the facile and manipulative approach, familiar to lawyers, where bits and pieces of tradition are put together for the sake of making a particular argument sound convincing (or at least plausible). The other is an authentic participation in tradition, which affirms its values and authority in an ongoing engagement with a changing social reality (illustrated, for example, by Noonan's essay on contraception). That difference, while it may not be determinative of outcome, is nevertheless the difference between shallowness and depth, between slickness and integrity, with respect to the relevant tradition. Thus, legal scholars might say of some especially sensitive analysis of case law, that it is a "good" legal argument; and they might do so even while not agreeing with the conclusion.

The difference to which we are pointing lies, again, in the willingness to accept tradition as in some sense authoritative, rather than, simply, as something to be used. (What that means in legal advocacy, where one's job is to argue for the client, fortunately need not concern us here.) With respect to ethics and our culture's religious traditions, the risk of accepting the authority of tradition is that one's own preferred position might not prevail. Fletcher, we think, refused to take that risk, producing a manipulative "Protestant" argument for utilitarianism that was clever enough to seem plausible and to convince many, but was not an honest engagement with the richness and complexity of his own Christian tradition, especially its insistence on humility.[66] However, in not taking that risk on the hard questions of life and death that he addressed, Fletcher lost the opportunity to speak to the uncertainties, anxieties, and ambivalences of most churchgoing Americans.

As the next two chapters will show, abortion as a morally and theologically debatable subject in our culture was quickly replaced (with Fletcher's "Protestant" stamp of approval) by abortion as a question of medical expertise and personal choice. This move was supported with the language of scientific rationalism and secularized religion. All too quickly, religious opposition then became hostile, defensive, and absolutist, and a dialogue that might really have spoken to Americans from within their own seriously considered religious traditions seemed to be lost.

8

A Tale of Two
Conferences

......

T he galloping process of secularization would effectively silence
mainline American religion as a distinct theological voice on the
abortion issue. Some holdouts, however, fully aware of proceeding against the stampede, sought for a time to address the issue as one
of *debatable public morality*, with appeals to theological sources regarded as
central to the ethical question. Their agenda included both the morality
of abortion and the separate issue of the legitimacy and extent of state
intervention in the decision-making process.

A striking example of such debate was a conference held in Washington,
D.C., in September 1967, sponsored by both the Joseph P. Kennedy, Jr.,
Foundation and the Harvard Divinity School.[1] A premise of the conference was that "if there is anything that is clear about the issue of abortion,
it is that it is complicated, delicate, and difficult," because "people who
come at it with honest, humane convictions have differences which are
not easily composed." It was assumed that public policy decisions with
respect to abortion would continue to be made in the "social-political
process." Yet the conference was held "in the hope that as the decisions
are made there will be responsible public debate, based on the facts and
issues as we understand them, and regard for our values of compassion,
freedom, and reverence for life."[2]

From the perspective of the current, polarized abortion debate, this
conference appears unusual. Contemporary pro-choice advocates would
probably see it as an instance of pro-life propaganda, given the recognition
of "reverence" for fetal life as an issue for public policy decision-making,
while pro-life advocates today would probably see it as a sellout, since
abortion is presented as morally ambiguous and not necessarily to be

regulated or criminalized even if regarded as an ethical wrong. What was particularly striking about the conference is that theologians, speaking from within their diverse moral traditions, were taken seriously as having an important role in the debate.

An outcome of the 1967 conference was the publication of *The Morality of Abortion: Legal and Historical Perspectives*, edited and introduced by John T. Noonan, Jr. Judging by the published volume, the participants were all wary of accelerating reform, yet not necessarily resolute in opposition, and they hardly spoke with one voice. Of the seven essays, five are explicitly theological,[3] one is rooted in a secular natural law tradition ("the universal respect for the value of human life"),[4] and the last essay is a legal brief in the nature of an attempted preemptive strike against the yet-to-be-decided *Roe v. Wade*.[5] Noonan's introduction grudgingly acknowledges a changing social reality.[6] Noonan saw three forces combining to change the rules with respect to abortion: first, professional autonomy in the name of science and expertise; second, the urgency of world population control; and third, an agenda of reproductive freedom, which, for Noonan, meant the combination of sexual freedom and rational control of consequences. The third force he perceived as a subset of a larger across-the-board resistance to the intrusion of traditional moralities into life-style issues.[7] The actual theological essays, three Protestant and two Catholic, share the assumption that abortion is an issue of *public morality*, to be discussed as such. The collection offers a variety of positions, from categorical moral absolutism[8] to post-Vatican II Catholic pragmatic flexibility[9] to even a version of Protestant contextual ethics.[10] Few of the essays offer easy answers; the common thread is in treating the issue as a hard one, and calling for the application of ethical insight derived from theological tradition.

The essay by James Gustafson, "A Protestant Ethical Approach,"[11] illustrates the potential for a Protestant ethical approach to abortion that neither surrendered to secular liberal individualism, nor sought refuge in simplistic fundamentalism. Gustafson begins by rejecting the perspective from which the "traditional Catholic arguments about abortion" are made.[12] He sees that perspective as formal, deductive, abstract, physical (life viewed as "biological" fact without encompassing "concern for the emotional and spiritual well-being of the mother or the infant"), and too indifferent to social and historical reality ("this particular mother, her particular relationships, and her past spiritual as well as physical history").[13] While Gustafson rejects what he sees as the excessively categorical rationalism of the natural law tradition as applied to the issue of abortion, he does not claim that one can abandon principle altogether. He rejects only the rationalism that serves "to reduce spiritual and personal individuality to abstract cases." [14] With such an approach, "[t]he sense of human compassion for suffering and the profound tragedy which is built into any situation in which the taking of life is morally plausible are gone." [15] On the other hand, he makes clear that the "alternative" to overly abstracted rationalism is "not to wallow in feeling and visceral responses." [16] To illustrate his approach, Gustafson offers a hypothetical case of a woman who became pregnant after being raped by her former husband and three other men in an act he characterizes as one of "sadistic vengeance." [17] A careful and deliberate analysis leads him to conclude that as a moral counselor (he was a pastor and a preacher before he became an academic theologian), he would affirm the moral propriety of an abortion for this particular woman. Despite his choice of that extreme hypothetical (probably chosen because the standard Catholic position would be no abortion), he also notes that his approach could be made applicable to other cases, such as "unwed girls, or older married women with large families, etc." [18] He is less certain, but not close-minded, about situations where "the social and emotional conditions do not appear to be beneficial for the well-being of the mother and the child." [19]

On the other hand, Gustafson is clear about his "moral biases: life is to be preserved, the weak and the helpless are to be cared for especially, the moral requisite of trust, hope, love, freedom, justice, and others are to be met so that human life can be meaningful." [20] His approach to the particular problem affirms that "[l]ife is to be preserved rather than destroyed," that "[t]hose who cannot assert their own rights to life are especially to be protected," but that "[t]here are exceptions to these rules." [21] At the core of Gustafson's theological worldview are both the "sense of a powerful Other," understood as the "sovereignty of God," and the "centrality of piety," an "attitude of reverence, awe, and respect which implies a sense of devotion and of duties and responsibilities as well." [22]

Gustafson's approach surely offered a basis for rethinking the abortion issue in a moral/theological context that might have supported significant liberalization of restrictive laws. This is not to suggest that he represented the "correct" Protestant line; the point is more that serious debate was possible. Dramatically opposed to Gustafson in the same volume, for example, stands Paul Ramsey, a Protestant theologian who had for years been battling "ethical relativism," favoring a deontological approach more akin to the Catholic natural law tradition. [23] Ramsey's absolute opposition to abortion resembles that of the Catholic traditionalists, although his detailed reflections on embryonic and fetal development seem to concede a potential moral basis for differential treatment of first trimester abortions, and he is not convinced that criminalization is appropriate.[24] Ramsey deploys not only the Catholic rational/scientific case for fetal personhood, but also the Protestant ethical tradition of Karl Barth. Given Ramsey's zeal, his effort to appropriate the Barthian tradition is understandable; yet in so doing he distorts and manipulates Barth's own position.[25] Ramsey enlists Barth's support, in fact, by quickly eliding Barth's actual treatment of the abortion issue and turning instead to Barth's adamant opposition to euthanasia. The latter was hardly surprising, given Barth's experience with Nazi Germany.

In the Noonan volume it becomes clear that Catholics as well as Protestants were willing to engage in open-minded dialogue on the abortion issue.[26] The eminent Catholic theologian Bernard Häring contributed an essay called "A Theological Evaluation."[27] Häring, a self-styled "Catholic of the post-Vatican II era," observes that "the characteristic note in Catholic theology today is one of critical searching," and while reaffirming the church's adherence to its traditional teaching on abortion, he nevertheless points out that there are "those who think that the teaching of the Catholic Church might be 'susceptible to gradual development through a process of refinement.'"[28] The remainder of the essay seeks to explore such possible "refinements."[29] More striking than the careful and tentative content of Häring's essay is its tone. He notes, for example, that Gustafson's position is "at least not very far from the position of Catholic thinkers of the past which we have reviewed."[30] Häring's ecumenical mission is clear: "The official position of the Catholic Church, which in most respects is well grounded, will be weakened in the eyes of Protestants and of many critical Catholics unless we give a clear account of the different degrees of certainty of our general presuppositions, and acknowledge the intellectual difficulties regarding some hard cases which are now falling under the official condemnation of the Church, although they were freely discussed in earlier centuries."[31] Implicitly critical of the church's intransigence with respect to contraception, Häring chides: "[t]he Church's condemnation of abortion is only fully credible if at the same time all possible effort is made to eliminate the chief causes of abortion."[32] His suggested "refinements" include reconsideration of "mechanical" lines, such as that between "direct" (impermissible) and "indirect" (allowable) abortion.[33] Showing his solidarity with Gustafson, Häring reminds the reader that there is a distinction between the level of moral theology and that of pastoral counseling.[34] On the counseling level, "a Catholic moralist might come to almost the same conclusion and even to almost the same way of friendly discourse as Gustafson. Pastoral prudence looks not only to the general principles but also to the art of the possible."[35] While Häring concedes that he would not actually recommend the course of abortion, he also affirms that he might well "refrain from all rigid judgment."[36]

Although the movement within Catholic theology was incremental at best, within the more general Catholic culture of the post-Vatican II era there was ferment in progress. In 1970, the same year that the Noonan volume was published, Daniel Callahan wrote *Abortion: Law, Choice and Morality*, which is perhaps still the best single book on the subject. Callahan, who had been an editor at *Commonweal* magazine, concedes that he set out to defend the traditional Catholic position and changed his view in the course of the project, which took him four years. While affirming the basic principle of the "sanctity of life,"[37] Callahan nevertheless calls for the repeal of prohibitory abortion laws in favor of more permissive regulatory ones.[38] He does not favor complete repeal of legislation, nor does he favor an absolute right to abortion on demand; he believes that a public moral debate should be sustained.[39] His firm conviction that abortion does raise serious moral issues leads him to reject the extremes that we are accustomed to today:

> The Catholic position says that the only moral question of importance is when human life begins. Once that has been determined (or believed determined), then all other possible questions and considerations become irrelevant. The "woman's right" position proceeds in the same way, the difference being that it locates the critical moral factor in the desire of the woman. Thus in neither position is room left for an integration of other possibly relevant data or for a balancing of rights.[40]

Callahan's position might best be characterized as "constrained choice." He believes there are serious "social" interests in pursuing such goals as a "desire to limit an excessively large number of repeated abortions to forestall a primary reliance on abortion for birth-control purposes rather than contraception" and to "lead women to consider abortion a serious and not a trivial choice," but also a "desire to maximize female freedom."[41] He does not accept a version of personal autonomy that leads to the rampant subjectivity of all value, with the consequent abandonment of *public* moral discourse: "Abortion does not seem to me the kind of moral issue which is just 'solved' once and for all; it can only be coped with."[42]

Even though Callahan's position placed him in sharp disagreement with traditional Catholics, his book was nevertheless a valid entry in the debate that marked out a boundary of legitimate discourse. In the early 1970s, Stanley Hauerwas, a Protestant theologian who taught theology at the University of Notre Dame, and now teaches at Duke University, wrote a pair of review-essays that cover Callahan's book, his traditionalist counterpart Germain Grisez, and the essays in the Noonan volume.[43] While his own position with respect to the appropriate theological teaching on abortion is closer to the traditional Catholic one than to Callahan's, Hauerwas finds serious flaws in the arguments at both extremes. And despite his own affinity for the more traditional view, he is sensitive to the dangers of rhetorical excess that we have come to know so well:

> I wish to make clear I do not agree with those who argue that once possible exceptions to the taking of life are admitted in connection with abortion then Auschwitz is somehow right around the corner. There is clearly no logical relation between these, nor is it clear that there is even a psychological relation. I must admit I have always found rather unconvincing the argument that suggests that the granting of possible exceptions for certain kinds of abortion would be to undermine the value of "sanctity of life" in the face of our nation's military spending alone, not to mention the degradation of life we are willing to tolerate in our ghettos. If what we have now is sanctity of life, then perhaps it could stand to be undermined.[44]

Along with debate over the substantive morality of abortion, a somewhat independent issue of church-state relations was being discussed. Not every religiously rooted moral position translates, even from a theological perspective, into a demand for secular enforcement through legislation. On the other hand, the mere fact that a moral position is deeply rooted in religious belief does not preclude the assertion of that position in the secular public realm, as many liberals would assert.

The role of religion in public life was conceded during this period to be a serious moral and political issue. Häring, for example, acknowledges the constraints of pluralism, even as he affirms that "in a pluralistic society one of the most urgent duties of the churches and of humanist ethicists is to contribute to the formation of a mature conscience."[45] He recommends that the church reduce its "undue emphasis on [the] battle for penal legislation" and that it remember that it is only within the church that the mere existence of a teaching is an argument for its validity; for others, real dialogue will be necessary.[46] And he recognizes that "[i]t cannot be the task of a pluralistic state to protect the religious teaching of a church where this does not coincide with the common good of the respective society."[47] If it is going to participate in the public debate, the church must provide "reasons and motives that could be convincing to sincere and intelligent people who are not under Church authority."[48]

Häring's seemingly prudential analysis of the church-state issues with respect to the looming abortion debate is best understood as firmly rooted in the Catholic tradition of debate about the relationship between religious and secular morality. At stake in this debate is the *theological position* on the respective roles of spiritual and temporal authority. For American Catholics in particular, the issue was heightened by its appearance in a concededly pluralistic society.

The tradition of John Courtney Murray, who died before the onset of the public abortion debate, cautioned against imposing particularistic religious faith on the secular political process[49]—although Murray's commitment to secularism was problematic, since he simultaneously attempted to find traditional Catholic moral positions on freedom and dignity already realized in a shared American secular morality. Abortion, like other issues emerging from the chaos of the 1960s—the Vietnam War, nuclear weapons, and capital punishment, for example—served to unhinge Murray's fragile solution. Instead of the facile equivalence of common good and Catholic tradition as realized by American shared secular morality, the reality was a fragmented American public morality, with a dominant secularism standing in opposition to, not serving as the realization of, religious moral traditionalism.

There were many legislative options facing would-be abortion reformers in the late 1960s, ranging from liberalization of criminal laws to decriminalization in favor of a substantive "indications" policy, with or without procedural delegation, to total repeal of restrictive legislation. In the context of that debate, many responsive options not necessarily amounting to an all-out campaign to retain harsh penal laws were available to the Catholic church and its theologians. At one extreme, the church might simply have served the privatized role of "bearing witness," or trying to instruct and guide the faithful to serve as an exemplary moral community on the issue. Further options included general appeals to the common good rather than the pursuit of specific legislative goals (for example, Joseph Cardinal Bernardin's consistent ethic of life)[50] or a secular morality that insisted on something less than the most extreme Catholic position. Father Robert Drinan represents another available role, that of moral advocate in the public realm without insistence on legal implementation of that position for those in disagreement.[51] Common to all these positions is the assumption that the church has a role in the formation of a public moral position on the question of abortion, as should other religious communities whose traditions have spoken to that issue.

Legal decision-making thus calls for a delicately nuanced sensitivity to the complexity of church/state relations, one that appreciates not only the importance of the state's freedom *from* religion, but also the importance of religion's contribution *to* free debate in a democracy. But in relation to the abortion issue, genuine debate and sensitivity to nuance were not to prevail. By way of recapturing a lost moment, consider the cautionary words of Alan Guttmacher, then-president of Planned Parenthood-World Population and active advocate of abortion reform: "I am opposed to [abortion on demand] for the U.S. in 1967. I believe that social progress is better made by evolution than revolution. Today, complete abortion license would do great violence to the beliefs and sentiments of most Americans. Therefore I doubt that the U.S. is as yet ready to legalize abortion on demand, and I am therefore reluctant to advocate it in the face of all the bitter dissension such a proposal would create." [52]

Neither Guttmacher himself, nor his fellow reformers, would heed his 1967 warning. Indeed, by 1968, reformers would be calling for medicalization, secularization, and legalization of abortion. The impetus for that movement came in part from an unlikely source—the U.S. Supreme Court. In the late 1960s the Court, despite its traditionally conservative role, was reaching its all-time historical peak of activism on behalf of equality and personal liberty interests. In 1965, in fact, it had initiated the move that would, within less than a decade, lift the abortion debate out of the legislative arena. In a problematic and puzzling 6–2 decision containing six opinions, the Court in *Griswold v. Connecticut* struck down Connecticut's archaic law forbidding the use of contraception. [53] It did so by explicitly announcing the existence of a constitutional right to "privacy." [54]

By that time, few outside the Catholic church supported such restrictions, but officially the church still advocated their enforcement, thereby deeply associating itself with what many took to be an oppressive intrusiveness. The church's historic tendency to focus on personal sexual behavior as the single most important moral issue—a peculiar obsession many American Protestants shared—only intensified the public perception that an increasingly secular society should be protected from an authoritarian and outmoded church-based moralism. Whereas Noonan, in his arguments against abortion, was genuinely advancing an ethic grounded on loving regard for human life, many took the church simply to be insisting, in its abortion policy, on one strict, unrealistic prohibition after another. That liberals saw only negativity in the church's position resulted in part from the church's own past mistakes and also from the "life-style" emphasis of the 1960s.

By the late 1960s some liberal theologians were ready to entirely discard any theological concern with the issue of abortion in favor of rational secular individualism. The striking contrast between these theologians and their more traditional and troubled colleagues becomes evident by comparing the treatment of abortion as an ethical issue in Noonan's *The Morality of Abortion*[55] with the treatment of the same issue at a conference one year later. In a manner reminiscent of the Carnegie Foundation's support of Gunnar Myrdal's *An American Dilemma*,[56] which helped retool liberal consciousness to support civil rights reform,[57] the 1968 abortion conference represents an establishment-backed call for liberalization and eventual repeal of restrictive abortion laws in furtherance of medical professionalism, population control, and the rationalization and secularization of ethics in the name of freedom.[58] The sponsor of the conference was the Association for the Study of Abortion. Its president, Robert Hall of the Columbia University Medical School, believed that "[c]ountries with stringent abortion laws have buried their heads in the sands of time."[59]

The introduction to the conference, entitled "Abortion Law Reform—The Moral Basis,"[60] was a clarion call issued by John D. Rockefeller III. His talk evidenced genuine concern for the fate of children born into adverse circumstances: "*The New York Times* recently reported that cases of child abuse are steadily increasing in the United States. Child abandonment and infanticide are serious problems in some countries. All over the world, unwanted children are being permanently harmed both physically and psychologically through hunger, neglect, and abuse. Is this not a moral issue of the first order?"[61] Nor did he fail to mention, albeit briefly, that liberalized abortion laws should be combined with concern for the "most fundamental rights of children—to be wanted, loved, and given a reasonable start in this world."[62] Nevertheless, there was a disquieting tone to the proposed solution—put crudely, to eliminate the unborn children rather than the conditions that made their childhood so bleak. His conclusion was to call first for liberalization of abortion laws, leading as soon as possible to repeal, leaving the decision "with the conscience and need of the patient and the professional experience and guidance of the physician."[63] He also advocated promotion of family planning and contraception, for he did not "favor liberalizing abortion laws for the purpose of fostering abortion as a method of birth control."[64]

The first plenary session of invited participants at the conference, entitled "The Ethical Aspects of Abortion,"[65] seems to have been structured to neutralize any lingering theological concern. The first two presenters were an embryologist whose conclusion amounted to a refutation of ensoulment at conception,[66] and a historian with a careful, critical review of Noonan's account of church doctrine.[67] For the "Protestant position," the conveners brought Joseph Fletcher himself, the author of *Situation Ethics*, to celebrate those Protestants who advocated a "free and responsible ethics of abortion"—especially Unitarians, who had decided in 1968 in favor of leaving the abortion decision in the hands of "duly licensed physicians and their patients."[68] In a telling case of a clouded crystal ball, Fletcher, seemingly unaware of conservative evangelicalism, observed that "[t]he majority of Protestant churches have remained silent and will probably stay that way until the question is resolved for them in the social-cultural debate. They will not give much leadership, even if their opposition to medically responsible abortion is not as plainspoken and theologically sophisticated as Catholicism's."[69] He conceded that some Protestants had actually taken "the Catholic position," oddly naming Karl Barth and Dietrich Bonhoeffer.[70] Nevertheless, in Fletcher's "modern world of scientific biology and medicine" we could rely on "an ethics of responsible decision rather than submission to inflexible moral laws."[71] In such a world, he said, "traditional church positions become more and more archaic."[72] Indeed, the entire history of both legislative and theological restriction of abortion he reduced to a "motivation" of "conscious and unconscious male chauvinism."[73] A sentiment like "a life is a life" is just "tautolog[y]," a case of mere "feeling," "sublogical," "an attitude only."[74] According to Fletcher, the "task is to reeducate people on a deeper level than logic," to "the level of empirical fact and a situational versatility which fits the realities of modern life."[75] Going even further than Rockefeller's opening address, Fletcher concluded that abortion was the "best method of birth control."[76]

For a Jewish counterpart to Fletcher, the conveners found Reform Rabbi Israel Margolies, who wanted nothing to do with "holier-than-thou religionists" overly preoccupied with "sin," deeming such behavior "spineless and irrational subservience to the dogmatism of theologians . . . unbecoming to the rational and largely moral society of a great nation."[77] He therefore called on us to "disavow the old taboos" and "assert proudly and honestly that, as creative partners of God, we reserve the right to build our families purposefully and joyfully, not accidentally and reluctantly."[78]

Nevertheless, a more poignant dimension to Rabbi Margolies's participation in the ethics panel emerged in the follow-up discussion. Margolies listened to three successive testaments to the secular/rational character of the abortion issue, followed by a concerned question about potential life from Daniel Callahan. Callahan's question was dismissed by Fletcher, whose only baseline was the utilitarian one, what will "augment our sense of well-being."[79] At that point Margolies suddenly shed his complacent veneer of secularism, reverting to the very theology he had earlier dismissed as so "unmodern":

> I also believe that there is something very special about what we call the soul, the spiritual nature of man. If you deny this and lean entirely on the rational you are in danger of falling into the kind of trap that occurred in Nazi Germany, which was by all objective judgment a highly rational society. We used to refer in German to the Luftmensch— "people who live on air." This was a people of philosophers, musicians, and scientists, and yet it was out of this company that the kind of philosophy was able to come which, having no consideration for the spiritual nature of man, was able to condemn a certain segment of the population to extinction in the interest of its own point of view. . . . I think this is why the religious emphasis at the beginning of this conference certainly has a place.[80]

However grudgingly, the conveners gave the penultimate slot on the ethics panel to Thomas J. O'Donnell, a "traditional Catholic," who stated the prevailing Catholic opposition to abortion.[81] O'Donnell was followed by what was touted as a "liberal Catholic view." Its advocate, Joseph Donceel, dissented from the theory of "immediate animation" (ensoulment at conception) in favor of "mediate" or "delayed" animation, but he did so by rejecting the basic dualistic premises of Western Enlightenment rationalism and by locating theological error in the deference of Catholic thinkers to Cartesian scientific rationalism.[82] Citing Aquinas, Donceel argued for the notion of hylomorphism, under which both body and soul proceed together from conception through vegetative and animal states, toward true hominization: "Hylomorphism holds that the human soul is to the body somewhat as the shape of a statue is to the actual statue. The shape of a statue cannot exist before the statue exists. . . . The human soul can exist only in a real human body."[83] Donceel found this theory consistent not only with the dynamics of fetal development, but with the most advanced epistemological philosophy of the time—the existential phenomenology of Maurice Merleau-Ponty.[84] The upshot of Donceel's position was that "a prehuman embryo cannot demand from us the absolute respect which we owe to the human person;" however, "it deserves a very great consideration," and "only very serious reasons should allow us to terminate its existence."[85]

The panel conversation was lurching dangerously out of control. Participants who had been assembled to give polite, deferential religious sanction to the requirements of enlightened secularism found themselves in an arcane discussion of ensoulment theory that was, at the same time, a sophisticated modern epistemological challenge to the whole tradition of Enlightenment dualistic rationality. Ralph Gampell of Stanford Law School expressed the view that this whole unfortunate debate should be kept, at all costs, away from courts and legislatures: "When you are dealing with the courts and legislatures I think that the matter of ensoulment is not irrelevant, for if you tell them that we are dealing with a choice between two lives in being, they will move away from you in holy horror. I think that such a proposition does have Nazi overtones that society would recognize. If you are going to persuade legislatures, you have to say that there is maternal, but not fetal life in being."[86]

Gampell hoped that he could trap O'Donnell by asking why spontaneous abortions were not given the rites of the church. O'Donnell informed him that rites *were* given, in the form of conditional baptisms, although he conceded that it was not "one of our clerical duties . . . to watch over every missed menstruation."[87] He then pointed out that the church's primary concern was not "about the soul surviving or not"—on that question the church had no lack of confidence—but rather about the moral state of American society.[88] Finally, George Corner, speaking as a medical biologist and philosopher, closed the unraveling discussion by stating that "many great problems of our responsibility to each other—abortion, moral restraint, penal law—can never be settled by delimiting fixed stages of development of body or soul."[89]

The 1968 conference was otherwise dominated by secular voices. Gampell, like many other participants, thought the solution lay with the medical profession. A practicing physician with a law degree who, with Herbert Packer, taught a law and medicine course at Stanford, Gampell had coauthored a law review article with Packer in 1959 calling for the decriminalization of "therapeutic abortions" in favor of procedural delegation to committees of doctors, who would gain plenary control over the process.[90] The authors called for the repeal of dysfunctional criminal law, seeing the problem of therapeutic abortion as one calling for the deliberate application of informed medical judgment. Their solution would both privatize the issue and transfer authority over it to the realm of medical expertise. Alan Guttmacher, however, while zealous in his quest for abortion reform, was candidly skeptical about the application of medical expertise to decisions whether to abort or not. At the 1968 conference he posed the question to Joseph Fletcher himself:

> And what kind of judgment is the physician to make? What are you endowing us with to make the wise decision? We are not religionists. Most of us are not psychiatrists. We are not social workers. We're just plain doctors. And on what basis are we going to say to a woman, "Yes, you should" or "No, you shouldn't have an abortion?"

Fletcher's response was that abortion should be available if there are no "medical contraindications." Guttmacher replied that there "is no woman we can't abort, so this idea that a certain proportion of patients cannot be aborted is not a medical concept."[91] It was an instance of ironic reversal that Guttmacher found himself explaining to Fletcher (the theologian) what Niebuhr had tried for so long to explain to the celebrators of scientific expertise about the limits of that expertise with respect to questions of moral responsibility.

Nevertheless, by 1968, when the Gampell and Packer article was reprinted in Guttmacher's *The Case for Legalized Abortion Now*,[92] the cutting edge of advocacy with respect to abortion reform had become the privacy right enunciated by the Supreme Court in *Griswold*. Particularly influential was the nearly fifty-page article "Federal Constitutional Limitations on the Enforcement and Administration of State Abortion Statutes," published in 1968 by Roy Lucas,[93] who would go on to be an important legal activist for abortion rights. Eschewing the incrementalism of legislative reform, Lucas called for the constitutionalization of choice. Given the legal rhetoric to which we have become accustomed since *Roe v. Wade*, it is difficult to recall how startling it was for Lucas to assert in 1968 that "[a]lthough interests at stake in the abortion controversy are diverse, subtle, novel, and sensitive, the case appears ultimately to fit within the classical framework of governmental interference with important interests of individual liberty and to be capable of resolution in traditional constitutional terms."[94] He concluded that

> [a] right to abortion by consent performed by a licensed physician can be strongly asserted in at least three related forms within the Bill of Rights and fourteenth amendment framework—first, as a fundamental right of marital privacy, human dignity, and personal autonomy

reserved to the pregnant woman acting on the advice of a licensed physician; second, as a penumbral emanating from values embodied in the express provisions of the Bill of Rights themselves; or, third, as a necessary and altogether reasonable application of precedent, namely, *Griswold v. Connecticut*.[95]

While Lucas's law review article displayed the understandable self-assurance of advocacy, it was far from certain in 1967 and 1968 that litigation would lead to abortion as constitutionally protected privacy. Another early abortion rights activist, Harriet Pilpel, noted at the 1968 conference, in the panel entitled "Abortion and Constitutionality: The Means of Assessing and Testing the Constitutionality of Abortion Law in the United States," that even losing test cases could have a valuable education effect: "So whether or not we are eventually successful in declaring clauses unconstitutional in this area, the fact that attacks are mounted and the public is educated as to the infirmities in the laws will become, I think, extremely useful."[96]

Accompanying the zeal for solving the abortion problem through constitutional litigation was a striking contempt, even distaste, for sectarian religion, religiously rooted morality, or even the notion that abortion might raise a serious question of morality from a theological perspective. It was routinely assumed that Protestants and Jews overwhelmingly favored extreme liberalization, and even repeal, of abortion laws, supporting the characterization of "the sole major organized body opposing all abortion reform—officials of the Roman Catholic Church."[97] According to Lucas, "[t]o make the decision that a fetus *ought to be considered* a human being is a subjective belief of religious character," and "[t]here is no valid state interest in implementation of religious belief sufficient to serve as a basis for legislation."[98]

The distinction between "developing fetal tissue," on the one hand, and "fully established human life," on the other, thus becomes the only appropriate distinction in the secular realm of legislation. Accordingly, the secular moral value of choice itself becomes the only allowable position. To allow otherwise would contradict "the ethical value of not forcing the subjective moral assumptions of one group upon all other groups."[99] We are told by Lucas that, according to H. L. A. Hart, "the unimpeded exercise by individuals of free choice may be held a value in itself with which it is *prima facie* wrong to interfere."[100]

Curiously, however, when he was requested to offer an establishment clause perspective on the abortion issue at the conference, Lucas took a position in the panel on abortion and constitutionality seemingly at odds with his law review article:

> Now, I will try to summarize the separation of church and state position. This is perhaps the final argument which can be raised, that the laws regulating abortion are laws respecting an establishment of religion. The quickest way to sum this up is to show that the abortion restrictions arise out of a metaphysical theory that the fertilized ovum is a human being entitled to the protection of ultimate birth and life. But in the same sense, all of the statements in the Decalogue can be said both to be religious and to represent some state interest.
>
> The chief obstacle to knocking out the abortion laws on the establishment of religion point, even though you can prove that maintenance of the laws is religiously motivated, is the argument of the other side that there is a state interest in protecting the sanctity of life. This is an argument not easily dismissed.[101]

Despite such concessions, the basic constitutional argument ruled out of order any sectarian claim about preserving the sanctity of life, gradually turning the legal abortion debate into an all-or-nothing affair obsessively focused on who does or does not have "rights."

The opponents of reform took up the challenge. The 1970 Noonan volume, for example, contains one entry that was written in 1970, after the California Supreme Court had invalidated its state abortion law on constitutional grounds,[102] which, unlike the other essays that had come from the 1967 conference, reflects the stark and uncompromising posturing of later pro-life legalists.[103] If the abortion rights strategy was to load the constitutional argument on the mechanical category of "privacy," then the equally mechanical pro-life response was to load everything on the category of "person" by definitionally including the fetus as person for all purposes. Just as creationists took on their evolutionist adversaries by appropriating through "creation-science" the status of secular positivism,[104] abortion opponents, heeding the warnings of those like Lucas, reprocessed their own position as firmly rooted in secular constitutional legalism. The particular essay written by Noonan and his colleague David Louisell displays for the most part a facile, manipulative conceptualism with an unrelenting insistence on deduction based on the all-or-nothing category of "human being."[105] In fact, it is exactly the sort of legalism that has become standard fare in pro-life tracts and is strikingly at odds with the sensitivity and deliberation of the theological essays in the same volume.

Then came *Roe v. Wade*, ensuring that the defenders of choice would be situated in a context that was almost exclusively legalistic and rights-based. Like all legalisms, it invited interminable legalist debate. The pro-choice legal arguments rested on the secular morality that was being developed to shore up the liberal activism of the Supreme Court. So starkly secular did the pro-choice position become that a leading liberal theorist would, in fact, argue that successful theological opposition to the pro-choice position would amount to an unconstitutional establishment of religion— which crudely oversimplified what was nonetheless a subtle and difficult question of church-state relations, from the perspective of both theology and law.[106]

Although *Roe* secularized the abortion issue through the insulating effect of the privacy right, a growing opposition to *Roe* became ever more resolutely absolutist in theologically defending the pro-life position. Triggered in part by reaction to *Roe* itself, Catholics and fundamentalists formed an alliance (hitherto unheard of) in opposition to abortion, with some fundamentalists quite self-consciously seizing on abortion as a vehicle for reasserting religion to counter what seemed to be an establishment of secularism.[107]

9

Is Compromise
Possible?

......

While we agree with Laurence Tribe that *Roe* was "not unconstitutional,"[1] we do think, in retrospect, that the decision may be fairly characterized as a mistake for three combined reasons: it was legally problematic at best, sociologically inaccurate, and politically disastrous. As to the first, the path of precedent from *Griswold* (the Connecticut birth-control case, itself legally problematic) to *Roe* was far from clear.[2] As the Court moves in particular cases from clearer realms of text and tradition to more open-ended interventions, circumspection and prudence become a necessary part of the constitutional calculus.

In *Roe*, for example, the Court could have refrained from the absolutism of the privacy right rationale and invoked instead the due process approach of Justice Harlan (in *Griswold*).[3] On those grounds it might have overturned the extreme Texas statute (which criminalized all abortions except to save the mother's life) as incompatible with constitutional "liberty," while merely remanding, or even summarily upholding, the statute in the companion case of *Doe v. Bolton*,[4] which involved a version of the reform statute from the 1962 American Law Institute's Model Penal Code. That due process rationale would have provided constitutional mandate for the ongoing process of abortion reform, without at the same time dismissing as legally irrelevant a continued ethical, theological, and political debate.

Such an approach would also have been consistent with other areas of constitutional law where the Court has intervened to check the most egregious practices, but has otherwise been willing to defer to state decision-making processes. With respect to obscenity, for example, the basic norm is that local, community standards of decency should prevail, yet the Court overrode those local standards when the state of Georgia held the film *Carnal Knowledge* to be constitutionally obscene.[5] Similar instances of limited intervention against a backdrop of general respect for state process are to be found in the areas of racial gerrymandering[6] and access to public education.[7]

Sociologically, as Alan Guttmacher had recognized, successful abortion reform requires some degree of public consensus. Abortion is a moral issue with sincere and deeply felt positions on both sides. Such moral division had simply ceased to exist with respect to state prohibition of contraceptive use by married couples (*Griswold*), despite the official Catholic position favoring prohibition. Thus, the privacy right rationale of *Griswold*, while in fact easily ridiculed for its shaky doctrinal basis, nevertheless resonated with a generally shared public conviction that the state should not intrude into birth-control decisions. When the Court extended the same rationale to include abortion, however, it met with quick and hostile resistance since public consensus on abortion simply did not exist. The Court fairly concluded that a consensus was emerging on the need for some liberalization of strict laws, but it was wrong in supposing that it could shape that consensus into support for abortion as a purely private option, constrained for two trimesters by medical concerns alone. The sociological error in *Roe* was the failure to appreciate the potential for serious religious opposition to its authorization of abortion on demand until viability.

The special problem posed by *Roe*, however, did not stem simply from the fact of public division on the abortion issue. Surely, for example, public division had existed on the question of racial segregation. On that issue, however, the Court could reach back to recapture the ethical agenda of the Civil War amendments and convincingly seize the moral high ground.[8] On abortion, in contrast, the legal rationale was problematic, and there were plausible moral arguments on both sides.

Probably one of the Court's goals in *Roe* was therapeutic: By leading the way in abortion reform as it had in civil rights, and by lifting the question out of the state decision-making process, it could prevent divisive struggles in state legislatures across the country. Politically, however, the effect of *Roe* was more inflammatory than therapeutic, as we can see with the advantage of hindsight. *Roe* triggered an opposition that would become increasingly absolutist in theologically defending the pro-life position.[9] Many Catholics, along with their church, decided that if *Roe* represented America's official secular morality, then the comfortable alliance of Catholicism with Americanism could not hold. One of our

Catholic colleagues recalled for us his experience of family discussions during the period just before and after *Roe*. His recollection, which finds support in the scholarly literature,[10] is that prior to *Roe* there was much debate about the particulars of concededly inevitable abortion reform. *Roe* itself, however, was perceived as an outrageous and enormous shock, to be opposed by all. He also observed that for many Catholics who had refused to comply with the church's teaching on contraception, opposition to *Roe*, in its clear moral purity, offered an opportunity to reaffirm commitment to the church's ethical tradition.

Meanwhile, conservative Protestant evangelicals, allied with Catholics to oppose *Roe*, seized on abortion as a vehicle for reasserting religion in what seemed to be an increasingly secular world.[11] Francis Schaeffer himself depicted the abortion decision as the extreme example of what was in fact a clash of competing worldviews, with the "totally humanistic" threatening to smother the "Judeo-Christian." For him, the Supreme Court represented an "elite" who were "arbitrarily" forcing "a totally secular concept" onto an unwilling majority.[12] This worldview theme expressed an authentic Christian pro-life sentiment, which, in turn, would be exploited by opportunistic Republicans[13] to their great political advantage. Republican party political promises would suggest that all of America could be remade according to a single Christian standard, as if sin could be eradicated and pluralism eliminated by political and legal action. These false promises served to trivialize and cheapen what were in fact difficult questions of church/state relations and public morality.

There is reason to believe, over the dissent of apologists for *Roe*,[14] that the state legislative process might have resolved the abortion issue through compromise more successfully than did the Court, even though many legislative compromises would not have been perfect from either the pro-life or pro-choice perspective. In the five years preceding *Roe*, sixteen liberalized abortion laws had been enacted in states with 41 percent of the nation's population. Among the most sweeping were those signed in New York by Governor Nelson Rockefeller and in California (much to his later regret) by Governor Ronald Reagan. As historian Michael Barone notes: "[B]y the time the *Roe v. Wade* decision was issued, about 70% of the nation's population lived within 100 miles—an easy two hours' drive—of a state with a legalized abortion law. And just as the Supreme Court was speaking, legislatures in almost all of the states were going into session; many would probably have liberalized their abortion laws if the court had not acted."[15]

This is not to suggest that the legislative path would have been a neat, linear one, or that remaining restrictions would not have imposed, as always, a disproportionate burden on poorer women. That route would, however, have allowed the widespread and deeply felt religiously rooted concern about abortion to be considered. Moreover, given all of the strife occasioned by this singularly divisive issue over the past twenty years, it is likely that abortion is now in fact less widely available, especially to the poor, than it was in the early 1970s or might have been some years later, had a workable moral consensus emerged.[16]

Mirroring the religiously rooted absolutist opposition to abortion that arose after *Roe v. Wade* was an equally absolutist emergent feminism that made abortion rights its political and moral centerpiece in the 1970s. Revisionist historians would like to portray the events leading up to *Roe* as part of a vast women's movement[17] and to recast the entire abortion struggle as one against "male control of procreation."[18] The historical record is otherwise. The actual process was more complicated and heavily dependent on the role of male, as well as female, law and health professionals.

The modern American abortion reform movement began with the American Law Institute's Model Penal Code reform, influenced by British jurist Glanville Williams, with subsequent and important support for reform/repeal coming from those concerned with both population control and medical autonomy (for example, Alan Guttmacher and Robert Hall, respectively). The publicity of the 1962 Sherri Finkbine case (Arizona mother and TV "Romper Room" host who had taken thalidomide) then captured public attention. As the 1960s drew to a close, distinctively feminist voices began to join the others; but it is easy to forget, for example, that *Ms.* did not even appear until 1972.[19]

Kristin Luker makes two points about the women (lawyers, public health officials, and physicians) who "argued forcefully and effectively" on behalf of legislative reform in California: "First, with very few exceptions, they were, like their male colleagues, professionals who had been trained in and were affiliated with elite institutions. Second, their arguments in favor of the bill were virtually indistinguishable from those of their male peers. . . . The language of a *right* to abortion, however, was not to be found in their claim."[20] And, as Faye Ginsburg points out, the lobbying efforts that helped produce the legislative successes gained strength from an affiliation of groups, many of which were still dominated by men: the American Medical Association (AMA) (1967), the American Civil Liberties Union (ACLU) (1969), Planned Parenthood-World Population (1969), and the National Organization for Women (NOW) (1968).[21]

The assertion, now so familiar, that abortion rights are by definition women's rights serves to reinforce extreme polarization on this issue. Most activist opposition to abortion comes from women.[22] These women are often dismissed by pro-choice feminists as bearers of "false consciousness" (to use the familiar characterization of left politics) or simply as dupes of manipulative males seeking control of their bodies. The characterization is bound to be demeaning. Moreover, when opposition to abortion becomes by definition "antifeminist,"[23] those who promote "pro-life feminism"[24] are treated as an oxymoron (at best) by both sides of the polarized abortion conflict. Once abortion rights became the single most headlined, non-negotiable demand of the feminist movement, some pro-life women came to reject anything called feminism, and therefore to reject feminist positions to which they might otherwise have been drawn (e.g., expanded health care for women and children, family leave time, etc.). One of the real tragedies of the abortion conflict is the extent to which women have thus become needlessly divided against each other.

A serious contributing factor to that division lay in the particular rationale relied on by Roe, which was then adopted and defended by the feminist movement. The rhetoric of choice is rooted in Roe's notion of privacy right, and it tends to correspond with the rhetoric of property. The claim of privacy as autonomy is one of self as owner, as having dominion. One can easily imagine the pro-choice Republican who can use the same (libertarian) rhetoric to defend abortion rights and unregulated plant closings (a live example is Governor William Weld of Massachusetts).[25] Ultimately, that secular, Enlightenment rhetoric of autonomy is bound up with a celebration of "self" as the final arbiter, the trump to all moral claim. In that context, by immunizing abortion from the legislative process, Roe could be read as sanctioning, or even "encouraging,"[26] routine use of abortion for the instrumental realization of self-interest, and, as Elizabeth Fox-Genovese has pointed out, this message is conveyed despite the very troubled particularity of most decisions to abort.[27] In effect, the secular discourse of choice rules the difficult moral questions both politically and legally out of bounds.

Consider, for example, the hypothetical that is often treated as a close-out argument for choice—the Thomson violinist case.[28] Philosopher Judith Thomson took up the challenge of defending the right to choose abortion even if the personhood of the fetus is conceded. Her hypothetical is that of a person who finds herself waking up having been involuntarily plugged into a life support system for a famous violinist who will otherwise die unless the hapless and involuntary supporter is kept so connected and confined for nine months. The case has the advantage of pointing out that imposing an obligation of unselfishness on women runs contrary to the usual libertarian legal (and cultural) assumption that one should be perfectly free to be perfectly selfish. Certainly nobody is obliged by law to provide medical life support for another. Yet because the pro-choice position found itself framed so completely by Roe, and therefore by the issues of a woman's "right," defense of that libertarian right became oddly aggressive, as in Tribe's account of the violinist case. "Indeed, just about everybody would agree with Professor Thomson that no law could justly compel you to take this situation lying down, at least if the violinist were an uninvited intruder—and perhaps even if he had been invited but had overstayed his welcome."[29] As Tribe does successfully argue, the problem with Roe is not its supposed unconstitutionality, but the failure of its "rights" methodology to grapple with the moral issue.[30] More exactly, the language of rights, as formulated by Roe, and even more glaringly by the Thomson hypothetical, seems to exclude analysis of precisely those points one would want to consider in order to do a careful ethical analysis of the problem.

There are, of course, many ways in which Thomson's case, morally, is simply different from abortion—in some ways easier, in some ways harder. As the careful Aristotelian philosopher Rosalind Hursthouse argues, many of those contextual differences are precisely the ones that would require emphasis if one were to frame the issue in terms of virtue or, the supposed correlative to rights, the question of duty.[31] For Thomson, those contextual differences can be ruled irrelevant since the issue is framed so starkly as a question of rights alone. Because the only analytic presupposition is a self with rights, the only analytically appropriate question is whether the self's rights have been invaded, not the substantive question of virtue. This is, of course, the Enlightenment version of rights and unconstrained human agency, wrenched, as Maritain said, from the context of a moral order, as if (going back to d'Entrèves) one could logically separate the question of rights from the moral foundation on which we build a conception of duty.

As feminists came to recognize, one obvious problem with the rhetoric of choice is the extent to which it fails to capture a complex social reality in which choice contains its own coercions. Many women tell abortion counselors that they "have no choice," that they "have to" have an abortion.[32] Economic pressure is the most frequently cited reason, but other coercions include male pressure for sexual pleasure without consequences (Playboy supports pro-choice, of course),[33] internalized social norms of success and independence, and even parental pressure.

More recently, drawing back from the libertarian rhetoric of choice, feminists have adopted a "reproductive freedom" claim. That claim, however, either repeats the problematic of choice or, as in some of the more recent literature, becomes a generalized demand for equality. That equality argument suggests that the consequences of biological difference between men and women are inherently unfair, so that the state must cancel them out lest it be guilty of discrimination.[34] As applied to abortion, this model is both reductionist (male vs. female is the only relevant line of demarcation) and totalizing (all men vs. all women), pitting all male (oppressors, never pregnant) against all women (victims, subject to pregnancy). We think this model simply fails to speak to the experience of most women with respect to the abortion issue.

The secular rights rationale of *Roe*, as adopted by feminists in the 1970s, was undeniably empowering in its affirmation of the capacity of women to take control of their own lives, to act as moral agents in the face of the conventional expectation that they passively accept preordained roles of dependency and self-abnegation. The language of rights, after all, is the language of membership in the moral community. Yet in its stark purity, the assertion of the unqualified right to individual autonomous choice as the foundation for moral and political thought ran counter to the religious traditions of most American women. One effect of *Roe* was to privilege that Enlightenment discourse as appropriate, rational, *public* discourse, while implicitly labeling other moral traditions private, subjective, and probably irrational.

Thus, while pro-life extremist women seemed oddly blind to the liberating aspects of *Roe*, pro-choice extremists seemed oddly blind to the moral limitations of *Roe*'s starkly secular vocabulary, and especially to its inability to speak to the ambivalent women in the middle—women who could not accept the hard-edged literalism and self-righteous ethical reductionism of the religious antiabortion extremists, yet who found the absolutism of the "right" to abortion on demand morally troubling.

In fact, by so enthusiastically embracing the secular vocabulary of *Roe*, liberal feminists tended to ignore the complex relationship between American women and their religion. It is too often a commonplace among pro-choice feminists that religion is some sort of monolithic "other" that exists over and against the lives of women in America, as an oppressive force to be held at bay by the powers of legalistic, secular neutrality. It is as if "religion" and "women" were separate categories, with religion representing either all men or some vague notion of "societal" domination.[35] In its most extreme form, the entire history of Judeo-Christian religion is reduced to a story of patriarchical domination, with consequent calls for

total rejection of that tradition, or at least, the fashioning of an appropriately androgynous "feminist theology" with all traces of patriarchy rooted
out.[36] To the extent these judgments reflect assumptions about American women, they are flatly contradicted by historical and contemporary
experiential reality.

Religion is not only of paramount significance to the lives of many, if
not most, American women, but there is a long and continuing record of
active, empowering involvement of women in churches, probably more
than in any other American institution.[37] This is not to suggest a clear
record of progress toward equality; many struggles continue. What is clear,
however, is the variousness of women's experience with religion, and
a continuing commitment, evidenced by the sheer numbers of women
taking part in church life, to personal fulfillment through religious experience.

Female church membership in America has always exceeded male
membership; in the nineteenth century, women made up two-thirds to
three-fourths of the members of Protestant denominations. While that
gap has narrowed, women have consistently retained their numerical majority, despite a history of male domination.[38] These gender differences
in religious commitment remain a distinct feature of American life. This
fact cannot be "relegated to the dark corners of the past," says sociologist
Robert Wuthnow, for "religion remains a vital aspect of the public and
private lives of the vast majority of American women." Thus, "nearly three-
quarters consider themselves church members. Half attend religious services at least once every week and more than two-thirds attend at least
once a month. Four in ten claim they pray more than once a day. Seven
in ten say their relation to God is very important to their self-worth. And
three-fourths consider their religious faith the most important influence
on their life."[39]

Nevertheless, when feminism began to receive full media attention in
the 1970s, its appeal seemed strongest to those among whom religious
commitment was weakest. Feminism thus became linked, fairly or unfairly, with the "new class" ideology of secularism and permissive life-style
freedom, a linkage clearly strengthened by Roe.[40] This was so despite the
fact that ordination of women had begun to take hold in many churches
(not all, of course) by the 1970s. In fact, by 1980 the proportion of professional women in the clergy was actually higher than in either law or
medicine.[41]

But the feminists who had begun to treat Roe v. Wade as the sine qua non
of their movement surely had their worst suspicions about religion con-

firmed when Catholics and conservative Protestants became the backbone of the emerging right-to-life movement. Many women viewed this coalition as yet another manifestation of the conservative religious tradition which held that women ranked below men in a divinely ordained hierarchy. "As long as . . . men are men and women are women, then women are to be subject to their husbands as unto the head."[42] Even Billy Graham, who endorsed equal pay for equal work, worried that "women's liberation" would damage the family since it flouted biblical teaching about spousal relationships: "God has appointed you husbands to be the head of the home. When a woman opposes that order, she rebels against the will of God."[43]

At its most extreme, the conservative position on a woman's role drew on a German "orders of creation" doctrine that held a woman's subservience to be built into the natural order before the Fall, and therefore not of human origin and not even relativized, or rendered provisional, by the gospel.[44] Many women find even this extreme doctrine less demeaning than one might suppose, because it is one part of an overall mediation between the gospel message of complete equality before God, on the one hand, and the need for some beneficial ordering of worldly relations in family, church, and polity, on the other. In theory the same doctrine imposes on men the discipline of responsibility and humility before God, as well as sanctioning male authority. Nevertheless, with sound theological warrant, churches that were more liberal could reject such doctrine and seek as well theological engagement with the challenge posed by feminism. It was a challenge to be taken seriously, not just for political reasons, but because it raised hard questions about the relation between the scriptural narrative itself and the history of power relations within the ongoing human tradition that interprets it.

In fact, in the liberal denominations (e.g., Episcopalian, Presbyterian), members, clergy, and especially church bureaucrats were becoming deeply influenced by the claims of the feminist movement.[45] During the 1970s an active women's movement within these churches worked to promote ordination for women (with a great deal of success, despite the inevitable instances of opposition and rejection, as with other professions), to root out sexism in tradition and practice (with some success), and in general to promote equality for women within the Christian churches. In Reform Judaism as well, a majority of women members saw themselves as feminists.

Ideally, as the abortion debate unfolded, both liberal (e.g., Presbyterian) and moderate (e.g., United Methodist) denominations should have been in a position to provide an alternative to the absolutist conservative religious opposition to abortion and the utterly secularized claims of the pro-choice extreme. That alternative might have spoken to the real moral concerns of those who found themselves in the ambivalent and troubled middle. Even before *Roe*, in fact, some churches had issued resolutions calling for reform, or even repeal, of abortion laws.[46] Yet once *Roe* was in place, the question before the churches was inevitably framed as "Should we oppose or support *Roe*?" This version of the issue tended to close off full theological analysis of the two critical questions that the churches really needed to address: (1) "What should our own moral position on abortion be?" (2) "What should we appropriately expect to be the relationship between our position and state law?" The second question was at least as complex as the first, for a number of alternatives were available.

The peculiar role of a church (or denomination) in a pluralist culture transforms a question like abortion into a connected pair of issues, each offering a continuum of possibility, with a number of solutions representing points of intersection. One continuum is the substantive moral question, which, on abortion, offers a range from abortion as murder unless the unintended consequence of an effort to save the mother's life (the traditional Catholic view) to abortion on demand until the birth of a live child (the pure libertarian position). The other continuum is the relationship between sectarian doctrine and secular law, which on abortion offers a range from the privatized bearing of witness in one's own tradition (making no demand on secular law at all) to the legislative realization of one's own doctrine in public law (positive law must coincide with sectarian moral position).

If one imagines the two continua, respectively, as the X and Y axes of analytic geometry, the pairing of various points on the two axes yields an array of coordinate solutions. The important point is that both questions are serious theological issues, and that only by answering both does one take a public policy position. Moreover, it is at least geometrically obvious that there are many compromise possibilities. The mere fact that a particular tradition would urge the prohibition of all or most abortions as a moral matter does not mean that its adherents must insist that the state take the same position. That solution, depending on how it is graphed, occupies one extreme corner. Nor must one's tradition necessarily abjure any public role whatsoever, which is just another extreme corner of the graph. It may well be that a careful theological accommodation to pluralism would lead to a preference in the public realm for less than one's full sectarian position but more than the passivity of isolated privatism.

With *Roe* in place, however, the liberal and mainline churches found it easier to avoid such complex theological analysis by simply endorsing the Supreme Court's decision. Anxious to disavow the extreme Christian doctrine of female subordination promoted by some anti-*Roe* activists, and sensitive to feminist suspicion of all patriarchical tradition, the authors of most mainline church resolutions on abortion seemed to look to their own traditions and doctrines in order to rationalize (in the manner of legal advocacy) a predetermined result that would fully accord with *Roe*.[47] The alternative would have been to look to theological tradition with an open mind, seeking guidance on this troubling issue, and thereby providing a distinctive theological voice. That voice, as is being conceded more forthrightly today, would have recognized that most of those traditions did affirm the moral worth of fetal life (which may be different from the "personhood" issue) and probably also had a "theological presumption against abortion,"[48] although such presumption might not have meant prohibition in each individual case, and did not necessarily, by itself, answer the question of the state's role.

The position of the Presbyterian Church (USA) illustrates what occurred. In its 1983 document "Covenant and Creation: Theological Reflections on Contraception and Abortion,"[49] the church took the position that "in the exceptional case in which a woman is pregnant and judges that it would be irresponsible to bring a child into the world given the limitation of her situation, . . . it can be an act of faithfulness before God to take responsibility for intervening in the natural process of pregnancy by terminating it, an act consistent with the obligation of responsible stewardship toward natural processes generally."[50] Such a decision may be based on a woman's decision that she lacks "the emotional, physical and financial services to carry a pregnancy to term." Her consequent decision to terminate the pregnancy will be regarded as an "expression of human responsibility": "The morality (or immorality) of a particular abortion is not contingent on the kind of problem that prompts its consideration, but on the seriousness of that problem in the particular case. We affirm the value of decision-making empowered by the Holy Spirit."[51] That statement alone is not necessarily inconsistent with serious Protestant contextual ethics, although, as with all Protestant contextualism, it runs the danger of being ultimately indistinguishable from mere utilitarianism.

Eager, however, to embrace every detail of the *Roe* opinion, the report proclaims that, with respect to *Roe*'s trimester formulation, the church "can affirm this decision, then, for religious reasons as well as medical, as it upholds the inviolability of human life."[52] As to the charge that *Roe* turns the abortion decision into "an entirely private choice," we are told that a "structure of accountability" is "built into the Court's decision" since the "decision to terminate a pregnancy must be made by the patient in consultation with her physician."[53] Having thus agreed with the complete medicalization of the issue, the report assures us that responsible physicians will of course refuse to perform abortions for the purpose of sex selection[54]—as if that refusal could somehow be rooted in medicine, rather than ethics and theology. As to whether there is a recognizable conflict of "rights" or even "interests" between fetal life and maternal choice, the report makes clear that its theological understanding of the morality of abortion does not differ from the legal understanding of Roe. In fact, with a cite to Carol Gilligan, the report insists that a theory which views the morality of abortion as an issue involving a conflict of rights or interests represents in its "highly abstract quality" the "typically masculine pattern of logic superimposed on a decision-making process that falls primarily to women."[55]

The underlying premise of the report is a vision of freedom that seems more in accord with the Enlightenment and with our contemporary "republic of choice"[56] than with the Calvinist tradition of the Presbyterian church, which had once emphasized a freedom realized in obedience to God.[57] Nevertheless, the report states: "While we would today reject Calvin's exclusively masculine language in reference to God, we are grateful for [his] clear and strong affirmation of human freedom and responsibility in God's provision for us."[58]

The Presbyterian aim was sincere, and the report's portrayal of women facing abortion decisions was especially sympathetic and caring. Nevertheless, the final Presbyterian position was in substance difficult to distinguish from the situation ethics of Joseph Fletcher,[59] and impossible to distinguish from the legal position of Roe v. Wade. There is some accuracy, then, to the charge leveled by Francis Schaeffer that "theological liberalism" had become no different from "secular humanism."[60]

The Presbyterians themselves, as if to confirm the contradictions lurking within their position, hastily (two years later) amended their document to provide: "We are disturbed by abortion which seems to be elected only as a convenience or to ease embarrassment. We affirm that abortion should not be used as a method of birth control."[61] One is driven to ask, why? The original report remained otherwise intact.

A dissident Methodist has characterized (we think fairly) his own church's similar position on abortion as "intentionally ambiguous, noteworthy for little else than its tone of muddled compromise and obfuscation—in short, a sort of blank-check view of morality that assures United Methodists that issues like abortion are purely personal, private and subjective, without theological or biblical relevance."[62]

This blank-check endorsement of *Roe*, of course, only deepened the suspicions that had already been dividing American churches along the lines of the traditionalist/modernist schism. True to caricature, pro-life extremists seemed intolerant, overly literal, and insensitive to the reality of sin in an imperfect world; and they ignored the complexity of church/state relations in a pluralist, liberal democracy. Yet, also true to caricature, the mainline denominations seemed pathetically overeager to make a hasty, uncritical covenant with every latest pronouncement of the secular culture. Many among the churchgoing public were dissatisfied with both extremes.

For a time, some attempt was made to articulate an alternative view through a moderate Protestant pro-life organization, American Citizens Concerned for Life (ACCL). The ACCL opposed permissive abortion laws, yet found much pro-life talk too Catholic or too absolutist and pro-life strategies too narrow and too simple.[63] This group was especially sensitive to feminist concerns and believed strongly in social service efforts on behalf of women and children, reasoning that legal protection of the fetus would not come without protections for pregnant women first. After thirteen years of trying, ACCL gave up as an organization for lack of support from liberal Protestants. Once again, what was lost was the possibility of a different voice, one that might have spoken to the fact of genuine ambivalence in the Protestant congregations whose leaders had so assuredly supported choice in its extreme form. That ambivalence, and even opposition, would soon emerge as a significant force.

What a serious theological voice might contribute to the otherwise polarized state of the abortion debate depends, of course, not only on its substantive moral content, but on the difficult and delicate question of the appropriate role of religion and theological discourse in public political debate. The most secular version of the pro-choice position, which many took to be embodied in *Roe*, would argue that any successful theological opposition to abortion on demand amounts to an unconstitutional establishment of religion.[64] We think that position crudely oversimplifies what is a subtle and difficult question of church/state relations from the perspectives of both law and theology. In fact, one positive outcome that might emerge from the tortured history of the abortion controversy is a recognition of exactly how difficult the question of church/state relations really is, of why it does not reduce itself easily to formulaic solution, but requires instead a high level of cultural sensitivity from both church and state.

Legal scholars have tended to view the church/state problem from, as it were, the "outside," from the point of view of one who is not part of any religious tradition, but who is instead a neutral arbiter among them and a representative of the secular state. That point of view assumes that there are no religious or moral truths or, if there are such truths, that they are appropriately experienced and realized only in the context of one's private life.[65] The fact/value dichotomy that d'Entrèves rejected is implicit to the outsider perspective.

From that perspective, religion might well be viewed as a generally positive social force, contributing good works and a potpourri of sound values. Even when religion is not so viewed, however, the outsider legalist will still treat private religious choice and expression as basic "autonomy rights," to be protected by the First Amendment's free exercise clause.

On the other hand, when a particular religion's truth claims enter the public square and threaten the neutrality of the secular order, that intrusion is deemed a violation of the establishment clause. Ever lurking in the background is the haunting historical memory of fierce early modern European religious wars, during which numberless people were slaughtered for the sake of religious truth.[66] America's constitutional disestablishment represented, at least in part, an effort to insure peace in a religiously pluralist country.

Even from the perspective of the outsider, however, the relation between privately chosen religious traditions and the public square is more complex than it first appears. Constitutional law scholars are aware of the paradoxical relation between the free exercise and the establishment clauses. Protecting the free exercise rights of one tradition might seem, from the nonadherent's perspective, an illegitimate instance of establishment.[67] Even more complex, however, is the elusive relation between religion and liberal democracy itself. Many of the ideals of the liberal state are, of course, surviving fragments of originally religious values—freedom (from the Reformation), respect for justice, and the personhood rights of others (from the natural law tradition), etc. In fact, in the 1830s Alexis de Tocqueville, very much the dispassionate outside observer, noted a close "affinity"[68] between American religion and American democracy. In the face of death, he said, religion is a form of "hope." Unbelief he termed an "accident," and faith "the only permanent state of mankind."[69] If that faith becomes too troubled, observed Tocqueville, it resolves itself in bursts of anarchy or, especially, servility.[70] Indeed, he stated, "I am inclined to think that if faith be wanting [in a person], he must be subject; and if he be free, he must believe."[71]

In part, religion promotes civil liberty simply by promoting the moral self-governance that makes coercive political regulations unnecessary. Freedom does not become unbridled selfishness, but self-interest "rightly understood."[72] Tocqueville's point, however, was not simply that churches provide a valuable civic function by training people to conform to conventional morality. An established church does that much, without having any special "affinity" for democracy. Nor did he simply mean that religion provides ideological legitimation for the social/political order, although American churches have sometimes played that bland role.

Instead, as George Kelly has argued, Tocqueville was describing a religious spirit that he associated with Calvinist Protestantism—one that insisted on clear separation of church and state, but at the same time fostered a "structured politics of involvement"[73] in which religious conviction and political organization reinforced each other. As Kelly explains, Tocqueville argued that religion provided people with both "hope and pause,"[74] for it is an "unknown providence" that "liberates them for cooperative satisfactions in the res publica."[75] Religion in the United States provides both an incentive to act responsibly in the world, and it also offers that "pause" which makes complete allegiance to any political order impossible. This is why religion provides a counterforce to totalizing secular ideologies, whether of the right or left—so long, that is, as churches resist the temptation to identify themselves too fully with the state.

This combination of "hope" and "pause" relates directly to the social implications of death, in ways not usually recognized by the outsider legalist perspective. Peter Berger, an insightful sociologist of religion, writes: "Death radically challenges all socially objectified definitions of reality— of the world, of others and the self. Death radically puts in question the taken-for-granted, 'business-as-usual' attitude in which one exists in everyday life. . . . Insofar as the knowledge of death cannot be avoided in any society, legitimations of the reality of the social world in the face of death are decisive requirements in any society. The importance of religion in such legitimation is obvious."[76] Death may be the one "essential" reality of the natural world, a reality that is simultaneously mundane and ultimate, a profane occurrence that forces us to confront the possibility of the sacred. If it is difficult to legitimate our reality at all in the face of death, then it is all the more difficult to acknowledge in uncompromising terms our pervasive social responsibility for death. That abortion is such a case can neither be deemed not so by semantics nor successfully hidden from view by secularizing and "privatizing" it.

The traditional role of religion has been to facilitate the contact between the sacred and the profane. It would thereby provide, Tocqueville said, the "hope" in the face of death that would make possible a politics of responsible freedom. As Barth wrote, "Here is the kingdom of death, the brutal tyranny of fate which became the fate of nature."[77] Nevertheless, a "person should not lie in the chains of the cosmos. . . . The Kingdom of God is a kingdom of the freed and the free. . . ."[78] Yet this freedom, this "hope" even in the face of death, also radically challenges our socially objectified definitions of reality, no less than death itself, and makes total allegiance to any human political order at best provisional. Thus, believers will "freely" fulfill their civic duties in utmost, earnest responsibility precisely because they alienate themselves from any existing political order. If the state were "someday to recognize the threat posed by this revolutionary method, then there will be sufficient time to prove ourselves as martyrs."[79]

The relation between religion and politics in our democracy is, in other words, a dialectic of freedom and responsibility in which the relation of church and state is linked to the meaning of life and death itself. Religion cannot dictate civil law; and justice is not Christian love. It is not the business of coercive state power to achieve a Schaefferite moral reclamation. Yet, Tocqueville warned us, without an independent religious culture to shape the political and legal culture, there is only the coercive power of the state, and abject servility before it.

Thus, even from the outsider perspective, there is no neat categorical answer to the "right" relation between religion and secular law. Ironically, the question is answered best only when it does not arise. When churches (and/or other "mediating structures") function with full vigor, providing the community with moral guidance, civil law will be required only as a last resort, to which, ideally, one need have recourse only rarely. In such a setting it would be a matter of relative indifference whether, for example, penal law addresses a question like abortion. Churches themselves, through their own freely chosen disciplines and in diverse ways, would uphold an underlying cultural respect for life, even while providing necessary contextual judgments in pastoral counseling, as well as providing a community of help and support for those who need it. That, of course, would be the model of churches as ideally functioning mediating structures, which not only lessens the need for a state-coerced morality, but also insures that the minimal morality embodied in the law will be widely shared and therefore relatively uncontroversial.

Conversely, as churches fall short of that ideal, secular law becomes more necessary to the social order as the main expression of the culture's moral norms. At the same time, the norms reflected in the law become more controversial and arguably sectarian, for there is no shared moral culture on which to draw. In the face of the resulting controversy, it is tempting for the outsider legalist to leap to the supposed neutrality of the "secular" solution—that is, to cleanse law of all vestiges of sectarian religious traditionalism and to appeal instead to the supposedly neutral authority of, for example, the Constitution. In so doing, however, one forgets the coercive character of such "cleansing," that it can become, as with abortion, a non-neutral substitution of one morality for another,[80] which will lead to further conflict in the form of fresh efforts to contest the moral arena through law. In turn, those efforts may be destructive to the very religious groups that undertake them. It has often been noted that the United States has remained so religious precisely because it lacks a history of official establishment. While it is always tempting for churches to seek aid from the coercive arm of the state, the effect on religious life is dispiriting and demeaning,[81] and the resulting alliance with politics leads quickly to the idolatry that too confidently associates some party, agenda, or candidate with divine providence itself.

At that point, the church/state analysis must address as well the "insider's" perspective, the point of view of believers trying to work out the correct relation between their own religious tradition and the modern liberal state. Again, no easily defined model presents itself, suggesting that there may be no single right answer to the church/state dilemma.[82] The earliest Christian churches, in their days of martyrdom, at least enjoyed the luxury of political innocence.[83] The great pact with Constantine, allowing for the spread of Catholic Christianity throughout the West, ended that innocence forever—nor could it be regained by the Reformation, despite the Protestant emphasis on a purified church to be kept ever separate from coercive political rule. No claim of separation can completely absolve churches of responsibility for a political order they have helped to shape. Indeed, even the most extreme Protestant separationists will usually concede that some minimal civil power is necessary for human life to be possible. While all human institutions—political, legal, even religious— are prone to evil, in a fallen world institutional structures have a valuable role to play in protecting human society from chaos. Thus, they may be a sign of God's patience and mercy, and, at least provisionally, require responsible Christian involvement.[84]

Protestant tradition in the United States in fact offers a diversity of roles for the church in relation to the legal order. Baptists, for example, at one time disavowed all church involvement with the state.[85] Roger Williams was singularly extreme on this point, drawing a line between state and church not out of love for democracy and civil liberty, but to maintain the purity of the church. For Williams, to link the state to religion would make the church a "filthy dunghill and whorehouse of rotten and stinking whores and hypocrites."[86] Luther and Calvin had been less purist, but separation of spheres was basic to Reformation thought, deemed crucial to protect religious freedom and liberty of conscience.[87] Lutherans, especially, have a long tradition of pessimism with respect to the political sphere and thus to the role of law. That pessimism can, perhaps ironically, lead to extreme conservatism. Episcopalians, however, with their history rooted in England's established Anglican church, and with their own long tradition of natural law thought, have probably been more open to a close, positive church/state connection than other American denominations, but even for Episcopalians the right relation is not easily defined.[88]

Within modern American democracy, the complexity of the Protestant's relation to state authority is deepened by the very fact of separation rather than establishment. Separation is more congenial to the Protestant tradition than to the Catholic[89] and is rooted, in fact, in Reformation theology itself. At another level, however, many of the premises on which toleration is now based are simply at odds with the underlying religious viewpoint. Liberalism's sharp split between public and private, its parallel split between fact and value, and its assumption that one can do "justice" without a conception of the good life have all served to trivialize the role of religion. To use a now well-known description, the serious Protestant is thus to some degree a "resident alien" in the liberal state.[90] The person who sees the world through the transforming lens of faith does not relegate that new vision to the realm of the private and personal while politely continuing to see the rest of the (public) world as secular. Instead, from the point of view of the believer, participation in the scriptural narrative allows one to see the whole world *as it really is.*[91]

This perspective does not require biblical literalism or political conservatism, nor does it require the more typically Catholic belief in the objectivity and universality of natural law. If, for example, one sees current events as informed by the biblical narrative, one might view our modern American combination of widespread violence, abortion, suicide, and environmental devastation as evidence of a people choosing death, not life, and thus as a sign, in turn, of that loss of hope which occurs with the loss of faith. From that perspective, the notion that abortion is only about private choices simply makes no sense, even though, from the same perspective, one certainly might not see criminal law as a solution to that cultural dilemma.

Stanley Hauerwas, the influential Methodist theologian, has dramatically described the breakdown of the public/private distinction that should ideally occur within the church community itself. The church, he says, should not hesitate to inquire as to an individual's wealth or make demands relating to marriage. All aspects of life are subject to the traditional disciplines of the church, which must be learned as a craft from those with authority.[92] Notably, for Hauerwas, this does not mean that the same disciplines should be imposed by civil law, for the assumptions of liberal democracy, such as the public/private distinction, are too distorting for accurate translation of church discipline into a public code of justice. The person well-schooled in church discipline will be able to *act* more righteously, in the public arena as elsewhere, but not necessarily in a way that can be scripted by the state.[93]

This problem of translation reveals the extent to which the church/state dilemma, from both the insider and the outsider perspective, is a problem of epistemology itself. Many who have been advocating the reintroduction of religious discourse into the public square assume some version of a natural reason (and natural law) that would make it possible for the believer and nonbeliever to use the same moral vocabulary—to, as Richard Neuhaus affirms, "engage one another in a shared world of discourse." That shared vocabulary should not, Neuhaus insists, be dependent on religious faith, lest it be subject to the totalizing claims of those religious movements he considers less "rational," such as the conservative evangelicals.[94] Some commentators, in fact, have argued that such a conception of reason is required if the tension between the religion clauses of the First Amendment is ever to be resolved.[95]

Modern secular philosophers, however, have consistently challenged the intelligibility of all "religion talk," denying it any public validity or relevance—as in Philosophy 101. In response, for a time theologians tried to demonstrate the propositional truth of religion's claims and/or their foundational rootedness in human experience.[96] More recently, however, foundationalism in general has been abandoned by philosophers, and with it any conception of an acultural, neutral "reason" operating independently of tradition.[97] In one sense, this antifoundationalism would seem to deny the possibility of any "public" dialogue about moral truth at all. Hence, Richard Rorty's defense of liberal democracy lies precisely in the fact that within it we are free to be disenchanted—to enjoy a light-minded aestheticism toward questions of moral truth rather than earnestly endeavoring to find "reasoned" answers.[98] Thus, while lessening the pressure on theologians to provide a philosophical defense of religion, modern antifoundationalism also raises the specter of pure relativism as to public moral questions, seemingly inviting postmodernism's violence as well as its playfulness.

David Tracy, with the assurance that comes from being rooted in a tradition (Catholicism) that has, as it were, "seen it all" when it comes to both philosophical argument and political forms, remains determined to establish grounds for public religious and moral dialogue in order to rescue religion from its societal definition as a "sometimes useful, sometimes dangerous, usually harmless 'private option.'"[99] Otherwise, he says, theology would not be true to its own task, since "any serious theocentric construal of reality demands publicness."[100] Moreover, a failure of responsible publicness means we would be left with an unsatisfactory choice (Tracy wrote in 1981) between the "pathos of privateness or coercive theological nonsense"[101]—by the latter meaning the Moral Majority. Tracy's work is philosophically and hermeneutically sophisticated, employing notions of dialogue and rhetoric rather than wooden propositional truth, while also conceding the finitude and historicity of distinctive religious traditions. Whether his approach can adequately establish the "publicness" he seeks, especially within the skeptical antifoundational academy (his intended audience), may still be an open question.[102]

Also in the Catholic tradition and closely identified with Tracy is the recent work of legal scholar Michael Perry, who argues persuasively for the legitimacy of religious content in public moral and political debate.[103] Perry's ideal is one of ecumenical discourse. Thus, he finds less congenial religious expression unwilling to concede a commitment to "fallibilism" and "pluralism" and wonders whether appeals that are simply "sectarian" or "authoritarian" can contribute meaningfully to public (and inevitably pluralist) conversation.[104] The question remains, however, whether there must be a stark choice between ecumenical "publicness," on the one hand, and sectarian "privateness," on the other.

Some Protestant theologians, for example, freed by modern philosophical skepticism (e.g., Rorty) to abandon defensive philosophical foundationalism, are exploring the meaning of religion as a cultural-linguistic tradition, as in the model of Geertzian anthropology.[105] The biblical narrative tradition can best be understood, they argue, as an interpretive tradition organized around a narrative text (the Bible—which Barth considered a "vast, loosely structured nonfictional novel").[106] This means that the distinctiveness of religious traditions can be stressed, since religion is best understood as a kind of language that is interiorized by the one who responds to the narrative and becomes part of its hermeneutic tradition. Thus, in the name of narrative, theology can boldly reject the pressure to conform to the rest of culture or to produce false moral universals and can concentrate instead on a thick description of its own tradition.

On the surface, this largely neo-Barthian cultural-linguistic narrative approach raises the specter of cultural relativism, and also, perhaps, the danger of a defensive sectarianism as well, by seeming to suggest that any single religious tradition constitutes just one culture among many, with no claim to universal truth and thus no claim to be heard in the public square. Yet that specter arises, according to theologian Ronald Thiemann, only if we accept the "grand and seductive" Either/Or of foundational philosophy itself—that there is either a fixed rationally demonstrable foundation for our knowledge, or "we cannot escape the forces of darkness that envelop us with madness, with intellectual and moral chaos."[107] That false either/or choice itself assumes a neutral "rationality" existing entirely independent of tradition, which modern philosophy has exposed as an impossibility. In fact, it may be that the collapse of foundationalism, and with it the sharply drawn fact/value distinction, will open the way for the "outsider perspective" to assimilate less skeptically the religious ethical tradition, without ascribing to any particular tradition a complete monopoly on truth. At the level of moral philosophy, Jeffrey Stout (a nonbeliever) has argued[108] for exactly that assimilation of theology, as has English philosopher Mary Midgley (also a nonbeliever).[109]

There is a gap, of course, between assimilation at the level of neopragmatic ethical theory (as with Stout) and assimilation at the level of public square decision-making, where coercive state power inevitably comes into play.[110] Nevertheless, the stark foundationalist either/or dichotomy that Thiemann criticizes is in fact the dichotomy that is assumed when "private" religion is excluded from the public arena. That dichotomy has been rendered especially suspect by our modern understanding of science itself—that it, too, is an interpretive tradition with its own presuppositions and with a reasoning process that is not acultural, but embedded within its own hermeneutic tradition. This modern understanding of science, however, does not render science's claims to knowledge meaningless or its claim for public attention unwarranted.

Perhaps, in fact, the subtlety of the church/state problem might better be understood by recognizing the parallel dilemma confronted by science in its relation to public life. Both science and religion must reconcile their publicness with their independence. We are so accustomed to the publicness of science (as Truth) and the mandated independence of religion (as Superstition) that we fail to appreciate the shared and similarly fragile situation of both traditions. Science, like religion, resides in a well-ordered, autonomous community of tradition, a community that sustains itself only through a complex and subtle interplay of authority and free critical inquiry. Science, too, no less than religion, must remain dedicated to the "internal goods" of its own practice, lest it accommodate too completely to the demands of the dominant culture and thereby lose its own distinctive credibility.[111]

Science as a community is regularly threatened by the lure of the marketplace (a core dilemma of intellectual property) and by the opportunistic appropriation of its claims to truth in the service of preset political agendas. And its "truths" are just as fragile as those of theology. As Mary Midgley has argued,[112] science represents more than the search for particular facts; its unifying urge for intellectual order takes it beyond "mindless, meaningless collecting." Aesthetic criteria of elegance and order are an essential part of "shaping scrappy data into usable patterns." Indeed, the intellectual constructions of science "present problems of belief which are often quite as difficult as those of religion, and which can call for equally strenuous efforts of faith." Believers are expected to "bow to the mystery, admit the inadequacy of their faculties, and accept paradoxes." Thus, it can be said of science, as of religion, that it transcends experience and asks for faith.

Yet, despite all of these risks, no one urges that we close off public space from the scientific voice. Some would claim, of course, that the true measure of scientific superiority is instrumental. Yet even employing that criterion, perhaps we have reached the cultural limits of secular Enlightenment individualism with respect to both the personal happiness of individuals and the physical life of our planet. As Mary Midgley argues: "[I]t must emerge that a whole set of communal aspects of life, which used to be despised and attributed to the corrupting influence of religion, now appear as both necessary and understandable in terms of the sciences. They are not just instruments of political oppression but essential conditions of life."[113] And, continuing with Midgley, perhaps an openness to the religious voice might reacquaint us with notions like "conventionality, identification with one's group, the fear of hubris, of novelty and excess, loyalty, respect for one's elders, and general awe at the mysterious otherness of nature"[114]—notions that are, after all, part of the culture of science as well.

With an appreciation of religious tradition alongside that of science, and with a full awareness of the limits of both as claimants to ultimate public truth, we might seriously and respectfully be able to engage with each other on issues like environmental ethics. Such questions will require, after all, a combination of scientific understanding and ethical sensitivity, going to the meaning of our relationship to nature and (the theologian would insist) to God as well, or at least to those ultimate powers that bear down on us (to use James Gustafson's phrase).[115] For that to happen, theology must be, as Stout says, sufficiently "distinctive to be interesting, but sufficiently critical to be respected,"[116] and it must offer more than what atheists already know. A new, Fletcheresque version of the cost/benefit analysis, for example, will not be helpful, for such we have in abundance; what we need is elucidation of the deeper meaning of human responsibility. Our relationship to nature is a public moral question that will require both (coercive) public regulation and voluntary cooperation. As with abortion, the potential for divisiveness is great, for environmentalism will inevitably involve public limits on human agency, imposed in the name of ethical responsibility.

Polarization on environmental ethics already seems well-entrenched in our political realm. So too, of course, with abortion. During the 1992 election campaign, the political platform of one side (the Republicans) insisted on advocating a "human life" amendment to the Constitution that would automatically ban all abortions (a position so extreme that even conservative columnist William Buckley, Jr., dissented from its inclusion). On the other side, the Democrats' platform called for nothing less than a return to the undiluted purity of Roe v. Wade and would not allow the "politically incorrect" governor of Pennsylvania (a popular Democrat who dissents from this view) to speak at the party's national convention.[117]

Nevertheless, in both law and theology there are some signs of movement toward genuine compromise. In law, we have a new Supreme Court case, one of the parties to which was that same governor of Pennsylvania. In Planned Parenthood of Southeastern Pennsylvania v. Casey,[118] three members of the Supreme Court, all of whom had been appointed by Republican presidents elected on a plank of absolutist opposition to abortion (O'Connor and Kennedy, appointed by Reagan; and Souter, appointed by Bush) offered with their controlling vote a new voice that may yet lead to workable compromise on the abortion issue.

The Court in Casey considered five provisions of Pennsylvania law that regulated abortions: informed consent, a twenty-four-hour wait with mandatory counseling, parental consent for minors, spousal notification, and mandatory record-keeping and reporting. All but one, the spousal notification, were upheld. More significantly, however, the justices in upholding those restrictions nevertheless declined to overrule Roe v. Wade itself. On this crucial issue, the vote was 5–4, with dissenting Justices Antonin Scalia, Clarence Thomas, and Byron White, along with Chief Justice William Rehnquist, calling for the immediate demise of Roe.

While upholding the basic rule of Roe, the "right of the woman to choose to have an abortion before viability," the Court also made clear that the state's "important and legitimate interest in potential life" exists throughout pregnancy, not just after viability. Accordingly, the state is empowered to regulate for the protection of fetal life, even where such regulations have the effect of making abortions more costly, but only so long as the regulations do not place an "undue burden on a woman's ability to make this decision," defined as "placing a substantial obstacle in the path of a woman seeking an abortion of a nonviable fetus." Undue burden is to be assessed in light of social facts, not as an abstract formalism, opening the way for further analysis of even the restrictions upheld in Casey. Permissible regulation does, however, include state authority to try to persuade women not to abort.

In approaching Casey with some small optimism, we recognize that earlier we characterized Roe itself as a "mistake," legally, sociologically, and politically. We also recognize that insofar as Casey makes absolute the pre-viability option of abortion, its allowance for protection of fetal life rings hollow for pro-life activists. Nevertheless, we would urge caution in repeating a mistake of judgment. The premise of Roe was a backward one: that the Court could freeze reality and make the abortion issue disappear. Forgotten was an inevitable dynamic of law, that judicial decisions contain a historical agency of their own. Thus, the precipitous overruling of Roe, which would immediately send the issue back to the state legislatures with no constitutional guidelines, might similarly loose a dynamic that would be worse than accepting with patience a gradual realignment on this painful question.

We do not suggest that the Casey decision is, by itself, in fact a final version of successful or workable compromise on this issue. It seems probable that real compromise will mean, as it does in many Western European countries, a public policy that allows abortion while regulating it to some degree and also seeking ways to discourage it. Compromise may mean retreating back from the line of viability with respect to presumptively legal abortions. Lines could be drawn, for example, at sixteen weeks, twelve, or ten—perhaps as consistent with the start of brain waves, which, in its scientific objectivity and consistency with the determination of death, should hold some appeal for natural law theorists. Even now, nearly 90 percent of abortions occur in the first trimester. While the

Court in *Casey* reaffirmed the viability line, the provisions at issue did not raise that question, and future cases may see future adjustments. Other approaches to compromise might include required statements of reasons for abortion after some specified duration of pregnancy, or even from the beginning; or reliance on positive, communitarian ways of affecting choices by helping women, not penalizing them. From our perspective, allowing for such compromises would have more ethical integrity than the often ignored political compromises that did in fact occur with a supposedly unmodified version of *Roe* in place—e.g., denial of public funding as upheld in *Harris v. McCrae*, [119] and de facto nonavailability of abortion for many, with no additional social mechanisms in place to help women cope with pregnancy. These results victimized the most politically vulnerable (generally the poor) without directly addressing the moral value of fetal life. Our main point here, however, is simply that compromise means that each side must give up something important.

In theology as well, there may be signs of compromise. By way of backdrop and as antidote to the usual strident pro-life tone, consider the view of noted Catholic moral theologian Richard McCormick (professor of Christian ethics at Notre Dame). McCormick wants to be faithful to Catholic tradition and sensitive to contemporary conditions. He regards himself as occupying the "extreme middle." [120]

For McCormick, the abortion debate raises the "general problem for the Catholic community of moral pluralism and public policy," or, more specifically, "what is to be done at the policy level when people disagree on the moral level that is the basis of the policy?" [121] He rejects the notion that there is no relation between law and morality, noting that in the heat of the American debate on the subject, "the very relationship between morality and law has been obscured." [122] From his perspective, the proper concern of law is the welfare of the community, which "cannot be unrelated to what is judged promotive or destructive to human beings, to what is morally right or wrong." [123]

Thus, the mere fact that an act is "private" does not exempt it from law. On the other hand, to be feasible, "law must rest on a sufficiently broad shared conviction or on a very fundamental moral or constitutional principle that people are reluctant to deny." [124]

What do we do when we are faced with profound conflict, where there is not agreement on the basic underlying equation? Some have suggested that present policy is a reasonably adequate way of living with conflict (no one forces another to have an abortion; no one forces another to carry a pregnancy). However, that is a deceptively simple point of view. What represents a better way of living with conflict will depend to some extent on what one supports as the resolution of the conflict. For example, if I grant that the conflict makes prohibitive law impracticable, but I believe (as a moral position) that nascent life is human life deserving of protection and hope that others come to share this view, then I might think the Supreme Court's decision [Roe v. Wade] simply deepens the difficulty of arriving at a resolution since it allows free abortion in a way that further blunts our sensitivities to the sanctity of nascent life. Widespread abortion is, after all, self-perpetuating. . . .

What is to be done? Any moral position, whether that of Vatican II or that of the Supreme Court, is going to be experienced as an imposition. . . . Indeed, the Supreme Court . . . should have remanded the matter to legislature. . . . [C]onditions are such that any legal disposition of the question must be accompanied by hesitation and large doses of dissatisfaction. That means that it is the right and duty of conscientious citizens to continue to debate the matter, to attempt to persuade in the public forum.[125]

Only a thoroughgoing insistence on the secular version of freedom described earlier renders irrelevant, as a matter of public policy, the concerns of those like McCormick, who would at least have us confront our obligation toward life regarded as a gift from God.

Setting a tone not unlike that of McCormick, the usually liberal (and pro-choice) ecumenical weekly, Christian Century, recently published a startling editorial in the wake of the Casey decision.[126] Author David Heim carefully points out that he would not argue that "the fetus is a person" or that "abortion is tantamount to killing a person." Nevertheless, he says, when he thinks about how "to live a responsible life before God, responding to creation with care and trust as a creature," then "the strong presumption is against abortion." That presumption, he recognizes, cannot simply be dismissed as the sectarian, private, esoteric belief "of a particular tribe," because the "sacredness of life concerns all communities." Heim also recognizes that his theological presumption, especially when translated into the public realm, is not absolute. At that point he confronts the claim of "choice": "Supporting 'choice' as a public policy easily implies that all choices have the same moral weight and that whatever one decides is morally irreproachable. The best public policy response to this dilemma is to seek abortion laws that, while allowing abortion, restrict it (except in the obvious exceptional cases) to the early weeks of pregnancy and regulate it in such a way as to convey the moral (and medical) seriousness of the act."

Other current developments suggest that Heim's view is not unrepresentative. The Presbyterians, from whose 1983 pro-choice report we quoted at length, have in recent years conducted a national debate, the "National Dialogue on Abortion Perspectives" (with four different points of view represented).[127] Through extensive surveys, they discovered the deep ambivalence within their own membership,[128] and they have issued a new report, theologically serious in its approach, reflecting with sensitivity the tentative and troubled character of the issue.[129] Similar developments have occurred with the American Baptists, who have moved toward the center from their traditional pro-choice view on the issue,[130] and with the United Methodists, whose strong pro-choice position has become increasingly controversial within that denomination.[131] Robert Cooper, for example, who is pastor of one of the largest and growing Methodist congregations in the urban South, thinks that it is not enough for his church to give its carefully measured acceptance of a woman choosing abortion as "the lesser of two evils." Cooper would have the church spell out more clearly that abortion is essentially "a moral tragedy, not a moral right."[132]

One also finds evidence of some change of tone and, perhaps, a reaching toward the center, coming from the other side. On July 14, 1992, the New York Times published an advertisement signed by a number of people who have been publicly supportive of or at least sympathetic to the pro-life position. The advertisement, entitled "A New American Compact: Caring About Women, Caring for the Unborn," takes what we have described as a feminist pro-life position, and impliedly concedes a reality of compromise in calling for legislative resolution of the issue undertaken with "serious public moral reflection" by an American people "capable of rising above partisanship on a matter of this gravity."[133]

Afterword

......

We will not offer any particular solution to the abortion question. Our goal has been to explore the issue as one appropriate for moral debate, and to question whether either side has the close-out resources (morally or politically) to compel its own solution. That exploration has led us to affirm the moral (and theological) integrity of compromise. In so doing, we dissent from the usual insistence, especially in elite institutional settings,[1] that theology be relegated to the status of irrational, supernatural, or backward.

There is, of course, more than a little irony in that elitist insistence, given the particular Enlightenment sources of our secular rationalism. Kant, we are told, was ashamed once when he was discovered praying.[2] More to the point, the very notions of "freedom" and "equality" so central to Enlightenment moral and political thought were historically and philosophically rooted in theology, as both Alasdair MacIntyre and Charles Taylor have so effectively demonstrated.[3] Thus, even as they rejected medieval concepts like "teleology" or "natural hierarchy," turning instead to a modern emphasis on notions like "passions" (Hume) or "reason" (Kant), Enlightenment philosophers took for granted that the resultant substantive morality would reflect Calvinist (Hume) or Lutheran (Kant) values.[4] Even John Stuart Mill saw in utilitarianism the realization of assumed Christian values.[5] We have inherited these post-Enlightenment structures of thought, which form the basis of our secular moral discourse.

Detached from their theological origins, however, our moral positions, even when articulated as such, appear as little more than masks for expressions of personal preference. We are so accustomed to thinking of "self-interest" as the basis of market economics, for example, that we can no longer understand the morally corrective notion of self-interest, "rightly understood,"[6] which might form the basis for responsible capitalism, as an antidote to our unabashed greed and consumerism.[7] Similarly, our inherited assumption of dominion over nature has become pure instrumentalism in the realization of human goals, losing its grounding in stewardship, humility, and respect. So long as there is public consensus on an issue, we can pretend that our moral vocabulary is about "something." As soon as consensus breaks down, however, as with both animals/nature and abortion, respective positions become incommensurable.

To insist that we privilege the secular even in the face of such breakdown is to repeat a venerable and recurring human folly—to universalize one's own physical or temporal moment and then project its understanding across space and time. Thus, the "choice" worldview of elite professionals is universalized as that of all citizens—or all women—but the lived reality of those women, especially their religious reality, is ignored.

So too with history. Just as Christianity, like it or not, is compelled by its origins to be engaged in permanent dialogue with Judaism,[8] and as Protestantism is similarly consigned to a never-ending dialogue with Catholicism,[9] our secular culture, despite its pretensions, cannot outgrow its theological roots. When Dr. Robert Hall, the abortion reformer/repealer, proclaimed that countries with stringent abortion laws have "buried their heads in the sands of time,"[10] he surely implied that fate for religion itself. Ironically, it seems that today all three of the great isms of the twentieth century that sought to displace religion as the source of human meaning and possibility—Marxism, Freudianism, and Existentialism—are rapidly fading blips on the screen of history.[11]

The more durable adversary of religion in our culture has been science, which has often threatened, and in the twentieth century nearly succeeded, in claiming the realm of truth for its own.[12] Nevertheless, science itself, through which nature becomes more known, more manageable, and more amenable to our wishes, need not, as we have observed, conflict with religion. In fact, when science proceeds provisionally, cognizant of doubt, in a spirit of humility and finitude, it is not only compatible with a religious sensibility, but may be regarded as part of a shared enterprise.[13]

Science becomes wicked only when its practitioners, or those who deploy the power it unleashes, become infused with pride, with the attitude that we can know everything and do anything. As Bonhoeffer noted in 1944, reflecting on our impulse to be "independent of nature":

Nature was formerly conquered by spiritual means, with us by technical organization of all kinds. Our immediate environment is not nature, as formerly, but organization. But with this protection from nature's menace there arises a new one—through organization itself.

But the spiritual force is lacking. The question is: What protects us against the menace of organization? Man is again thrown back on himself. He has managed to deal with everything, only not with himself. He can insure against everything, only not against man.[14]

As Bonhoeffer wrote those words, he was confined in Tegel prison in Berlin and subjected regularly to bombing raids by the Allied forces seeking to destroy Hitler's Nazi empire. The success of that military technology would help to create a faith in science, technology, and expertise that would permeate the postwar culture of both the victors and the vanquished, but especially that of the United States, which had lost lives but never experienced the bombs. There is at least some tragic irony in the fact that our most recent instance of shared, collective national celebration was occasioned by the success of American technology in the Persian Gulf War.

Despite the best efforts of enterprises like the *Natural Law Forum*, which tried to suggest that the legacy of World War II and the Nazis was a profound moral and spiritual agenda, its more lasting legacy was the triumph and extension of science. Issues traditionally regarded as moral ones could be recast as questions of "medical judgment," or submitted to the expertise of "social science." Profound dilemmas like that of sin, once thought basic to the human condition, could be recast as occasions for "therapy."[15]

The same culture produced a generation, of which we were a part, that had little use for humility, denied our own sinfulness, and lacked any sense of restraint or limits. In retrospect, a number of appropriate responses to oppressive conditions led to a culture of unrestrained excess. Thus, the Supreme Court's long-overdue interventions with respect to race and reapportionment set the stage for bypassing more cumbersome political processes and instead relying on federal courts to implement a new moral and political agenda with wave after wave of new "rights." Similarly, our reaction to the oppressive conventionality of the 1950s, especially with respect to matters of sex and gender role, led us to reject any and all moral orthodoxy in the name of "life-style freedom," to the point of defying all religious tradition in assuming we had a "right" to "happiness."[16] And more to the point, a sensible effort to modernize repressive abortion laws became a claim of absolute right to abortion on demand, with some 1.5 million abortions as the current annual norm in the United States.

Luxuriating in what theologians would call pridefulness, we took on the transformative utopian fantasy, which is perhaps the undoing of all revolutions, that a select elite could through mere human agency transform the entire social/cultural world around it and discard all inconsistent tradition to the rubbish heap of history. In that euphoric process, we surely forgot our finitude. Ernest Becker, anthropologist and critic of therapy as religion, posed this question back in 1973 (the year *Roe v. Wade* was decided):

> What do we mean by the lived truth of creation? We have to mean the world . . . as it would appear to creatures who assessed their true puniness in the face of the overwhelmingness and majesty of the universe. . . . What are we to make of a creation in which the routine activity is for organisms to be tearing others apart with teeth of all types—biting, grinding flesh, plant stalks, bones between molars, pushing the pulp greedily down the gullet with delight, incorporating its essence into one's own organization, and then excreting with foul stench and gasses the residue. Everyone reaching out to incorporate others who are edible to him. . . . not to mention the daily dismemberment and slaughter in "natural" accidents of all types: an earthquake buries alive 70 thousand bodies in Peru, automobiles make a pyramid heap of over 50 thousand a year [back in 1973] in the U.S. alone, a tidal wave washes over a quarter of a million in the Indian Ocean. Creation is a nightmare spectacular taking place on a planet that has been soaked for hundreds of millions of years in the blood of all its creatures. The soberest conclusion that we could make about three billion years is that it is being turned into a vast pit of fertilizer. But the sun distracts our attention, always baking the blood dry, making things grow over it, and with its warmth giving . . . hope. . . .[17]

Such a depiction is congenial to the theological tradition that runs all the way from Jonathan Edwards to Dietrich Bonhoeffer, both of whom had absorbed the lessons of Enlightenment rationality and were prepared to deal in their respective ways with a world come of age. If God reveals Himself in nature, He surely does so on His terms, not ours. We tend to forget what God reminded Job with relentless interrogation—that we, after all, are not the authors of creation.[18] In a fallen world, there is no particular basis for immediate optimism, nor is there occasion for despair.

Perhaps, as Christopher Lasch suggests, the best we can do is to exchange optimism for hope, and recall our own limits.[19]

And the limit that marks our finitude regularly and relentlessly is death. We can neither avoid death, as some pro-choicers would have us do, by renaming the fetus as tissue, or, as the meat industry does, with its cellophane packages backed with sponge pads; nor can we conquer death, as some pro-lifers would have us do, by simply compelling the birth of all the unborn, or as animal activists would do, by banning all hunting or by mandating vegetarianism.

The starting point for a discussion about abortion ought to be the frank recognition that the issue is life or death. To abort a fetus is to kill, to prevent the realization of a human life. But to say that much is not to answer the moral question involved. In the "successful" Gulf War, we (Americans) killed many thousands of people, some of them civilians, others exposed to danger against their will. That we choose to kill does not make it wrong on that score alone; but we surely need a vocabulary for talking about life-and-death issues in moral terms that underscore the seriousness of any choice for death. Our religious traditions have served for many hundreds of years to offer hope in the face of despair, to offer life in the face of inevitable suffering and death. We discard those traditions at our peril.

Notes

......

Introduction

1 See, e.g., H. Gorey, "Supreme Confidence," *Time*, Sept. 24, 1990, at 46: "[T]he bachelor from Weare, N.H., keenly senses that he has been chosen by Bush and history to cast perhaps the deciding vote on whether to overturn *Roe v. Wade*, the landmark 1973 decision that made abortion legal in all states." See also Bob Cohn, "The 'Soon-to-Be' Supreme," *Newsweek*, Sept. 24, 1990, at 27. "To the frustration of committee liberals and women's rights activists, Souter unflappably insisted on his prerogative to avoid the all-important question of abortion."

2 410 U.S. 113 (1973); see also Doe v. Bolton, 410 U.S. 179 (1973) (*Roe*'s companion case).

3 112 S.Ct. 2791 (U.S. Sup. Ct., June 29, 1992). Two justices (Blackmun, Stevens) would have reaffirmed *Roe* in basically undiluted form; three justices (Souter, O'Connor, Kennedy) chose to "reaffirm" *Roe* while simultaneously giving the states wider latitude in regulating abortions; four justices (Rehnquist, Scalia, Thomas, White), dissenting, would have overruled *Roe* immediately.

4 "Abortion's Antipolitics," *Wall Street Journal*, Aug. 17, 1992, at A6.

5 A review of opinion poll data, with due respect for its fallibility, leaves one with the impression that some 20–25 percent of the American public believe that abortion should be illegal in all or nearly all circumstances, some 20–25 percent believe that it should be legal in all circumstances, and the rest will vary depending on the form of the question, the timing of the abortion (first trimester versus later trimesters), or the reason for the abortion (rape or physical danger to the mother vs. family size or simply inconvenience). See, e.g., Celeste Michelle Condit, *Decoding Abortion Rhetoric: Communicating Social Change* 147–51, 167–68, 170 (U. of Illinois Press, 1989); and the following essays in *Abortion: Understanding Differences* (ed. Sidney Callahan & Daniel Callahan, Plenum Press, 1984): Daniel Callahan, "The Abortion Debate: Is Progress Possible?" at 309, 313; Mary Segers, "Abortion and the Culture: Toward a Feminist Per-

spective," at 229, 232–34; and Mary Ann Lamanna, "Social Science and Ethical Issues: The Policy Implications of Poll Data on Abortion," at 1–23.

On the distinction between opinion polls and "public opinion," the latter reflecting the actualities of disproportionate power in the process of opinion-formation, *see* Condit, *supra*, at 7–8. According to Daniel Callahan, who has written extensively on this issue, "the public has never been unambiguously prochoice or prolife; some 60% of the public falls in a zone of ambivalence and nuance." "An Ethical Challenge to Prochoice Advocates: Abortion and the Pluralistic Proposition," 117 *Commonweal* 681–87 (1990).

6   Brigitte Berger & Peter L. Berger, *The War Over the Family: Capturing the Middle Ground* 74 (Anchor Press/Doubleday, 1983).

7   *See* Leo Ribuffo, "The Complexity of American Religious Prejudice," in *Right Center Left: Essays in American History* (Rutgers U. Press, 1992), at 68–69.

8   James Hunter, *Culture Wars: The Struggle to Define America* (Basic Books, 1991), at 329 n.22 ("There is little doubt that the controversy over abortion is a central part of the larger conflict. Indeed, it has crystallized the antagonism between the orthodox and the progressive as no other issue has").

9   Berger & Berger, *supra* note 6, at 75–77.

10   Laurence H. Tribe, *Abortion: The Clash of Absolutes* (Norton, 1990). From an advocacy perspective, the strategy of Tribe's book is to keep the two sides as far apart as possible, especially emphasizing the pro-life position as necessarily incapable of compromise, thereby leaving the reader who is unwilling to criminalize all or nearly all abortions with no choice but to reaffirm *Roe v. Wade*. For a similar reaction to Tribe's book, *see* "Recent Publications," 25 *Harv. C.R.-C.L. L. Rev.* 625–29 (1990). For instance, the author notes that "[w]hile [Tribe] critiques both the pro-life and pro-choice proponents [, his] desire for compromise is somewhat thwarted by his apparent intent to fuel pro-choice advocates with criticism of the pro-life position." *Id.* at 626. Tribe's repeated rejection of potential areas of compromise is troubling in view of what he proclaims to be the purpose of his book. As a result, the book may demonstrate the very intractability of the positions on abortion that he seeks to mediate. He fails to deliver fully on his promise to set the stage for compromise. *Id.* at 629. For a particularly glaring example, consider Tribe's assertion that "[b]y the late 1960s as many as 1,200,000 women were undergoing illegal abortions each year: more than one criminal abortion a minute." *Supra*, at 41. *See* James C. Mohr, *Abortion in America: The Origins and Evolution of National Policy, 1800–1900* 254 (Oxford U. Press, 1978), where this sentence appears: "By the late 1960's estimates of the number of illegal abortions performed in the United States each year ranged from 200,000 to 1,200,000." *Id.* (On the difficulties implicit in making such calculations, *see* Condit, *supra* note 5, at 37 n.4). While Tribe's "as many as" is not technically inaccurate, from the perspective of our own legal training and experience we think the difference between Mohr's very qualified statement, and Condit's careful evaluation, on the one hand, and Tribe's coverage of the same issue is the difference between a scholarly agenda and an advocacy agenda. For a critical yet, we think, fair assessment of the Tribe volume, *see* Michael McConnell, "How Not To Promote Serious Deliberation About Abortion," 58 *U. of Chicago L. R.* 1181–1202 (1991).

11   Tribe takes this position (*supra* note 10, at 78–79). *See, e.g.,* Frances Olsen, "Comment: Unraveling Compromise," 103 *Harvard L. Rev.* 105 (1989), characterizing *Roe* as a "political, legal, and social compromise." *Id.* at 107. Thus, "*Roe v. Wade* was a compromise. The case legalized most abortions but it did not grant the plaintiffs everything they wanted. . . ." *Id.* For a characterization of *Roe* from the pro-life side as something other than compromise, *see* John T. Noonan, Jr., *A Private Choice: Abortion in America in the Seventies* 10–12 (Life Cycle Books, 1979). As Noonan sums up: "Vis-a-vis the childbearing woman who wanted an abortion, the unborn child was valued by *The Abortion Cases* [*Roe v. Wade* and *Doe v. Bolton*] at zero before viability and as less than a whole human being after viability." *Id.* at 119. This is not to affirm Noonan's characterization, but merely to suggest that the assertion of *Roe v. Wade* as "compromise" is substantially belied by both the substantive positions of its critics and the politics that followed the decision. For more on Noonan, who is a significant figure in the history we seek to relate, *see* chapter 2, *infra*.

12   With respect to the issue of "compromise," even Condit (*supra* note 5) in her otherwise excellent study leaves her readers perplexed. Condit's book is a sophisticated and studiously unbiased historical account of abortion as situated in public discourse from 1960 to 1985. Her careful and critical depiction of the rhetorical moves used by both sides (described as the "heritage tale" of the illegal abortion for pro-choice; Condit, *supra* note 5, at 22–42, or the "Pro-Life Human History," *id.* at 43–58) makes the book a rarity in an area usually characterized by the production of polemical excess, not by reflection on its content. Yet Condit seems determined from the outset to have her story end with "legal and cultural consensus." *Id.* at xii. In her strongest statement on the issue, at the end of a chapter reviewing prime-time television coverage of abortion in the early 1980s, Condit announces that the "general acceptance of a compromise position on the abortion issue" serves to refute the "social pessimists," like Alasdair MacIntyre, who see such issues as instances of moral "incommensurability." *Id.* at 141. Conceding that "rationally generated" compromise was not possible, Condit nevertheless claims that the ambivalence revealed in scenes such as a long dialogue between Cagney and Lacey on the television drama series of that name reveals the existence of "pragmatic resolution" or "working compromise." *Supra* note 5, at 142, 126–33.

The assertion of compromise depends on a number of problematic items of evidence: that, basically, *Roe v. Wade* was itself a compromise; that, even if not a compromise, it somehow authoritatively settled the abortion issue; and that the "public" in some sense agreed to live with it and settled down to proceed from there. Thus, Condit says that in *Roe* the Court "constructed a compromise" (*id.* at 112), yet on the same page she recognizes that the compromise was rooted in an "individualism" that "exacts a clear price" and that the rhetoric of "choice" itself leads to no-choice in the form of being held "economically responsible for all such choices" (*id.*). More significantly, she does not consider how *Roe* might be considered not a compromise at all, but a pro-choice victory. For one thing, her study discounts the importance of religion in this debate. She recognizes that "religion has been the underlying motivation and world view of most pro-life activists" (*see id.* at 215–16 n.1), but she cannot bring herself to seriously consider theological issues as such. Her very statement of the "compromise" achieved by the 1980s belies its credibility or stability: "The compromise negotiated about abortion framed it as a women's choice but also as an undesirable moral act. Abortion was to be legally permitted but not publicly financed. It was to be undertaken primarily in the first term of pregnancy" (id. at 199). (Nothing in Roe, which specifically bans any regulation of abortion on behalf of fetal life until after "viability," serves to limit abortion to the "first term of pregnancy.") Against that background, it should have been no surprise, as Condit points out, that activists on both sides became increasingly militant, self-righteous, and unwilling to enter into dialogue with the other side, preferring the purity of their own posturing. Id. at 159–60, 164–66. Ultimately, the compromise that Condit insists on depends on the precedential immortality of Roe. Although Webster v. Reproductive Health Services, 492 U.S. 490 (1989), was decided after her book had gone to press, Condit does agree that Webster "substantially alters the consensus and conditions that obtained during the period examined by this book." Supra note 5, at 198. These issues are clouded even more, of course, by the recent decision in Casey, which we discuss in chap. 9, infra.

13   E.g., Tribe, supra note 10. See also Rosalind P. Petchesky, Abortion and Women's Choice: The State, Sexuality, and Reproductive Freedom (Northeastern U. Press, 1984). According to Condit, "Petchesky appears to believe that any moral decision is merely an inappropriate ploy by men to control women." Supra note 5, at 16 n.7. We think the pro-choice characterization also fits Roger Rosenblatt, Life Itself: Abortion in the American Mind (Random House, 1992). While he tries to hear what people are actually saying about the issue, he nevertheless simply reaffirms the Roe status quo and seems incapable of comprehending a religious worldview. For a good review, see Elizabeth Fox-Genovese, "Society's Child," New Republic, May 18, 1992, at 39–43.

14   E.g., Noonan, supra note 11. In his introduction, Noonan appeals to readers who are confused and concerned about this issue by promising to address those who, given the cultural reality of the United States at this time, "hold that abortion, like war, is a social necessity." Id. at 4. The remainder of the book, while containing some fair criticism, especially with respect to the jurisprudence of Roe v. Wade, is basically a relentless pro-life tract, often propagandistic in argument, which never addresses the particular concerns of those who are troubled about abortion yet regard it as a necessity in at least some cases. Compare these thoughts with those of James Gustafson, who may have been the source of the war analogy: "As the morally conscientious soldier fighting in a particular war is convinced that life can and ought to be taken 'justly,' but also 'mournfully,' so the moralist can be convinced that the life of the defenseless fetus can be taken, less justly, but more mournfully." "A Protestant Ethical Approach," in The Morality of Abortion: Legal and Historical Perspectives 122 (ed. John T. Noonan, Jr., Harvard U. Press, 1970). Gustafson's treatment of abortion is contextual and particular, rather than abstract and categorical, with due respect for the life-and-death character of the issue. See chap. 8, infra.

More difficult to situate is Mary Ann Glendon, Abortion and Divorce in Western Law: American Failures, European Challenges (Harvard U. Press, 1987). We strongly disagree with the hostile denunciation Glendon received in Jane Cohen's review-essay, "Comparison-Shopping in the Marketplace of Rights," 98 *Yale L.J.* 1235 (1989), which displays an unabashed hostility toward the pro-life position. Glendon does call for legislative compromise on the abortion issue, using the various European approaches to illustrate the possibility of compromise, and she correctly points out that the "rights" approach, as deployed by either side, is not consistent with such compromise. She clearly regards *Roe v. Wade* as a social policy failure; we think one can take this position without thereby being or becoming a pro-life extremist. The question raised by Glendon, however, is what insights can be derived from the European experience, given the differences in culture. Can we imagine American legislation that would successfully combine the objective of easy availability of first-trimester abortions with a publicly mandated attitude of respect for unborn lives, as she suggests occurs under the 1975 French law? One must concede that a post-*Roe v. Wade* world might reveal possibilities of compromise that are not now regarded as such, so long as *Roe* is the perceived enemy of pro-life advocates. Thus, one leaves the Glendon book uncertain as to whether the European experience reveals or suggests a common ground of moral debate that might be the basis for real compromise. The possibility, even historically, of such a common ground is a major theme of the present book. We therefore regard our basic agenda as consistent with Glendon's.

A number of works, in addition to Condit (*supra* note 5), stand out for their willingness to take both sides seriously, regardless of the author's own views. *See, e.g.*, Hyman Rodman, Betty Sarvis, & Joy Walker Bonar, *The Abortion Question* (Columbia U. Press, 1987), whose authors *predict* (not recommend) "that ultimately U.S. policy will permit early abortions and prohibit late abortions, and that the intensity of the abortion controversy will subside by the first decade of the twenty-first century" (*id.* at 171). For sociological profiles of the women activists on both sides, *see* Faye D. Ginsburg, *Contested Lives: The Abortion Debate in an American Community* (U. of California Press, 1989); Kristin Luker, *Abortion and the Politics of Motherhood* (U. of California Press, 1984). For good philosophical treatments, *see* Rosalind Hursthouse, *Beginning Lives* (Basil Blackwell, 1987) (neo-Aristotelianism); Richard Posner, *Sex and Reason* (Harvard U. Press, 1992), at 272–90 (utilitarianism); L. W. Sumner, *Abortion and Moral Theory* (Princeton U. Press, 1981) (utilitarianism). Despite its vintage, Daniel Callahan, *Abortion: Law, Choice, and Morality* (Macmillan, 1970), still stands out as a "must-read" for anyone interested in this issue.

Strikingly unusual for this field is *Abortion: Understanding Differences* (*supra* note 5), which offers a rare instance of actual dialogue between proponents of the two sides. All but one of the twelve contributors are women (the exception being Daniel Callahan), who not only present their views in essays, but also, with few exceptions, comment directly on the views of other contributors. The overall result is a rich and thought-provoking dialogue, perhaps facilitated by the fact that the Callahans themselves, who are spouses, are on opposite sides of this issue (she is pro-life; he is pro-choice).

15   In this regard, the role of explicitly theological or religious discourse in public debate becomes important. The book may be regarded as part of the larger

ongoing discussion of that issue. For discussions advocating a place for religion in the public sphere, *see* Kent Greenawalt, *Religious Convictions and Political
Choice* (Oxford U. Press, 1988); Richard Neuhaus, *The Naked Public Square: Religion
and Democracy in America* (W. B. Eerdmans, 1984); Michael Perry, *Love and Power: The
Role of Religion and Morality in Public Power* (Oxford U. Press, 1991) and *Morality, Politics & Law* (Oxford U. Press, 1984), at 180–84; Jean Elshtain, "Muddled Language
Makes for Wearying Debate," *Christianity and Crisis*, Oct. 29, 1984, at 399–401;
Frederick M. Gedicks, "Public Life and Hostility to Religion," 78 *Virginia L. Rev.*
671 (1992); Edward Gaffney, "Politics Without Brackets on Religious Convictions: Michael Perry and Bruce Ackerman on Neutrality," 64 *Tul. L. Rev.* 1143
(1990); Perry, "Comment on the Limits of Rationality and the Place of Religious Conviction: Protecting Animals and the Environment," 27 *William &
Mary L. Rev.* 1067 (1986). For an excellent example of such discourse, *see* Milner S. Ball, *Lying Down Together: Law, Metaphor and Theology* (U. of Wisconsin Press,
1985), as well as his more recent *The Word and the Law* (U. of Chicago Press, 1993).
For our own views, in the public school context, *see* Elizabeth Mensch & Alan
Freeman, "Losing Faith in Public Schools," *Tikkun*, March/April 1992, at 31–36.

For some debate about these issues, *see Religion, Morality and the Law: NOMOS
XXX* (ed. J. Roland Pennock & John W. Chapman, NYU Press, 1988); Stephen
Carter, "The Religiously Devout Judge," 64 *Notre Dame L. Rev.* 932 (1989); Daniel
Conkle, "Religious Purpose, Inerrancy, and the Establishment Clause," 67 *Indi-
ana L.J.* 1 (1991); Edward Gaffney, "Biblical Religion and American Politics:
Some Historical and Methodological Reflections," 1 *J. L. and Religion* 171–240
(1983); Sanford Levinson, "The Confrontation of Religious Faith and Civil
Religion: Catholics Becoming Justices," 39 *DePaul L. Rev.* 1047 (1990); Michael
McConnell, "Christ, Culture, and Courts: A Niebuhrian Examination of First
Amendment Jurisprudence," *DePaul L. Rev.* (forthcoming); Howard Vogel, "The
Judicial Oath and the American Creed: Comments on Sanford Levinson's 'The
Confrontation Between Religious Faith and Civil Religion,'" 39 *DePaul L. Rev.*
1107 (1990); "Symposium on the Religious Foundations of Civil Rights Law,"
5 *J. L. & Religion* 1–108 (1987) (especially the panel discussion from 95–108).

On the revival of interest in law and religion, *see generally* Howard Vogel,
"A Survey and Commentary on the New Literature in Law and Religion," 1
J.L. & Religion 79 (1983). For some constitutional implications of a fresh look
at religion in American public life, *see* Frederick Gedicks & Roger Hendrix,
"Democracy, Autonomy, and Values: Some Thoughts on Religion and Law in
Modern America," 60 *S. Cal. L. Rev.* 1579 (1987); Michael McConnell, "The Ori-
gins and Historical Understanding of Free Exercise of Religion," 103 *Harvard L.
Rev.* 1409 (1990).

16 We were struck particularly by the autobiographical accounts in *Abortion: Understanding Differences, supra* note 5. Condit, as well, carefully introduces herself as
"a career woman (not solely a homemaker) who has never faced an unwanted
pregnancy and who has adequate resources to insure a relatively high degree
of control over her fertility." Condit, *supra* note 5, at xii.

17 For a philosophical and historical reevaluation of what purports to be moral
discourse in our culture, concluding with the reality of incommensurability,
see Alasdair MacIntyre, *After Virtue* (2d ed., U. of Notre Dame Press, 1984). For
his specific application of the problem to abortion, *see id.* at 6–7. Our use of

MacIntyre for our introductory quotation underscores our indebtedness to him. *See* epigraph, *supra*.

Appreciating his critical insights, however, does not compel us to embrace either his solution, Aristotelianism, or his more recent work. We are thus content to follow him through the first eight chapters of *After Virtue*, without necessarily agreeing that the question he poses at the beginning of chapter 9, "Nietzsche or Aristotle?," is the correct question after all. Alasdair MacIntyre, *After Virtue*, *supra*, at 109. Our position may be similar to MacIntyre's with respect to Nietzsche and Sartre, that they were "at their philosophically most powerful and cogent in the negative part of their critiques." *Id.* at 22. On his more recent work, *see* Martha Nussbaum, "Recoiling from Reason," *New York Rev. of Books*, Dec. 7, 1989, at 36 (reviewing MacIntyre, *Whose Justice? Which Rationality?* U. of Notre Dame Press [1989]).

For an approach that parallels that of MacIntyre's, *see* Lloyd L. Weinreb, *Natural Law and Justice* (Harvard U. Press, 1987). For Weinreb's position on MacIntyre, *see id.* at 251–59. For some insightful attempts to describe the actuality of moral discourse in a world of incommensurability, *see* Gerald Frug, "Argument as Character," 40 *Stanford L. Rev.* 869 (1988); Steven Winter, "Transcendental Nonsense, Metaphoric Reasoning and the Cognitive Stakes for Law," 137 *U. of Pennsylvania L. Rev.* 1105 (1989). *See also* Gerald Wetlaufer, "Rhetoric and Its Denial in Legal Discourse," 76 *Virginia L. Rev.* 1545 (1990) (discussing the particular rhetoric of law).

18   *See, e.g.*, Lisa Cahill, "Abortion, Autonomy, and Community," in *Abortion: Understanding Differences*, *supra* note 5, at 261–76; Sidney Callahan, "Value Choices in Abortion," in *id.*, at 285–301; Jean Elshtain, "Reflections on Abortion, Values, and the Family," in *id.*, at 47–72; Mary Meehan, "More Trouble Than They're Worth?: Children and Abortion," in *id.*, at 145–70. *See generally* "Abortion and the Law: Perspectives on a Painful Dilemma," *Sojourners*, Nov. 1989, at 14–22. For recognition that one might in good faith as a feminist support a pro-life position, *see* Kathleen McDonnell, *Not An Easy Choice: A Feminist Re-Examines Abortion* (South End Press, 1984); Ruth Colker, "Feminist Litigation: An Oxymoron? A Study of the Briefs Filed in *William L. Webster v. Reproductive Health Services*," 13 *Harvard Women's L.J.* 137, 161–64 (1990); Ruth Putnam, "Being Ambivalent About Abortion," *Tikkun*, Sept.–Oct. 1989, at 81–82. Thus, we cannot accept the charge that "pro-life feminism, as currently formulated, is a contradiction in terms," as expressed by Katha Pollitt in her hostile review of Ginsburg, *Contested Lives*, *supra* note 12. *See* Pollitt, "Everything's Up to Date in North Dakota," *Tikkun*, Jan.–Feb. 1990, at 57–60; *see also* Glendon, *supra* note 12, at 50–58 (abortion as a woman's issue); Victor Rosenblum & Thomas Marzen, "Strategies for Reversing *Roe v. Wade* Through the Courts," in *Abortion and the Constitution: Reversing Roe v. Wade Through the Courts*, at 195, 205–6, (ed. Dennis J. Horan, Edward R. Grant, Paige C. Cunningham, Georgetown U. Press, 1987). On this issue, as well as others, we find both feminist and congenial the distinctive voices of, e.g., Jean Elshtain, *Power Trips and Other Journeys: Essays in Feminism as Civic Discourse* (U. of Wisconsin Press, 1990); Elizabeth Fox-Genovese, *Feminism Without Illusions: A Critique of Individualism* (U. of North Carolina Press, 1991); Mary Ann Glendon, *Rights Talk: The Impoverishment of Political Discourse* (Free Press, 1991).

19   For examples of the "reproductive freedom" approach, *see* Rosalind P. Pet-

chesky, *supra* note 13; Susan Estrich & Kathleen Sullivan, "Abortion Politics: Writing for an Audience of One," 138 *U. of Pennsylvania L. Rev.* 119 (1989); Sylvia Law, "Rethinking Sex and the Constitution," 132 *U. of Pennsylvania L. Rev.* 955, 1016–28 (1984); Isabel Marcus, "A Response to Michael J. Quirk: Who's Directing Traffic?," *Tikkun*, March–April 1990, at 93–94.

We of course recognize that regulatory abortion laws speak directly to the lives of women, as they do not to men, and that one should at least be wary of moral pronouncements largely developed by male theologians when only women are the recipients of their instruction. Thus, in an important sense abortion is properly regarded as a woman's issue. Nevertheless, we cannot accept that those perceptions lead necessarily to the successful deployment of "reproductive freedom" as a definitive argument that renders abortions, at least within the *Roe v. Wade* scheme, immunized from any meaningful public moral debate. As mothers know (and the one of us with that capability has had four full-term pregnancies), *from experience*, there is a time when the experience of "being pregnant" becomes the experience of nurturing and protecting a small life. The point is not to suggest that we recriminalize abortions, but to appreciate that there is more to the pro-life position than can be flicked away with words like "freedom" or "choice." *See* Condit, *supra* note 5, at 74 n.5. Condit also notes that the "reproductive freedom" claim belongs more to the world of academic feminists and activists than to the stories and lives of "ordinary" women. *Id.* at 76–77 n.25. And at some point the claim of "freedom" collapses back into the rhetoric of "choice." *See* Lawrence M. Friedman, *The Republic of Choice: Law, Authority, and Culture* 182–85 (Harvard U. Press, 1990). Friedman's book is simultaneously a historical sociology and celebration of "choice" as the dominant cultural motif for our contemporary notion of "freedom." Yet his discussion of abortion, the issue that surely tests the dominance of "choice," ends in nothing but the conflict, confusion, and incommensurability we have described earlier, casting some doubt on Friedman's entire thesis.

20   Robert Wuthnow, *The Restructuring of American Religion: Society and Faith Since World War II* 226 (Princeton U. Press, 1988). The gap between female and male membership in churches is lessening. In 1985, 73 percent of women and 63 percent of men were church members. *Id.* at 226 n.15. Notably, however, a gender gap persists even when young women with college educations and full-time jobs are compared with male counterparts. "Rather than being simply a peripheral issue that can be relegated to the dark corners of the past, religion remains a vital aspect of the public and private lives of the vast majority of American women." *Id.* at 226.

21   On the middle-class tilt of the public discourse of "choice," *see* Condit, *supra* note 6, at 188, 194–96; McDonnell, *supra* note 18. Moreover, a growing literature is questioning, on both epistemological and moral/political grounds, the more extreme versions of feminist "essentialism," which universalize the experience of all women as against that of all men, often reducing at the same time all social/cultural issues to ones of gender. Thus, a number of authors have suggested that claims made on behalf of all women may reflect little more than the experience and privilege of white middle-class professional women.

See, e.g., E. Spelman, *Inessential Woman: Problems of Exclusion in Feminist Thought* (Beacon Press, 1988); Angela Harris, "Race and Essentialism in Feminist Theory," 42 *Stanford L. Rev.* 581 (1990); Marlee Kline, "Race, Racism and Feminist Legal Theory," 12 *Harvard Women's L.J.* 115 (1989). *See also* Clifford Geertz, "A Lab of One's Own," *New York Review of Books*, Nov. 8, 1990, at 19 (questioning the existence of "feminist" science). To allow women their particularity would welcome the richness and difference of their experiences, including religious and cultural differences, which is a strength of Ginsburg, *supra* note 14. The usual left response that the women on the wrong side (pro-life) must be victims of "ideology" or "false consciousness" seems increasingly facile and outmoded. Cf. Clifford Geertz, "Ideology as a Cultural System," in *The Interpretation of Cultures* 193–233 (Basic Books, 1973).

22   We do not intend to suggest that this is a simple dichotomy. Starkly sectarian views may well play a valuable role in public moral dialogue. The bottom line is a willingness to engage in such dialogue. For an excellent introduction to these issues, *see* panel discussion with Richard Neuhaus, Robert Cover, Lisa Cahill, 5 J. L. & *Religion* 95–108. For more discussion of these issues, *see* chap. 9, *infra*.

23   *See* Elizabeth Mensch, "The History of Mainstream Legal Thought," in *The Politics of Law: A Progressive Critique* 13, 24–33 (2d ed., ed. David Kairys, 1990). *See also* George Armstrong Kelly, *Politics and Religious Consciousness in America* 274 (Transaction Books, 1984).

24   As noted, MacIntyre perceives the same problem with his version of Aristotelianism as the only solution. *See supra* note 17. *See also* his *Three Rival Versions of Moral Enquiry: Encyclopedia, Genealogy, and Tradition* (U. of Notre Dame Press, 1990).

25   *See, e.g.*, Theodore Caplow, Howard M. Bahr, & B. Chadwick, *All Faithful People: Change and Continuity in Middletown's Religion* (U. of Minnesota Press, 1983); Jackson W. Carroll, Douglas W. Johnson, & Martin E. Marty, *Religion in America: 1950 to the Present* (Harper & Row, 1979); Andrew M. Greeley, *Religious Change in America* (Harvard U. Press, 1989); Marty, *A Nation of Behavers* (U. of Chicago Press, 1976); Marty, *Pilgrims in Their Own Land: 500 Years of Religion in America* 461–77 (Little, Brown, 1984); *The New Religious Consciousness* (ed. Charles Y. Glock & Robert N. Bellah, U. of California Press, 1976); A. James Reichley, *Religion in American Public Life* 243–339 (Brookings Institution, 1985); *Religion and Twentieth-Century American Intellectual Life* (ed. Michael J. Lacey, Cambridge U. Press, 1989); Wade Clark Roof & William McKinney, *American Mainline Religion: Its Changing Shape and Future* (Rutgers U. Press, 1987); Wuthnow, *supra* note 20.

For the most recent survey data about Americans and religions, *see Religion in America 1992*, published by the Princeton Religion Research Center, which uses the resources of the Gallup Organization in its polling (George Gallup, Jr., is executive director of the center). In 1991, for example, 58 percent of adults rated religion as "being very important in their lives," the highest measurement this factor has received since 1972. *Id.* at 10–11. Based on more than 40,000 interviews conducted in 1991, Gallup found that 89 percent of American adults single out a religious faith or denomination as their preference; for 82 percent that faith is Christianity. *Id.* at 34. When compared with European countries, Americans (at 81 percent) rank second only to Italy (83 percent) in considering themselves religious persons and rank first (8.2 on a scale of 10) on the importance of God in one's life, with only Ireland close behind (8.0). Id. at 70. Moreover, Gallup concludes from the recent surveys that there "may be a new upswing in religious belief and practice." Id. at 10.

26   Thus we will give scant attention to the Jewish theological position on abortion. For the most part, Jewish teaching on abortion is rooted in the particularistic and technical realm of halakah (Jewish law). And from that realm come a variety of positions on the issue, ranging from a traditional opposition to all but a narrow category of therapeutic abortions to a liberal pro-choice position supported by Reform Jewish theologians. The most thorough review of this issue that we have found concludes that Jewish law prohibits abortion "for less than a serious reason" and mandates "a solemn awareness of the potential life involved." For the author, David Feldman, serious reasons include pain to the mother, but not "ordinary pain," and certainly not "economic or social inconvenience." Birth Control in Jewish Law 251–94 (NYU Press, 1968). For other examples of the restrictive view, see Immanuel Jakobovits, "Jewish Views on Abortion," in Abortion and the Law 124–43 (ed. David T. Smith, Press of Western Reserve U., 1967); Fred Rosner, "The Jewish Attitude Toward Abortion," in Contemporary Jewish Ethics 257–69 (ed. Menachem Marc Kellner, Sanhedrin Press, 1978); Isaac Klein, "Abortion and Jewish Tradition," in Contemporary Jewish Ethics, supra, at 270–78. For liberal Jewish positions, see Balfour Brickner, "Judaism and Abortion," in Contemporary Jewish Ethics, supra, at 279–83; Israel Margolies, "A Reform Rabbi's View," in 1 Abortion in a Changing World 30–33 (ed. Robert E. Hall, Columbia U. Press, 1970) (to be discussed further infra, chap. 8). For the view that Jewish law "presents a number of central opinions that, when carried to their logical conclusions, lead to a range of possible rulings on abortion in Jewish Law," see Rachel Biale, "Abortion in Jewish Law," Tikkun, July–Aug. 1989, at 26. Moreover, in our experience (largely in the academic world), ethnic Jews have preferred and even insisted on the propriety of secular, not theological, moral discourse: "American Jews, especially the liberal-to-moderate majority, have long held that integration would be fostered by advancing the tolerant pluralism of middle-class liberalism and adopting a universalistic ethic, allowing them at least nominal continued identification as Jews." Wade Clark Roof & William McKinney, supra note 25, at 225. On the outsider-as-insider motif in American Jewish experience, focusing on the particular case of Felix Frankfurther, see Robert A. Burt, Two Jewish Justices: Outcasts in the Promised Land 37–61 (U. of California Press, 1988).

Against this background, one rarely finds examples of particularistic Jewish tradition being deployed in more universal terms as part of public moral discourse. In our own field, however, two notable exceptions stand out: Edmond Cahn and Robert Cover, both of whom were lost, tragically, to untimely death. See, e.g., Cahn, Confronting Injustice: The Edmond Cahn Reader (ed. Lenore L. Cahn, Little, Brown, 1966); Cahn, The Moral Decision: Right and Wrong in the Light of American Law (Indiana U. Press, 1955); Cahn, The Sense of Injustice (NYU Press, 1949). See generally Cover, "Bringing the Messiah Through the Law: A Case Study," in Religion, Morality & the Law: NOMOS XXX 201–17 (ed. J. Roland Pennock & John W.

Chapman, NYU Press, 1988); Cover, "Obligation: A Jewish Jurisprudence of the Social Order," 5 J. L. & Religion 65–74 (1987); Cover, "The Supreme Court 1982 Term—Foreword: NOMOS and Narrative," 97 Harvard L. Rev. 4 (1983); Bruce Ledewitz, "Edmond Cahn's Sense of Injustice: A Contemporary Reintroduction," 3 J. L. & Religion 277 (1985) (analyzing Cahn, Sense of Injustice, supra, and its relation to modern thought). Another such voice, drawing explicit inspiration from Cover, may be emerging. See Winter, "The Cognitive Dimension of the Agon Between Legal Power and Narrative Meaning," 87 Mich. L. Rev. 2225, 2225 n.3 (1989). See also Guyora Binder, "Representing Nazism: Advocacy and Identity at the Trial of Klaus Barbie," 98 Yale L.J. 131, 1372–83 (1989) (Jewish author discussing Jewish identity); Robert A. Burt, "Constitutional Law and the Teaching of Parables," 93 Yale L.J. 455 (1984) (Jewish author discussing New Testament parables); Arthur Jacobson, "The Idolatry of Rules: Writing Law According to Moses, with Reference to Other Jurisprudences," 11 Cardozo L. Rev. 1079 (1990).

The Mormon position on abortion is not unlike the traditional Jewish one, discouraging abortion in all cases, but allowing exception of the "hard cases" of rape or health of the mother. The LDS (Church of Jesus Christ of Latter-Day Saints) church, however, encourages its members to read and study the scriptures and to pray to the Lord for personal confirmation about the scripture's meanings. Liberal LDS members feel that the idea of free agency, central to church belief, conflicts with laws against abortion. (We are indebted to Fred Gedicks and Christine Jepsen for educating us.)

Finally, we are well aware of and applaud the efforts of Ruth Colker. See Colker, "Feminism, Theology, and Abortion: Toward Love, Compassion, and Wisdom," 77 California L. Rev. 1011 (1989). Colker placed the abortion issue in a generalized theological setting, with its sources, for her, in selected Buddhist and Catholic writers, along with one Jewish source, Martin Buber. Id. at 1011 n.2. See generally Colker, Abortion and Dialogue (Indiana U. Press, 1992). Our own effort, which to some extent parallels Colker's, is to recover a more historically specific theological debate within explicitly Christian tradition, given both the overwhelming presence of Christianity in American culture and the particular Christian character inherent in much of the pro-life position.

1   Evil, Good, and Beyond

1   See, e.g., Guyora Binder, "Representing Nazism: Advocacy and Identity at the Trial of Klaus Barbie," 98 Yale L.J. 1321, 1329–30 (1989). We recognize that there is a vast literature on this point, not without dissent. There is certainly support for the point of view expressed by, e.g., William O. Douglas, An Almanac of Liberty 96 (Doubleday, 1954) ("the crime for which the Nazis were tried had never been formalized as a crime with the definiteness required by our legal standards. . . ."). See generally William J. Bosch, Judgment on Nuremburg (U. of North Carolina Press, 1970).

2   For good discussions, see e.g., Robert Burt, The Constitution in Conflict (Belknap Press, 1992), at 1–33; Edward A. Purcell, "Alexander Bickel and the Post-Realist

Constitution," 11 *Harvard Civil Rights-Civil Liberties L. Rev.* 521–64 (1976) (reviewing the large contribution to this discussion of Alexander Bickel).

3   *See* the discussion in chapter 6, *infra*.

4   For a recent example, *see* Richard Neuhaus, *America Against Itself: Moral Vision and the Public Order* (U. of Notre Dame Press, 1992). Describing the disintegration of the New Left (of which he had been a part), Neuhaus describes the civil rights movement as the "last great movement for social change in America that was morally unambiguous" (at 54). In the same book, without quite explicitly drawing the Nazi parallel with respect to abortion, he does so with respect to euthanasia (at 140–51); and, bringing the themes full circle, he explains his opposition to abortion in part by reference back to his experience as a pastor to a poor, black church in the 1960s. Most of the people in his congregation should not have been "brought into the world" if one were to follow the "quality of life" guidelines then being promulgated by a Princeton University professor. Neuhaus, of course, saw them as "God's people" (at 125–26).

A powerful example is the April 1978 telecast of *Holocaust*, for four successive evenings, which was watched by more than 120 million Americans, more than two-thirds of the adult population. Robert Wuthnow notes that more people watched the show than voted in either the 1976 or 1980 presidential elections, and that no TV show (other than the perhaps equally telling example of *Roots*) had ever attracted so large a viewing audience. He calls the event a "public moral ritual." *See Meaning and Moral Order: Explorations in Cultural Analysis* (U. of California Press, 1987), at 123–45. While attesting to the awesome power of these images of good and evil, we do not suggest that the actual human beings who were proponents of segregation, or even adherents of Nazism, can be dismissed themselves as exemplars of perfect evil. Nothing is that simple. As Randall Kennedy has suggested, writing about segregation, the tendency to conclude that "the losing side—the side supporting *de jure* segregation— was wholly bereft of morality or reason" is to succumb to the all too seductive pattern of "victor's history." *See* Kennedy, "Martin Luther King's Constitution: A Legal History of the Montgomery Bus Boycott," 98 *Yale L.J.* 999–1067, at 1005 (1989). Similarly, with respect to Nazism, none of us can be absolutely certain that *at the time* we would have recognized what, in retrospect, we understand to be its obvious evil. For a sensitive description of why German conservative Lutherans, disillusioned with the degeneracy of Weimar culture, embraced the *volk* spirit of Nazism, *see* Robert Theimann, *Constructing a Public Theology: The Church in a Pluralist Culture* (Westminster/John Knox Press, 1991), at 75–80. Martin Luther King, Jr., took from St. Augustine the firm belief that one should "hate the sin" but "love the sinner."

5   This is the question posed, for example, by Thomas Mann in his long and searching novel, *Doctor Faustus* (1948), whose lead character, Adrian Leverkuhn, is a bizarre fusion of Beethoven and Nietzsche.

6   *See* the discussion in chapter 3, *infra*.

7   In the 1960s Stanley Milgram began a series of experiments in human obedience to the commands of authority. The experiment was calculated to test the extent to which an individual would take harmful action against an innocent person in compliance with the command of an authority figure. In his basic

experiment, roughly two-thirds of the subjects administered what they believed to be extremely serious, painful shocks to the innocent victim, achieving a level of compliance well beyond that predicted by lay and expert opinion solicited before the experiments were conducted. For the full report, *see* Milgram, *Obedience to Authority* (Harper & Row, 1974).

8   *See* Gunnar Myrdal, *An American Dilemma* (Harper & Bros., 1944).

9   *See* David Southern, *Gunnar Myrdal and Black-White Relations: The Use and Abuse of* "An American Dilemma," 1944–1969 (LSU Press, 1987), at 102. *See also* Mary Dudziak, "Desegregation as a Cold War Imperative," 41 *Stanford L. Rev.* 61 (1988).

10 The Skokie case is Collin v. Smith, 578 F.2d 1197 (7th Cir.), *cert. denied*, 439 U.S. 916 (1978). The issue was recently before the Supreme Court in R.A.V. v. St. Paul, 112 S.Ct. 2538 (1992), and it remains unsettled. For a sample of the debate on the issue, *compare* Lee Bollinger, "Book Review," 80 *Mich. L. Rev.* 617 (1982) (reviewing Neier, "Defending My Enemy: American Nazis, The Skokie Case, and the Risks of Freedom"), *with* Mari Matsuda, "Public Response to Racist Speech: Considering the Victim's Story," 87 *Mich. L. Rev.* 2320 (1989).

11 William Brennan, *The Abortion Holocaust: Today's Final Solution* (Landmark Press, 1983), at 5. For a deeply critical response to this rhetoric, *see* Robert Brown, "Abortion and the Holocaust," *Christian Century*, Oct. 31, 1984, at 1004–5 (the analogy is "repugnant, incorrect and divisive").

12 On the use of fetal imagery by pro-life activists, *see* Celeste Michelle Condit, *Decoding Abortion Rhetoric: Communicating Social Change* (U. of Illinois Press, 1989), at 79–92.

13 *See* Robert Wuthnow, *The Restructuring of American Religion: Society and Faith Since World War II* (Princeton U. Press, 1988), at 213.

14 Ronald Reagan, *Abortion and the Conscience of the Nation* (T. Nelson, 1984), at 19, quoted in Condit, *supra* note 12, at 50. For other examples, *see* John T. Noonan, Jr., *A Private Choice: Abortion in America in the Seventies* (Free Press, 1979), at 81–84; *Abortion and the Constitution: Reversing Roe v. Wade Through the Courts* (ed. Dennis J. Horan, Edward R. Grant, & Paige C. Cunningham, Georgetown U. Press, 1987), at 15, 17, 57, 92–93.

15 *E.g.*, Justice Scalia, dissenting, in Planned Parenthood of Eastern Pennsylvania v. Casey, 112 S.Ct. 2791 (U.S. Sup. Ct., June 29, 1992).

16 This concept has been employed to recharacterize the culture and fervent religious belief of lower-middle-class people as a kind of psychopathology. *See* Christopher Lasch, *The True and Only Heaven: Progress and Its Critics* (Norton, 1991), at 445–65. *See also*, as an example, Robert Jay Lifton & Charles Strozier, "Waiting for Armageddon," *New York Times*, Aug. 12, 1990, § 7, at 1, 24–25 (offering their generalizations about "50 million Americans" who are "fundamentalist Christians").

17 *See* James Hunter, *Culture Wars: The Struggle to Define America* (Basic Books, 1991), at 13–17. The editor of the *Daily Californian* (student-run newspaper at the University of California, Berkeley) recently rejected a pro-life advertising supplement, citing as precedent the paper's previous rejection of an ad arguing that the Holocaust was a hoax. Both, she said, were "regarded as misleading and offensive by the staff." "Pro-Choice, Anti-Speech," *Wall St. Journal*, Nov. 30, 1992, at A12.

18   Peter Irons, "Little Rock, 1957. Wichita, 1991," *New York Times*, Saturday, Aug. 10, 1991, at sec. 1, p. 19, col. 1 (late ed., final).

19   Pro-Choice Network of Western New York v. Project Rescue Western New York, Civ. No. 90-1004A, U.S. Dist. Ct., W.D.N.Y., Feb. 14, 1992, at 47–48 (Judge Richard Arcara).

20   *E.g.*, Peter Singer, *Animal Liberation* (Avon Books, 1977): "Under the Nazi regime in Germany, nearly 200 doctors, some of them eminent in the world of medicine, took part in experiments on Jews and Russian and Polish prisoners. Thousands of other physicians knew of these experiments, some of which were the subject of lectures at medical academies. Yet the records show that the doctors sat through medical reports of the infliction of horrible injuries on these 'lesser races' and then proceeded to discuss the medical lessons to be learned from them without anyone making even a mild protest about the nature of the experiments. The parallels between this attitude and that of experimenters today toward animals are striking." *Id.* at 76–77. *See also* Gary Francione, " 'Harassment' and 'Terrorism,' " *The Animals' Voice*, Oct. 1990, at 53. "[T]hose who have a reverence for *all* life may legitimately regard as the *real* "terrorists" those who kill, torture, and maim, nonhumans for commercial gain." *Id.*

21   *See* Albert Gore, *Earth in the Balance: Ecology and the Human Spirit* (Houghton Mifflin, 1991), at 177, 275.

22   *The Animals' Voice*, Dec. 1990. This magazine is intended "to reach mainstream audiences with our message of animal rights" (at 7). Similar pictures are to be found at 10–15, 33–47. Singer makes use of similar photographs to support his philosophical argument. *See supra* note 20, at 140 (photo insert).

23   Singer, *supra* note 20, at 1–26. For a sympathetic yet critical treatment of the analogy, *see* Mary Midgley, *Animals and Why They Matter* (U. of Georgia Press, 1983), at 98–111. *See also* Tom Regan, *The Case for Animal Rights* (U. of California Press, 1983), at 226–28, 312–15.

24   The December 1990 issue of *The Animals' Voice* contains a full-page advertisement for itself and its related foundation, the Compassion for Animals Foundation, which explicitly invokes the tradition of Garrison, including the quoted words.

25   *See* James Jasper & Dorothy Nelkin, *The Animal Rights Crusade: The Growth of a Moral Protest* (Free Press, 1992), at 174–76.

26   *Id.*

27   *See, e.g.*, Constance Holden, "Universities Fight Animal Activists," *Science*, Jan. 6, 1989, at 17–19 (citing the example of the former Stanford University president, Donald Kennedy).

28   Quoted in Jasper & Nelkin, *supra* note 25, at 23–24.

29   Jean Elshtain makes the point about women as activists in her excellent (and sympathetic to the issue) article, "Why Worry About the Animals?," *Progressive*, March 1990, at 17–23. Women have traditionally played a disproportionate role in the antivivisectionist movement. *See* Coral Lansbury, *The Old Brown Dog: Women, Workers, and Vivisection in Edwardian England* 83, 198 n.4 (U. of Wisconsin Press, 1985). *See also* Harriet Ritvo, *The Animal Estate: The English and Other Creatures in the Victorian Age* 157–66 (Harvard U. Press, 1987) (discussing history of the anti-

vivisectionist movement during the nineteenth century). A notable exception to the whiteness of the movement is novelist Alice Walker. *See, e.g.,* Walker, "Am I Blue? Ain't Those Tears in Those Eyes Tellin You?," *Ms.,* July 1986, at 29 (discussing the feelings animals have toward humans). The animal rights movement is also one of the largest instances of mass political energy in our culture. *Newsweek* reported in May 1988 that "Congress had received more mail on the subject of animal research than any other topic." Adler, "Emptying the Cages: Does the Animal Kingdom Need a Bill of Rights?," *Newsweek,* May 23, 1988, at 59.

30   Twentieth Century Fox 1987.

31   Rosalind Hursthouse, *Beginning Lives* (Basil Blackwell, 1987), at 155–56. One striking exception is political scientist Jean Elshtain, who is sympathetic to both the plight of animals and the unborn, but is not an absolutist on either issue. *Compare* Elshtain, *supra* note 29 (animals), with her "Reflections on Abortion, Values, and the Family," in *Abortion: Understanding Differences* (ed. Sidney Callahan & Daniel Callahan, Plenum Press, 1984), at 47–72. Elshtain is also the only person we are aware of, other than ourselves, who acknowledges that her view of the abortion issue was informed, at least in part, by her earlier view of the animals issue. For our own previously published views on animals, *see* Alan Freeman & Elizabeth Mensch, "Scratching the Belly of the Beast," *Tikkun,* Sept.–Oct. 1989, at 34–38, 92–93, 95–96, reprinted in *Animal Experimentation: The Moral Issues* (ed. R. Baird & S. Rosenbaum, Prometheus Books, 1991), at 161–78.

32   Carol J. Adams, "Abortion Rights and Animal Rights," *Between the Species* 7, no. 4 (Fall 1991): 181–89, who is also the source for the quotes in the remainder of the paragraph.

33   *See, e.g.,* Midgley, *supra* note 23, at 33–44 (examining emotions toward animals and seeking to justify those emotions); Richard Rorty, *Philosophy and the Mirror of Nature* 188–92 (Princeton U. Press, 1979). Rosalind Hursthouse illustrates the gap between analytic philosophy and "ordinary morality" with her apt example "We can't take Laura on holiday, why don't we drown her?" to which the ordinary morality response would be, "But that would be *killing a baby!*" The context is her review of two philosophical traditions, one of which would regard as irrelevant the fact of "killing," while the other would regard as equally irrelevant that the victim is a baby. *Supra* note 31, at 179–80.

34   *See* Regan, *supra* note 23, at 319.

35   *Id.*

36   *See* Peter Singer, *Practical Ethics* 122–26 (Cambridge U. Press, 1979), which is what prompted Rosalind Hursthouse to ask: "Would not one expect someone arguing against the way we slaughter animals to be rather 'pro-life' in general, and hence against abortion and infanticide?" *Supra* note 31, at 155–56. She goes on to criticize Singer's utilitarianism for both its inconsistency and its failure to give even adequate protection to animals. *Id.* at 155–58. For a utilitarian who takes both issues seriously, however, and is committed to consistency, *see* L. Sumner, *Abortion and Moral Theory* (Princeton U. Press, 1981). For his specific views on animals, *see id.,* at 139–40, 198–200.

On the other hand, conceding the difficulty of positing absolutist, universally valid ethical norms may compel hesitation even with respect to practices like infanticide, which seem so morally repugnant to most of us. Consider two culture-specific examples. Anthropologist Nancy Scheper-Hughes observed the practice of "selective neglect" (or "passive infanticide"), whereby mothers in poverty-stricken northeastern Brazil, with a great deal of stoicism and equanimity, decide whether particular infants are "thrivers and survivors" or "born already 'wanting to die.'" "Death Without Weeping: Has Poverty Ravaged Mother Love in the Shantytowns of Brazil?," *Natural History*, Oct. 1989, at 8, 10. The mothers nurture those perceived as survivors, while "stigmatized, doomed infants were left to die, as mothers say, *a mingua*, 'of neglect.'" *Id.* The local Catholic churches have been at odds with themselves over the practice. The traditional approach was "patience and resignation" in the face of domestic tragedy, with elaborate funerals for the deceased infants. *Id.*, at 16. Newer, liberation theology priests, however, find themselves opposed to condoning in any way the cultural accommodation of infanticide. *Id.* Families on the verge of starvation among the Inuit people of the Far North would also sometimes place newborn infants in the snow to die. Yet, according to legend, this could be done only before the child had been named, for, if named, the child would acquire a soul and, if killed, become an *angiak*, a "child of the living dead," who, even as its flesh decayed, would live on as a spirit, seeking revenge. For a vivid mythological account, *see* "Furies of the Far North," in *Tales of Terror* 70, 74–76 (Time-Life Enchanted World Series, 1987).

37   John Finnis, "Natural Law and the Rights of the Unborn," in *Abortion and the Constitution, supra* note 14, at 119. Writer John Lofton characterizes "caring for animals more than people" as "moral insanity." "Moral Insanity Has Turned American Value System Topsy-Turvy," *Buffalo News*, Sept. 23, 1990, at H-11.

38   For a good summary, *see* James Serpell, *In the Company of Animals: A Study of Human-Animal Relationships* 122–30 (Basil Blackwell, 1986). For a sampling of these views, as well as some of their critics, *see Animal Rights and Human Obligations* 51–169 (ed. Tom Regan & Peter Singer, Prentice-Hall, 1976). On Kant's position with respect to animals, which denied them the status of "moral agent," but imposed duties of kindness toward them so as not to stifle human feelings toward one another, *see id.*, at 122–23. *See also* Hursthouse, *supra* note 31, at 94–96 (describing the extension of Kant's "person" to nonhuman beings and how this would change the way humans treat nonhuman "persons"); Regan, *supra* note 23, at 84–85 (determining the Kantian sense of autonomy does not apply to animals while the preferential sense of autonomy does); Sumner, *supra* note 36, at 140 (examining Kant's position and A. I. Meldon, *Rights and Persons* 204 (U. of California Press, 1977), where Meldon writes that, because only humans are capable of moral agency, these natural rights belong to humans.

39   Milan Kundera, *The Unbearable Lightness of Being* 288 (trans. Michael Henry Heim, Harper & Row, 1984). For our own critique of such dualism, *see* Freeman & Mensch, "Scratching the Belly of the Beast," *Tikkun*, Sept.–Oct. 1989, at 34–38, 92–93, 95–96.

40   John Finnis, *Natural Law and Natural Rights* 194–95 (Oxford U. Press, 1980). Rosalind Hursthouse, writing in the same Aristotelian tradition, disagrees. *See* Hursthouse, *supra* note 31, at 237–47.

41   Rorty, *supra* note 33, at 191. Rorty is talking about the problem of constituting

a moral "community," to which our moral prohibitions will extend, a crucial issue with respect to both animals and fetuses. He concludes that it is "notorious that moral philosophers are of little help in deciding what is to count as a moral agent, as having dignity rather than value." Id. at 191. He concludes: "The emotions we have toward borderline cases depend on the liveliness of our imagination, and conversely. Only the notion that in philosophy we have a discipline able to give good reasons for what we believe on instinct lets us think that 'more careful philosophical analysis' will help us draw a line between coldness of heart and foolish sentimentality." Id. See also, Midgley, supra note 23, at 28–32 (discussing membership/community issue and focusing on its complexity); Lloyd L. Weinreb, Natural Law and Justice (Harvard U. Press, 1987) at 301 n.26 (examining whether animals "count as significant others").

42   So concludes Kent Greenawalt, with respect to both animals and abortion. See his Religious Convictions and Political Choice (Oxford U. Press, 1988), at 98–110 (animals), and 120–37 (abortion). For our similar conclusion with respect to animals, see Freeman & Mensch, supra note 31.

43   John Rawls, A Theory of Justice (Belknap Press, 1971), at 504–12.

44   Martin Luther King, Jr., "Letter from Birmingham Jail," 80 Christian Century, June 12, 1963, at 767–73; "Any law that uplifts human personality is just. Any law that degrades human personality is unjust."

45   See chap. 9, infra.

46   See Harper's Bible Dictionary (ed. Paul J. Achtemeier, Harper & Row, 1985), at 213, 219–20.

47   Lynn White, Jr., "The Historical Roots of Our Ecological Crisis," in Machina ex Deo: Essays in the Dynamism of Western Culture 75 (MIT Press, 1968).

48   See, e.g., William Leiss, The Domination of Nature 29–35, 188–90, 196–97 (Braziller, 1972).

49   See sources cited in introduction, supra.

50   See generally Elijah Judah Schochet, Animal Life in Jewish Tradition: Attitudes and Relationships (Ktav, 1984). We recommend especially his "Biblical Portrait." Id. at 9–79.

51   Genesis 1:26–28.

52   A number of injunctions laid down in the Torah speak specifically to the decent treatment of animals. The obligation to rest on the Sabbath includes the obligation to provide a day of rest for all domestic animals and beasts of burden. Deuteronomy 5:14. The muzzling of an ox, while he treads grain on the threshing floor, is forbidden, for the animal is entitled to enjoy food, as is any human laborer. Deuteronomy 25:9; 23:25–26. An animal fallen beneath the weight of its burden must be assisted to rise, even if it is the beast of one's enemy. Deuteronomy 22:4; Exodus 23:4–5. Beyond enunciating specific prohibitions, scripture also expresses the deep kinship of people and animals, who share a common mortality. "For that which befalleth the sons of men befalleth beasts; even one thing befalleth them: as the one dieth, so dieth the other; yea, they have all one breath; so that man hath no preeminence above a beast: for all is vanity. All go unto one place; all are of the dust, and all turn to the dust again." Ecclesiastes 3:19–21. Whatever words scripture uses to describe life—a mist, a fleeting breath, a cloud, a dream, a shadow, a flower, or

grass—apply to both people and animals. *See* Schochet, *supra* note 50, at 52–53. Similarly, as Schochet points out, biblical terminology reflects the unity of humans and beasts. *Ruach hayyim* ("spirit of life") can refer to both people and animals, as can *nefesh hayyah* ("living creature"). The word *Basar* ("flesh") refers literally to the softer parts of the body of an organism, or to the body in general, or to humanity; and the phrase *kol Basar* ("all flesh") can denote *all* living creatures, animal as well as human. While *Basar* can refer to food, more generally it connotes "frailty," the perishable nature of all living entities. *See id.* at 53. Indeed, animals are specifically included in God's covenant with Noah: "Behold, I establish my covenant with you . . . and with every living creature that is with you, of the fowl, of the cattle, and every beast of the earth with you[.]" Genesis 9:9–10. Not surprisingly, then, the prophetic, messianic vision, depicting the final fulfillment of the covenant, is a vision of renewed harmony among all members of the animal kingdom:

> The wolf shall dwell with the lamb
> And the leopard shall lie down with the kid;
> And the calf and the young lion and the fatling together;
> And a little child shall lead them.
> And the cow and the bear shall feed;
> Their young ones shall lie down together;
> And the lion shall eat straw like the ox,
> And the sucking child shall play on the hole of the asp,
> And the weaned child shall put his hand on the adder's den.
> (Isaiah 11:6–9)

In this passage, Isaiah harkens back to the Garden of Eden, which was, as described in the first chapter of Genesis, a time of peaceful vegetarianism for both people and animals; the fulfillment of the covenant means a return to such a state. This message is emphasized by Hosea as well, who describes the time when God would once again renew his loving relationship with the errant Israel: "And I will make for you a covenant on that day with the beasts of the field, the birds of the air, and the creeping things of the ground; and I will abolish the bow, the sword, and war from the land; and I will make you lie down in safety. And . . . I will betroth you to me forever; I will betroth you to me in righteousness and in justice, in steadfast love, and in mercy." (Hosea 2:18–19).

53   "Is it for the oxen that God is concerned? Does he not speak entirely for our sake?" I Corinthians 9:9–10. Later, he explains that the passage is really about the right of preachers, like Paul himself, to be paid a suitable wage. I Timothy 5:17–18.

54   Thomas Aquinas, "Difference Between Rational and Other Creatures," in *Animal Rights and Human Obligations*, supra note 38, at 58–59.

55   *See* John Passmore, *Man's Responsibility for Nature: Ecological Problems and Western Traditions* 13 (Scribner's, 1974) (quoting John Calvin, *Institutes of Religion*, bk. 1, at 182 [trans. F. Battles, 1961]).

56   *See, e.g.*, Thomas Aquinas, "On Killing Living Things and the Duty to Love Irrational Creation," in *Animal Rights and Human Obligations*, supra note 38, at 118–21.

57 *See* Susan Bratton, "The Original Desert Solitaire: Early Christian Monasticism and Wilderness," 10 *Environmental Ethics* 31 (1988).

58 David Tracy, *Dialogue with the Other* 5 (W. B. Eerdmans, 1991).

59 *See* Paula Cooey-Nichols, "Nature as Divine Communication in the Works of Jonathan Edwards" (unpublished Ph.D. dissertation, Harvard U., 1981). *See also* Ball, *Lying Down Together: Law, Metaphor and Theology* (U. of Wisconsin Press, 1985), at 184 nn.16–17 (comparing Edwards's Trinitarian theology of nature with Karl Barth's Christocentric views); Wilson Kimnach, "Jonathan Edwards' Pursuit of Reality," in *Jonathan Edwards and the American Experience* 102–17 (ed. Nathan O. Hatch & Harry S. Stout, Oxford U. Press, 1988) (discussing religion as experience and spiritual awareness).

60 *See* Andrew Linzey, "The Place of Animals in Creation: A Christian View," in *Animal Sacrifice: Religious Perspectives on the Use of Animals in Science* 115–48 (ed. Tom Regan, Temple U. Press, 1986) (citing Paul Tillich, 2 *Systematic Theology*, pt. 3, 96 [1978]).

61 Quoted in *id.* at 119 (quoting Tillich, *supra* note 60, at 96).

62 James M. Gustafson, 1 *Ethics from a Theocentric Perspective* 91 (U. of Chicago Press, 1981), at 82–105.

63 Stephen R. L. Clark, *The Moral Status of Animals* 195 (Clarendon Press, 1984).

64 *Id.* Clark is both an avid advocate for animals and an opponent of abortion. On abortion, *see id.* at 74–75, 128.

65 On the theological importance of the notion of limits in our relation to both the family and the environment, *see* Gustafson, *supra* note 62, at 105–6.

66 James Tonstead Burtchaell, *The Giving and Taking of Life: Essays Ethical* 123–24 (U. of Notre Dame Press, 1989).

67 *Newsweek*, Sept. 24, 1990, opposite 67 (Buffalo regional edition).

68 On the serious practical and theoretical differences between animal rights advocates and those favoring a deeper and more comprehensive environmental ethic, *see* J. Baird Callicott, "Animal Liberation: A Triangular Affair," 2 *Environmental Ethics* 311 (1980). On the problem of even defining what we mean by an objective ecosystem, and the consequent quandary for environmental ethics, *see* B. Boyer, "Ecosystem, Legal System, and the Great Lakes Water Quality Agreement" (unpublished manuscript on file with authors).

69 For an excellent review of the literature, attesting to the persistence of some irreducible "biosocial" basis for gender differences, *see* Carl Degler, *In Search of Human Nature: The Decline and Revival of Darwinism in American Social Thought* (Oxford U. Press, 1991), at 293–327. Notably, the author concludes his book with an epilogue about animals. *See id.* at 329–49.

70 For this account, we are indebted to Coral Lansbury's brilliant and persuasive account of this brief alliance. *See generally supra* note 29.

71 Anna Sewell, *Black Beauty: Autobiography of a Horse* (1877).

72 Lansbury, *supra* note 29, at 86–87.

73 *Id.* at 112–29.

74 *Id.* at 84.

75 *See* C. Merchant, *The Death of Nature: Women, Ecology, and the Scientific Revolution* 171 (Harper & Row, 1989). *See generally id.* at 164–90.

76   *Id.* at 168.

77   *Id.* at 169–70. *Compare* the similar terminology used by noted historian of science Thomas S. Kuhn in characterizing Baconian science. "Mathematical versus Experimental Traditions in the Development of Physical Science," in *The Essential Tension: Selected Studies in Scientific Tradition and Change* 31, 41–59 (U. of Chicago Press, 1977). "[T]hey wished to see how nature would behave under previously unobserved often previously nonexistent, circumstances." *Id.* at 43. Kuhn also uses the phrases "the control of nature" (*id.* at 48); "[t]o experiment or to constrain nature was to do it violence" (*id.* at 55); and the "impetus toward power over nature through manipulative and instrumental techniques" (*id.* at 59). *See generally* Leiss, *supra* note 48. For debate about the "eco-feminism" movement emerging from the perception that women have a peculiar historical, cultural, or biological affinity with "nature," see Jim Cheney, "Eco-Feminism and Deep Ecology," 9 *Environmental Ethics* 115 (1987); Warwick Fox, "The Deep Ecology-Ecofeminism Debate and Its Parallels," 11 *Environmental Ethics* 5 (1989); Karen Warren, "Feminism and Ecology: Making Connections," 9 *Environmental Ethics* 3 (1987); Warren, "The Power and the Promise of Ecological Feminism," 12 *Environmental Ethics* 125 (1990); Michael Zimmerman, "Feminism, Deep Ecology, and Environmental Ethics," 9 *Environmental Ethics* 21 (1987).

78   With respect to the study of animals, for example, there has been a gradual but dramatic revolution in scientific thought in recent years. Many careful researchers have come to recognize the need to study animals in their own settings to learn about the animals' cultures and ways of life in stark opposition to the presumptuous claims of laboratory experimenters. Virtually demolished are the twin presuppositions that have been the compelled orthodoxy of animal scientists: the injunction against anthropomorphism and the insistence that the principle of parsimony comports with the behaviorist view of animals. The upshot is a rejection of Baconian science in favor of practices more akin (yet notably careful and painstaking) to Aristotelian scientific tradition. For an excellent overview by a noted scientist, *see* Donald R. Griffin, *Animal Thinking* (Harvard U. Press, 1984). *See also* Vicki Hearne, *Adam's Task: Calling Animals by Name* 224–44 (Knopf, 1986). Most people are aware of the breakthroughs in knowledge achieved by Jane Goodall with respect to chimpanzees, and by Diane Fossey with respect to gorillas (see the movie, *Gorillas in the Mist,* Warner Brother's Universal Pictures, 1989); there are, in fact, many other examples revealing the reality of animal culture. *See, e.g.,* Cynthia Moss, *Elephant Memories* (Morrow, 1988) (elephants); Shirley C. Strum, *Almost Human* (Random House, 1987) (baboons); Barry Holstun Lopez, *Of Wolves and Men* (Scribner's, 1978) (wolves); Elizabeth Thomas, "Reflections: The Old Way," *New Yorker,* Oct. 15, 1990, at 78 (lions). *See generally* Degler, *supra* note 69, at 329–49.

79   *See* Faye D. Ginsburg, *Contested Lives* (U. of California Press, 1989), at 172–93.

80   Sidney Callahan, "Value Choices in Abortion," at 296–97, in *Abortion: Understanding Differences* (ed. Sidney Callahan & Daniel Callahan, Plenum Press, 1984). Callahan regards her view as "holistic," *id.* at 291, and sums up her outlook, in contrast to the "Enlightenment model of a rational, pragmatic human being": "Feelings of sacrificial love and gifts of self to others are called for. Empathy

and nurturing feelings are focused on the fetus, which is fiercely identified with, either as a family member or as a powerless, helpless being in need of protection. Communal memberships and the giving and receiving of love are seen as the highest emotional fulfillments, and attractions to achievement and independent autonomy are secondary" (Id. at 300).

81   See Ginsburg, supra note 79, at 227–47.

82   Id. at 236.

83   One of the more insightful studies of the culture of domesticity traces its relation to the religious experience of women in the nineteenth century. See Barbara Leslie Epstein, The Politics of Domesticity: Women, Evangelism, and Temperance in Nineteenth-Century America (Wesleyan U. Press, 1981). Epstein compares the First Great Awakening, the Second Great Awakening, and the temperance movement specifically from the vantage point of female experience. During the First Great Awakening, which occurred in Calvinist New England in the mid-eighteenth century, Epstein found little or no relation between the intense experience of conversion and gender hostility; in general, men's and women's experiences were similar. Id. at 11–44. At that time, of course, the farm/household still functioned as the primary social and economic unit, despite some Calvinist fears that an emerging merchant class and acquisitive culture would destroy the old order. Id. at 24–30. Responsibility for the farm and household was basically a shared one, despite some gender-specific tasks. Notably, too, the shared category "parent" was culturally far more significant than "mother" or "father" as distinct from each other, and parents were considered deserving of huge respect. Id. at 33. New England Calvinist theology still assumed female subordination to males, but all earthly relations of subordination (which were justified as designed for social cohesion and the exercise of social responsibility) were viewed as contingent and provisional; the primary concern was one's relationship to God, and in that women were equal to men. Women were relatively better off in Calvinist New England than were women elsewhere at the time (better off than under the common law, for example). A man who abused his wife (or even dared, as in one case, to call her "servant") was both morally and legally answerable to the whole community. See id. at 23.

By the time of the Second Great Awakening, the emergence of a market economy (with the most significant economic relations taking place outside the family for many of the middle class) facilitated the creation of "domesticity" as a female-dominated sphere separate from market relations. This sphere was in part the creation of women themselves, although it was also a response to the constraints imposed by the dominant culture, especially limits on full female participation in economic and political life. Increasingly, religion became associated with domesticity, although church hierarchy was still male-dominated. Then, Epstein finds, the conversion experience became an arena in which women acted out gender antagonism. By claiming to be answerable to Christ even over and above their husbands, women were empowered to defy growing male resistance to religion. When women did draw men into the Awakening, there was some victory in seeing them submit to an authority even greater than worldly male power—yet the victory could only be partial, since the only available cultural categories rendered male conversion a (temporary) victory of domesticity as against a dominant male culture. *See id.* at 45–87.

In the WCTU, middle-class female resentment against the isolation and economic dependency of domesticity was, in a sense, projected onto the single issue of drinking. *Id.* at 103–4. Even while that projection limited the scope of feminist analysis within the temperance movement, appeal to religion and domestic values did empower women to assert themselves. Under the leadership of Frances Willard, the WCTU took on a broad range of issues relating to female inequality, including suffrage, labor conditions for both men and women, and legal issues relating to sexual abuse. While the WCTU never lost its middle-class, Protestant, essentially Victorian perspective, especially in relation to sex, it did push that frame of reference to its limits and in some important ways transcended it. *Id.* at 146. According to Epstein, there is still some tendency for feminist ideology to draw on the perspective of a relatively privileged middle class. In modern times that means an educated, secular perspective that does not necessarily speak to the concerns of the working class on issues such as family and abortion. *Id.* at 150.

84   *See* Joan Williams, "Gender Wars: Selfless Women in the Republic of Choice," 66 NYU L. Rev. 1559 (1991); "Virtue and Oppression," in *Virtue:* NOMOS XXXIV (ed. John W. Chapman & William A. Galston, NYU Press, 1992), at 309–37.

85   *See* Joan Williams, "Deconstructing Gender," 87 Mich. L. Rev. 797 (1989) (arguing that feminists can attack "male norms" without appealing to domesticity).

86   *See generally* Sara M. Evans, *Born for Liberty: A History of Women in America* 45–92 (Free Press, 1989); Jay Fliegelman, *Prodigals and Pilgrims: The American Revolution Against Patriarchical Authority, 1750–1800* (Cambridge U. Press, 1982); Michael Grossberg, *Governing the Hearth: Law and Family in Nineteenth-Century America* (U. of North Carolina Press, 1985); Janet Wilson James, *Changing Ideas About Women in the United States, 1776–1825* (Garland Press, 1981); Linda K. Kerber, *Women of the Republic: Intellect and Ideology in Revolutionary America* (U. of North Carolina Press, 1980); Suzanne Lebsock, *The Free Women of Petersburg: Status and Culture in a Southern Town, 1784–1860* (Norton, 1984); Mary Beth Norton, *Liberty's Daughters: The Revolutionary Experience of American Women, 1750–1800* (Little, Brown, 1980); Frances Olsen, "The Family and the Market: A Study of Ideology and Legal Reform," 96 *Harvard L. Rev.* 1497 (1983).

87   *See generally* Merchant, *supra* note 75. Rosemary Ruether offers a sympathetic, yet cautionary account of a similar venture launched at the end of the nineteenth century, when a disparate group of "post-Christian" women sought to recover an ancient, pre-Christian, matriarchal worldview and in so doing largely projected their preexisting Victorian familial values onto their premodern "discoveries." *See* "Radical Victorians: The Quest for an Alternative Culture," in 3 *Women and Religion in America: 1900–1968* (ed. Rosemary Ruether & Rosemary Skinner Keller, Harper & Row, 1986), at 1–47.

88   Quoted in Stephen Clark, *From Athens to Jerusalem: The Love of Wisdom and the Love of God* 166 (Oxford U. Press, 1985). Clark himself has written with passion and sophistication about moral issues with respect to animal/human relationships. *See The Nature of the Beast* (Oxford U. Press, 1982); *Moral Status of Animals,*

supra note 63; "Animals, Ecosystems, and the Liberal Ethic," *Monist*, Jan. 1987, at 114–31. On the variousness of female experience among nonhuman animals, *see* Bettyann Kevles, *Females of the Species: Sex and Survival in the Animal Kingdom* (Harvard U. Press, 1986).

89   The observers in question are Charles Darwin and Herman Melville. *See* Donald Worster, *Nature's Economy: A History of Ecological Ideas* 118–19, 120–21, 124–25 (paperback ed., Cambridge U. Press, 1987).

90   *See id.* at 122.

91   *See id.* at 115–29.

92   Annie Dillard, *Pilgrim at Tinker Creek* (Harper's Magazine Press, 1974), at 6.

93   *Id.* at 63.

94   *Id.* at 229.

95   *Id.* at 135.

96   *Id.* at 171.

97   *Id.* at 159–81.

98   *See* Gustafson, *supra* note 62, at 105–6.

99   Robert A. Pois, *National Socialism and the Religion of Nature* 35, 38 (Croom Helm, 1986) (quoting Hitler).

100   Consider the advice of a Nazi scientist: "A new National Socialist science cannot create, as if by sorcery, arbitrary and amateurish world systems and conceptions—only infinite damage could come of this. Rather, it must reverentially immerse itself in nature itself, and in the great Nordic discoverers and interpreters of nature, to find there the essence of German being in glorious abundance. . . . 'Natural science is not a root, but a blossom. Let us take care of the roots. The blossom will appear by itself.' "

101   Pois, *supra* note 99, at 59.

102   *See* Binder, *supra* note 1, at 1345–49.

103   For the quote and its context, *see* Mary Ann Glendon, *Abortion and Divorce in Western Law* (Harvard U. Press, 1987), at 26, 25–33.

104   The familiar "Hand formula" from tort law, derived from Learned Hand's opinion in United States v. Carroll Towing Co., 159 F.2d 169 (2d Cir. 1947). If the cost, or "burden" (B), of preventing an accident is greater than the loss to be avoided (L), discounted by the likelihood of its occurrence (P), then failure to prevent the accident is not to be regarded as negligence. *See generally* Charles O. Gregory & Harry Kalven, Jr., *Cases and Materials on Torts* 76–77 (2d ed., Little, Brown, 1969).

105   *See* Jonathan Kozol, *Rachel and Her Children: Homeless Families in America* (Crown, 1988), at 181–84.

2   *Natural Law and Catholic Tradition*

1   For a brief summary that accords with the anecdotal recollection, *see* Iris Murdoch, *The Sovereignty of Good* 48–49 (Schocken, 1971).

2   Jeffrey Stout, *Ethics After Babel: The Languages of Morals and Their Discontents* 105 (Beacon Press, 1988). We are also indebted to Stout (at 160) for the notion of "moral abomination" as applied to Nazi crimes against humanity, discussed in the text accompanying notes 4–5, *infra*.

3 See, e.g., Frederick Douglass, "What to the Slave Is the Fourth of July?," in My
   Bondage and My Freedom 349 (Ebony Classics, 1970) ("the great principles of politi-
   cal freedom and of natural justice, embodied in that Declaration of Indepen-
   dence"). The familiar Lincoln example is, of course, the Gettysburg Address
   ("Fourscore and seven years ago . . ."). See Garry Wills, Lincoln at Gettysburg: The
   Words that Remade America 101–8 (Simon & Schuster, 1992).

4 See Taylor Branch, Parting the Waters: America in the King Years 740 (Simon & Schuster, 1988).

5 Ronald Steel, Walter Lippmann and the American Century 491 (Little, Brown, 1980).

6 Id. at 492.

7 Id. (quoting Walter Lippmann, The Public Philosophy [1955]).

8 See J. Austin, The Province of Jurisprudence Determined & the Uses of the Study of Jurisprudence (Humanities Press, 1965).

9 See Elizabeth Mensch, "The History of Mainstream Legal Thought" in The Politics of Law: A Progressive Critique 13, 21–29 (ed. David Kairys, 2d ed., Pantheon
   Books, 1990), and sources cited therein.

10 "Statement of Policy," 1 Natural Law Forum 3 (1956).

11 1 Nat. L.F., facing 1 (1956).

12 6 Nat. L.F., at vi (1961).

13 7 Nat. L.F., at iii (1962). International scholars were also included, since the
    goal was to establish a firm basis for law generally, not just for the English
    and American common law tradition. Included were, e.g., A. P. d'Entrèves
    (Turin University and Oxford); Felice Battaglia (University of Bologna); Guido
    Fassò (University of Parma); Eustaquio Galan (University of Valladolid, Spain);
    Eduardo Garcia Maynez (National University of Mexico); Freiherr von der
    Heydte (University of Würzburg, Germany); Jacques Leclercz (University of
    Louvain, Belgium); Luis Legaz y Lacambra (University of Santiago de Compos-
    tela, Spain); Luis Cabral de Mancada (University of Ciombra, Portugal); Radha-
    binod Pal (University of Calcutta); René Théry (École Libre du Droit, Facultés
    Catholiques, Lille); Antonio Truyol (Universities of Lisbon and Murcia); Erik
    Wolf (U. of Freiburg). See 1 Nat. L.F., facing 1 (1956).

14 O'Meara, "Foreword," 1 Nat. L.F. 1–2 (1956) (O'Meara was then dean of Notre
    Dame Law School). For another entry in the natural law revival, see Brent
    Patterson, The Forgotten Ninth Amendment: A Call for Legislative and Judicial Recognition
    of Rights Under Social Conditions of Today (Bobbs-Merrill, 1955). In his foreword,
    Roscoe Pound hailed the book for its contribution to the "marked revival of
    natural law ideas throughout the world." Patterson believed that the Ninth
    Amendment was the constitutional text through which we could reaffirm that
    "[i]ndividual freedom and the recognition and development of the spiritual
    nature of mankind are the essence of democracy" (id. at 1) and that they recall
    the "inherent natural rights" with which individuals are "endowed by their
    Creator." Id. at 4. For Patterson, individual freedom meant the recovery of "the
    identity of the religious, spiritual, and noble principles upon which this gov-
    ernment was founded." Id. at 58. Moreover, it was clear to him that the price of
    individual liberty was acceptance of obligations and duties, such as the "obli-
    gation to maintain a reverent belief in God as the guide of the destiny of this
    nation, and to encourage an attitude of gratitude, humility, and worship of the

Supreme Being." *Id.* at 78–79. Why the fuss over an obscure book? Because, ironically, ten years later, the Patterson book would figure prominently as support for the majority in Griswold v. Connecticut, 381 U.S. 479 (1965), the case that announced the privacy doctrine that supplied the basis of *Roe v. Wade.* For further discussion of *Griswold, see infra,* chap. 8.

15 *See generally* 1 *Nat. L.F.,* at 5–166 (1956).

16 Edmond Cahn, *The Moral Decision: Right and Wrong in the Light of American Law* (Indiana U. Press, 1955).

17 Cahn was applauded for his resistance to legal positivism, yet chided for contextualism, intuitionism, and his rejection of what he saw as the absolutism and authoritarianism of the natural law tradition. *See* Witherspoon, "Book Review," 1 *Nat. L.F.* 146, 163 (1956) (reviewing *The Moral Decision*). Lost in this dismissal of Cahn was a serious Jewish entry in the possibility of genuine dialogue between the essentialist and rationalist morality of natural law, on the one hand, and the morality of context and particularity, also rooted in religious tradition. Cahn, for one, drew on both the Jewish and Christian biblical traditions. He bemoaned the decline of religious discourse in public moral debate; he was hardly a legal positivist: "From ancient times, religion has exalted the value of individual personality and has summoned men to understand their neighbors as nearly as possible after the manner of God's understanding, for—we are told—in his eyes all men, created in his image, are equal and alike, yet every man is distinct, unique, and filled with the splendor of human dignity. This is religion's own insight. Applied wholeheartedly in the law, it could help us shape decisions of individualized and creative justice." "A Lawyer Looks at Religion," in *Confronting Injustice: The Edmond Cahn Reader* (ed. Lenore L. Cahn, Little, Brown, 1966), at 207, 220. "It is time to recognize that the foremost existential question of our era is not whether one believes in God but whether what one believes about Him is sufficiently worthy. . . . The highest aim of the religious enterprise is to persuade a just, righteous, and compassionate God that He can believe in us." "The Binding of Isaac: A Case Study," in *Confronting Injustice,* at 232, 240. *See also* "The Pathology of Organized Religion," in *Confronting Injustice,* at 220. For a serious and sophisticated attempt by a Protestant theologian to locate Cahn in moral dialogue about the limits and possibilities of natural law by juxtaposing him with Catholic theologian Jacques Maritain, *see* Paul Ramsey, "Jacques Maritain and Edmond Cahn: The Egypt of the Natural Law," in *Nine Modern Moralists* 209 (Prentice-Hall, 1962), and "Jacques Maritain and Edmond Cahn: Man's Exodus from the Natural Law," in *Nine Modern Moralists,* at 233.

18 McDougal, "Law as a Process of Decision: A Policy-Oriented Approach to Legal Study," 1 *Nat. L.F.* 53, 71 (1956).

19 *Id.* at 67.

20 *Id.*

21 *See* A. P. d'Entrèves, "The Case for Natural Law Re-Examined," 1 *Nat. L.F.* 5 (1956). D'Entrèves's works at the time included *The Medieval Contribution to Political Thought* (Prentice-Hall, 1925); *Dante as a Political Thinker* (Clarendon Press, 1952); *Aquinas: Selected Political Writings* (Basil Blackwell, 1948); and *Natural Law* (Hutchinson's U. Library, 1951).

22 For a good review of the different approaches to "fundamental rights" juris-prudence, *see* Paul Brest, "The Fundamental Rights Controversy: The Essen-tial Contradictions of Normative Constitutional Scholarship," 90 *Yale L.J.* 1063 (1981).

23 D'Entrèves, "The Case for Natural Law Re-Examined," at 7.

24 H. L. A. Hart, *The Concept of Law* (Clarendon Press, 1961).

25 H. L. A. Hart, "Definition and Theory in Jurisprudence" (an inaugural lecture delivered before the University of Oxford on May 30, 1953).

26 D'Entrèves, "The Case for Natural Law Re-Examined," at 13.

27 *Id.* at 16.

28 *Id.* at 15.

29 *Id.* at 16 (citing Arthur L. Goodhart, *English Law and the Moral Law* [F. B. Roth-man, 1953]).

30 *Id.* at 17 (citing Goodhart, *supra* note 29, at 30).

31 *Id.* at 18–20.

32 For analytic purposes, d'Entrèves insists on this distinction between law, an externality involving coercion, and morality, involving the internal processes of motive. *Id.* at 20–21.

33 *Id.* at 21.

34 *Id.*

35 *Id.* at 24.

36 *Id.*

37 *Id.* at 25.

38 *Id.* at 25 (paraphrasing Jean-Jacques Rousseau, *Social Contract* 109 [1898]).

39 *Id.* (paraphrasing Rousseau, *supra* note 38, at 114).

40 *Id.*

41 *See* Elizabeth Mensch & Alan Freeman, "A Republican Agenda for Hobbesian America?," 41 *U. of Florida L. Rev.* 581, 584–88 (1989), and sources cited therein.

42 D'Entrèves, "The Case for Natural Law Re-Examined," at 26.

43 *Id.*

44 *Id.* at 34.

45 *Id.*

46 *Id.* at 35 (quoting Heinrich Rommen, *The Natural Law* 161 [Herder, 1947]).

47 *Id.*

48 *Id.*

49 *Id.* at 34–36.

50 *Id.* at 41–42.

51 Jacques Maritain, *Man and the State* 88–89 (U. of Chicago Press, 1951).

52 *E.g.*, Cardinal John J. O'Connor, "Abortion: Questions and Answers" (A spe-cial edition of Cardinal O'Connor's newsletter, "From My Viewpoint," *Catholic New York*, June 14, 1990).

53 Maritain, *supra* note 51 at 85 (citing Sophocles, *Antigone*, at ii, 452–60).

54 *Id.* at 85–88.

55 This position implicates both epistemology and, again, ontology. D'Entrèves thus insists that one cannot simply retreat into Hobbesian epistemological subjectivity, but must confront the world as an objective reality. His example comes from Coleridge by means of C. S. Lewis. In describing a natural wonder

as "sublime" one is not just saying "I have feelings associated in my mind with the word 'sublime' " (d'Entrèves, "The Case for Natural Law Re-Examined," at 45). Rather, one is saying something about the quality of the natural wonder itself, something not captured by the word "pretty." Just as some responses to a natural wonder are more "just," "ordinate," or "appropriate" than others, so in human societies and human nature itself, "[t]here are certain ultimate standards or values which determine approval or disapproval, assent or dissent; and I believe that it is these same values that determine our judgments as to whether a law is 'just' or 'unjust': in other words—to use a very ancient language that is perfectly appropriate at this point—whether we are bound in conscience to obey it or not" (Id.).

56 Id. at 22.

57 Id.

58 Thomas Aquinas, Summa Theologica, at i–ii. 96.2, quoted in Maritain, supra note 51, at 168.

59 Id. For a discussion of the Thomistic perspective on law as applied to abortion, see M. Cathleen Kaveny, "Toward a Thomistic Perspective on Abortion and the Law in Contemporary America," The Thomist, pgs. 343–96 (1991).

60 D'Entrèves, "The Case for Natural Law Re-Examined," at 39 (stating "no lesser authority than Professor Maritain").

61 Id. at 47 (quoting Leo Strauss, Natural Right and History 9 [U. of Chicago Press, 1953]).

62 See Stout, supra note 2 at 220–21.

63 Maritain, supra note 51, at 91.

64 Id. at 91.

65 Id. at 91–92. See also d'Entrèves, Natural Law 40–41, supra note 21 (also stressing "inclination").

66 Maritain, supra note 51, at 93–94. He cites as one rudimentary truth that "[taking] a man's life is not like taking another animal's life." Id. at 93.

67 See Ramsey, supra note 17, at 215–23.

68 Maritain, supra note 51, at 90.

69 See Alasdair MacIntyre, After Virtue 51–78 (2d ed., U. of Notre Dame Press, 1984).

70 D'Entrèves, "The Case for Natural Law Re-Examined," at 39.

71 Maritain, supra note 51, at 82.

72 Id. In effect, he is here criticizing not only the Enlightenment formulation of rights, but the parallel and aggressive Baconian approach to nature, which had replaced the Aristotelian respect for beings in their essence with a Reason that conquers and subdues. D'Entrèves draws that analogy explicitly in Natural Law (1951). Grotius is cited as the first promulgator of a natural law wholly premised on Enlightenment rationalism—a secular natural law that would remain true "even if God did not exist," so great was the capacity of unaided natural reason. This was clearly a departure from medieval natural law theorists, who would never have so completely separated natural law from theology, thereby separating what Aquinas and the later Schoolmen had taken pains to join (id. at 52) when they reconciled Aristotle with Christianity. Enlightenment natural law, moreover, was so determined to celebrate the capacity of human "geometrizing" reason that it also rejected the Aristotelian attention

to the historical world of actual, factual reality. Hence, "[i]f natural law consists in a set of rules which are absolutely valid, its treatment must be based upon an internal coherence of necessity. In order to be a science, law must not depend on experience, but on definitions, not on facts, but on logical deductions. . . . Such a science must be constructed by leaving aside all that undergoes change and varies from place to place." *Id.* at 53. The specifically Enlightenment version of natural law formed the basis of Langdell's assertion that law was a science; when Holmes asserted the role of "experience," he was not necessarily rejecting the medieval (Aristotelian) conception of natural law, but only the particular, arguably distorted, form it took during the Enlightenment. On Langdell, Holmes, and law as "science," *see* S. Presser & J. Zainaldin, *Law and Jurisprudence in American History: Cases and Materials* 712–34 (2d ed., West Pub. Co., 1989).

73   Maritain, *supra* note 51, at 83.

74   *Id.* D'Entrèves made essentially the same point in his book, emphasizing the contractarian nature of the political theory that thereby evolved, its basic features shared by Hobbes, Locke, and Kant—Hobbes simply drove the point, relentlessly, to its logical end-point. *Natural Law, supra* note 21, at 55–57. On Hobbes, *see* Mensch & Freeman, *supra* note 41, at 585–600. D'Entrèves also points to the implicit radicalism of the Enlightenment rights formulation. *See supra* at 57–61. D'Entrèves is less unequivocally critical of the Enlightenment than is Maritain, however. *See generally id.* at 48–62.

75   *See* d'Entrèves, "The Case for Natural Law Re-Examined," at 41–45.

76   John T. Noonan, Jr., "*Tokos* and *Atokion*: An Examination of Natural Law Reasoning Against Usury and Against Contraception," 10 Nat. L.F. 215 (1965).

77   *Id.* at 224, 229–31.

78   *Id.* at 224.

79   *Id.* at 222–23.

80   *Id.* at 233.

81   *Id.* at 224–25, 234–35.

82   *Id.* at 235.

83   *Id.*

84   John T. Noonan, Jr., "Abortion and the Catholic Church: A Summary History," 12 Nat. L.F. 85 (1967).

85   *Id.* at 125.

86   *Id.* at 126.

87   *Id.* at 128–29.

88   *Id.* at 129.

89   *Id.* at 126.

90   *Id.* at 121–25. There was vigorous debate even about such a limited exception and about whether "intention" was really a proper basis for distinction. *Id.*

91   *Id.* at 124–25.

92   *But see* Robert George, "Human Flourishing as a Criterion of Morality: A Critique of Perry's Naturalism," 63 Tulane L. Rev. 1455, 1464–74 (1989).

93   Noonan, *supra* note 84, at 131.

94   John O'Connor, On Humanity and Abortion, 13 Nat. L.F. 127 (1968).

95   *Id.* at 130–31.

96   Id. at 131.

97   Margaret Mead, "Some Anthropological Considerations Concerning Natural Law," 6 Nat. L.F. 51, 52 (1961).

98   O'Connor, *supra* note 94, at 131.

99   Id. at 131–33.

100 John T. Noonan, Jr., "Deciding Who Is Human," 13 Nat. L.F. 134 (1968).

101 Id. at 137.

102 Noonan, *supra* note 85, at 131.

103 Noonan, *supra* note 100, at 138.

104 Id. at 140.

105 John T. Noonan, Jr., "Book Review," 7 Nat. L.F. 169 (1962) (reviewing Hart, *The Concept of Law*).

106 John T. Noonan, Jr., *Persons and Masks of the Law* 111 (Farrar, Straus & Giroux, 1976) (analyzing Palsgraf v. Long Island RR, 248 N.Y. 839, 162 N.E. 99 (1928)). This is an elegant depiction, using the famous *Palsgraf* case, of the process by which the legal system depersonalizes the plaintiff. Noonan also describes the number of deaths and injuries that occurred each year from the operation of the railroads—a statistically necessary sacrifice if the railroads were to keep running. Id. at 129–30.

107 *See* chap. 8, *infra*.

108 John Rawls, "Distributive Justice: Some Addenda," 13 Nat. L.F. 51 (1968).

109 Robert Nozick, "Moral Complications and Moral Structures," 13 Nat. L.F. 1 (1968).

110 Maritain, *supra* note 51, at 83. There is clearly a revival of interest in the natural law tradition in moral philosophy. *See, e.g.*, John Finnis, *Natural Law and Natural Rights* (Oxford U. Press, 1980); Russell Hittinger, *A Critique of the New Natural Law Theory* (U. of Notre Dame Press, 1987); MacIntyre, *supra* note 69; and even in mainstream legal thought, *see* Lloyd L. Weinreb, *Natural Law and Justice* (Harvard U. Press, 1987). For a variety of contemporary views, *see generally* "Natural Law Symposium," 38 Cleveland State L. Rev. 1–250 (1990).

111 The utilitarian side is realized most fully, in legal thought, in the "law and economics" school. *See* Richard A. Posner, "The Ethical and Political Basis of the Efficiency Norm in Common Law Adjudication," 8 Hofstra L. Rev. 487 (1980). *See generally* Posner, *Economic Analysis of Law* (3d ed., Little, Brown, 1986).

112 *E.g.*, Ronald Dworkin, *Taking Rights Seriously* (Harvard U. Press, 1977). At the extreme, however, they become (conservative?) libertarians. *E.g.*, Robert Nozick, *Anarchy, State, and Utopia* (Basic Books, 1974).

113 The most celebrated of such in the 1970s was John Rawls, *A Theory of Justice* (Belknap Press, 1971), which sought to combine Kantianism with the contractarian tradition to defeat utilitarianism. Rawls's initial and ambitious aim was the alchemical one of turning procedure (contracting) into substance (morality), but he gradually yielded to the fuzzy reality of intuitionism. For a good critique, *see* Robert Paul Wolff, *Understanding Rawls* (Princeton U. Press, 1977).

114 Louis Midgley, "Karl Barth and Moral Natural Law: The Anatomy of a Debate," 13 Nat. L.F. 108 (1968).

115 Id. at 123–26.

3   *Protestant Ethics: The Legacy of Barth and Bonhoeffer*

1   *See* Eberhard Jungel, *Karl Barth: A Theological Legacy* 25–26 (Westminster Press, 1986) (describing the state of Karl Barth's theology when he took part in drafting the Barmen Declaration). Meeting in Barmen on May 31, 1934, the first synod of the Confessing Church adopted the Barmen Theological Declaration, written principally by Barth. Barth refused to take the unconditional oath of loyalty to the führer, which led to his dismissal from the chair of systematic theology at Bonn; although he successfully appealed the dismissal, he was pensioned off, and German publication of his works was prohibited. Following his June 1935 expulsion from Germany, he returned to Basel, where he continued to oppose Hitler and produce as well his monumental works in theology, which included the multivolume *Church Dogmatics*. *Id.* at 26. For a description of (Calvinist) Barth's relationship to the more hesitant Lutherans, *see* Ronald Thiemann, *Constructing a Public Theology: The Church in a Pluralist Culture* 75–79 (Westminster/John Knox Press, 1991).

2   Eberhard Bethge, *Dietrich Bonhoeffer: Man of Vision, Man of Courage* 296–97 (trans. Eric Mosbacher et al., Harper & Row, 1970) (quoting Barmen Declaration).

3   Edwin H. Robertson, *The Shame and the Sacrifice: The Life and Martyrdom of Dietrich Bonhoeffer* 117 (Collier Books, 1988) (quoting Barmen Declaration).

4   *See* Frederick O. Bonkovsky, "The German State and Protestant Elites," in *The German Church Struggle and the Holocaust* 124, 138–39 (ed. Franklin H. Littell & Hubert G. Locke, Wayne State U. Press, 1974). On Barmen, *see also* Eberhard Bethge, "Troubled Self-Interpretation and Uncertain Reception in the Church Struggle," *id.* at 167, and Arthur C. Cochrane, "The Message of Barmen for Contemporary Church History," in *id.* at 185.

5   *See* Barth, "NO!: Answer to Emil Brunner," in Emil Brunner, *Natural Theology* 65, 96 (trans. Peter Fraenkel, Centenary Press, 1946). *See also* Barth, *The Church and the Political Problem of Our Day* (Scribner's, 1939); *The German Church Conflict* (John Knox Press, 1965); Jørgen Glenthøj, "Karl Barth and the German Salute," 32 J. Church & State 309 (1990).

6   On the institutional failure of the German churches, both Protestant and Catholic, *see* Sarah Gordon, *Hitler, Germans and the "Jewish Question"* 246–62 (Princeton U. Press, 1984); J. S. Conway, "The Churches," in *The Holocaust: Ideology, Bureaucracy, and Genocide* 199 (ed. Henry Friedlander and Sybil Milton, Kraus International, 1980) [hereinafter *Holocaust*]; Beate Ruhm Von Oppen, "The Intellectual Resistance," in *Holocaust*, at 207; E. Wolf, "Political and Moral Motives Behind the Resistance," in *The German Resistance to Hitler* 193, 196–227 (U. of California Press, 1970). For more encyclopedic coverage, see J. S. Conway, *The Nazi Persecution of the Churches, 1933–45* (Basic Books, 1968); *German Church Struggle, supra* note 4; *see also* Richard Gutteridge, *The German Evangelical Church and the Jews, 1879–1950* (Barnes & Noble, 1976).

7   *See* Jungel, *supra* note 1. See also Clifford Green, *Karl Barth: Theologian of Freedom* 20 (Collins Liturgical Publications, 1989). Barth's one regret in relation to Barmen was the failure to make solidarity with the Jews a "decisive feature" of the text. *Id.*

8   A singular resource available to those who wish to learn about Bonhoeffer

is the 836-page biography by his friend Bethge, *supra* note 2. For an introduction to Bonhoeffer himself, *see* Dietrich Bonhoeffer, *The Cost of Discipleship* (trans. R. Fuller, 2d ed., Macmillan, 1959), through which one can glimpse the intensity and commitment of his faith. *See also Letters and Papers from Prison* (3d ed., Macmillan, 1967), which speak for themselves, and his posthumous *Ethics* (Macmillan, 1955). For an uncanny call for Americans to look to Bonhoeffer and Albert Camus for inspiration once the religious boom of the 1950s had subsided, *see* Peter Berger, "Camus, Bonhoeffer and the World Come of Age— II," 76 *Christian Century* 450 (1959). Sociologist Berger is the coauthor of the often-cited Berger & Thomas Luckmann, *The Social Construction of Reality* (Doubleday, 1966). For a sampling of the vast literature on Bonhoeffer and the ethical implications of his life and thought, *see A Bonhoeffer Legacy: Essays in Understanding* (ed. A. J. Klassen, W. B. Eerdmans, 1981); James H. Burtness, *Shaping the Future: The Ethics of Dietrich Bonhoeffer* (Fortress Press, 1985); *Ethical Responsibility: Bonhoeffer's Legacy to the Churches* (ed. John D. Godsey & Geoffrey B. Kelly, E. Mellen Press, 1981); Ernst Feil, *The Theology of Dietrich Bonhoeffer* (Fortress Press, 1985); Robin Lovin, *Christian Faith and Public Choices: The Social Ethics of Barth, Brunner and Bonhoeffer* 126–78 (Fortress Press, 1984); *New Studies in Bonhoeffer's Ethics* (ed. William J. Peck, E. Mellen Press, 1987). There is reason to believe that the legacy of Bonhoeffer played a significant role in sustaining the religious resistance in East Germany that led to the dramatic collapse of the Communist regime in 1989. It is more than fortuitous that the roundtable discussions that paved the way for new government began at a recently constructed Protestant conference center in East Berlin called the Dietrich-Bonhoeffer-Haus. *See* Richard Pierard, "Religion and the East German Revolution," 32 J. *Church & State* 501, 505 (1990). On the political role of the East German Evangelical Church, *see generally* John Burgess, "Church-State Relations in East Germany: The Church as a 'Religious' and 'Political' Force," 32 J. *Church & State* 17 (1990).

9   *See* George Armstrong Kelly, *Politics and Religious Consciousness in America* (Transaction Books, 1984), at 156–57. For a similarly critical account of 1950s American Protestantism and its consequent unreadiness for Bonhoeffer's thought, *see* Martin E. Marty, "Introduction," in *The Place of Bonhoeffer: Problems and Possibilities in His Thought* 9, 18–20 (ed. Martin E. Marty, SCM Press, 1962).

10   Kelly, *supra* note 9, at 156–57.

11   *See* Louis Midgley, "Karl Barth and Moral Natural Law: The Anatomy of a Debate," 13 *Nat. L.F.* 108, 113–16 (1968).

12   *Id.* at 116–21.

13   Thiemann, *supra* note 1, at 79.

14   Peter L. Berger, "The Social Reality of Religion" 79 (1967), quoted in Kelly, *supra* note 9, at 160.

15   *See infra,* chap. 6.

16   *Id.*

17   *See* Garry Wills, *Under God: Religion and American Politics* 89 (Simon & Schuster, 1990). Wills's particular, yet representative, examples are historians Henry Steele Commager and Arthur Schlesinger, Jr. *See id.* at 86–93. A striking example of such "serene provincialism" is the treatment of religion in that bastion of literary sensibility, the *New York Times Book Review.* The December 2, 1990, issue

offers us the "best" (14) and most "notable" (309) books of 1990. Of the 323 titles listed, only six of the "notable" ones (and none of the "best") were in the category "Religion," the same number as "Science Fiction" or "Spies and Thrillers." By way of comparison, the category "Autobiography and Biography" contains fifty-one entries, many of whose subjects are so obscure as to be esoteric. Of the six titles actually listed under "Religion," none is a theological work. Two are about the politics of the Catholic church, one offers a sociological profile of American Catholics, and another is from the "Bible as literature" school, coming with the imprimatur of the elite critic Harold Bloom. *Id.* at 69. Two of the books, while not works of theology, share our perspective about the importance of religion as such in American life. One is Wills *supra*; the other is Robert Coles, *The Spiritual Life of Children* (Houghton Mifflin, 1990).

For Coles, our "cosmological yearnings" may actually offer "a little help in knowing what this life is about," for "the issue is the nature of our predicament as human beings, young or old—and the way our minds deal with that predicament, from the earliest years to the final breath" (at 7). He therefore regards it as "particularly ironic to find both Freudian and Marxist thought so arrogantly abusive when the subject of religion comes up" (at 7–8). And arrogance and abuse are just what one finds in the same *New York Times Book Review* when it offers a secular liberal review of the "fundamentalist" publishing scene, which lumps together all manner of various strands of religious belief to take a lot of cheap shots. *See* Robert Jay Lifton & Charles Strozier, "Waiting for Armageddon," *New York Times Book Review*, Aug. 12, 1990, at 1, 24–25. For a sampling of the critical response elicited, *see* "Letters," *New York Times Book Review*, Sept. 9, 1990, at 46. Ironically, if the thousands of books sold in "religious" stores were counted in the weekly tabulations, they would probably dominate the *Times*'s best-seller list.

18   *See* Elizabeth Mensch & Alan Freeman, "A Republican Agenda for Hobbesian America?" 41 *U. Fla. L. Rev.* 581, 587–88, 587 n.14 (1989). Again, note the link between Baconian rationalism and the rationalism of Enlightenment versions of natural law, as in Grotius. *See* A. P. d'Entrèves, *Natural Law: An Introduction to Legal Philosophy* 50 (Hutchinson's U. Library, 1951).

19   Karl Barth, 3 *Church Dogmatics*, pt. 3, at 124 (J & T. Clark, 1960).

20   *See* Mensch & Freeman, *supra* note 18, at 587–88, 587 n.14. More specifically, Aquinas had sought to reconcile notions of natural law, drawn largely from the Romans, and the Aristotelian conception of both politics and nature, with the Augustinian perception that human sin renders the Earthly City naught but illusion and vanity. *See* d'Entrèves, *supra* note 18, at 36–37. Aquinas himself insisted that "[i]f 'Grace does not abolish Nature,' neither does nature abolish grace"—the law of nature is "only a step, although a necessary step, towards perfection." D'Entrèves observes that the "proud spirit of modern rationalism is lacking." *Id.* at 45. Nevertheless, the harmony Aquinas sought to establish between human and Christian values was bound to be unstable; and the Reformation was a reassertion of the Augustinian side of that unstable medieval "harmony." *See, e.g.*, Perry Miller, *The New England Mind* 3–34 (Macmillan, 1939).

21   Karl Llewellyn, for one, became acutely aware of this correspondence: "I am

therefore driven back upon faith, as conditioned by temperament. The important factors of temperament seem to be: a rebelliousness; an optimism and interest in underdogs; an insistence on seeing clean. . . . But it promptly appears that the rebelliousness does have something to work on. I can meet the Lord without reservation, and just merge into the work He seems to want; and do it for us and Him. But I don't want any intermediaries. It has taken me thirty years to get here. And the Lord understands the stiff neck quite as well as He understands the drive for craftsmanship and the fact that only by driving for technique could I have reached the deeper things. . . . Yet the whole job is a sort of rebel job. It is like appeal[ing] to Jesus before there was Paul. It is essential heresy, in that I am trying to do a Paul my way. Because what Paul did was to put structure, carrying-power, under Jesus' teachings. I find I feel about Paul the same way I feel about great lawyers whom I think to have gone sometimes off the track. He over-intellectualized, so far as he wrote. . . . Let me then stay as close as I may to Jesus and to Paul's living rather than—or better, together with—his writing. With this, 'rebel' and 'non-rebel' begin to line up. I observe with amusement that I am duplicating in religion a twenty-year road in legal work. But I think the Lord is equally amused. He never let me meet Him until I had cut under 'authoritative' hogwash in law, and then gone on and sweated into contact with the real tradition. He was out of sight and hearing while I was merely fighting authoritative nonsense, or trying to 'construct' nonsense of my own. It was only when I began to feel for the real underneathness, as vouched in the tradition, and then to work toward giving workable form to that, that the Lord let me meet Him. As if He had left some jobs of creation over for His creatures to do, and watched to say 'Good kid'; 'Now go on and do the next one better.' . . . I don't trust any intermediary machinery. My whole contact with the Lord depends on having gotten down under machinery, and on finding that when I managed to start working the real juice of human need into more effective machinery, the Lord stepped in and took over. But direct. So I can't go through any Church that won't leave me that direct contact, even if I do have to join up." Karl Llewellyn, Position re: Religion (1943) (Karl Llewellyn Papers, University of Chicago Law School). We are grateful to Michael McConnell for providing us with a transcription of the document.

On the importance of religion in Llewellyn's life, see William L. Twining, Karl Llewellyn and the Realist Movement 87–90, 123–24, 423–24 (Weidenfeld & Nicolson, 1973).

22 For a clear statement of the centrality of that message, see Barth, 3 Church Dogmatics, pt. 3, at 124; Rumscheidt, "The First Commandment as Axiom for Theology: A Model for the Unity of Dogmatics and Ethics," at 143, in Theology Beyond Christendom: Essays on the Centenary of the Birth of Karl Barth, May 10, 1886 (ed. John Thompson, Pickwick Publications, 1986). The relation between the critical mode and the affirmation of "God is God" is clarified in such Barthian passages as: "In announcing the limitation of the known world by another that is unknown, the Gospel does not enter into competition with the many attempts to disclose within the known world some more or less unknown and higher form of existence and to make it accessible to men. The Gospel

is not a truth among other truths. Rather, it sets a question-mark against all truths. The Gospel is not the door but the hinge. The man who apprehends its meaning is removed from all strife, because he is engaged in a strife with the whole, even with existence itself. Anxiety concerning the victory of the Gospel—that is, Christian Apologetics—is meaningless, because the Gospel is the victory by which the world is overcome. By the Gospel the whole concrete world is dissolved and established." Barth, *The Epistle to the Romans* 35 (6th ed., Oxford U. Press, 1933). For a brief, yet evocative, portrait of Barth drawn from personal experience and emphasizing the distinction between "religion" and "the Word," see Milner Ball, *The Word and the Law* 76–82 (University of Chicago Press, 1993).

23   Rumscheidt, *supra* note 22, at 150–51.

24   Jungel, *supra* note 1, at 32 (quoting *Karl Barth Der Römerbrief* 7 [1919]). Barth's later work could be described to some extent as a move from dialectics to assertion, yet it never became undialectical. *See generally id.* at 33–51.

25   *Id.* at 66 (quoting Barth, *Epistle to the Romans* 10 [2d ed., 1922]).

26   *Id.* at 50. In *Epistle to the Romans*, Barth, citing Kierkegaard, said that "Jesus as the Christ . . . can be comprehended *only* as Paradox" (at 29) (emphasis added). Thus, "[a]s Christ, Jesus is the plane which lies beyond our comprehension. The plane which is known to us, he intersects vertically, from above." *Id.* This is somewhat different geometrizing than that associated with Enlightenment rationalism and Enlightenment versions of natural law.

27   *See* Jungel, *supra* note 1, at 67.

28   *Id.* at 68.

29   *Id.* at 67–68. For the continued difficulty of describing the relation between motion and rest, compare Morris Kline, *Mathematics in Western Culture* 404–5 (Oxford U. Press, 1964) with Gary Zukav, *The Dancing Wu Li Masters: An Overview of the New Physics* 122–29 (Bantam Books, 1979). *See also* Barth, *Epistle to the Romans*, at 46, for the Platonic assertion that "behind the visible there lies the invisible universe which is the Origin of all concrete things." For Barth, however, that recognition never becomes simple idealism. For example, referring to the "irony of intelligence," he states: "We know that God is He whom we do not know, and that our ignorance is precisely the problem and the source of our knowledge. We know that God is the Personality which we are not, and [that] this lack of Personality is precisely what dissolves and establishes our personality. The recognition of the absolute heteronomy under which we stand is itself an autonomous recognition; and this is precisely *that which may be known of God.* When we rebel, we are in rebellion not against what is foreign to us but against that which is most intimately ours, not against what is removed from us but against that which lies at our hands." *Id.* at 45–46.

30   For the following discussion we are indebted to C. Rasmussen, "Karl Barth on St. Anselm: A Theological Response to the Dilemma of Liberal Theory" (unpublished manuscript on file with authors). On Barth and Anselm, *see also* Harold Nebelsick, "Karl Barth's Understanding of Science," in *Theology Beyond Christendom* 165, 193–205, *supra* note 22.

31   Rasmussen, *supra* note 30, at 17.

32   *Id.* at 20.

33 This particular analogy is ours. For a discussion of the definition of "infinity," see Peter Wolff, *Breakthroughs in Mathematics* 129–30 (New American Library ed., 1970): "An infinite quantity is not enumerable—it cannot be counted. And conversely, anything which can be counted—any quantity, no matter how large, to which a number can be assigned—is by that token not infinite. No number can ever be said to be infinite, for every number always has a next one; hence the former number cannot be called infinite, since there is at least one number greater than it. In fact, a good definition of infinity states that infinity is larger than any number you may name and that consequently, infinity itself is not a number." *See also* Kline, *supra* note 29, at 395–409.

34 *Compare:* "God is He Whom we do not know," an "ignorance" that is then both "the problem" and the "source of our knowledge." *See supra* note 29 (quoting Barth).

35 Barth, 3 *Church Dogmatics*, pt. 3 at 127.

36 *Id.* Barth was not denying the existence of order in the natural world. He affirmed: "It is not chance which rules but constancy, not caprice but faithfulness. All occurrence, inasmuch as it takes place at all, takes place within the framework of a definite rule." *Id.* at 128. Nevertheless, he insisted, "[w]e will acknowledge this the more seriously and proclaim it the more effectively, the more scrupulously we cease trying to equate even one of the laws known to us, even the law which we perceive with what we imagine to be the greatest clarity and certainty, with the order and form or constance and faithfulness which rule in that causal nexus, with the rule to which all occurrence within it is subject. Only as we cease doing that do we give evidence that in the laws perceived and described and formulated by us we are aiming at real law; at the ordering and forming which takes place in the occurrence itself and not simply in our experience and thinking, which is not merely an ordering and forming but also an effecting and calling forth of the actual occurrence itself. It is remarkable enough that the less we believe that the laws known to us have anything at all to do with the real foreordination of creaturely occurrence, the more they really have to do with it, the more clearly they testify by their own particular, that is, noetic, clarity and certainty that there are indeed valid laws, that in the causal nexus in which each individual activity has its place and by which it is conditioned there does rule a unitary and—we can now legitimately use the description of Goethe and say—an 'eternal' law. . . ." *Id.*

Barth's insights about the subject/object problem in Enlightenment science bear a close resemblance to those of America's greatest theologian, Jonathan Edwards, whose analysis of Newtonian physics and Lockean epistemology was more sophisticated and "modern" than that of any of his eighteenth-century contemporaries. As both Barth and Edwards understood, the world is more relentlessly "objective" than any human statement of its laws can describe. *See* Perry Miller, *Jonathan Edwards* 43–99 (Meridian Books, 1949).

37 For a full discussion of Barth's notion of theology as science *see* Nebelsick, *supra* note 30, at 165–214.

38 *Id.* at 197.

39 *See* Werner Heisenberg, *Physics and Beyond: Encounters and Conversations* 205, 210–12 (trans. Arnold Pomerans, Harper & Row, 1971). Barth had not realized the

parallels between his theology and modern physics, assuming natural science remained struck in its "premodern" positivist mode. Barth, after all, was still battling the tendency of "liberal" religion to humble itself before the arrogant rationalism of post-Enlightenment scientific rationalism. Given that misunderstanding, he declined to join the Göttingen Theologian-Physicists conversations (1949–61), despite the efforts of his friend Gunter Howe, and lost the opportunity to engage Heisenberg, who was a member of the group. See Nebelsick, supra note 30, at 199–200. Heisenberg himself saw in the variety of religious formulations "the clear impression that all such formulations try to express man's relatedness to a central order." Heisenberg, supra, at 214. With respect to ethics, moreover, the meaning of that "central order" was clear. Secular "pragmatism" offered little on its own: "If we ask Western man what is good and what is evil, what is worth striving for and what has to be rejected, we shall find time and again that his answers reflect the ethical norms of Christianity even when he has long since lost all touch with Christian images and parables. If the magnetic force that has guided this particular compass—and what else was its source but the central order?—should ever become extinguished, terrible things may happen to mankind, far more terrible even than concentration camps and atom bombs." Id. at 217. For an account of Heisenberg's own ambiguous (at best) relationship with Nazism, see David Cassidy, Uncertainty: The Life and Science of Werner Heisenberg (W. H. Freeman, 1992), at 418–522 (he "refused to leave Germany during the 12 years of Nazi rule"). Placing him in context, however, Cassidy notes the reality that "scientists everywhere, no matter how devoted they may be to the search for truth and universal understanding, will work for their governments, whether worthy or loathsome, and that many will serve their governments by fashioning the weapons of war and destruction." Id. at 522.

40   Nebelsick, supra note 30, at 174.

41   Id. at 182–83. No science could be more dialectical, since God is both its object and subject: "God may be known only as he reveals himself. He is both the object of knowledge and the means by which knowledge of himself may be gained." Id. at 199. See also id. at 203.

42   Jungel, supra note 1, at 59 (quoting Barth, "Biblical Questions, Insights and Vistas," in The Word of God and the Word of Man 66 [1928]). Thus, Barth read the Bible as self-demythologizing: "The biblical piety is not really pious; one must rather characterize it as a well-considered, qualified worldliness." Id. In addition, Barth believed: "Jesus simply ha[d] nothing to do with religion. The meaning of his life is the actuality of that which is not actually present in any religion—the actuality of the unapproachable, the unreachable, the incomprehensible, the realization of the possibility, which is not a matter of speculation: 'Behold, I make all things new!'" Id. (quoting Barth, supra, at 88).

43   See Thiemann, supra note 1, at 81 (quoting Schleiermacher).

44   Id.

45   See Brunner, "Nature and Grace," in Natural Theology, supra note 5, at 15.

46   See Barth, supra note 5, at 65 (answering Brunner).

47   Brunner, supra note 45, at 28–30.

48   Id. at 31.

49   *Id.* at 36–37.

50   *Id.* at 39–40.

51   *Id.*

52   Barth, "Answer to Emil Brunner," *supra* note 5, at 96. On the importance of this doctrine, *see generally* Thiemann, *Revelation and Theology* 9–111 (U. of Notre Dame Press, 1985).

53   *Id.* This point is often obscured both by Protestant critics of natural law and by Thomists who want to make it more accessible to non-Christians. Calvin considered it axiomatic when he used the term *lex naturae*, although its axiomatic status was of course lost during the Enlightenment. *See* Thiemann, *supra* note 52 at 10–12, dealing with "knowledge" of revelation.

54   Barth, "Answer to Emil Brunner," *supra* note 5, at 95.

55   *Id.* at 105.

56   *See* Jungel, *supra* note 1, at 54–61. *See also* E. Feil, *The Theology of Dietrich Bonhoeffer* 161–64 (trans. Rumscheidt, Fortress Press, 1985) (on Barth's concept of religion).

57   On Bonhoeffer's response to Nietzsche, *see* Bethge, *supra* note 2 at 84–86, 772–73. On Nietzsche, *see* Alasdair MacIntyre, *After Virtue: A Study in Moral Theory* 110–20, 256–59 (U. of Notre Dame Press, 1984). Nietzschean criticism was effective in overcoming the constraints of Enlightenment rationalist complacency, which would otherwise engulf Christianity. The challenge remained, however, to reclaim Christianity from Nietzschean criticism. For Bonhoeffer, this necessarily meant affirming the "this-worldliness" of Christianity: "The Christian is not a '*homo religiosus*' but simply a man, as Jesus was a man . . . I don't mean the shallow and banal this-worldliness of the enlightened, the busy, the comfortable, or the lascivious, but the profound this-worldliness characterized by discipline, and the constant knowledge of death and resurrection." *Letters and Papers from Prison* 201 (Macmillan, 1953). *See also* Burtness, *supra* note 8, 106–7, 46; R. Lovin, *supra* note 8, at 126–27, 139–43; James W. Woelfel, *Bonhoeffer's Theology: Classical and Revolutionary* 68–71 (Abingdon Press, 1970).

58   *See*, e.g., Burtness, *supra* note 8 at 43–51, 54–59; Jungel, *supra* note 1, at 45. Similarly: "Who is my neighbour? Does this question admit of any answer? Is it my kinsman, my compatriot, my brother Christian, or my enemy? . . . The answer is: 'You are the neighbour. Go along and try to be obedient by loving others.' Neighbourliness is not a quality in other people, it is simply their claim on ourselves. Every moment and every situation challenges us to action and to obedience. We have literally no time to sit down and ask ourselves whether so-and-so is our neighbour or not. We must get into action and obey—we must behave like a neighbour to him." Bonhoeffer, *supra* note 8, at 67–68 (the context is that of the lawyer who insists on a preliminary fuss about membership in the "neighbor" category before he can obey the commandment; *see* Luke 10:25–29). Likewise: "This concept of correspondence to reality certainly needs to be defined more exactly. It would be a complete and a dangerous misunderstanding if it were to be taken in the sense of that 'servile conviction in the face of the fact' that Nietzsche speaks of, a conviction which yields to every powerful pressure, which on principle justifies success, and which on every occasion chooses what is opportune as 'corresponding to reality.'

'Correspondence with reality' in this sense would be the contrary of responsibility; it would be irresponsibility. But the true meaning of correspondence with reality lies neither in this servility towards the factual nor yet in a principle of opposition to the factual, a principle of revolt against the factual in the name of some higher reality. Both extremes alike are very far removed from the essence of the matter. In action which is genuinely in accordance with reality there is an indissoluble link between the acknowledgement and the contradiction of the factual. The reason for this is that reality is first and last not lifeless; but it is the real man, the incarnate God. It is from the real man, whose name is Jesus Christ, that all factual reality derives its ultimate foundation and its ultimate annulment, its justification and its ultimate contradiction, its ultimate affirmation and its ultimate negation. To attempt to understand reality without the real man is to live in an abstraction to which the responsible man must never fall victim; it is to fail to make contact with reality in life; it is to vacillate endlessly between the extremes of servility and revolt in relation to the factual." *Ethics* 228.

59   Barth, 3 *Church Dogmatics*, pt. 4, at 9.
60   *Id.* at 7.
61   *Id.* at 9–10.
62   *Id.* at 10 (quoting Bonhoeffer).
63   *Id.* at 11.
64   *Id.*
65   *Id.* at 13.
66   *Id.*
67   *Id.* at 10–11. Barth explains: "At a safe distance from the ethical battlefield—like a staff officer of the Lord—he manipulates for himself and others a method of correct decisions—correct in the sense of the law. . . . He has in fact made God's will and command the prisoner of this law and his application of it. Casuistry is a mastering of the command and therefore of God Himself, which is certainly conceivable in every kind of philosophical and religious paganism, but is quite impossible in Christianity. Since this is incompatible with the knowledge of grace which God shows to men even in His command, it is a mastering of which a man who knows that he lives by God's grace will not make himself guilty. Casuistry is a violation of the divine mystery in the ethical event." *Id.* at 11.
68   *Id.* at 13. What is required is not "external conformity" but "genuine agreement." *Compare* A. P. d'Entrèves, "The Case for Natural Law Re-Examined," 1 *Nat. L.F.* 5 (1956), on the relation between outward conformity and inner conviction.
69   Barth, 3 *Church Dogmatics*, pt. 4, at 14.
70   *Id.*
71   *Id.* at 14–15 (quoting Bonhoeffer). Compare the legend of the Grand Inquisitor in Dostoyevsky's, *The Brothers Karamazov*. The Inquisitor, an aged cardinal of the church, confronts the Prisoner, who is Christ: "For fifteen centuries [the Inquisitor declares] we have been wrestling with thy freedom. . . . Instead of taking men's freedom from them, Thou didst make it greater than ever! Didst Thou forget that man prefers peace, and even death, to freedom of choice in

the knowledge of good and evil? Nothing is more seductive for man than his freedom of conscience, but nothing is a greater cause of suffering. And behold, instead of giving a firm foundation for setting the conscience of man at rest forever, Thou didst choose all that is exceptional, vague and enigmatic; Thou didst choose what was utterly beyond the strength of men, acting as though Thou didst not love them at all—Thou who didst come to give Thy life for them! Instead of taking possession of men's freedom, Thou didst increase it, and burdened the spiritual kingdom of mankind with its sufferings forever. Thou didst desire man's free love, that he should follow Thee freely, enticed and taken captive by Thee. In place of the rigid ancient law, man must hereafter with free heart decide for himself what is good and what is evil, having only Thy image before him as his guide. But didst Thou not know that he would at last reject even Thy image and Thy truth, if he is weighed down with the fearful burden of free choice? They will cry aloud at last that the truth is not in Thee, for they could not have been left in greater confusion and suffering than Thou has caused, laying upon them so many unanswerable cares and unanswerable problems. So that, in truth, Thou didst Thyself lay the foundation for the destruction of Thy kingdom." Paul Louis Lehmann, *Ethics in a Christian Context* 326–27 (SCM Press, 1963) (quoting *The Brothers Karamazov* 276–80). This captures the dilemma of the Reformation. Lehmann's contrast is between an ethics of rationalist prescription and *koinonia*, the fellowship-creating presence of Christ: "The ethical reality of the church is the building up of itself in love. . . ." *Id.* at 54. *See generally id.* at 45–73.

72   See Bonhoeffer, *Cost of Discipleship*, at 43–47. *See also* Robertson, *supra* note 3 at 143–48.

73   See Bonhoeffer, *Ethics*, at 197–98.

74   For an account of Bonhoeffer's family background and education, *see* Bethge, *supra* note 2, at 3–64.

75   See Burtness, *supra* note 8, at 149–56.

76   Bonhoeffer, *Ethics*, 240. *See id.* at 231–44; Lovin, *supra* note 8, at 5; J. Woelfel, *supra* note 57, at 153–54. For a good example of Bonhoeffer's disagreement with Kant, see his essay, "What Is Meant by 'Telling the Truth'?" in *Ethics*, at 326–34.

77   See Bonhoeffer, *Letters and Papers from Prison*, 202; Woelfel, *supra* note 57, at 68–71.

78   See Woelfel, *supra* note 57, at 70–71. For a version of the myth, *see* I. D'Aulaire & E. P. D'Aulaire, *Book of Greek Myths* 140 (paperback ed., Doubleday, 1962).

79   Bonhoeffer, *Ethics* 106.

80   Burtness, *supra* note 8, at 106–7.

81   Bonhoeffer, *Ethics* 143–46.

82   See Burtness, *supra* note 8, at 70–71.

83   Bonhoeffer, *Letters and Papers from Prison* 195–96.

84   See Lovin, *supra* note 8, at 138–39.

85   Bonhoeffer, *Ethics* 221.

86   Bethge, *supra* note 2, at 559.

87   *Id.* (quoting Bonhoeffer's letter).

88   For a summary of Bonhoeffer's involvement in the "conspiratorial resistance," *see* Bethge, *supra* note 2, at 696–702. For the detail, *see id.* at 626–96. *See also* Robertson, *supra* note 3, at 156–58, 161, 199–201, 210–13, 218–20, 263–65.

89   Bonhoeffer, *Letters and Papers from Prison* 198.

90   Bonhoeffer, *Ethics* 166.

91   Bonhoeffer, *Letters and Papers from Prison* 210. This leads to Bonhoeffer's notion of the "church for others," which is basic to his ethical worldview: "The Church is the Church only when it exists for others. To make a start, it should give away all its property to those in need. The clergy must live solely on the free-will offerings of their congregations, or possibly engage in some secular calling. The Church must share in the secular problems of ordinary human life, not dominating, but helping and serving. It must tell men of every calling what it means to live in Christ, to exist for others. In particular, our own Church will have to take the field against the vices of hubris, power-worship, envy, and humbug, as the roots of all evil. It will have to speak of moderation, purity, trust, loyalty, constancy, patience, discipline, humility, contentment and modesty. It must not underestimate the importance of human example (which has its origin in the humanity of Jesus and is so important in Paul's teaching); it is not abstract argument, but example, that gives its word emphasis and power." *Id.* at 211. For an excellent and thorough account of Bonhoeffer's theology as developed in his prison writings, *see* Bethge, *supra* note 2, at 757–95.

92   *See* Paul Ramsey, "Jean-Paul Sartre: Sex in Being," in *Nine Modern Moralists*, 71–109 (Prentice-Hall, 1962).

93   Barth, 3 *Church Dogmatics*, pt. 3, at 346. Similarly, Barth says sarcastically, "[w]e cannot but admire the virile address and resolution" with which Sartre sets the question of evil behind him, and he calls Sartre the "most virile of modern existentialists." *Id.* at 339.

94   *Id.* at 346–47; *see also* Bonhoeffer, *Letters and Papers from Prison* 188–89.

95   Barth, 3 *Church Dogmatics*, at 340.

96   *Compare id.* at 348–56 (animals) *with id.* at 415–23 (abortion). With respect to animals, as is usually the case with Barth, the moral responsibility is a grave one: "And the nearness of the animal to man irrevocably means that when man kills beast he does something which is at least very similar to homicide. We must be very clear about this if we maintain that the lordship of man over animals carries with it the freedom to slaughter them. Those who do not hear the prior command to desist have certainly no right to affirm this freedom or cross the frontier disclosed at this point." *Id.* at 352–53.

  Thus, for Barth, "If there is a freedom of man to kill animals, this signifies in any case the adoption of a qualified and in some sense enhanced responsibility. . . . The slaying of animals is really possible only as an appeal to God's reconciling grace, as its representation and proclamation. It undoubtedly means making use of the offering of an alien and innocent victim and claiming its life for ours. Man must have good reasons for seriously making such a claim." *Id.* at 354–55. *See also* James F. Gustafson, *Protestant and Roman Catholic Ethics* 35–36 (U. of Chicago Press, 1978) (discussing Barth's treatment of the relationship between God, man, and nature).

97   Barth, 3 *Church Dogmatics*, pt. 4, at 417.

98   *Id.*

99   *Id.* at 417–18.

100   *Id.* at 417.

101   *Id.* at 418.

102   *Id.* at 420. *See also* Gustafson, *supra* note 96, at 30–31.

103   *See* Barth, 3 *Church Dogmatics*, pt. 4, at 417–21. On the dialectic of freedom and obedience in Barth's theological ethics, *see* Lovin, *supra* note 8, at 18–44. As to the particular freedom of women, Barth approved of feminist impatience with "typologies" of gender role that defined for women their special "nature." Barth ridiculed the way in which "contingent, schematic, conventional, literary and half-true indicatives" are turned into false "imperatives." Both men and women "will justifiably refuse to be addressed in this way." Barth, 3 *Church Dogmatics, supra* note 19, pt. 4, at 153. To that extent he fully agreed with Simone de Beauvoir, although he rejected the view that one could transcend sexual difference altogether (*id.* at 162), asserting that the difference was a constant question, and riddle; male and female should always be learning from one another. *Id.* at 167. He insisted on retaining a sequential ordering of male before female, but not as male "privilege or advantage" or "any kind of self-glorification," but as a special male obligation to, in humility, create conditions of freedom. *Id.* at 170.

104   Barth, 3 *Church Dogmatics*, pt. 4, at 419, 422–23.

105   Bonhoeffer, *Ethics*. Central to Bonhoeffer's ethics was his simultaneous rejection of (Kantian) rational moral absolutism and what he saw as its "existential" counterpart, radical individual subjectivized atomism: "The ethical, in this sense of the formal, the universally valid and the rational, contained no element of concretion, and it therefore inevitably ended in the total atomization of human society and of the life of the individual, in unlimited subjectivism and individualism. When the ethical is conceived without reference to any local or temporal relation, without reference to the question of its warrant or authority, without reference to the concrete, then life falls apart into an infinite number of unconnected atoms of time, and human society resolves itself into individual atoms of reason. It makes no practical difference whether one interprets the ethical as a purely formal universally valid principle or whether one refers it to the 'existential' decision which the individual takes completely anew at every separate 'moment.' The underlying factor is always that the ethical is destroyed by its being detached from its concrete relations. . . . [S]ociety consists solely in the concrete and infinitely manifold relationships of responsibility of men one for another." *Id.* at 272. On Bonhoeffer's notion of "responsibility," *see* Lovin, *supra* note 8, at 139–47.

106   Bonhoeffer, *Ethics* 131.

107   *Id.*

108   *Id.*

109   *Id.*

4   *The Fragile Umbrella of Pluralism: American Religion in the 1950s*

1   On churches as "mediating structures," *see* Peter L. Berger & Richard John Neuhaus, *To Empower People: The Role of Mediating Structures in Public Policy* 1–8, 26–34 (American Enterprise Institute for Public Policy Research, 1977); J. Philip

Wogaman, "The Church as Mediating Institution: Theological and Philosophical Perspective" and "The Church as Mediating Institution: Contemporary American Challenge," in *Democracy and Mediating Structures: A Theological Inquiry* 69–105 (ed. Michael Novak, American Enterprise Institute for Public Policy Research, 1980).

2   *See* Robert Wuthnow, *The Restructuring of American Religion: Society and Faith Since World War II*, at 26 (noting that church contributions increased by 64 percent while personal consumption increased by only 50 percent). Our debt to Wuthnow throughout this section will be apparent.

3   *Id.* at 36.

4   *Id.* at 17.

5   *Id.* at 15. In 1946, 66 percent of Americans attended services at least once a month, and 42 percent attended every week. *Id.* at 16.

6   *Id.* at 66.

7   Will Herberg, *Protestant-Catholic-Jew* 274 (Doubleday, 1955). *See* William G. McLoughlin, "Is There a Third Force in Christendom?" in *Religion in America* 47–48 (ed. William G. McLoughlin & Robert N. Bellah, Houghton Mifflin, 1968).

8   *See* Michael W. Hughey, *Civil Religion and Moral Order: Theoretical and Historical Dimensions* 143 (Greenwood Press, 1983). "Parsons echo[ed] Herberg . . . in arguing that the Three dominant 'faiths' of American society . . . have come to be integrated into a single socio-religious system [and that] . . . the basic value pattern common to all three faiths has been at least partially institutionalized at a higher level of generality." *Id.* (quoting Talcott Parsons, "Introduction to Max Weber," in *The Sociology of Religion* [1964]). The core value matrix was the Protestant one of responsibility for positive action in the world, the instrumental activism of ascetic Protestantism. Hughey's book explores the extent to which this was always the value system of *some* in American life (largely the successful WASPs of Main Street America and also of Parsons himself), but not of others. See, for example, Hughey's critique of Warner's more celebratory sociological description of the Memorial Day parade in Newburyport, *id.* at 109–23.

9   Peter L. Berger, *The Noise of Solemn Assemblies* (Doubleday, 1961).

10   Gibson Winter, *The Suburban Captivity of the Churches: An Analysis of Protestant Responsibility in the Expanding Metropolis* (Macmillan, 1962).

11   *See* Leonard I. Sweet, "The 1960's: The Crises of Liberal Christianity and the Public Emergence of Evangelism," in *Evangelicalism and Modern America* 36 (ed. George Marsden, W. B. Eerdmans, 1984).

12   This vividly assembled list is taken from William G. McLoughlin, "How Is America Religious?" in *Religion in America*, at ix. With respect to Billy Graham, his seeming blandness was deceptive, however; the same Graham who lined his platforms with celebrities—and was even scorned by his mentors for selling out to popularity, liberalism, and compromise—believed as fervently as one could in an errorless Bible, the Virgin Birth of Jesus, His death and resurrection, and the Second Coming. The lesson to be learned from Graham was skillful packaging. *See* Martin E. Marty, *Pilgrims in Their Own Land: 500 Years of Religion in America* 410–14 (Little, Brown, 1984). *See also*, on Graham's "sophistication," "obvious sincerity, his charismatic appeal, and his adroit salesmanship," McLoughlin, *supra* note 7, at 60–61.

13   Leo Ribuffo, *Right Center Left: Essays in American History* 60 (Rutgers U. Press, 1992).

14   Garry Wills, *Bare Ruined Choirs: Doubt, Prophecy, and Radical Religion* 260 (Double-day, 1972). Paradoxically, Wills's *Under God: Religion and American Politics* (Simon & Schuster, 1990) celebrates both the vitality of religion in American public life and the way in which the tradition of separation contributes to that vitality.

15   Wuthnow, *supra* note 2, at 44.

16   *Id.* at 46.

17   *Id.* at 48.

18   *Id.* at 49.

19   *Id.* at 50.

20   These themes resonate with religious discourse at the turn of the century, when religious leaders were describing their social role in relation to impending class warfare, also perceived as a period of moral crisis. *See* Elizabeth Mensch, "Religion, Revival and the Ruling Class: A Critical History of Trinity Church," 36 *Buffalo L. Rev.* 427, at 533 (1987).

21   *See* Wuthnow, *supra* note 2, at 58–60, 66–67. This was, of course, also the assumption of legal academics who turned to religion after the war.

22   *See supra* note 1.

23   Wuthnow, *supra* note 2, at 53.

24   *Id.* at 52.

25   *Id.* at 50.

26   *Id.* at 61.

27   *Id.* at 62–64. The same view dominated secular thought as well—for example, in Gunnar Myrdal's assumption that racism was basically a problem of attitude, a gap between America's core creed and its behavior that could be corrected with a change in attitude. *See An American Dilemma: The Negro Problem and American Democracy* (Harper & Bros., 1944). *See* Freeman, "Racism, Rights, and the Quest for Equality of Opportunity: A Critical Legal Essay," 23 *Harv. C.R.-C.L. L. Rev.* 295, 349–50 (1988). According to David W. Southern, close acquaintances of Myrdal could not talk him out of "his optimistic perception of social reform propelled by the 'American Creed.' . . . Myrdal asserted that if the discrepancy between the creed and the deed were exposed, it would die like a germ in powerful sunlight." Southern, *Gunnar Myrdal and Black-White Relations: The Use and Abuse of "An American Dilemma," 1944–1969* (Louisiana State University Press, 1987), at 32–34.

28   Wuthnow, *supra* note 2, at 15.

29   *Id.* at 81–82. Dean Acheson and President Harry Truman were unable to speak at the opening because of a snowstorm that day. *Id.*

30   *Id.* at 140–41. The older strict fundamentalism was viewed as lacking in "brotherliness." *Id.* at 173.

31   Such churches, however, were still sometimes viewed as too "bureaucratic" and too given to emphasizing "science, literature, and philosophy, rather than salvation." *Id.* at 176 (quoting a New York lawyer who was active in these evangelical movements). On the NAE, *see also* Martin E. Marty, *A Nation of Behavers* 86–88 (U. of Chicago Press, 1976).

32   Wuthnow, *supra* note 2, at 178.

33   *Id.* at 180. *See also* George Marsden, "Evangelicals and the Scientific Culture: An Overview," in *Religion and Twentieth-Century American Intellectual Life* (ed. Michael J.

Lacey, Cambridge U. Press, 1989), at 45–47. For a sympathetic account of the theological seriousness at a modern counterpart of those schools, Criswell College (an evangelical Bible school in Dallas), *see* Mike Bryan, *Chapter and Verse: A Skeptic Revisits Christianity* (1991).

34 Robert Wuthnow, *supra* note 2, at 180.

35 *See* Bendroth, "The Search for 'Women's Role' in American Evangelicalism, 1930–1980," in *Evangelicalism and Modern America* 123, at 132–34 (ed. George Marsden, W. B. Eerdmans, 1984).

36 Wuthnow, *supra* note 2, at 185–87.

37 *Id.* at 56–57, 140–41.

38 *Id.* at 140–41.

39 Paul Blanshard, *American Freedom and Catholic Power* (Beacon Press, 1949).

40 *See generally id.*; Wuthnow, *supra* note 2, at 74–77.

41 Catholics were solidly in the mainstream by 1976. Wuthnow, *supra* note 2, at 86–87.

42 Wills, *supra* note 14, at 42.

43 *Id.* at 24.

44 Wuthnow, *supra* note 2, at 61.

45 For a description of this turn in theology generally, *see* George A. Lindbeck, *The Nature of Doctrine: Religion and Theology in a Post Liberal Age* 19–25 (Westminster Press, 1984) (without specific reference to the 1950s as such).

46 Wuthnow, *supra* note 2, at 31.

47 *Id.* at 33–34.

48 *Id.* at 15.

49 Kenneth D. Wald, *Religion and Politics in the United States* 9 (St. Martin's Press, 1987).

50 Peter Berger has written with special perceptiveness on this subject, employing essentially an antitrust model. The move from "monopoly" (establishment) to a competitive "market" in religion creates conditions for a vigorous religious life, which is one reason why the United States is more "religious" than Europe. There, the old forms of establishment led to anticlericalism during the Enlightenment and a general sapping of religious spirit. The danger of the competitive model lies in a kind of consumerist "taste" mentality in religion—anything goes, so long as it sells, and churches will engage in intense efforts to do successful product differentiation, within a still essentially stabilized, standardized market. *See The Sacred Canopy* 137–48 (Doubleday, 1967). Writing in 1967, Berger was perhaps too pessimistic, or even cynical, in this respect. The current vitality of American religion is not just an expression of rampant individualism or consumer preference, but a complex interaction of individual and community, of personal choice and established tradition. To run the consumer model too far is to assimilate religion to the range of styles or experiences selected in the marketplace. This is what Lawrence Friedman does to describe the only form of religion that fits with his "republic of choice," with religion as no more than just another expression of personal autonomy and individual experience. *See The Republic of Choice* 164–69 (Harvard U. Press, 1990). While there are validating examples, like the young nurse, Sheila Larson, described in the book *Habits of the Heart*, who has fashioned for herself a religion she calls "Sheilaism" (her "own little voice"), the actual context is

more complicated. Robert N. Bellah et al., *Habits of the Heart* 219–49 (U. of California Press, 1985). While choice and freedom are certainly part of the American religious scene, one must not lose sight of the distinctive character of religion, as opposed to other objects of choice (cars, clothes, music, movies), especially insofar as that character represents a quest for shared meaning that is ultimately at odds with secular autonomous individualism. On the varieties of flourishing American religious experience in this regard, *see* Wills, *supra* note 14, *passim*. For a recent journalistic account, which is sensitive to the problem of consumer orientation, and striking for its placement, *see* Kenneth Woodward, "A Time to Seek: With Babes in Arms and Doubts in Mind, A Generation Looks to Religion," *Newsweek*, Dec. 17, 1990, at 50.

51   *See* Elizabeth Mensch, "History of Mainstream Legal Thought," in *The Politics of Law: A Progressive Critique* 13, at 24–31 (2d ed., ed. David Kairys, Pantheon Books, 1990).

5   Protestant Fundamentalism

1   *See* Peter L. Berger, *The Sacred Canopy*, at 105–25 (Doubleday, 1967). The process of secularization could be said to have started with the Old Testament emphasis on an utterly transcendent God whose relationship with human beings is historical, not manifested within natural forces or located in particular places. Medieval Catholicism was more "sacral" than Protestantism, which represented a return to a more biblical faith, but even during the medieval period, the rivalry of pope and king represented a refusal to subsume the temporal world within a single, all-embracing sacral order. The "sacral"/"secular" dichotomy, while useful, might also be too slick. *See* Harvey Cox, *The Secular City: Secularization and Urbanization in Theological Perspective* (Macmillan, 1965).

2   George Marsden, "Evangelicals and the Scientific Culture: An Overview," in *Religion and Twentieth Century American Intellectual Life* (ed. Michael J. Lacey, Cambridge U. Press, 1989), at 32. Marsden has been a consistently knowledgeable and insightful interpreter of the fundamentalist controversies. *See also* his "Evangelicals, History, and Modernity," in *Evangelicalism and Modern America* 94–102 (ed. George Marsden, W. B. Eerdmans, 1984).

3   Marsden, "Evangelicals and the Scientific Culture," at 34 (citing Charles Darwin, *On the Origin of Species by Means of Natural Selection* [J. Murray, 1859]).

4   "The most formidable American scientific opponent of Darwin was Harvard's Louis Agassiz, a Unitarian. The most formidable supporter was Agassiz's colleague, Asa Gray, an evangelical." *Id.* at 35.

5   *Id.* at 36. In fact, Gray was something of an animal rights proponent, reading Darwin, who himself abhorred cruelty to animals, as emphasizing our kinship with nonhuman animals and thereby extending our ethical community: "We are sharers not only of animal but of vegetable life, sharers with the higher brute animals in common instincts and feelings and affections. It seems to me that there is a sort of meanness in the wish to ignore the tie. I fancy that human beings may be more humane when they realize that, as their dependent associates live a life in which man has a share, so they have rights which man is bound to respect." 70 *Monist* 98, 103 (1987) (quoting Asa Gray, *Natural Science*

and Religion: Two Lectures Delivered to the Theological School of Yale College 54 [Scribner's 1880]). See generally James Rachels, Created from Animals: The Moral Implications of Darwinism 83–86, 98–113 (Oxford U. Press, 1990).

6   Andrew Dickson White, A History of the Warfare of Science with Theology in Christendom (abridged ed., Free Press, 1965).

7   Id. at 38 (quoting Huxley).

8   See Rachels, supra note 5, at 83.

9   Marsden, "Evangelicals and the Scientific Culture," at 41.

10   Bruce Kuklick, "John Dewey, American Theology, and Scientific Politics," in Religion and Twentieth Century American Intellectual Life, at 82.

11   Id. at 85.

12   Id.

13   Marsden, "Evangelicals and the Scientific Culture," at 42.

14   Kuklick, supra note 10, at 83.

15   Id. at 87–88. David Hollinger, similarly, has described the essentially religious vocabulary and assumptions that were used to celebrate ostensibly nonreligious science early in the century. He calls this the "intellectual gospel." Modern scholars have come to appreciate the complexity of the interplay between scientific and religious thought: now only embittered fundamentalists and, at the other extreme, only "a few die-hard village atheists . . . [fail to] realize how anachronistically Victorian is the vision of a triumphant science eventually replacing religion." "Justification By Verification: The Scientific Challenge to the Moral Authority of Christianity in Modern America," in Religion and Twentieth-Century American Intellectual Life, at 116. Hollinger points out that in theological terms, the notion of justification by verification, the basic premise of scientific positivism, is a form of Arminianism—in contrast to the doctrine of justification by faith. Id. at 118. In that sense, it was more Methodist than Calvinist. For the importance of Methodist Arminianism, with its optimism about human possibility, in American culture, see George Armstrong Kelly, Politics and Religious Consciousness in America 84–85 (Transaction Books, 1984).

16   For a perceptive account of that confrontation, see Garry Wills, Under God: Religion and American Politics (Simon & Schuster, 1990), at 97–114 (arguing persuasively that Bryan's real opponent was not "science," but the amoral nihilism of those who had misappropriated Darwin, such as H. L. Mencken in his publicizing of Nietzsche).

17   Id. at 104.

18   Richard Wightman Fox, "The Niebuhr Brothers and the Liberal Protestant Heritage," in Religion and Twentieth-Century American Intellectual Life, 2.

19   Id. at 107.

20   Id. at 108–9.

21   Moreover, scientific reason, no less than theology, depended on communal "faith" in inquiry, a commitment that could not be verified on purely scientific grounds. Id. at 109. Fox's perceptive essay also explores more fully the differences between Reinhold Niebuhr's thought and that of H. Richard Niebuhr. Reinhold, in his earlier years, was drawn to Marxism, whereas H. Richard was more influenced by Barth. See also Langdon Gilkey, "Social and Intellectual Sources of Contemporary Protestant Theology," in Religion in America 156–57

(1968), for a brief account of Reinhold Niebuhr's importance. For a more complete account, *see* Richard Wightman Fox, *Reinhold Niebuhr* (Pantheon Books, 1985). For more on Reinhold Niebuhr, *see* Christopher Lasch, *The True and Only Heaven: Progress and Its Critics* 369–93 (Norton, 1991).

22   Linda Holler, "Is There a Thou 'Within' Nature?: A Dialogue with H. Richard Niebuhr," 17 J. *of Religious Ethics* 81 (1989) (quoting Niebuhr).

23   *Id.* (quoting Niebuhr).

24   *See generally,* Holler, *id.* at 81–102.

25   *See* Gilkey, *supra* note 21, at 157.

26   *See* Kuklick, *supra* note 10, at 92.

27   *See* Elizabeth Mensch & Alan Freeman, "Religion as Science/Science as Religion: Constitutional Law and the Fundamentalist Challenge," Tikkun, Nov.–Dec. 1987, at 64.

28   The distinction is made far too flippantly. Today, for example, three in ten Americans count themselves as evangelicals, but many evangelicals are not fundamentalists. Pentecostals, for example, are not, nor are many black Baptists. Many evangelicals are also not political conservatives—probably roughly one in four white evangelicals see themselves as on the "left" of the political spectrum, as do most black evangelicals. *See* Grant Wacker, "Uneasy in Zion: Evangelicals in Postmodern Society," in *Evangelicalism and Modern America* 18 (1984). Indeed, white southern Baptists, the largest evangelical denomination, were largely Democratic in the earlier part of the twentieth century; they strongly favored the New Deal programs that attacked poverty, and that commitment to social welfare programs was still strong in the 1940s and 1950s. *See* Kenneth D. Wald, *Religion and Politics in the United States* (St. Martin's Press, 1987), at 185. The Democrats began to lose favor among evangelicals only in the 1960s, probably partly in response to John F. Kennedy's Catholicism. *Id.* Even in the 1980s, evangelical support for the Jerry Falwell New Right agenda was far more mixed than is commonly supposed, suggesting the inadequacy of labels such as "conservative" or "liberal." Pro-family issues are the ones that have gained the most support, but even then support is surprisingly mixed. Careful interviews in 1983 showed majorities among evangelicals supporting school prayer, a pro-Israel policy, and tuition tax credits for parochial schools. On the other hand, majorities *also,* contrary to common perceptions, supported the distribution of birth control information in the schools, favored passage of the Equal Rights Amendment, and rejected the view that AIDS was a form of divine retribution. On issues of increased defense spending, the nuclear freeze, and abortion, evangelical opinion was split, with no single view prevailing. Notably, Falwell was less popular among respondents than was the National Organization for Women. *See id.* at 192–93. Common groupings within Protestantism, however, are usually made as follows:

    Liberal Protestants—Episcopalians, Presbyterians, and United Church of Christ (composed of Congregationalists). These were once the "big three," dominating American culture. They emerged from the fundamentalist controversies with modernists firmly in control, and they generally have been "liberal" both in biblical interpretation and commitment to political action. Now this grouping represents slightly less than 10 percent of the American population, although it remains influential because its members are represented disproportionately among civic and business leaders, despite its waning membership in the population generally.

Moderate Protestants—Methodists, Disciples of Christ, Northern Baptists, Lutherans, and Reformed. This grouping accounts for about one-fourth of the religious population and is the largest Protestant grouping. Traditionally, it has not had the same access to power as did the old-line group; it has tended to be middle-class in status and outlook; in some senses the Methodists, with their Arminian theology, stressing good works and optimism, along with sound organizational structures and a practical rather than theoretical approach to theology, are the most "American" denomination. Diversity within this grouping is wide in both theology and politics, but cultural influences are strong.

African American Protestants—Black Americans have been primarily Methodist or Baptist in background, but their churches took distinct form and were not subsumed within the broader denominational structures. Churches were a vital part of the African American experience, second only to family life as a source of identity, strength, and solidarity. African Americans have a high level of religious commitment relative to other groups. When compared with other groups, they tend to be evangelical and "conservative" on family issues, while more politically "liberal" in other respects.

Conservative Protestants—The largest denomination is the Southern Baptist; others include Churches of Christ, Church of the Nazarene, the Assemblies of God, Seventh-Day Adventists, and many independent fundamentalist Pentecostal and Holiness groups. The grouping accounts for 16 percent of the American population. Many are members of the National Association of Evangelicals. Despite a good deal of diversity, most emphasize the conversion experience, biblical authority, and the importance of morality in personal life. They are more inclined than most to see the forces of good and evil, God and the Devil, played out in the world of concrete events.

Taken altogether, Protestants still make up the majority religious faith. Nevertheless, roughly one-fourth of the American population is now Catholic —slightly larger than the "moderate Protestant" grouping. Like black and conservative Protestants, Catholics have a high level of religious commitment. As Protestantism became more fragmented after the 1970s, Catholicism entered the mainstream. After Vatican II, Catholic churches seemed more Protestant and therefore typically more American than they had in the past. Catholics had entered the socioeconomic mainstream as well. Importantly, Catholics have been able to articulate a unified and coherent moral position on a number of issues in a way that Protestants have not.

Jews represent 2 to 3 percent of the American population in three groups, Reformed, Conservative, and Orthodox. Jews have relatively low rates of attendance at services, and synagogue and temple involvement are weak, but communal ethnic bonds are strong. No other major group has had to struggle so hard with the conflict between commitment to faith and assimilation into the American mainstream.

Other faiths include Mormons, Jehovah's Witnesses, Christian Scientists,

Unitarian-Universalists, and Muslims (the latter now approximate Episcopalians in numbers), which have been important in American life despite low percentages of the population. Nonaffiliates comprise about 7 percent; most are more indifferent to religion than hostile to it. For a succinct summary of these groupings, *see generally* Wade Clark Roof & William McKinney, *American Mainline Religion: Its Changing Shape and Future* 85–99 (Rutgers U. Press, 1987).

29   *See* Marsden, "Evangelicals and the Scientific Culture," at 25–26. Marsden points out that "Princeton theology" has had more influence in the twentieth century than the nineteenth.

30   *See* Robert M. Baird, "Schaeffer's Intellectual Roots," in *Reflections on Francis Schaeffer* 47 (ed. Ronald W. Ruegsegger, Academic Books, 1986).

31   *Id.* at 53.

32   *See* Eberhard Jungel, *Karl Barth: A Theological Legacy*, 70–82 (Westminster Press, 1986).

33   Karl Barth, *The Epistle to the Romans*, 447–48 (6th ed., Oxford U. Press, 1963).

34   *See* Thiemann, *Revelation and Theology*, 78–79, 94–95.

35   Baird, *supra* note 30, at 53–55.

36   *See* Ronald L. Numbers, "The Dilemma of Evangelical Scientists," in *Evangelicalism and Modern America*, at 156. *See also*, George Marsden, "A Case of the Excluded Middle," in *Uncivil Religion: Interreligious Hostility in America* 132–56 (ed. Robert N. Bellah and Frederick E. Greenspahn, Crossroad Press, 1987).

37   Richard Rorty, *Philosophy and the Mirror of Nature* (paperback ed., Princeton U. Press, 1979). His influence in this regard has extended to legal thought as well. *See, e.g.*, Joan Williams, "Rorty, Radicalism, Romanticism: The Politics of the Gaze," 1992 *Wisconsin L. Rev.* 131, 134–43.

38   For an argument that the Bible as such *cannot* save foundationalism in theology, *see* Nicholas Wolterstorff, *Reason Within the Bounds of Religion* (2d ed., W. B. Eerdman, 1984), at 58–62.

39   Baird, *supra* note 30, at 61–63.

40   Clark H. Pinnock, "Schaeffer on Modern Theology," in *Reflections on Francis Schaeffer*, at 179.

41   *See* Wills, *supra* note 16, at 318–28 (on both Schaeffer and Terry).

42   Baird, *supra* note 30, at 81.

43   On this important doctrinal point, Schaeffer tended to waffle, for fundamentalists prefer to believe in a wooden consistency between the objectivity of natural fact and the objectivity of scripture; serious Calvinists are more skeptical about the ultimate reliability of the evidences a fallen natural world can ever present to a fallen reason. *Id.* at 55–58. *See also* Marsden, "Evangelicals and the Scientific Culture," at 23–25 (discussing Kuyper, a presuppositionalist).

44   *See* Ronald Ruegsegger, "Francis Schaeffer on Philosophy," in *Reflections on Francis Schaeffer* 107–28.

45   *See* Garry Wills, "Evangels of Abortion," *New York Review of Books*, June 15, 1989, at 18–21. *See also* Wills, *supra* note 16, at 322–24.

46   Francis A. Schaeffer & C. Everett Koop, *Whatever Happened to the Human Race?* (1979).

47   *See* Hollinger, "Schaeffer on Ethics," in *Reflections on Francis Schaeffer* 245–56. On

the problematic character of making a literal, biblical case against abortion, to the point where some of the passages relied on might support reverence for "all life" (i.e., even animal?), see Wills, supra note 16, at 318–20. Wills notes that even St. Augustine could not find a text in scripture that answered the question of the soul's origin. Id. at 318.

48   See Richard Neuhaus, America Against Itself: Moral Vision and the Public Order 129 (U. of Notre Dame Press, 1992). On the dramatic changes among American evangelicals in general, and fundamentalists in particular, in response to Roe, which was seen as confirming the sense that the "moral foundations of American society were crumbling," see A. James Reichley, Religion in American Public Life 316–17 (Brookings Institution, 1985); Robert Wuthnow, The Restructuring of American Religion 199–201, 212–13 (Princeton U. Press, 1988).

49   As pointed out by Leo Ribuffo, "The Complexity of American Religious Prejudice," in Right Center Left: Essays in American History (Rutgers U. Press, 1992), at 63. Ribuffo's "God and Jimmy Carter," id. at 214–48, is insightful about Carter, his ambivalent approach to the abortion issue, and to religion and politics.

6   The 1960s: The Secularization of Mainline Religion

1   James Hunter, Culture Wars: The Struggle to Define America 43–51 (Basic Books, 1991).
2   Bruce Kuklick, "John Dewey, American Theology, and Scientific Politics," in Religion and Twentieth-Century American Intellectual Life (ed. Michael J. Lacey, Cambridge U. Press, 1989), at 88–89; he is quoting J. Phillips, "John Dewey and the Transformation of American Intellectual Life, 1859–1904," at 309 (Ph.D. dissertation, Harvard University, 1978).
3   Van A. Harvey, "On the Intellectual Marginality of American Theology," in Religion and Twentieth-Century American Intellectual Life, at 180, quoting Burton J. Bledstein, The Culture of Professionalism: The Middle Class and the Development of Higher Education in America (Norton, 1978).
4   Id. at 181.
5   Id.
6   Id. (quoting Bledstein).
7   Id.
8   Id.
9   Id. at 185–86. Harvey describes the fourfold compartmentalization of theology schooling, which originated in Germany. He gives special emphasis to the expertise now required for biblical studies, arguing that the effect has been to rob public discourse of the language of moral and communal commitment, which once was the special integrative province of theology. Id. at 186–92.
10   See Christopher Lasch, The True and Only Heaven: Progress and Its Critics (Norton, 1991), at 509–29. See also Alvin W. Gouldner, The Future of Intellectuals and the Rise of the New Class (Continuum, 1979).
11   Robert Wuthow, The Restructuring of American Religion: Society and Faith Since World War II (Princeton U. Press, 1988).
12   Id. at 158.
13   Government employees, in fact, manifested "new class" life-style attitudes even irrespective of educational level. Harvey, supra note 3, at 186.

14 In 1955, approximately $4.50 was donated to religion for every dollar given to education; by 1970 the ratio declined to $2.90. *Id.* at 159.

15 A. James Reichley, *Religion in American Public Life* (Brookings Institution, 1985), at 242.

16 *Id.; see also,* James F. Findlay, "Religion and Politics in the Sixties: The Churches and the Civil Rights Act of 1964," 77 J. *American History* 66, 69–70 (1990). The complete letter was first published in the ecumenical weekly *Christian Century*. *Id.* at 69.

17 Taylor Branch, *Parting the Waters: America in the King Years 1954–63* (Simon & Schuster, 1988), at 740.

18 *See* Richard Wishtman Fox, "The Niebuhr Brothers and the Liberal Protestant Heritage," in *Religion and Twentieth-Century American Intellectual Life,* at 100.

19 *See* Wuthnow, *supra* note 11, at 145–47.

20 Branch, *supra* note 17, at 760–61. (We are relying on Branch for our account generally.) The graphic power of that image contained some irony: the boy had not intended to become part of the demonstration, and the incident convinced him he had been "with a bad crowd" when he stopped to observe the demonstration. *Id.*

21 *Id.* at 755.

22 *Id.* at 881–82.

23 *Id.* at 892–93.

24 *Id.*

25 Dietrich Bonhoeffer, *Letters and Papers from Prison* (3d ed., Macmillan, 1967).

26 For the importance of this book during the period, *see* Emil L. Fackenheim, "On the Self-Exposure of Faith," in *Religion in America* 205 (ed. William G. McLoughlin and Robert N. Bellah, Houghton Mifflin, 1968). On the connection made to civil rights, *see* William Stringfellow, *Dissenter in a Great Society: A Christian View of America in Crisis* 94–95 (Holt, Rinehart & Winston, 1966). For Bonhoeffer's direct understanding of American racism's challenge to American religion, *see* Donald Shriver, Jr., "Faith, Politics, and Secular Society: The Legacy of Bonhoeffer for Americans," in *Ethical Responsibility: Bonhoeffer's Legacy to the Churches* (ed. John D. Godsey & Geffrey B. Kelly, E. Mellen Press, 1981), at 205; *see also* Eberhard Bethge, *Dietrich Bonhoeffer: Man of Vision, Man of Courage* (trans. Eric Mosbacher et al., Harper & Row, 1970), at 109–10. The racial issue was, in fact, the one American social issue with which Bonhoeffer allowed himself to become involved during his stay in New York in 1930–31. *Id.* His subsequent description of the American race problem to his brother, Karl-Friedrich, in Germany, was so powerful as to elicit the following reply: "I am delighted you have the opportunity of studying the Negro question so thoroughly. I had the impression when I was over there that it is really *the* problem at any rate for people with a conscience and, when I was offered an appointment at Harvard, it was a quite basic reason for my disinclination to go to America for good, because I did not want either to enter upon that heritage myself or to hand it on to my hypothetical children. It seems impossible to see the right way to tackle the problem." *Id.* at 110 (quoting a letter of Jan. 24, 1931). Moreover, according to Bethge, "[n]ot suspecting the heritage he would have to enter upon in his own country, Karl-Friedrich continued: 'At all events, our Jewish

question is a joke in comparison; there cannot be many people left [in 1931] who maintain they are oppressed here. At any rate, not in Frankfurt. . . .' " *Id.*

27   Findlay, *supra* note 16, at 69.

28   *See generally* C. Eric Lincoln & Lawrence H. Mamiya, *The Black Church in the African American Experience* (Duke U. Press, 1990); Anthony Cook, "Beyond Critical Legal Studies: The Reconstructive Theology of Dr. Martin Luther King, Jr.," 103 *Harvard L. Rev.* 985, 1015–23 (1990).

29   For a recent sympathetic reanalysis of the Social Gospel movement, *see* William M. King, "An Enthusiasm for Humanity: The Social Emphasis in Religion and Its Accommodation in Protestant Theology," in *Religion and Twentieth-Century American Intellectual Life*, at 49.

30   King sought a middle ground between the excessive optimism of Social Gospel and evangelical liberalism and what he perceived as the despair implicit in Barth's neo-orthodoxy, given its emphasis on "the intractable nature of sin and evil and the relative futility of utopian aspirations." Cook, *supra* note 28, at 1028. For a discussion of King's theology, *see id.* at 1012–44.

31   Branch, *supra* note 17, at 896. (The specific issue discussed was the one of pacifism.)

32   In California in 1968, for example, one-quarter of the Protestant clergy took an active part in civil rights demonstrations. Wuthnow, *supra* note 11, at 146.

33   Findlay, *supra* note 16, at 71.

34   *Id.* at 71–73. Quickly appointed to the staff was Anna Hedgeman, a savvy and shrewd African American woman who knew how to do effective political organizing.

35   *Id.* at 78–79.

36   *Id.* at 84–85. An executive from that group wrote: "The God of the Gospel is also the God of justice, and holds society and government responsible for equality under the law." *Id.* at 85.

37   Garry Wills, *Bare Ruined Choirs: Doubt, Prophecy, and Radical Religion* (Doubleday, 1972), at 148–49. Wills is critical of the extent to which the church became embroiled in the details of political pressure and funding.

38   Branch, *supra* note 17, at 892.

39   Harvey Cox, *The Secular City: Secularization and Urbanization in Theological Perspective* (Macmillan, 1965).

40   *Id.* at 241 (quoting Bonhoeffer).

41   *Id.* at 15–26.

42   *Id.* at 58.

43   *Id.* at 64.

44   *Id.* at 65.

45   *Id.* at 64.

46   *Id.* at 73–74.

47   *Id.* at 83.

48   *Id.* at 114.

49   *Id.* at 62.

50   *Id.* at 63.

51   *Id.*

52   *Id.*

53   *Id.* at 125–26.

54   *See* Elizabeth Mensch, "History of Mainstream Legal Thought," in *The Politics of Law: A Progressive Critique* 13 (2d ed., ed. David Kairys, Pantheon Books, 1990).

55   *See* David O'Brien, "Catholic Contentiousness: The Public Consequences of Denominational Disputes," in *Uncivil Religion: Interreligious Hostility in America* (ed. Robert N. Bellah and Frederick E. Greenspahn, Crossroad Press, 1987), at 163–64.

56   Reichley, *supra* note 15, at 288.

57   *Id.*

58   The state was relinquished to the merely human and provisional, and social pluralism was acknowledged, but only as a fact of a fallen world. *See id.*

59   Neal, "Catholicism in America," in *Religion in America* 326.

60   *Id.* at 323–24.

61   *Id.* at 324.

62   *Id.* Catholic theologians were, in fact, writing on similar themes. For example, Johannes Metz wrote "to Christianize the world means in its basic sense to make the world more worldly, to bring it to its own. . . . [Grace] calls and guides the world into its perfect secularism." Cox, "Afterword," in *The Secular City Debate* 191–92 (ed. Daniel Callahan, Macmillan, 1966) (quoting Metz, "A Believer's Look at the World: A Christian Standpoint in the Secularized World," in *The Christian and the World*, at 93. Similarly, the Jesuit theologian Karl Rahner wrote: "If the world of the future is a world of rational planning, a demythologized world, a world secularized by the creature in order that it may serve as the raw material for man's activity, then this whole modern attitude . . . is basically a Christian one." *Id.* at 192 (quoting Rahner, "Christianity and New Man," in *The Christian and the World*, at 228).

63   Neal, *supra* note 59, at 313.

64   Wills, *supra* note 37, at 90–91.

65   *Id.* at 90.

66   Cox, "Beyond Bonhoeffer? The Future of Religionless Christianity," in *The Secular City Debate* 206; Michael Novak, "Christianity: Renewed or Slowly Abandoned?" in *Religion in America* 385.

67   Cox, *Beyond Bonhoeffer?* at 206.

68   *Id.* at 207.

69   *See* Stanley Hauerwas, *After Christendom?* (Abingdon Press, 1991), at 54. (Not about Bonhoeffer specifically.)

70   Eberhard Jungel, *Karl Barth: A Theological Legacy* (Westminster Press, 1986), at 32 (quoting Karl Barth, *Der Römerbrief* 7 [1919]).

71   Cox, *Beyond Bonhoeffer?* at 207–8. Cox noted Bonhoeffer's dismay when he visited the United States and found students at Union Theological Seminary laughing out loud at passages from Luther on sin and forgiveness. *Id.* at 207. On the other hand, this does not mean, of course, that there is no point in trying to rid theology of dead myths and excessive dependence on philosophical modes of thought. Daniel Callahan, from the Catholic perspective, wrote that God "reveals Himself in history rather than in the philosopher's study, [and] . . . speaks

through the language of events rather than that of timeless essences." Callahan, "Toward a Theology of Secularity," in *The Secular City Debate* 95 (pointing
out that few Catholic theologians would dissent).

72   Summarized in Wolfhart Pannenberg, *Christian Spirituality* (Westminster Press,
1983) at 78–80.

73   Thomas J. J. Altizer, *The Gospel of Christian Atheism* (Westminster Press, 1966). Altizer's work is described well in Fackenheim, *supra* note 26, at 216–18.

74   *See* Pannenberg, *supra* note 72, at 80–83.

75   Fackenheim, *supra* note 26, at 217 (quoting Thomas J. J. Altizer & William
Hamilton, *Radical Theology and the Death of God* 157 [Bobbs-Merrill, 1966]). Fackenheim argues that Altizer was untrue to Hegel, whom Barth had understood
more accurately than modern death-of-God Hegelians (at 228 n. 41).

76   John A. T. Robinson, *Honest to God* 51–54 (Westminster Press, 1963). *See also* Callahan, "The Quest for Social Relevance," in *Religion in America* 339–40.

77   Paul Matthew Van Buren, *The Secular Meaning of the Gospel* (SCM Press, 1963).

78   *Id.* at 81–106. *See also* Callahan, "Quest for Social Relevance," at 340, and
Fackenheim, *supra* note 26, at 214–16. Fackenheim describes two different
standpoints—the one within and the one outside the circle of faith. Empiricism accepts as objective data only those things that are accessible to one
outside the circle; "thus the objective realm is confined to 'the world,' which
in turn is empirical data and the hypotheses needed to explain them." *Id.* at
215. With that stance taken as one's basic presupposition, faith does reduce
itself to attitude, as Van Buren argued. From the vantage point of faith, however, in its own self-understanding, "faith is a committed confrontation of the
world . . . and in this confrontation of the world, . . . it takes itself as receptive
of an objective truth accessible only in the believing attitude and inaccessible
otherwise. Linguistic empiricism poses as a refutation of faith; in fact, it merely
takes its stand outside the circle of faith, in a circle of its own in which the
world of God is not heard and only 'data' are given." *Id.* In the face of
the various God-is-dead celebrators of secularism, Fackenheim argued that the
Jewish response should be wary. Traditionally, Jews had found in secular liberalism freedom from the oppression of a Christianizing culture. Fackenheim
is urging reappraisal of that Jewish position. *Id.* at 220, 223.

79   Wills, *supra* note 36, at 91.

80   Leonard I. Sweet, "The 1960's: The Crises of Liberal Christianity and the Public Emergence of Evangelism," in *Evangelicalism and Modern America* (ed. George
Marsden, W. B. Eerdmans, 1984), at 35. Cox's Christocentrism was more authentic, but he was not part of the God-is-dead movement.

81   *See* George D. Younger, "Does the Secular City Revisit the Social Gospel?" in
The Secular City Debate 78–79.

82   Callahan, *Toward A Theology of Secularity*, at 98. Hence, the inner contradiction
in Cox, which Wills points to. If one truly embraces secularization, then why
refer to biblical categories at all? *See* Wills, *supra* note 36, at 92.

83   Cox, "Cox on His Critics," in *The Secular City Debate* 87.

84   Callahan, *supra* note 71, at 99.

85   Richard Rubenstein, "Cox's Vision of the Secular City," in *The Secular City Debate*
132, 142–43.

86 *Id.* at 142–43.

87 Callahan, *supra* note 71, at 99. Similarly, from Richard Rubenstein: "There is something very success-oriented about his theology. He approves the mobility and anonymity of the city, but says hardly enough about the hideous price the poor have had to pay in rootlessness, disorientation and suffering as a result of these phenomena. Anonymity and mobility can be enormously helpful to successful, highly educated young men who are part of what *Life* magazine recently called the 'take-over' generation. They constitute an impossible burden for the millions of Americans who lack the personal, social or psychological resources with which to take advantage of the new freedom." *Supra* note 85, at 139.

88 Andrew Greeley, "An Exchange of Views," in *The Secular City Debate* 101.

89 Rubenstein, *supra* note 85, at 140.

90 *Id.* at 138. Cox, who did not quite agree with Greeley as a matter of sociology, acknowledged Rubenstein's critique fully. *See* Cox, *supra* note 62, at 181. He admitted it was not the mark of the mature person to flippantly jettison the past. He has also spent years, since then, studying other religious traditions at a very particular level. *See Many Mansions* (Beacon Press, 1989).

7   Schism

1   370 U.S. 421 (1962).

2   *Id.* at 446, 449 (Stewart, J., dissenting). Garry Wills suggests that a singular failure of the Dukakis presidential campaign was its failure to understand that the Pledge of Allegiance issue worked so well for George Bush because the pledge is the only remaining instance where the words "under God" may be invoked ceremonially in a public school. Wills, *Under God: Religion and American Politics* (Simon & Schuster, 1990), at 80–82.

3   374 U.S. 203 (1963).

4   *Id.* at 313 (Stewart, J., dissenting).

5   A. James Reichley, *Religion in American Public Life* (Brookings Institution, 1985), at 147. In contrast, Graham did support civil rights on religious grounds. See Robert Wuthnow, *The Restructuring of American Religion: Society and Faith Since World War II* (Princeton U. Press, 1988), at 188.

6   Reichley, *supra* note 5, at 149.

7   Kenneth D. Wald, *Religion and Politics in the United States* (St. Martin's Press, 1987), at 129. In 1984, Reagan supported an amendment to permit prayer in public institutions, including schools. It was supported by fifty-six senators, but not by the sixty-seven votes needed for passage. *Id.* at 130.

8   *Id.* at 132.

9   Wald points out that survey results are not unambiguous, however. *Id.* Given widespread political support for allowing prayer and Bible-reading, it is surprising that political action has not led to results. That may be because of de facto tolerance for the practice in areas when feelings run especially strong, combined with the fact that support is stronger among the less-educated and, therefore, less-powerful voters.

10 Harvey Cox himself had favored neutrality in public schools but distinguished

that from an "intolerant religion of secularism." Cox, *The Secular City: Secularization and Urbanization in Theological Perspective* (Macmillan, 1965), at 100. He opposed prayer in the schools, but praised the California State Board of Education for stating that a "point of view denying God" would be as inappropriate as to "promote a particular religious sect." *Id.* Whether those distinctions are workable is highly debatable, but they are central to the American church/state dilemma.

11   Langdon Gilkey, "Social and Intellectual Sources of Contemporary Protestant Theology," in *Religion in America* (ed. William G. McLoughlin and Robert N. Bellah, Houghton Mifflin, 1968), at 163–64.

12   *Id.* at 163.

13   See David O'Brien, "Catholic Contentiousness: The Public Consequences of Denominational Disputes," in *Uncivil Religion* (ed. Robert N. Bellah and Frederick E. Greenspahn, Crossroad Press, 1987), at 158–59 (analyzing various public statements of American Catholic bishops).

14   See Lisa Cahill, "The Catholic Tradition, Morality, and the Common Good," 5 J.L. & Religion 75, 77–82 (1987); *see also* Daniel Callahan, "Quest for Social Relevance," in *Religion in America, supra* note 11, at 356.

15   See Garry Wills, *Bare Ruined Choirs: Doubt, Prophecy, and Radical Religion* (Doubleday, 1972), at 241–50.

16   Pope Paul VI, *Humanae Vitae: Acts Apostolicae Sedis* (1968) reprinted in *The Papal Evangelicals, 1958–1981*, at 223 (1981).

17   John T. Noonan, Jr., "*Tokos and Atokion:* An Examination of Natural Law Reasoning Against Usury and Against Contraception," 10 *Nat. L.F.* 215 (1965).

18   See Wills, *supra* note 15, at 176–87.

19   See Mark Noll, "Catholics and Protestants Since Vatican II," in *Uncivil Religion,* at 99–101.

20   See Wuthnow, *supra* note 5, at 132–33. These stereotypes were based on a 1984 Gallup survey and a church official's report. This is, of course, matched by an equally caricatured version of traditionalists—intolerant, morally rigid, fanatical, unsophisticated, close-minded, simplistic, smug, self-righteous, having a loveless, dogmatic faith, etc. *Id.*

21   This is not, of course, to say that religious groups did not, in the past, try to influence legislation, and succeed. Those that proliferated after the 1960s were those that were specifically concerned with dealing with government. See Wuthnow, *supra* note 5, at 115–16. The number of religious groups with a specific purpose—those representing workers within ecclesiastical institutions (managers, secretaries, etc.) as well as those representing various women's concerns (both pro- and antifeminist) also increased significantly. *Id.* at 107–12. Before 1960, some denominations had already located themselves in Washington, D.C. As early as 1946, Baptists had appointed a lobbyist to "watch the Catholics." *See* Reichley, *supra* note 5, at 244. A 1951 study by Ray Ebersole found sixteen church offices located in Washington. *Id.* at 245. Even the NCC's Washington office, however, was originally directed "not to engage in efforts to influence legislation," a prohibition dropped specifically for the purpose of the Civil Rights Act of 1964. *Id.* For an account of church activity on behalf of the act, *see id.* at 246–50. Catholics were less inclined to use direct lobbying

and more inclined to work through parish constituents, but that difference was not considered divisive—only complementary. *Id.* at 248.

22 Wuthnow, *supra* note 5, at 123–24.

23 *Id.* at 125–30.

24 *See* Reichley, *supra* note 5, at 244 ("The Churches Come to Washington"). For a serious Catholic justification of the impact that churches can have on social reform, *see* Callahan, "Quest for Social Relevance," at 358–63.

25 Reichley, *supra* note 5, at 277.

26 *Id.* at 277–78.

27 *Id.* at 314–27.

28 Cox, *supra* note 10 at 225–26. The church is the "eventful moment" in which barriers are being struck down, and a radically new community beyond the divisiveness of inherited labels and stereotypes is emerging. *Id.* at 226.

29 Harvey Cox, "The 'New Breed' in American Churches: Sources of Social Activism in American Religion," in *Religion in America*, at 374–75. On the dilemma of professionalization and specialization, *see* Bryan Wilson, "Religion and the Churches in Contemporary America," in *Religion in America*, at 99–102.

30 Wuthnow, *supra* note 5, at 145–46; *see also* Wald, *supra* note 7, at 246; Cox, *supra* note 29, at 374–75.

31 Wuthnow, *supra* note 5, at 146–49.

32 Wald, *supra* note 7, at 242; Cox, *supra* note 29, at 371–72. Saul Alinsky said that the churches were "now taking the leadership in social change." *Id.* at 371.

33 Cox, *supra* note 29, at 381.

34 There is some surprise in this, given the importance of Paul Louis Lehmann's work, a sophisticated examination of philosophy that stressed the importance of "koinonia," or Christian community, as the basis of ethics. Lehmann, *Ethics in a Christian Context* (SCM Press, 1963). For a time, koinonia was a trendy term until, it was said, the churches had "koinonitis," but too little attention was devoted to sustained communities over time as part of a historic religious tradition. *See* Leonard I. Sweet, "The 1960's: The Crisis of Liberal Christianity and the Public Emergence of Evangelism," in *Evangelicalism and Modern America*, (ed. George Marsden, by W. B. Eerdmans, 1984), at 42–43. Sweet's work is an excellent summary of the 1960s. Churches tried to meet the needs of congregations but not bring them into a historic tradition, which is part of the task of theology.

35 *See, e.g.*, Wuthnow, *supra* note 5, at 186.

36 Cox, *supra* note 29, at 371–72 (quoting Alinsky).

37 *Id.* at 375–76.

38 Karl Barth, *The Epistle to the Romans* (6th ed., Oxford U. Press, 1963), at 478.

39 *Id.* at 478–80.

40 *Id.* at 480.

41 On the continuing need for ministers to concern themselves with such matters, see William A. Clebsch, "American Religion and the Cure of Souls," in *Religion in America*, at 249–68.

42 Wuthnow, *supra* note 5, at 161–62.

43 One of the most important changes is that religious participation used to increase with education; by the end of the 1960s that was no longer true. *See id.*

44 On changing patterns generally, see Wade Clark Roof & William McKinney, *American Mainline Religion: Its Changing Shape and Future* (Rutgers U. Press, 1987), at 161–79.

45 Wuthnow, *supra* note 5, at 192.

46 Cox is an exception. His critique of consumerist sexuality—the idols of *Playboy* and the American Girl of Miss America—is one of the most insightful parts of *The Secular City*. See 192–216.

47 Joseph Fletcher, *Situation Ethics: The New Morality* (Westminster Press, 1966).

48 See Roof & McKinney, *supra* note 44, at 62.

49 See, e.g., Fletcher, *supra* note 47, at 64–67, 77.

50 *Id.* at 18–21.

51 *Id.* at 91.

52 *Id.* at 189.

53 *Id.* at 133.

54 *Id.* at 139.

55 *Id.* at 33, 37, 62. Fletcher criticizes Barth's disapproving attitude.

56 For critical responses to Fletcher in this regard, see Richard A. McCormick, *How Brave a New World?: Dilemmas in Bioethics* 45–46, 334–35 (Doubleday, 1981); Paul Ramsey, *Ethics at the Edges of Life: Medical and Legal Intersections* 204 (Yale U. Press, 1978) ("Fletcher is simply a sign of our times"). See also James F. Gustafson, *Protestant and Roman Catholic Ethics* 38–40 (U. of Chicago Press, 1978).

57 See Joseph Fletcher, "Indicators of Humanhood: A Tentative Profile of Man," *Hastings Center Report* 2, no. 5 (Nov. 1972).

58 Francis A. Schaeffer & C. Everett Koop, *Whatever Happened to the Human Race?* (revised ed., Marshall, Morgan & Scott, 1980).

59 See Fletcher, *supra* note 47, at 33.

60 Joseph Fletcher, *Moral Responsibility: Situation Ethics at Work* 123 (Westminster Press, 1967).

61 *Id.*

62 *Id.* at 145.

63 *Id.* at 124.

64 Joseph Fletcher, "Reflection and Reply," in *The Situation Ethics Debate* 249, 263 (comp. Harvey Cox, Westminster Press, 1968).

65 James Davison Hunter, *Culture Wars: The Struggle to Define America* (Basic Books, 1991), at 44–45.

66 For a Protestant approach to ethics that does try to take theological tradition seriously, especially the tradition of humility, but is also sensitive to "real world" choices that must be made, see James F. Gustafson, *I & II Ethics from a Theocentric Perspective* (U. of Chicago Press, 1981).

8 A Tale of Two Conferences

1 The published account is *The Morality of Abortion: Legal and Historical Perspectives* (ed. John T. Noonan, Jr., Harvard U. Press, 1970), which included contributions by John Noonan, Paul Ramsey, James Gustafson, Bernard Häring, George Williams, John Finnis, and David Louisell. The same conference produced an earlier volume published as *The Terrible Choice: The Abortion Dilemma* (Bantam Books, 1968) edited and written with the help of two physicians, Robert Cooke

and Andrew E. Hellegers; also assisting were Robert G. Hoyt and Herbert W. Richardson. The book contains a foreword by Pearl Buck; a list of participants (seventy-two in all); five "case studies" presented dramatically at the conference as occasions for discussion; transcripts of some of that discussion following each presentation; and summary chapters, first on the then-current law with respect to abortion, followed by chapters dealing with perspectives offered by social scientists, physicians, ethicists, and lawyers. Of the 72 participants, 15 are listed under "Medical," 12 under "Social Sciences," 15 under "Ethics," 15 under "Law," and 15 under "Representatives-at-Large." Twenty-three of the participants (not even including Noonan) are identifiable as religiously affiliated, members of the clergy, teachers of religion or in divinity schools, or representatives of religious organizations. Eight of the participants are women (identifiable by name). With respect to race, one can identify both Dorothy Height, then-president of the National Council of Negro Women, and Whitney Young, then-executive director of the Urban League. The group also included three college presidents (Mary Bunting, Arthur Flemming, and Theodore Hesburg), two Supreme Court justices (Abe Fortas and Potter Stewart), and a U.S. Senator (Mark Hatfield). Id. at xiii–xvi.

Preceding the title page of The Terrible Choice is a statement of the "Purpose and Origin of the First International Conference on Abortion," which offers an accurate overview of what follows in the published volume: "The first International Conference on Abortion that was interdisciplinary in nature was convened in Washington, D.C., in the fall of 1967 under sponsorship of the Harvard Divinity School and the Joseph P. Kennedy, Jr. Foundation." Conference planners for both organizations agreed:

—that abortion is a moral, social, and cultural matter, as well as a medical and legal problem, and that it should not be decided for all society by doctors or lawyers acting alone;

—that abortion is not an issue that divides Catholics, Jews, and Protestants along denominational lines, for some leading religious authorities from all groups oppose abortion while others justify it, albeit in limited cases;

—that abortion is an issue of vital importance to all, for it involves delicate questions that are basic to concepts of life, responsibility for retarded or otherwise disadvantaged children, and morality; . . .

—and finally, both groups agreed it was time to substitute thoughtful discussion among responsible experts for the emotional publicity given to those abortion cases involving rape, mental retardation, incest, or physical defects of the fetus like those caused by thalidomide poisoning, all of which taken together account for much less than 5 percent of all abortions.

2   Id. at 105.

3   All of these essays are included in The Morality of Abortion: Häring, "A Theological Evaluation"; John T. Noonan, Jr., "An Almost Absolute Value in History"; Paul Ramsey, "Reference Points in Deciding About Abortion"; James Gustafson, "A Protestant Ethical Approach"; and George Williams, "The Sacred Condominium."

4   John Finnis, "Three Schemes of Regulation," in Morality of Abortion.

5   David Louisell & John T. Noonan, Jr., "Constitutional Balance," in Morality of Abortion.

6   Morality of Abortion, at ix–xvii.

7   See id. at xv–xvii. Lawrence M. Friedman's The Republic of Choice (Harvard U. Press, 1990) may be seen as an extended elaboration of Noonan's cultural observation. Noonan, writing in 1970, described the promoters of this new culture as "[c]ollege students, journalists, lawyers, physicians, professors, and opinion-makers." "Introduction" to Morality of Abortion, at xvii.

8   E.g., Noonan, "An Almost Absolute Value in History," at 1 (Catholic); Ramsey, "Reference Points in Deciding About Abortion," at 60 (Protestant). Ramsey's position is a bit more complicated, however. He is quoted in The Terrible Choice as distinguishing abortion as a moral issue from its legal status: "[T]he churches and anyone else concerned with the moral ethos of this civilization ought to know that even now it is the morality of acts of abortion with which they should be chiefly concerned—not with proposed public policies that would use abortion law as an interim solution. I suggest . . . that those among us who believe that morally abortion is, or sometimes is, a species of the sin of murder might be able to distinguish this from any conclusion to the question whether such abortion ought to be defined as a crime in the penal code." The Terrible Choice, at 92 (quoting Ramsey, "Reference Points in Deciding About Abortion," at 63). Moreover, there is a basis in Ramsey's own essay for differential, more relaxed treatment of early abortions. On the other hand, Ramsey reacted to sweeping cultural change by becoming much more extreme in his opposition to abortion, even before Roe v. Wade. See Ramsey, "The Morality of Abortion," in The Ethics of Abortion (ed. Robert M. Baird & Stuart E. Rosenbaum, Prometheus Books, 1989), at 61 (this Ramsey essay was a reprint of one originally published in 1971).

9   Häring, supra note 3, at 123–45. The essay is striking because Häring had written some years earlier that "[t]he appeal to the Christian law of brotherly love as justification for the taking of innocent life and the killing of genuine motherliness is probably the lowest depth of error attainable and the sorry fruit of the victory of the birth control campaign." Daniel Callahan, Abortion: Law, Choice and Morality (Macmillan, 1970), at 4 (quoting Häring, Marriage in The Modern World). On the Catholic position generally, see Callahan, supra, at 409–47.

10 Gustafson, supra note 3, at 101–22. Gustafson's presentation at the 1967 conference was regarded as a "critique of the Roman Catholic approach" and a particular case study as well. The Terrible Choice, at 89.

11 Gustafson, supra note 3. A leading Protestant theologian, who taught for many years at the University of Chicago Divinity School and is now at Emory, Gustafson has written extensively and thoughtfully about ethics in the following books: Protestant and Roman Catholic Ethics (U. of Chicago Press, 1978); 1 Ethics from a Theocentric Perspective: Theology and Ethics (U. of Chicago Press, 1981); and 2 Ethics from a Theocentric Perspective: Ethics and Theology (U. of Chicago Press, 1984). For a brief sociological and personal portrait (written by his brother), see P. Gustafson, "A Sociological and Fraternal Perspective on James M. Gustafson's Ethics," in Religious Sociology: Interfaces and Boundaries 57 (ed. William H. Swatos, Greenwood Press, 1987).

12   *See* Gustafson, *supra* note 3, at 101–6.

13   *Id.* at 104.

14   *Id.* at 105.

15   *Id.*

16   *Id.*

17   *Id.* at 107.

18   *Id.* at 117 & n.4.

19   *Id.* at 116.

20   *Id.* at 114.

21   *Id.* at 116.

22   For a fuller account of his theological world view, *see* Gustafson, 1 *Ethics from a Theocentric Perspective*, at 163–78. In 1984, Gustafson briefly summarized his views on abortion: "The choice is always a morally serious one because fetal life has the possibility of developing into a unique human being with capacities for self-fulfillment and for contributions to the human community. There are circumstances in which it is morally justifiable, though it is always a tragic choice. Among those circumstances might be a familial situation in which the birth of another child and the resources needed for its care would severely jeopardize the survival and well-being of the family and its other members. Other courses of action for relieving such dire straits, however, ought to be taken by the family and by the community of which it is a part." Gustafson, 2 *Ethics from a Theocentric Perspective*, at 245–46.

     Consider the views of Paul Lehmann, another important Protestant contextual ethicist, who was a student of Barth and a close friend of Bonhoeffer. The following was reported to us in a letter from Milner Ball (Oct. 1990): "[I]t was reported to me that, in the question-answer period following a public lecture of his, Paul Lehmann was asked what he thought about abortion. He gave a long, complicated answer that mystified the audience. Frustrated, the questioner asked: 'Dr. Lehmann, are you against abortion—yes or no?' To which he responded: 'Yes . . . and no. In that order.'" Gustafson regards Lehmann as too "polemical" in his opposition to "absolutist ethics." *See* Gustafson, *supra* note 3, at 122. For an introduction to Lehmann, *see* Paul Louis Lehmann, *Ethics in a Christian Context* (SCM Press, 1963), at 122.

23   *See generally* Paul Ramsey, *Ethics at the Edges of Life: Medical and Legal Intersections* (Yale U. Press, 1978), at 60–100. Ramsey's principal mission, in *Nine Modern Moralists* (Prentice-Hall, 1962), is to show how the supposed moral relativists cannot evade some absolutism (or natural law), while neither can their absolutist counterparts evade the relativistic reality of context. Ramsey, at the time, was chairman of the religion department of Princeton University.

24   *See* Ramsey, *supra* note 3, at 78. Ramsey carefully distinguishes the moral issue of abortion from the legal one. Citing Aquinas for the proposition that "[h]uman law does not prescribe concerning all the acts of every virtue: but only in regard to those that are ordainable to the common good." *Id.* at 63, n.7 (citing *Summa Theologica*, at pts. 2 and 3). Ramsey follows Norman St. John-Stevas in offering three tests for telling when wrongful practices become fit subjects for legislation: "(1) the practice injures the common good substantially, (2) the law can be enforced equitably in its incidence, and (3) its enforcement does

not cause greater evils than those it represses." *Id.* at 63 & n.7. He concludes that "[t]hese criteria . . . would give us pause in passing from sin or wrong to crime." *Id.* at 63.

25   *See id.* at 91–95. Both Barth and Bonhoeffer have been distorted in the service of both sides of the abortion debate. John T. Noonan, Jr., for example, appropriates them for his own categorical opposition to abortion. *See A Private Choice: Abortion in America in the Seventies* (Free Press, 1979), at 60–61, 169. Similarly ignoring the dialectical reality of both Barth's and Bonhoeffer's ethics, Joseph Fletcher dismisses them both as Protestants who "take the Catholic position." *See* "A Protestant Minister's Position," in 1 *Abortion in a Changing World*, at 25, 26. (This took place at the 1968 conference.) For the Barthian position, *see* chap. 3, *supra.*

26   Reviewing the 1967 conference, the authors of *The Terrible Choice* concluded: "The official Catholic position is not so simple, so rigid, or so monolithic as is commonly thought. Cultural relativism was accepted as morally relevant to the abortion question by at least one Catholic theologian. One ought not to suggest that the Catholic Church's teaching is about to change in a substantive way; it is clear, however, that the teaching is susceptible of gradual development through a process of refinement. In discussion of a case history presented at the Conference, Father Johann [Rev. Robert O. Johann, S.J., Fordham University (Philosophy)] remarked in passing: 'The question I pose very seriously for the Catholic moralist is that we consider and . . . try to understand at least what is behind the perception of so many people . . . where dealing in particular with the fetus is felt, experienced, perceived as being something different from dealing with an infant.' Father Johann was here calling for theological reflection on the social facts" (87–88). Some at the conference, such as Noonan and his colleague, David Louisell, took the extreme pro-life position with which we are today familiar. Other Catholics, however, took a variety of positions. Robert Drinan of Boston College Law School advocated that "criminal law withdraw entirely from abortion control," yet he also expressed his fear that legalization of abortion would lead us to "institutionalize abortion as the contraception of the poor." *Id.* at 102. "If abortion were given on request, would this not in effect lead to the proposition that the poor can have the number of their children limited by the wishes of a white suburban affluent society?" *Id.* at 24. Richard McCormick, a noted Catholic medical ethicist, reminded the participants that there was a " 'tenable and respectable theory' preferred by a notable number of [Catholic] philosophers and theologians which holds that the soul is not infused at conception but rather at some later point, perhaps when the body develops recognizably human characteristics." *Id.* at 86. It has even been suggested that Catholic tradition itself offers a contextual ethics that might serve a quest for compromise with respect to the abortion issue. That tradition is the legal one of casuistry. *See* Albert R. Jonsen & Stephen Toulmin, *The Abuse of Casuistry: A History of Moral Reasoning* 333–38 (U. of California Press, 1988).

27   Häring, *supra* note 3, at 123.

28   *Id.* at 123–24.

29   *Id.* at 124–45.

30   *Id.* at 131–32.

31   *Id.* at 132.

32   *Id.* at 135.

33   *Id.* at 124, 135–38.

34   *See id.* at 139–42.

35   *See id.* at 140. It must be conceded that Häring's spirit of exploration and "re-finement" is not entirely welcome today. Archbishop Rembert G. Weakland of Milwaukee was recently disciplined by the Vatican (mandatory withdrawal of an honorary degree) for having criticized the tactics of antiabortion activists and for suggesting, not unlike Häring, that moral principles could not be a matter of law unless they enjoyed a "consensus of the population." P. Stein-fels, "Vatican Bars Swiss University from Honoring Archbishop of Milwau-kee," *New York Times,* Nov. 11, 1990, §1, at 20. Similarly, on the difficulties facing contemporary dissenters within the church on the abortion issue, *see* Barbara Ferraro & Patricia Hussey, with Jane O'Reilly, *No Turning Back: Two Nuns' Battle with the Vatican Over Women's Right to Choose* (Poseidon Press, 1990).

36   Häring, *supra* note 3.

37   Callahan, *supra* note 9, at 308.

38   *See id.* at 307–48, 448–83.

39   *Id.* at 448–83.

40   *Id.* at 467.

41   *Id.* at 477–78.

42   *Id.* at 486.

43   Stanley Hauerwas, "Abortion and Normative Ethics," in *Vision and Virtue: Essays in Christian Ethical Reflection* 127 (Fides Publishers, 1974); "Abortion: The Agent's Perspective," in *Vision and Virtue,* at 147–65.

44   Stanley Hauerwas, "Abortion: The Agent's Perspective", in *Vision and Virtue,* at 155–56. While seemingly not agreeing with Callahan's moderate pro-choice position, Hauerwas sees no easy answer: "It may be that issues such as abortion are finally not susceptible to intellectual 'solution.' I do not mean to suggest that we cease trying to formulate the problem in the most responsible manner possible, but rather that our best recourse may be to watch how good men and women handle the tragic alternatives we often confront in abortion situa-tions. . . . For no amount of ethical reflection will ever change the basic fact that tragedy is a reality of our lives. A point is reached where we must have the wisdom to cease ethical reflection and affirm that certain issues indicate a reality more profound than the ethical." "Abortion and Normative Ethics," in *Vision and Virtue,* at 146.

45   Häring, *supra* note 3, at 143. One need not believe in pluralism to accept it as a reality constraint. As A. James Reichley reports with respect to the great American Catholic theologian John Courtney Murray: "Murray doubted no more than Cardinal Ottaviani or Monsignor Ryan that 'religious pluralism is against the will of God.' But pluralism, he had decided, 'is the human condi-tion; it is written into the script of history.'" Reichley, *Religion in American Public Life* (Brookings Institution, 1985), at 287.

46   Häring, *supra* note 3, at 143.

47   *Id.* at 144.

48   *Id.*

49   *See, e.g.,* John Courtney Murray, "Religious Freedom," in *Freedom and Man* (ed. John Courtney Murray, P.J. Kenedy, 1965), at 131; Murray, "The Declaration of Religious Freedom: A Moment in Its Legislative History," in *Religious Liberty: An End and a Beginning* (ed. John Courtney Murray, Macmillan, 1966), at 15. This is not to say that Murray was a liberal, however: "The issue is drawn. Which is the myth and which is the reality? Is the myth in Nietzsche or in the New Testament? Is it in Marx or in Moses? Is it in Sartre of Paris or in Paul of Tarsus? Is God dead, as the prophet of the post-modern age proclaimed, or is he still the living God of more ancient prophecy, immortal in his being as He Who Is, deathlessly faithful to his promise to be with us all the days, even to the end of the epoch within which both the modern and the post-modern ages represent only moments in a longer dialectic of history?" *The Problem of God: Yesterday and Today* 120 (Yale U. Press, 1964) (presented as the inaugural series of St. Thomas More Lectures at Yale University in 1962).

50   *See* "Cardinal Bernardin's Call for a Consistent Ethic of Life," 13 *Origins* 491–94 (1983) (text of Dec. 6, 1983, address by Joseph Cardinal Bernardin at Fordham University in New York); "Cardinal Bernardin's St. Louis Address: Enlarging the Dialogue on a Consistent Ethic of Life," 13 *Origins* 705 (1984) (text of March 11, 1984, address by Bernardin at St. Louis University). Bernardin has insisted on "a consistent, pro-life philosophy, a 'seamless garment,' encompassing the church's positions on armaments, abortion, and the death penalty. Pro-life activists are furious at this seeming surrender to the liberals, allowing abortion to be swallowed up in a range of issues incapable together of mobilizing any considerable 'clout.' " David O'Brien, "Catholic Contentiousness: The Public Consequences of Denominational Disputes," in *Uncivil Religion* (ed. Robert N. Bellah and Frederick E. Greenspahn, Crossroad Press, 1987), at 156, 159. For expressions of such an ethic of life by pro-life feminists, *see* Sidney Callahan, "A Moral Obligation," *Sojourners*, Nov. 1989, at 18; Kathleen Hayes, "Fully Pro-Life," *Sojourners*, Nov. 1989, at 22. For discussion of economic rights and Catholic tradition, *see* Lisa Cahill, "The Catholic Tradition: Religion, Morality and the Common Good," 5 J.L. & Religion 75 (1987). For a critical challenge to the consistency of the American bishops with respect to their pro-peace and pro-life efforts, see Mary Segers, "A Consistent Life Ethic: A Feminist Perspective on the Pro-Peace and Pro-Life Activities of the American Catholic Bishops," in *Women, Militarism, and War: Essays in History, Politics, and Social Theory* 61–84 (ed. Jean Elshtain & Sheila Tobias, Rowman & Littlefield, 1990).

51   Robert Drinan apparently changed his mind on this issue sometime between 1965 and 1967; at the 1967 conference he took the position that the state should withdraw from abortion control through criminal law. *Compare* Drinan, "The Inviolability of the Right to Be Born," in *Abortion and the Law* 107 (comp. David T. Smith, Press of Western Reserve U., 1967) (essays originally solicited for a law review symposium in 1965–66), with *The Terrible Choice,* at 102. David O'Brien of Holy Cross College believes that Drinan, who later served as a U.S. congressman from Massachusetts, was "driven from office . . . by right-to-life agitation." O'Brien, "Catholic Contentiousness," at 156. On the Drinan matter, *see also* Garry Wills, *Under God: Religion and American Politics* (Simon & Schuster,

1990), at 241. The evolution of Drinan's views on abortion and law is described in Callahan, *supra* note 9, at 436–38.

52   Alan F. Guttmacher, "Abortion—Yesterday, Today, and Tomorrow," in *The Case for Legalized Abortion Now* 1, 12–13 (ed. Alan F. Guttmacher, Diablo Press, 1967).

53   381 U.S. 479 (1965). Given the dependence of *Roe v. Wade* on *Griswold* for its privacy rationale, it is important to recall just how problematic a decision *Griswold* was. Every justice but one (Tom Clark) wrote separately. Three of the justices (Goldberg, Warren, and Brennan) jointly wrote a concurring opinion. Harlan and White wrote separate opinions, concurring with Douglas's majority only in the judgment. *Id.* at 499 (Harlan, J., concurring); *Griswold*, 381 U.S. at 502 (White, J., concurring). Black and Stewart wrote separate dissents.

Douglas was so desperate to avoid the charge of "substantive" due process that he engaged in some amazing verbal legerdemain to prove that "privacy" was actually protected by the Bill of Rights, as incorporated through the Fourteenth Amendment, and therefore consistent with post-New Deal judicial review theory. *Griswold*, 381 U.S. at 481–85. Thus, privacy as physical security (Fourth Amendment) and privacy as confidentiality (Fith Amendment) became privacy as privacy, which therefore protected something new, privacy as autonomy. *See id.* at 484–85. There was also the play on the word "association," which took a First Amendment doctrine that protected membership confidentiality and transposed it through sheer formalism to protect martial "association." *See id.* at 482–84. And of course there was the frightening imagery of alien intruders in the marital bedroom (*id.* at 485–86) (remember how poor Bork got roasted on that one), which had nothing to do with the case, since the sanctity of the marital bedroom *as a place* was neither at issue nor secured by the decision. For an excellent and insightful critique of the Douglas opinion, drawing on linguistic philosophy, that was unfortunately lost in the liberal euphoria of the times, *see* Hyman Gross, "The Concept of Privacy," 42 NYU L. Rev. 34 (1967).

Even more problematic was the concurring opinion of Goldberg, Warren, and Brennan, which relied explicitly on the Ninth Amendment's reservation of "rights . . . retained by the people." *Griswold*, 381 U.S. at 487–88 (Goldberg, J., concurring). Just how problematic it was is evident if one looks at the major interpretive secondary source cited by the concurring justices (*id.* at 490 n.6, citing Bennett Patterson, *The Forgotten Ninth Amendment: A Call for Legislative and Judicial Recognition of Rights Under Social Conditions of Today* [Bobbs-Merrill, 1955]). As Justice Black realized, the Patterson book is an explicit call for a "revival of natural law" through the medium of the Ninth Amendment. *Griswold*, 381 U.S. at 518 n.12 (Black, J., dissenting). And the natural law sought by Patterson is one that is firmly rooted in theology.

The other four opinions, two of which were dissents, all agreed that this was a substantive due process case, inasmuch as the Court was defining the content of the word "liberty" in the Fourteenth Amendment. Justice Harlan, while concurring, was cautionary: "Judicial self-restraint . . . will be achieved in this area, as in other constitutional areas, only by continual insistence upon respect for the teachings of history, solid recognition of the basic values that underlie our society, and wise appreciation of the great roles that the doctrines of federalism and separation of powers have played in establishing and preserving American freedoms." *Griswold*, 381 U.S. at 501 (Harlan, J., concurring).

None of this is to say that *Griswold* was wrongly decided. But when the Court ventures to define the meaning of "liberty" as it did in *Griswold*, it is doing the same thing it did in the infamous Lochner v. New York, 198 U.S. 45 (1905), offering the public a particularized version of natural law and freedom. On the normative implications of judicial review, including a brief discussion of *Griswold*, *see* Richard Hiers, "Normative Analysis in Judicial Determination of Public Policy" 3 J.L. & *Religion* 77 (1985) (on *Griswold* in particular, *see id.* at 99–102). Whether *Griswold*'s particular vision accords with consensus or with publicly shared values is an inescapable element in the constitutional calculus. *Griswold* was easy in that regard, since Connecticut stood alone in 1965 in banning the use of contraceptives by married people.

In other areas of modern substantive due process, the Court has been careful not to stray too far from values rooted in consensus. *Compare, e.g.*, Village of Belle Terre v. Boraas, 416 U.S. 1 (1974) (groups of more than two unrelated persons not constitutionally entitled to live together), *with* Moore v. City of East Cleveland, 431 U.S. 494 (1977) (right of "extended family" to live together protected by substantive due process).

54   *Griswold*, 381 U.S. at 485.

55   *Morality of Abortion.*

56   Gunnar Myrdal, *An American Dilemma: The Negro Problem in American Democracy* (Harper & Bros., 1944).

57   *See* David W. Southern, *Gunnar Myrdal and Black-White Relations: The Use and Abuse of "An American Dilemma," 1944–1969* (Louisiana State U. Press, 1987), at 127–50.

58   The 1968 conference was held at Hot Springs, Virginia, November 17–20, 1968. It resulted in a two-volume publication, *Abortion in a Changing World* (ed. Robert E. Hall, Columbia U. Press, 1970). For a list of conference participants, *see* 2 *Abortion in a Changing World*, at 213–18.

Of the 93 participants, more than half (56) are identifiable as physicians or health professionals, as compared with 15 out of 72 at the 1967 conference. On the other hand, only 11 of the 93 are religiously affiliated, as compared with 23 out of 72 for the 1967 conference. Eleven of the participants were women, virtually the same percentage as the 1967 conference, with two female physician/medical school teachers (Sophia Kleegman and Natalie Shaines) being the only two participants listed for *both* conferences (which certainly amounts to a tiny overlap for two conferences ostensibly on the same subject held in the same area of the same country within a year of one another). *Id.*

Racially identifiable as nonwhite is Percy Sutton, borough president of Manhattan at the time. The 1968 conference was, however, much more genuinely international in representation than the earlier one. Whereas the 1967 conference listed participants from Canada and Western Europe (England, France, Netherlands, Sweden), the 1968 conference drew participants not only from Western Europe (England, Sweden, Belgium, Greece), but also from Eastern Europe (Czechoslovakia, Hungary, East Germany, Yugoslavia, the USSR), Africa (Nigeria), Asia (India, Taiwan, Korea, Japan), the Middle East (Turkey, Israel), and South America (Brazil, Chile). *Id.*

John T. Noonan's account of the 1968 conference is characteristically sarcastic but not inaccurate: "The conference was under the auspices of the Association for the Study of Abortion, that imperfectly disguised committee for the promotion of the abortion liberty. It was organized by Alan Guttmacher, Louis Hellman, and Planned Parenthood's chief lawyer, Harriet Pilpel. Announced as a meeting to 'discuss' abortion, the conference had the kind of ratio of proponents to opponents not uncharacteristic of pro-choice symposia—twenty of the pro-choice side to one of the other." *Supra* note 25, at 44.

59   Hall, "Commentary," in *Abortion and the Law* 224, 234.

60   Rockefeller, "Abortion Law Reform—The Moral Basis," in 1 *Abortion in a Changing World.*

61   *Id.* at xv, xvii.

62   *Id.* at xviii.

63   *Id.* at xix.

64   *Id.* at xx. Whitney Young at the 1967 conference had expressed some ambivalence, arguing vigorously, on the one hand, that if "abortions are a fact of life" in this country and "are engaged in substantially by people who can afford them," then the poor should have equal access, yet conceding that he was "a little suspicious when the first intervention, first concern as regards the Negro is around liberalizing sterilization laws and abortion laws, but the real concern is less with the human being involved and there is much more concern about increased Aid to Dependent Children and welfare caseloads." *The Terrible Choice,* at 64.

Dorothy Height, then-president of the National Council of Negro Women, felt that "[i]f we had the courage to deal" with problems like "poverty," "deprivation," and "racial discrimination," "it would allow these children to come into life really wanted." *Id.* at 19–20. And Eric Lincoln, at the time of Union Theological Seminary, reported: "[t]here is a very broad suspicion on the part of many Negroes that what appears to be a sudden concern with contraception and with abortion is thought by many to be a part of a very heinous plot to eliminate, or further control, not only the black minority in this country, but dark minorities everywhere." *Id.* at 24. At the 1968 conference, Percy Sutton, whose role in the panel on abortion and poverty was to "speak about abortion in the Negro ghetto," *supra* note 58, at 31, spoke only about the (real) problem of access and availability of abortions for poor women. *See id.* at 32–35.

Recent data reveal that while nonwhites have often, when surveyed, reported more opposition to abortion than whites (see, e.g., Wade Clark Roof & William McKinney, *American Mainline Religion: Its Changing Shape and Future* [Rutgers Univ. Press, 1987], at 209–13 [black Protestants]), abortion rates among nonwhites are dramatically higher than their white counterparts: "In 1981, based on reported data from thirty-four states, black (and other) women had approximately 240,000 abortions and white women approximately 580,000. The abortion ratio (number of legal abortions per 1000 live births) was 549 for black women and 329 for white women." Hyman Rodman, Betty Sarvis, & Joy Walker Bonar, *The Abortion Question* (Columbia U. Press, 1987), at 153. A 1989 study reports that "[i]n the mid-1980s, there were about 64 abortions per 100 live black births and 30 abortions per 100 white births in a 13-state reporting area." "Children and Families," in *A Common Destiny: Blacks and American Society*

509, 513 (ed. Gerald David Jaynes & Robin M. Williams, Jr., National Academy Press, 1989). The authors of *The Abortion Question* conclude from such data that "black women are currently exercising more reproductive control."

Perhaps the issue is more complicated and places in question the experiential meaning of "choice." Consider the following statement from a black mother, as reported by Robert Coles: "They say, no, no—no more kids; the welfare worker she tells you you're 'overpopulating' the world, and something has to be done. But right now one of the few times I feel good is when I'm pregnant, and I can feel I'm getting somewhere, at least then I am—because I'm making something grow, and not seeing everything die around me, like all it does in the street, I'll tell you. They want to give me the pill and stop the kids, and I'm willing for the most part; but I wish I could take care of all the kids I could have, and then I'd want plenty of them. Or maybe I wouldn't. I wouldn't have to be pregnant to feel hope about things. I don't know, you can look at it both ways, I guess." Callahan, *supra* note 9, at 506.

65 1 *Abortion in a Changing World*, *supra* note 58, at 3–57. Volume 1 reports on the five plenary sessions at the conference, and volume 2 reports on the ten subsequent panels, which ran, five at a time, simultaneously. Among the panels were discussions entitled "Abortion and Animation," "Abortion and Poverty," "Abortion and Morality," and "Abortion and Womankind."

66 George W. Corner, "An Embryologist's View," in 1 *Abortion in a Changing World*, at 3.

67 Cyril Means, "A Historian's View," in 1 *Abortion in a Changing World*, at 16.

68 Joseph F. Fletcher, "A Protestant Minister's View," in 1 *Abortion in a Changing World*, at 25.

69 *Id.* at 25–26.

70 *Id.* at 26.

71 *Id.*

72 *Id.*

73 *Id.*

74 *Id.* at 27.

75 *Id.* Fletcher elaborated on his views during the subsequent panel discussions. At the panel entitled "Abortion and Animation" (ensoulment), Fletcher proclaimed: "[T]his whole discussion is like the argument about the death of God—pointless because we cannot establish whether God was ever alive to begin with. All of the positions taken by people about animation are a matter of faith rather than empirical reasoning; therefore, the debate provides no foundation for social policy with respect to abortion. . . . Desirability—that is, a bill of goods and evils in any concrete situation realistically assessed in terms of human needs and social welfare—should decide whether we terminate a life in *utero* or postnatally just as we would in any case of self-defense or common defense." 2 *Abortion in a Changing World*, at 5. Fletcher went even further at the panel entitled "Abortion and Morality: The Relationship between Available Abortion and Sexual Freedom" (all seven of the panelists were men). Fletcher made clear that his goal was sex without consequences, that his moral position was maximization of human satisfaction. To that end, he announced that early abortion was "the best method of fertility control because it would

entail, if present research succeeds, the least discomfort and the least risk of failure due to emotion or carelessness and the least hazard of ineffectiveness." *Id.* at 93. Fletcher summed up his moral outlook: "I say, let's be done with all objective morality, that is to say, any notion in terms of scriptural law or natural law, that right and wrong and good and evil are intrinsic values, and take instead the view that all values are quite extrinsic, dependent upon the varieties of circumstances." *Id.*

By way of contrast with (and perhaps antidote to) Fletcher's shallow utilitarianism, consider recent efforts by federal judge Richard A. Posner to offer a utilitarian ethical analysis of the abortion issue. *Sex and Reason* (Harvard U. Press, 1992), at 272–290. Posner frankly concedes that a "critical" uncertainty is "v," the value of fetal life, concluding that his analysis must be "inconclusive even on its own terms." Before reaching that conclusion, however, Posner, illustrating what utilitarians do best, carefully clarifies the issues. He also suggests that while ultimately inconclusive, his analysis does suggest that "the extreme positions . . . are untenable."

76   Fletcher, "A Protestant Minister's View," in 1 *Abortion in a Changing World*, at 28.

77   Israel Margolies, "A Reform Rabbi's View," in 1 *Abortion in a Changing World*, at 32.

78   *Id.* at 33.

79   "Discussion," in 1 *Abortion in a Changing World*, at 46, 53.

80   *Id.* at 53.

81   Thomas J. O'Donnell, "A Traditional Catholic's View," in 1 *Abortion in a Changing World*, at 34.

82   *See* Joseph Donceel, "A Liberal Catholic's View," in 1 *Abortion in a Changing World*, at 39–45 (italics omitted).

83   *Id.* at 39–40.

84   *Id.* at 44.

85   *Id.* at 45. Curiously, the delayed animation notion has recently gained some scientific support as a way to solve the abortion dilemma. By defining the beginning of life to achieve symmetry with our standard for its termination, brain wave activity, Hans-Martin Sass of the Kennedy Institute of Ethics at Georgetown University has proposed that we "set the beginning of life at about 70 days after conception, when he says the brain has started to function and connections between nerve cells are rapidly forming." His model abortion law, fashioned accordingly, would legalize abortions only in the first ten weeks of pregnancy, except, perhaps, for medical indications. *See* Joan Beck, "Let's Use Scientific Basis to Fix Beginning of Life and Settle Abortion Issue," *Buffalo News*, Nov. 25, 1990, at G-7, col. 3; *see also,* Eike-Henner W. Kluge, *The Practice of Death* 88–100 (Yale Univ. Press, 1975); P. Steinfels, "Catholic Scholars, Citing New Data, Widen Debate on When Life Begins," *New York Times*, Jan. 13, 1991, § 4 (Week in Review), at 5.

86   *Discussion,* 1 *Abortion in a Changing World*, at 54.

87   *Id.* at 54–55.

88   *Id.* at 55–56.

89   *Id.* at 56–57. While there was no feminist presence as such at the 1968 conference, which was hardly atypical for the early abortion reform movement, one of the ten subsequent panels was devoted, almost in the manner of a

traditional "ladies" auxiliary," to "Abortion and Womankind: Abortion as an Inherent Right, an Occasional Prerogative, or a Special Privilege." 2 *Abortion in a Changing World*, at 191. The group consisted of eight of the eleven women listed as conference participants—four physicians, a psychologist, a social scientist, a lawyer, and Vera Houghton, chairman, Abortion Law Reform Association, London. (See the alphabetical entries of participants in *id*. at 213–18).

Mary Calderone, M.D., executive director of the Sex Information and Education Council of the United States and moderator of the panel, opened the session by reminding the group that "Dr. Robert Hall deliberately made this a panel of women so that we would approach the question as women." *Id*. at 193. The first third of the session consisted of reports and discussion with respect to incidence of abortion and surveys of attitudes toward abortion, especially in England where a reform law had recently been enacted. *Id*. at 193–201. Then Sophia Kleegman, M.D., professor of obstetrics and gynecology at New York University Medical Center, spoke from her forty-four years of medical practice, focusing on serious problems of poverty and illegal abortion, concluding that we should "have all legal restrictions removed entirely to allow physicians to take care of their patients within the framework of sound medical judgment and practice." *Id*. at 201–3, 215. Ruth Lidz, M.D., associate clinical professor of psychiatry at Yale, reported on her work in the "unwed mother" project at Yale, where she gave therapeutic counseling to women seeking abortions and then advocated for those she believed deserved the abortions (forty of forty-two she regarded as "deserved"). *Id*. at 204–6, 216. Her conclusion was somewhat cautious: "[W]hile I would like very much to have all restrictive abortion laws removed, I would like to caution that this is not going to settle all of our problems. It is two different things, to be pregnant and to have the child, and many women are very much mortified by becoming pregnant, but not by having a child." *Id*. at 205.

Next, Ruth Roemer, a lawyer and associate researcher in health law at UCLA, spoke in what we have come to regard as "rights terms": "[W]omen, particularly in the developed countries, are coming to regard abortion as a fundamental human right. . . . It is a right so fundamental, so personal to women, that its denial nullifies the right to freedom and to security of their person and of their families." *Id*. at 207. Roemer then called for the panel to "address itself to political action designed to make abortion freely available to women who want it." *Id*. at 208. Interpreting the call as a motion, Calderone replied that she "would like to include in it the motion that with every right go certain obligations." *Id*. Then things got a little heated:

Roemer: We are carrying out our obligations.
Calderone: Not with repeated unwanted pregnancies. The rights and obligations should balance.
R. Lidz: Yes. I think that I am also for removing the law. I am very much for that, but I do not think that will solve our problems. (*Id*. at 208)

Kleegman offered her view: "I do not believe in abortion on demand. I feel very strongly that if a woman asks for an abortion it is a medical problem, and I do not think physicians should be chaplains. When a woman requests an abortion, then I think it is important that she be given the opportunity to be seen by someone who is trained." *Id.* at 209. And Calderone would not let the moral issue go: "The point I want to make is that we have a picture of many young people marrying today because they know if things do not work out properly, they can get a divorce all too quickly. And to have young people growing up and saying, "Well, we can always get an abortion"—this is what I was driving at. This has already happened in Japan, where multiple abortions are carried out on the same woman. It is too easy." *Id.* at 209.

By way of testament to the diversity of viewpoints, Natalie Shaines, M.D., lecturer in psychiatry at Columbia University College of Physicians and Surgery (id. at 217), gave the last long statement of the session, seeing "the abortion problem [as] one manifestation of the power struggle between the sexes, with man fearful of and reluctant to surrender power, as is every group which is in command," and citing Simone de Beauvoir regarding male-female relations. *Id.* at 210–11.

90 Herbert L. Packer & Ralph Gampell, "Therapeutic Abortion: A Problem in Law and Medicine," 11 *Stanford L. Rev.* 417 (1959). This was consistent with Packer's approach to criminal law in other problem areas. *See The Limits of the Criminal Sanction* (Stanford U. Press, 1968).

91 *See* 2 *Abortion in A Changing World, supra,* at 107–8.

92 *The Case for Legalized Abortion Now* 147, *supra* note 52.

93 Roy Lucas, "Federal Constitutional Limitations on the Enforcement and Administration of State Abortion Statutes," 46 N.C.L. Rev. 730 (1968). On its significance, *see* Daniel Callahan, *supra* note 25, at 468–73.

94 Lucas, *supra* note 93, at 738.

95 *Id.* at 755–56.

96 2 *Abortion in a Changing World,* at 137.

97 Lucas, *supra* note 71, at 737. Interestingly, Milner Ball, who was a Protestant parish minister in the 1960s and who had not yet gone to law school, recalls the perception among his fellow theologians that the *Griswold* decision was basically a statement to the Roman Catholic church that it should not enact its doctrine into law. The Catholic church was presumed by Ball and his colleagues to exercise legislative power in Connecticut. Letter from Milner Ball to Elizabeth Mensch and Alan Freeman (Oct. 1990).

98 Lucas, *supra* note 71, at 760.

99 *Id.* at 751.

100 *Id.* at 751–52 (quoting H. L. A. Hart, *Law, Liberty, and Morality* 21 [1963]).

101 2 *Abortion in a Changing World,* at 160.

102 *People v. Belous,* 71 Cal. 2d 954, 458 P.2d 194, 80 Cal. Rptr. 354 (1969) (finding the phrase "necessary to preserve" the life of the mother insufficiently certain to satisfy due process requirements without violating constitutional rights), *cert.* denied 397 U.S. 915 (1970).

103 Louisell & Noonan, "Constitutional Balance," in *Morality of Abortion,* at 220.

104 *See* Elizabeth Mensch & Alan Freeman, "Religion as Science/Science as Religion: Constitutional Law and the Fundamentalist Challenge," *Tikkun,* Nov.–Dec. 1987, at 64.

105 *See* Louisell & Noonan, *supra* note 103, at 220–30, 244–58. They are on more

solid ground when they argue that the precedential route from *Griswold* to abortion is far from obvious. *See id.* at 233–34.

106　*See, e.g.,* David Richards, "Constitutional Privacy, Religious Disestablishment, and the Abortion Decisions," in *Abortion: Moral and Legal Perspectives* 148 (ed. Jay L. Garfield & Patricia Hennessey, U. of Massachusetts Press, 1984). Laurence H. Tribe himself made this argument back in 1973 and later repudiated it. *Compare* Tribe, "The Supreme Court, 1972 Term—Foreword: Toward a Model of Roles in the Due Process of Life and Law," 87 *Harvard L. Rev.* 1, 21–25 (1973), with Laurence H. Tribe, *American Constitutional Law* 1349–50 (2d ed., Foundation Press, 1988), and Laurence H. Tribe, *Abortion: The Clash of Absolutes* 116 (Norton, 1990).

107　*See* Reichley, *Religion in American Public Life,* at 319–27; *see also* Michael Barone, *Our Country: The Shaping of America from Roosevelt to Reagan* 565, 610 (Free Press, 1990); Christopher F. Mooney, *Public Virtue: Law and the Social Character of Religion* 16–17 (U. of Notre Dame Press, 1986); Wills, *supra* note 51, at 121. *See generally id.* at 15–93.

9　Is Compromise Possible?

1　Yet we remain unpersuaded by Tribe's defense of the decision in Laurence H. Tribe, *Abortion: The Clash of Absolutes* 77–112 (Norton, 1990).

2　For an elaboration of this point, *see* William Van Alstyne, "Closing the Circle of Constitutional Review from *Griswold v. Connecticut* to *Roe v. Wade*: An Outline of a Decision Merely Overruling *Roe*," 1989 *Duke L.J.* 1677.

3　*Griswold v. Connecticut*, 381 U.S. 479, 499 (1965) (Harlan, J., concurring).

4　410 U.S. 179 (1973).

5　*Compare* Miller v. California, 413 U.S. 15 (1973) (upholding enforcement of local standard for obscenity), with Jenkins v. Georgia, 418 U.S. 153 (1974) (holding the film *Carnal Knowledge* not constitutionally obscene despite contrary finding under local standards).

6　*Compare* Gomillion v. Lightfoot, 364 U.S. 339 (1960) (striking down racial gerrymandering), with Wright v. Rockefeller, 376 U.S. 52 (1964) (not striking down racial gerrymandering).

7　*Compare* San Antonio Independent School District v. Rodriguez, 411 U.S. 1 (1973) (denying constitutional right to equalized school financing), with Plyler v. Doe, 457 U.S. 202 (1982) (mandating access to public education for illegal aliens under equal protection clause).

8　*See* Robert A. Burt, *The Constitution in Conflict* 271–310 (Belknap Press, 1992). In comparing *Roe* to Brown v. Board of Education, 347 U.S. 483 (1954), he notes that the result of *Brown* was to "break the silence" on segregation by removing the advantage whites imposed for so long, thereby returning the issue to public debate. *Id.* at 347–50.

9　*See* Burt, *supra* note 8, at 346–47 (the Catholic church was "discreet" and "reticent" in its legislative dealings until *Roe* impelled a "publicly visible political campaign"); A. James Reichley, *Religion in American Public Life* 327–28 (Brookings Institution, 1985) (fundamentalists are ready for "martyrdom" because "they are certain they are on the side of the angels"); Robert Wuthnow, *The Restructuring of American Religion: Society and Faith Since World War II* 212 (Princeton U. Press,

1988) ("New Right leaders saw abortion as a moral evil bringing danger to the well-being of the entire society.").

10 See Reichley, supra note 9, at 319–27; see also Michael Barone, Our Country: The Shaping of America from Roosevelt to Reagan 565, 610 (Free Press, 1990); Christopher Mooney, Public Virtue: Law and the Social Character of Religion 16–17 (U. of Notre Dame Press, 1986); Garry Wills, Under God: Religion and American Politics 121 (Simon & Schuster, 1990). See generally id. at 15–93.

Reichley describes the lay Catholic reaction to Roe v. Wade: "The sweeping nature of the Court's decision practically guaranteed that opponents of abortion would fight back in a similarly draconian spirit. Many lay Catholics who had stopped listening to their bishops over contraception and had been prepared to accept some modification of absolutist laws against abortion were startled and outraged by the Court's contention that for the first six months of gestation, unborn life has no rights whatever. They agreed with the bishops that the Court's ruling violated the fundamental value attached to individual human life not only by Catholicism but by the entire Judeo-Christian tradition, and indeed by most forms of Western humanism. Catholic opponents of abortion . . . were psychologically prepared to accept defeat in those states which enacted abortion reform, though they clearly did not relish the prospect. But 'deciding this question in the courts . . . was steadfastly opposed by the anti-abortion forces because it undermined the process of negotiation and compromise and denied effective representation to the unborn.'" Supra note 9, at 292.

For the troubled experience of one such lay Catholic who was caught in the middle of the abortion issue as secretary of Health, Education and Welfare in the Carter administration, see Joseph A. Califano, Jr., Governing America: An Insider's Report From the White House and the Cabinet 49–87 (Simon & Schuster, 1981) (the chapter is called "Abortion").

11 See James Davison Hunter, Culture Wars: The Struggle to Define America 90–92 (Basic Books, 1991) (surveying the increased development of religious groups focusing on abortion); Wuthnow, supra note 9, at 319–20 ("abortion . . . became the unifying cause"). See Leo Ribuffo, "The Complexity of American Religious Prejudice," in Right Center Left: Essays in American History (Rutgers U. Press, 1992), at 68–69 ("Abortion may be the nation's most divisive cultural issue since Prohibition but, unlike Prohibition, it unites conservative Catholics and Protestants instead of dividing them.").

12 Francis Schaeffer, A Christian Manifesto, in American Political Theology: Historical Perspective and Theoretical Analysis 140 (ed. Charles W. Dunn, Praeger, 1984).

13 For an account of just how manipulative and successful this effort was, see Reichley, supra note 9, at 319–27.

14 E.g., Tribe, supra note 1, at 51.

15 Barone, supra note 10, at 756 n.14.

16 See R. Lacayo, "Abortion: The Future Is Already Here," Time, May 4, 1992, at 27. The author observes that the battle against abortion may be succeeding regardless of what the courts decide. "At this moment, abortion is not available in 83% of America's counties, home to nearly a third of American women of childbearing age. For reasons of professional pride, or fear, or economic pres-

sure, doctors have backed away from the procedure even where it remains available." Id. at 28. This is reiterated in another article, which notes that "[m]any of those who do [continue to perform abortions] are veteran practitioners who remember the coat-hanger days. . . . At present, the procedure is routinely taught in only a quarter of all OB-GYN training programs." "Abortion Angst," Newsweek, July 13, 1992, at 16, 18.

17 See Jane Cohen, "Comparison-Shopping in the Marketplace of Rights," 98 Yale L.J. 1235, 1242 n.24 (1989) (yearning for a "full, documented history . . . of the national and international involvement of the sixties women's movement in abortion reform in the decade that ended with Roe").

18 Celeste Michelle Condit, Decoding Abortion Rhetoric: Communicating Social Change 74 n.5 (U. of Illinois Press, 1989) (rejecting the "Feminist account, which attributes the entire contemporary controversy" to this theory).

19 See generally Daniel Callahan, Abortion: Law, Choice & Morality 448–83 (Macmillan, 1970); Faye D. Ginsburg, Contested Lives: The Abortion Debate in an American Community 35–42 (U. of California Press, 1989); Kristin Luker, Abortion and the Politics of Motherhood 73–113 (U. of California Press, 1984) (focusing on California); Hyman Rodman, Betty Sarvis, & Joy Walker Bonar, The Abortion Question 94–104 (Columbia U. Press, 1987) (emphasizing legal rights). Callahan, reflecting on the issue twenty years after the publication of his book, notes a shift in voice, observing that "the most striking ideological development" since the early 70s "has been the emergence into leadership positions in the prochoice movement of some feminists who have scanted many of the original arguments for abortion reform," shifting the "emphasis almost entirely to a woman's right to an abortion, whatever her reasons and whatever the consequences." See "An Ethical Challenge to Prochoice Advocates: Abortion and the Pluralistic Proposition," 117 Commonweal 681–87 (1990).

20 Luker, supra note 19, at 92–93.

21 Ginsburg, supra note 19, at 37–38.

22 Id. at 6–7, 43.

23 E.g., Jerome Himmelstein, "The Social Basis of Antifeminism: Religious Networks and Culture," 25 J. for the Scientific Study of Religion 1 (1986) (offering a "simple name" for opponents of abortion and ERA).

24 An articulate example is Sidney Callahan, "Abortion and the Sexual Agenda," in The Ethics of Abortion: Pro-Life vs. Pro-Choice 131 (ed. Robert M. Baird & Stuart E. Rosenbaum, Prometheus Books, 1989).

25 On Weld, see Christopher Lydon, "Hostile Takeover: The Republican Raid on Massachusetts," New York Times Magazine, Aug. 2, 1992, at 32–33, 50, 52–53. Weld is alleged to have said that permitting women to have abortions through the ninth month of pregnancy is a price he "would pay in order to have government stay out of the thicket" (Boston Herald, May 6, 1992, at 1). This report prompted an advertisement in the form of "An Open Letter to Governor William F. Weld," signed by more than five hundred women, suggesting that Weld's "abortion package is part and parcel of a cold and heartless attitude toward poverty and helplessness in our society: discourage poor people from reproducing, and dress the 'solution' up in the language of women's rights."

26 The claim of "neutrality" seems as problematic as its counterpart in Reitman v.

Mulkey, 387 U.S. 369 (1967), where the Court (affirming a decision of the California Supreme Court) struck down California's Proposition 14, which had "repealed" fair-housing laws by constitutionalizing freedom of choice in housing rentals or sales. *Id.* at 377. By removing the issue from the legislative process altogether (albeit by referendum), California was guilty of "encourag[ing]" racial discrimination in housing. *Id.* at 381. *Roe*, by judicial decision alone, similarly removed the abortion issue from the legislative process nationally by constitutionalizing freedom of choice.

27 *See* "Society's Child," *New Republic*, May 18, 1992, at 39–43.

28 Judith Thomson, "A Defense of Abortion," 1 *Phil. & Pub. Affairs* 47, 48–49 (1971) (reprinted in *The Problem of Abortion* 121–39 [ed. Joel Feinberg, Wadsworth Publishing Co., 1984]).

29 Tribe *supra* note 1, at 129–30. Would Tribe also suggest that economic regulation demanding employer self-sacrifice for moral purposes, such as mandatory family leave time, would be unconstitutional because it is antilibertarian?

30 *Id.* at 129.

31 *See* Rosalind Hursthouse, *Beginning Lives* (Basil Blackwell, 1987), at 181–94 (critical of Thomson). Thomson herself shows more sensitivity to this dimension of the problem, once she moves past the "rights" analysis of her hypothetical; yet it is the rights analysis which has been so often cited approvingly in the pro-choice literature. *See* Thomson, *supra* note 28.

32 Kathleen McDonnell, *Not An Easy Choice: A Feminist Re-examines Abortion* 68–80 (South End Press, 1984) (discussing inherent coercions in the concept of "choice").

33 *See id.* at 71–80.

34 Jean Bethke Elshtain, *Power Trips and Other Journeys: Essays in Feminism as Civic Discourse* 47 (U. of Wisconsin Press, 1990) (discussing the views of Alison M. Jagger). Specifically, Jagger writes: "We must remember that the ultimate transformation of human nature at which socialist feminists aim goes beyond the liberal conception of psychological androgyny to a possible transformation of 'physical' human capacities, some of which, until now, have been seen as biologically limited to one sex. This transformation might even include the capacities for insemination, for lactation and for gestation so that, for instance, one woman could inseminate another, so that men and nonparturitive women could lactate and so that fertilized ova could be transplanted into women's or even men's bodies. These developments may seem farfetched, but in fact they are already on the technological horizon; however, what is needed much more immediately than technological development is a substantial reduction in the social domination of women by men. Only such a reduction can ensure that these or alternative technological possibilities are used to increase women's control over their bodies and thus over their lives, rather than being used as an additional means for women's subjugation. Gayle Rubin writes: 'We are not only oppressed as women, we are oppressed by having to be women or men as the case may be.' " *Id.* at 89. Elshtain, however, insists that "[b]iological differences do count; the question is how." *Id.* at xxii. While there may be a long history in which to analyze "to what extent women were powerful or powerless," it is certainly known that "[e]very human society differentiates

maleness from femaleness, and widely differing societies have located complementary forms of power with the two sexes. . . . In dozens of societies, . . . neither sex was wholly dominant over the other, but each prevailed in demarcated areas of social life." Id. at 140. Consequently, most feminist philosophy more likely reveals "a combination of maternal and community imperatives, including caring and sharing, plus evoking 'rights' and 'choice' as absolutes or nearly so." By pushing for the androgynous, independent individual, the "new eugenics [of ultraliberals like Jagger] puts terrific pressure on feminists" against their more communal philosophies. Id. at 91.

Elshtain is not alone in her criticism of the overemphasis by some women on individualism as opposed to community. Elizabeth Fox-Genovese contends that "the vision of androgyny . . . abstracts too much from the varieties of life in different human bodies, proposing homogenization of the ways of being—of male and female—rather than advocating free access to social and cultural categories for very different beings." In fact, once this idealistic vision of androgynous people arrives, it soon "collapses into the gray interchangeability of cogs in some machine." *Feminism Without Illusions: A Critique of Individualism* 228 (U. of North Carolina Press, 1991). Once the state intervenes, furthermore, the "growing power over men guarantees its growing power over women, albeit as isolated individuals rather than as members of communities." Id. at 51. See also Mary Ann Glendon, *Rights Talk: The Impoverishment of Political Discourse* 74 (Free Press, 1991) ("A large collection of self-determining, self-sufficient individuals cannot even be a society").

The argument that gender should be relevant to the abortion decisions has not been ignored by traditional legal scholars, however. Robert Burt proposes "an alternative doctrinal formulation available in *Roe*" that could have changed the substance of the argument, "constitutional equality." *Supra* note 8, at 349. Under this analysis, abortion laws unequally prevent women from freely engaging in sexual relations; their bodies are unfairly "conscripted" for fetal protection in comparison to compulsory military conscription; or, perhaps in a manner Jagger would prefer, "abortion restrictions are part of a long-standing general pattern of state-imposed devaluation and oppression of women in family and political relations." Id. Attacking the problem with this approach, however, reveals a "paradox at the core of our constitutional scheme: that no coercion is legitimate, even if it is sometimes unavoidable." Id. at 350. Nothing that imposes on another would ever be considered constitutionally permissible. The only basis, in Burt's opinion, for overturning a "coercive imposition because of its inherent inequality" is to assure an "equal status of stalemate on the adversaries," not to give one the upper hand. Id.

Guido Calabresi attempts a more in-depth analysis of this equality argument, but arrives at a contrary conclusion. Although his primary focus is on assessing the nature of judicial review in different types of cases, he writes "anti-abortion laws impose a greater degree of control over women's lives and behavior that is not imposed on men." Since at the time of *Roe*, women were "an excluded group," the laws must be reviewed for this inequality. "It is . . . no answer to argue that if men became pregnant, anti-abortion laws would not exist. Indeed, that is just the point." Calabresi, "Foreword: Antidiscrimination and Constitutional Accountability (What the Bork-Brennan Debate Ignores)," 105 Harv. L. Rev. 80, 91 (1991). Calabresi sketches a series of possible equality balancers within antiabortion laws, e.g., requiring expectant fathers to become available for blood, bone marrow, or as sources for organ transplants. Alternatives may be to require them to undertake other "compulsory, lifesaving duties." Calabresi is forced to conclude that "[i]n the end, the 'outlandishness' of my proposals is just one more bit of evidence that the polity is totally committed to life only when others have to bear the burden of preserving it, and it reinforces the intuition that we would not have anti-abortion laws if men could become pregnant." Id. at 95.

35 Although she is much tougher on fundamentalism (with some justification, perhaps, as far as gender roles are concerned), consider, e.g., the view of Beverly Wildung Harrison, Our Right to Choose: Toward a New Ethic of Abortion (Beacon Press, 1983), at 58, speaking of "mainstream Christianity": "Deification of the male gender and trivialization of women and sexuality are not simply minor subordinate themes in an otherwise enlightened Christian theological world view. . . . the hold of patriarchal idolatry on Christianity goes to the heart of its story and sense of mission." See also R. Siegal, "Reasoning from the Body: A Historical Perspective on Abortion Regulation and Questions of Equal Protection," 44 Stanford L. Rev. 261, 293–97 (1992) (use of theological terms by doctors to justify their antiabortion social views).

36 E.g., Harrison, supra note 35, at 57–62, 96–103.

37 The relations of women to their churches have varied according to faith and according to their experiences of dominant American culture. Jewish immigrant women moved away from the religious institutions into less restrictive, secular roles in American society, until Conservative and Reform Judaism presented the opportunity to demand a greater level of participation in the synagogue as well. Ann D. Braude, Jewish Women in the Twentieth Century: Building a Life in America, in 3 Women and Religion in America: 1900–1968 (ed. Rosemary Radford Ruether & Rosemary Skinner Keller, Harper & Row, 1986), at 135.

Almost the reverse process can be found in the various branches of evangelical, holiness, and pentecostal traditions. There was an early thrust in the direction of male/female equality in the churches, including ordination. Letha Scanzoni & Susan Setta, "Women in Evangelical, Holiness, and Pentecostal Traditions," in Women and Religion in America, at 224–27. Since World War II a move toward female subordination in both church and family life has dramatically decreased women's roles, although some have powerfully resisted the trend. These women invoke both modern feminism and the egalitarianism that has always been part of the evangelical spirit. See Barbara Zikmund, "Winning Ordination for Women in Mainstream Protestant Churches," in Women and Religion in America, at 368–70. See also Esther Bruland, "Evangelical and Feminist Ethics: Complex Solidarities" 17 J. of Religious Ethics 139–60 (1989).

Despite their exclusion from church hierarchies, women in mainstream American Protestantism developed strong, active organizations built around their religion. Many women chose to form independent societies for missionary, relief, and evangelical work. For a thorough history, see Barbara Leslie Epstein, The Politics of Domesticity: Women, Evangelism, and Temperance in Nineteenth-

Century America (Wesleyan U. Press 1981). The strength of these separatist societies eventually led to their negotiated merger into the structures of the denominations, which, in turn, led gradually to greater equality within those structures. *See* Zikmund, *supra,* at 347. For a summary of progress in the various mainstream denominations, *see id.* at 340–48. The Catholic church, of course, has continued to insist on ordination for celibate males only. For a dissenting view, *see* Garry Wills, *Bare Ruined Choirs: Doubt, Prophecy, and Radical Religion* 329–37 (Doubleday, 1972). For a good historical overview of the roles of Catholic women, both in religious orders in the service of education and health care, and as lay social activists, epitomized by Dorothy Day and the Catholic Worker movement, which found in the preaching of the gospel an alternative to atheistic socialism, *see* Lorine M. Getz, "Women Struggle for an American Catholic Identity," in *Women and Religion in America,* at 175.

38   Margaret L. Bendroth, "The Search for 'Women's Role' in American Evangelicalism, 1930–1980," in *Evangelicalism and Modern America* 123 (ed. George Marsden, W. B. Eerdmans, 1984).

39   Wuthnow, *supra* n.9, at 226.

40   *Id.* at 227. *See also* Erling Jorstad, *Holding Fast/Pressing On: Religion in America in the 1980s* 135–36 (Greenwood Press, 1990); Wade Clark Roof & William McKinney, *American Mainline Religion: Its Changing Shape and Future* 30, 204 (Rutgers U. Press, 1987).

41   Wuthnow, *supra* note 9, at 228.

42   Bendroth, *supra* note 38, at 132 (quoting Charles Caldwell Ryrie, *The Place of Women in the Church* 68) (Moody Press, 1968).

43   Jorstad, *supra* note 40, at 135.

44   Scanzoni & Setta, "Women in Evangelical, Holiness, and Pentecostal Traditions," in *Women and Religion in America,* note 37, at 233–34. This doctrine was imported through a translation of Fritz Zerbst's *The Office of Women in the Church* (Concordia Pub. House, 1955). Cf. Bendroth, *supra* note 38, at 133–34. As Bendroth notes, the question is far from resolved within evangelicalism.

45   Wuthnow, *supra* note 9, at 227; Roof & McKinney, *supra* n.40, at 204.

46   *See, e.g.,* Religious Coalition for Abortion Rights, "We Affirm: National Religious Organizations' Statement on Abortion Rights" (Religious Coalition for Abortion Rights, 1991), which contains an introduction and thirty-one separate organizational statements. There are pre-*Roe* statements of the American Friends Service Committee (1970), the National Council of Jewish Women (1969), the Unitarian Universalist Association (1963), United Church of Christ (1971), and the Young Women's Christian Association of the U.S.A. (1970); *see also* Luker, *supra* note 19, at 123.

47   *See, e.g.,* Religious Coalition for Abortion Rights, *supra* note 46. From the introduction to the collection of organizational statements: "Widespread denominational support exists for the right of women to choose safe and legal abortion, but the public has been falsely led to believe that all religions are opposed to abortion rights. The religious pro-choice community has a deep respect for the value of potential human life and an equally deep commitment to women as responsible, moral decision makers. . . . The Coalition believes that the right of reproductive freedom is intrinsically tied to religious liberty. We oppose

any attempts to enact into secular law restrictions on abortion based on one particular theological definition of when the fetus becomes a person."

48 See, e.g., David Heim, "Pro-Choice: Saying Something Theological," 109 Christian Century 699–700 (1992).

49 Presbyterian Church (USA), General Assembly, The Covenant of Life and the Caring Community and Covenant and Creation: Theological Reflections on Contraception and Abortion 31–61 (Office of the General Assembly, Presbyterian Church (USA), 1985) (originally adopted by the 195th General Assembly, 1983).

50 Id. at 32.

51 Id. at 36.

52 Id.

53 Id. at 53.

54 Id.

55 Id. at 43–44.

56 In its starkest, but hardly unusual, form, our contemporary secular notion of freedom combines expectations of security (or entitlement) on the one hand, with unaccountability on the other. This vision is basically that of the spoiled suburban teenager who expects to be fed, clothed, and otherwise taken care of, but becomes indignant at authoritarian interference with life-style choice. As reported by Lawrence M. Friedman of Stanford Law School: "Contemporary individualism implies as large a menu of choices as possible for each human being; only in this way can people freely develop their selves, their personalities, their central core of being. . . . Modern individualism is far from inconsistent with security; indeed, it thrives on security, it depends on security. . . . The world of modern individualism . . . presupposes, in the West, a certain base of wealth and leisure, and, what is more, a basic floor of guarantees, entitlements, social services, and rights." The Republic of Choice 109 (Harvard U. Press, 1990). In fact, the entire Friedman volume is a celebration of this version of freedom, which is most aptly characterized by the word "choice."

57 According to Patrick Collinson, "Luther and all subsequent Protestants" (including Calvin) understand the "gospel of Christ" as follows: "The key to this transaction was faith, defined as a total and trustful commitment of the self to God, and in itself not a human achievement but the pure gift of God. 'Faith cometh by hearing and hearing by the word of God': fides ex auditu. Thereafter the justified Christian man, in himself and of his own nature a sinner but not seen as a sinner by God, brings forth those good works which consist in the love of God and neighbour, not slavishly to win any reward but gladly, that service which is perfect freedom." "The Late Medieval Church and Its Reformation (1400–1600)," in The Oxford Illustrated History of Christianity 233, 258–59 (ed. John McManners, Oxford U. Press, 1990). On the life and thought of Calvin, see generally William J. Bouwsma, John Calvin: A Sixteenth Century Portrait (Oxford U. Press, 1988). For a series of essays on the complex relationship between faith and freedom, see The World Treasury of Modern Religious Thought chap. 8 (ed. Jaroslav Pelikan, Little, Brown, 1990).

Vaclav Havel offers a view of freedom, which Calvin might also have found appropriate, as freedom confronting responsibility; it is a freedom that understands both gratitude and obligation, not toward people, but toward God. In a speech to Congress, he said: "[T]he salvation of this human world lies nowhere else than in the human heart, in the human power to reflect, in human meekness and in human responsibility. . . . We are still incapable of understanding that the only genuine backbone of all our actions, if they are to be moral, is responsibility. Responsibility to something higher than my family, my country, my company, my success—responsibility to the order of being where all our actions are indelibly recorded and where and only where they will be properly judged." Time, March 5, 1990, at 14, 15 (publishing the text of Havel's speech). Havel also has observed: "We are going through a great departure from God which has no parallel in history. . . . I feel that this arrogant anthropocentrism of modern man, who is convinced he can know everything and bring everything under his control, is somewhere in the background of the present crisis. It seems to me that if the world is to change for the better it must start with a change in human consciousness, in the very humanness of modern man." Vaclav Havel, Disturbing the Peace: A Conversation with Karel Hvizdala (trans. Paul Wilson, Knopf, 1990), at 11. See also id. at 181.

   We surely affirm that talking about freedom plus responsibility is an advance over freedom as unaccountability, yet we find ourselves unpersuaded that Robin West's appropriation of Havel is anything other than a tactical move to shore up the basic liberal agenda (e.g., Ronald Dworkin, whom she cites approvingly). We think West is being less than faithful to Havel's context, which, as she concedes, was opposition to bureaucratic totalitarianism, and to his content, which we think is as spiritual as it is secular, as the passages quoted above indicate. For West's rendition of Havel's notion of freedom and its application to abortion, see her "Foreword: Taking Freedom Seriously," 104 Harvard L. Rev. 43–47, 63–85 (1990).

   For a recent effort by Ronald Dworkin to refine Roe v. Wade (and allow for the limited restrictions upheld in Casey), see "Unenumerated Rights: Whether and How Roe Should Be Overruled," 59 U. of Chicago L. Rev. 381–432 (1992), as well as his "The Center Holds!" N.Y. Rev. of Books, Aug. 13, 1992, at 29–33. Dworkin's argument, which is not unlike that of Tribe (see Introduction supra) in its closure of the middle, depends ultimately on rigid dichotomies between "derivative" and "detached," on the one hand, and "responsibility" and "conformity," on the other.

58 Presbyterian Church (USA), supra note 49, at 32.
59 Joseph Fletcher, "Abortion and the True Believer," in Abortion: The Moral Issues (ed. Edward Batchelor, Jr., Pilgrim Press, 1982) (first published in Christian Century, Nov. 27, 1974). Fletcher criticizes two primary lines of thought underlying an antiabortion position. The first one tends to be religious, and is either metaphysical or revelatory. The metaphysical approach sees the fetus as containing the substance "person," so that aborting the fetus is the same as murdering an innocent person. Opponents using the revelatory argument claim they have learned that "God's eternal will has sanctified the fetus." Though often used together, these are not mutually inclusive stances. The second line of thought highlights ethical, rather than religious, arguments, concluding that there is greater value in the potential of a fetus as opposed to all other values, prefer-

ences, or choices. *Id.* at 141–42. Fletcher rejects the "dogmatic" or "absolutist" assertions that protecting the "person in the fetus" is always "the highest good (summum bonum)" or that the potential of a fetus must always be given a "first-order value . . . regardless of the situation or circumstances." *Id.* at 140, 142. The "great majority of us," he writes, view abortion as an ethical rather than religious matter, weighing "[w]hether present human value should be traded off for or subordinated to future fetal values" in assessing the "proportionate good." Approached in this way, a good case can sometimes be made for abortion, whether it happens to be for medical reasons or personal reasons." *Id.* at 142. "It is difficult if not impossible to see how church metaphysics or divine revelations or individual value preference can be imposed by law on those who do not believe them to be either true or wise." *Id.*

Charles Hartshorne also rejects the metaphysical "substance" argument, claiming that "[a] fetus is not a person but a *potential* person." "Concerning Abortion: An Attempt at a Rational View," *Christian Century,* Jan. 21, 1981, at 42, 44. A fetus lacks the qualities attributable to humans and persons; "[i]t cannot speak, reason or judge between right and wrong. It cannot have personal relations, without which a person is not functionally a person at all, until months . . . have passed. . . . A possible individual person is one thing; an actual person is another. If this difference is not important, what is?" *Id.* at 42–45. Hartshorne details the endless number of changes and factors that interplay between the stage of fertilized egg and the point of actual human. Identical twins receive different stimuli in the womb and develop differently, for example, despite their identical genetic makeup. Even infants are "not fully human" since they cannot, at that stage, do many of the same things that a fetus cannot do, such as reason or judge right from wrong. "But [infants are] much closer to that stage than is a three month old fetus." *Id.* at 43–44. "That persons have rights is a universal belief in our society, but that a fetus is already an actual person—about that there is and there can be no consensus." *Id.* at 45.

The emphasis in Hartshorne on the potential human in the fetus versus an actual human is a reflection of his belief in process theology. This school is grounded in the metaphysical and religious writings of Alfred North Whitehead. *See,* for example, Whitehead, *Process and Reality: An Essay in Cosmology* (Macmillan, 1929), and *Religion in the Making* (Macmillan, 1926). Process theologians have adopted the priority that Whitehead's metaphysics gave to an existential "becoming" as opposed to "being" or "substance" as the basis of reality. Becoming is events or processes through which entities interact in unconsciously choosing their potential. Actual entities are not substances, but moments in a temporal background of series of events. Subjectivity and free choice are key in the sociality in which these entities are necessarily part. Thus "each successive 'actual occasion [or entity]' creatively determines itself within limits as it responds to its grasp of the previous state to which it is the successor and of its [social] environment, including in the latter the lures of what it is possible for it to become." "Process Theology," in *Westminster Dictionary of Christian Theology* 467, 468 (ed. Alan Richardson & John S. Bowden, Westminster Press, 1983). Thus, the potentiality of the Hartshorne's fetus will be fulfilled through a continuous series of temporal events after which it can be called "actual" human. Process theology can also be helpful in providing a context for a woman's decision regarding abortion: "It is important for her to recognize . . . that her decisions are made in a world in which there is a call to do good, a call to be generous, a call to self-fulfillment. But it is also a world in which it is also certain that creation both recovers from wrong decisions and continues to be alive to the processes of creation. It is important for her to be open to the possibility that the way this 'works' is not best understood by natural law, but by forgiveness. . . . In this perspective, she may recognize that God's purposes include her freedom to choose, and that God's resources of imagination and forgiveness are available to heal, direct, and enrich her life whatever she decides. Her life may be lived responsibly and creatively with or without a pregnancy to complete and the gains and losses involved, though real, are not the last word on anything." Harrison, *supra* note 35, at 87–88, quoting Lamberg, "Becoming Human: A Contextual Approach to Decisions About Pregnancy and Abortion," in *Feminism and Process Thought* (ed. S. G. Daveney, E. Mellen Press, 1981). For more detail on process theology, *see generally, id.* at 84–90; John B. Cobb & David Ray Griffin, *Process Theology, An Introductory Exposition* (Westminster Press, 1976). *See also* Douglas Sturm, "Religious Sensibility and the Reconstruction of Public Life: Prospectus for a New America," in *Religion and American Public Life* (ed. Robin Lovin, Paulist Press, 1986).

60 Schaeffer, *supra* note 12, at 141.

61 Presbyterian Church (USA), *supra* note 49, at inside front cover.

62 W. H. Willimon, "A Uniquely Christian Stand on Abortion," *Christian Century,* Feb. 27, 1991, at 220, 221. Willimon is contrasting the positions of "The Durham Declaration: To United Methodists on Our Church and Abortion," promulgated by "about 30 people, . . . pastors, professors and lay-people" who are "increasingly uncomfortable with their church's stand—or lack thereof—on abortion." *Id.* at 220. He applauds the reliance on "biblical, theological and ecclesiastic language," as opposed to the "secular political or social science" terms of the church's official statement. *Id.* at 221. The official statement refers to a "degree of control" over reproduction regarding which the church is "reluctant to approve abortion" while simultaneously recognizing "the sacredness of the life and well-being of the mother." The church concludes, "a decision concerning abortion should be made only after thoughtful and prayerful consideration by the parties involved, with medical, pastoral, and other appropriate counsel." *The Book of Discipline of the United Methodist Church* 96 (1988) (the passage remains substantially unchanged in the 1992 version).

63 J. R. Kelly, "The Vanishing Middle in Abortion Politics," *Christian Century,* Aug. 3–10, 1988, at 708. The ACCL was formed at the same time as the National Right to Life Committee in May 1973 by Joseph A. Lampe, one of the latter organization's incorporators. It stayed out of the spotlight until a year later when Lampe and several others sought a more "pragmatic" approach. Lampe described the group's failure as the product of "[t]hings [being] too ideological. . . . [Y]ou had these two camps, and it was hard to position yourself in the middle and attract a constituency. We thought it was out there and it probably is. But these people are quiet." *Id.* at 709–10. Margaret Farley described the problem in 1974 as "an impasse not only in moral discourse, or in struggles between

wants and beliefs, or in political battles for different sorts of law. . . . It is, rather, an impasse in efforts either to mediate or to join issue between what are fundamentally opposing conscience claims, profoundly different experiences of moral obligation." Farley, "Liberation, Abortion and Responsibility," in *On Moral Medicine: Theological Perspectives in Medical Ethics* 434 (ed. Stephen E. Lammers & Allen Verhey, W. B. Eerdmans, 1987) (originally published in *Reflection* 71 9–13 (May 1974).

64   *See, e.g.*, David Richards, "Constitutional Privacy, Religious Disestablishment, and the Abortion Decisions," in *Abortion: Moral and Legal Perspectives* 148 (ed. Jay L. Garfield & Patricia Hennessey, U. of Massachusetts Press, 1984). Tribe himself made this argument back in 1973 and later repudiated it. *Compare* Tribe, "The Supreme Court, 1972 Term—Foreword: Toward a Model of Roles in the Due Process of Life and Law," 87 *Harvard L. Rev.* 1, 21–25 (1973), *with* Laurence H. Tribe, *American Constitutional Law* 1349–50 (2d ed., Foundation Press, 1988), *and* Tribe, *supra* note 1, at 116. *See generally*, F. M. Gedicks, "Public Life and Hostility to Religion," 78 *Va. L. Rev.* 671 (1992).

65   E.g., Bruce A. Ackerman, *Social Justice in the Liberal State* (Yale U. Press, 1980).

66   For continuing concern over religious warfare, *see, e.g.*, Jeffrey Stout, *Ethics After Babel* 223 (Beacon Press, 1988). Stanley Hauerwas points out that if the Enlightenment produced people incapable of killing each other in the name of God, it also produced people fully able to kill each other in the name of the nation-state. Hauerwas, *After Christendom?* 33 (Abingdon Press, 1991). Indeed, the withdrawal of religion from public life may lead the state to get into the business of "mystery and magic," since only the state can supply a public moral purpose. *See* Richard Neuhaus, *America Against Itself* 46 (U. of Notre Dame Press, 1992).

67   *See* Elizabeth Mensch & Alan Freeman, "Religion as Science/Science as Religion: Constitutional Law and the Fundamentalist Challenge," *Tikkun*, Nov.–Dec. 1987.

68   *See* George Armstrong Kelly, *Politics and Religious Consciousness in America* 42 (Transaction Books, 1984). Kelly's book is, in effect, an extended and complex meditation on the meaning of the "affinity" to which Tocqueville pointed, as well as one of the most sophisticated analyses of American church/state relations in the literature. Tocqueville also termed religion "first" among American political institutions; even though there was no direct connection between church and state, religion was of primary importance to American political freedom. *Id.* at 46. To the extent that Tocqueville overemphasized New England Calvinism as the model of American religion, his observations have been challenged. *See generally* Jon Butler, *Awash in a Sea of Faith: Christianizing the American People* 289–90 (Harvard U. Press, 1990) (contending that the historical reality was one of lively variousness and great sectarian diversity). On the importance of religion to those historic Americans, there is agreement. Of great contemporary significance is the debate over whether there was, is, or should be an American "civic" religion, derived more or less from Protestant tradition, and supplying Americans with a shared public basis for moral understanding. For an introduction to this debate, *see* Robert N. Bellah, *The Broken Covenant: American Civil Religion in Time of Trial* (Seabury Press, 1975); Robert N. Bellah & Phillip E. Hammond, *Varieties of Civil Religion* (Harper & Row, 1980); Robert N. Bellah,

R. Madsen, W. Sullivan, A. Swidler, & S. Tipton, *Habits of the Heart: Individualism and Commitment in American Life* 219–96 (U. of California Press, 1985); *Uncivil Religion: Interreligious Hostility in America* (ed. Robert N. Bellah & Frederick E. Greenspahn, Crossroad Press, 1987); Michael W. Hughey, *Civil Religion and Moral Order: Theoretical and Historical Dimensions* (Greenwood Press, 1983); Martin E. Marty, *The Public Church: Mainline-Evangelical-Catholic* (Crossroad Press, 1981); Richard Neuhaus, *The Naked Public Square: Religion and Democracy in America* (W. B. Eerdmans, 1984); *NOMOS XXX: Religion, Morality, and the Law* (ed. J. Roland Pennock & John W. Chapman, NYU Press, 1988); *see also*, Lovin, "Perry, Naturalism, and Religion in Public" 63 *Tulane L. Rev.* 1517 (1989).

69   Kelly, *supra* note 68, at 41.

70   *Id.* at 41.

71   *Id.* at 24.

72   *Id.* at 48. On the inverse relation between religious and political control, *see id.* at 25–26 (quoting Montesquieu): "He who has no religion at all is that terrible animal who can only feel his freedom when he is destroying or devouring." *Id.* at 26.

73   *Id.* at 27.

74   *Id.* at 43 (emphasis added).

75   *Id.*

76   *Id.* at 12 (quoting Berger). As Berger also writes: "Human life has always had a day-side and a night-side, and, inevitably, because of the practical requirements of man's being in the world, it has always been the day-side that has received the strongest 'accent of reality.' But the night-side, even if exorcised, was rarely denied. One of the most astonishing consequences of secularization has been just this denial. Modern society has banished the night from consciousness, as far as this is possible. The treatment of death in modern society, especially in America, is the sharpest manifestation of this." *A Rumor of Angels* 93 (Doubleday, 1969). Meanwhile, ultimate questions of life and death are not only suppressed in practice, but are "theoretically liquidated by relegating them to meaninglessness" in modern philosophy.

77   Eberhard Jungel, *Karl Barth: A Theological Legacy* 98 (Westminster Press, 1986) (quoting Barth).

78   *Id.* at 99.

79   *Id.* at 101. For Barth's own essentially Augustinian formulation of church/state relations, *see* Kelly, *supra* note 68, at 174–75. Kelly views Barth's formulation as similar to the practice adopted by the New England Calvinists. Notably, in a rerun of the Milgram experiment, those with either a high or low degree of religious commitment were significantly less likely to be obedient than those with a "moderate" commitment. The researchers explained: "In the Judeo-Christian tradition, a high value is placed on a strong, well-defined response to 'the will of God.' In fact, a decisive response even if negative is to be preferred over neutrality. The Biblical position is that the man who is undecided about basic religious issues is unable to be decisive when confronted by an ethical dilemma. His tendency is to forfeit his choice to any impinging power. On the other hand, having taken a definite religious stance, one is in a position to act in accord with conscience." Kenneth D. Wald, *Religion and Politics in*

the United States 283 (St. Martin's Press, 1987). For a discussion of the relationship between membership in a family with strong religious conviction and a willingness to be a rescuer of Jews during Nazism, *see* Neuhaus, *supra* note 66, at 104–19.

80   For the complexity of the relationship between government action and religion, showing that politics cannot be "inconsequential" to religion, even when calling itself "neutral," *see* Wuthnow, *supra* note 9, at 319.

81   *See, e.g.*, Hauerwas, "A Christian Critique of Christian America," in NOMOS XXX 110–33, *supra* note 68; Littell, "The Churches and the Body Politic," in *Religion in America* 24–44 (ed. William G. McLoughlin & Robert N. Bellah, Houghton Mifflin, 1968). The central, and somewhat paradoxical, argument of Wills's *Under God* is that American religion owes its continuing vitality and visible presence in public life to the American tradition of insistent church/state separation. *Supra* note 10.

82   The classic work describing the possible relationships between religious communities and the public sphere, from a theological perspective, is H. Richard Niebuhr, *Christ and Culture* (Faber and Faber, 1952). For a recent application of Niebuhr to First Amendment religion issues, *see* Michael McConnell, "Christ, Culture, and Courts: A Niebuhrian Examination of First Amendment Jurisprudence" (forthcoming, *DePaul L. Rev.*).

83   *See* Hauerwas, *supra* note 66, at 36.

84   Lesslie Newbigin, *The Gospel in a Pluralist Society* 208–9 (W. B. Eerdmans, 1989). Newbigin points out that there is an anarchic strain to Protestantism, but it usually does not predominate.

85   *See, e.g.*, Butler, *supra* note 68, at 257–62; Marty, *supra* note 68, at 150–54. For an excellent and sensitive anthropological account of a contemporary Baptist community, focusing specifically on its relation to law and dispute resolution, *see* C. Greenhouse, *Praying for Justice: Faith, Order, and Community in an American Town* (Cornell U. Press, 1986). For a reprint of a "liberal" Baptist sermon endorsing the pro-choice position on abortion, on theological grounds, *see* Paynter, "Life in the Tragic Dimension," in *Ethics of Abortion, supra* note 24, at 143–50.

86   Quoted in Marty, *supra* note 68, at 78. On Williams as the unlikely sponsor of religious toleration, *see id.* at 75–78; Wills, *supra* note 10, at 341–53.

87   For a good overview, *see* Collinson, *supra* note 57, at 257–63. On the challenge to the legitimacy of law posed by Reformation thought, *see generally* David Little, *Religion, Order and Law* (Harper & Row, 1969). *See also* Elizabeth Mensch, "Religion, Revival, and the Ruling Class: A Critical History of Trinity Church," 36 *Buffalo L. Rev.* 427, 456–57 (1988).

If God saves through grace, not good works, then of what value are the external forms of order, whether in church or state? As St. Paul himself had asked, "Do we then overthrow the law by this faith?" Romans 3:31. If the true community could be founded only on the free assent of the redeemed, was not law an empty shell, to be rightly discarded? Nevertheless, most Protestants believed that the true voluntarism of the moment of redemption—to be protected at all costs from state authority—must be distinguished from "mad men acting according to their frantick passions, who should be restrained with chaines, when they can not be restrained otherwise." *See* Perry Miller,

The New England Mind: The Seventeenth Century 392 (Harvard U. Press, 1967). In a fallen world, the state, unlike the churches, must preserve order through law's coercive power rather than abandon the world to its own "Satanic devices." *See* Harold Berman, "Conscience and Law: The Lutheran Reformation and the Western Legal Tradition," 5 J. L. & Religion 177, 190 (1987). In that sense, law was not illegitimate, and the way was open for the Christian prince to do much good in the world. Nevertheless, the church order of pure voluntarism, where the sword should not be wielded, was inevitably a "better" order than that enforced by law. Moreover, while neither Luther nor Calvin wholly rejected the notion of natural law, the sharp distinction between noncoercive church order and the legal order of the state rendered problematic the older, all-embracing scholastic identification of civil order with a divinely ordained natural harmony. In that sense, political order could be more utilitarian and positivist, although not necessarily un-Christian. *See generally id.*

On law as serving a subordinate, "functional" rather than "ethical" role, of exposing "crucial danger spots" or "boundary" situations, and thereby becoming "instrumental to the divine activity," *see* Paul Louis Lehmann, *Ethics in a Christian Context* 146–47 (SCM Press, 1963). For the complexity of Calvin's approach to civil law, *see* Mary Lane Potter, "The 'Whole Office of the Law' in the Theology of John Calvin," 3 J. L. & Religion 117 (1985). For Barth's reformulation of the relation between law and gospel, *see* Jungel, *supra* note 77, at 105–26. On the problematic character of law in Lutheran theology, *see* Martin Luther, "Of the Double Use of the Law," in *Martin Luther: Selections from His Writings* 139–45 (ed. John Dillenberger, paperback ed., Doubleday, 1961); Martin Luther, "Secular Authority: To What Extent It Should Be Obeyed," in *id.* at 363–402. For Milner Ball's effort, drawing on the theology of Calvin, Barth, and Bonhoeffer, to reformulate the metaphor of law as "medium" instead of the traditionally dominant one of "bulwark" against "chaos," *see* Lying Down Together: Law, Metaphor, and Theology 119–36 (U. of Wisconsin Press, 1985). *See also* his more recent *The Word and the Law* (U. of Chicago Press, 1993).

88   *See generally* Mensch, *supra* note 87, at 427.

89   *See* Hauerwas, *supra* note 66, at 69–82.

90   Stanley Hauerwas and W. Willimon, *Resident Aliens: Life in a Christian Colony* (Abingdon Press, 1989). For Hauerwas's description of public/private and fact/value, *see also, e.g.,* Hauerwas, *supra* note 66, at 58–68. *See generally,* Stanley Hauerwas, *Against the Nations: War and Survival in a Liberal Society* (1985) and "Symposium," 44 Theology Today 69 (Apr. 1987). On the other hand, Ronald Thiemann argues that serious Protestants should be attentive to "the resources liberalism might provide for the reconstruction of a political ethos that honors the pluralism of contemporary public life" and seek a more "nuanced engagement of Christian theology with America's predominant political philosophy" than Hauerwas thinks possible. Thiemann would want Christian theology to contribute "not to the death of liberal democracy but to its moral renewal." *See Constructing a Public Theology: The Church in a Pluralistic Culture* 24–25 (Westminster/John Knox Press, 1991). We take his view of liberalism as basically consistent with that of Jeffrey Stout (*supra* note 66, at 220–42) and as consistent with Stout's notion of moral bricolage (*e.g., id.* at 74–77). Richard Neuhaus, Lutheran (now turned

Roman Catholic) has more emphatically taken liberalism to be compatible with Christianity, and the two to be joined in their rejection of totalitarianism. *See* Neuhaus, "Christianity and Democracy," *Center Journal* (Summer 1983).

91   On religion as a "lens" through which the world is seen, *see* Newbigin, *supra* note 84, at 38. *See also* Hauerwas, "The Gesture of a Truthful Story," 42 *Theology Today* 181, 182 (July 1985): "For without the church, the world has no means to know that it is the world . . . 'the distinction between church and world is not something God has imposed upon the world by prior metaphysical definition, nor is it only something which timid or pharisaical Christians have built up around themselves. It is all of that in creation that has taken the freedom not yet to believe' " (quoting John Howard Yoder).

92   *See, e.g.,* Hauerwas, *supra* note 66, at 99–111.

93   Stanley Hauerwas, "Will the Real Sectarian Stand Up?" 44 *Theology Today* 87 (April, 1987).

94   Neuhaus, *supra* note 66. Neuhaus is editor of *First Things*, a journal dedicated to exploring those possibilities of dialogue.

95   Gramwell, "Religion and Reason in American Politics," in *Religion and American Public Life, supra* note 59, at 88. Gramwell argues that if religiously grounded assertions cannot be subject to the reasoned debate that the Founders thought possible, then both "outsider" legalists and believers will be stuck forever within the separationist/establishment quandary (*id.* at 107).

96   For a critical summary of these attempts, *see* George A. Lindbeck, *The Nature of Doctrine: Religion and Theology in a Postliberal Age* 15–32 (Westminster Press, 1984), discussing especially the very influential work of Karl Rahner and Bernard Lonergan. See also Nicholas Wolterstorff, "Can Belief in God Be Rational If It Has No Foundation?" in *Faith and Rationality: Reason and Belief in God* 135–86 (ed. Alvin Platinga and Nicholas Wolterstorff, U. of Notre Dame Press, 1983). For a summary of the extensive work of Wolfhart Pannenberg, directed toward an anthropology that would guard religion from the charge of subjectivism, see D. Holwerda, "Faith, Reason and the Resurrection," in *Faith and Rationality*, at 265.

97   The classic attack on foundationalism is Richard Rorty, *Philosophy and the Mirror of Nature* (Princeton U. Press, 1979).

98   Rorty, "The Priority of Democracy to Philosophy," as discussed in Stout, *supra* note 66, at 226–33, and Hauerwas, *supra* note 66, at 74–88. For criticism of the priority that Rorty gives to the private rather than the public realm, to the romantic self-creating "strong poets" rather than the moral claims of egalitarianism, *see* Joan Williams, "Rorty, Radicalism, Romanticism: The Politics of the Gaze," 1992 *Wisconsin L. Rev.* 143–55.

99   Tracy, "Defending the Public Character of Theology," *Christian Century* 350, 351 (April 1, 1981).

100   *Id.*

101   *Id.* at 353.

102   Tracy's major works are *Blessed Rage for Order* (Seabury Press, 1975) and *The Analogical Imagination: Christian Theology and the Culture of Pluralism* (Crossroad Press, 1981). For Stout's reservations, *see supra* note 66, at 164–66. The question is whether Tracy truly escapes the trap of foundationalism, especially the experiential

variety. *See also* Lindbeck, *supra* note 96, at 136. For a brief introduction to the complexity of Tracy's thought, *see* "The Uneasy Alliance Reconceived: Catholic Theological Method, Modernity, and Postmodernity" 50 *Theological Studies* 548–70 (1989).

103   Michael J. Perry, *Love and Power: The Role of Religion and Morality in American Politics* (Oxford U. Press, 1991).

104   Perry's critics have chided him for seeking to structure exclusionary rules of discourse. *See, e.g.,* David Smolin, "Regulating Religious and Cultural Conflict in a Postmodern America: A Response to Professor Perry," 76 *Iowa L. Rev.* 1067–1104 (1991) (evangelical Christian perspective); Sanford Levinson, "Religious Language and the Public Square," 105 *Harvard L. Rev.* 2061–79 (1992) (inclusionary liberal perspective). Such criticisms, Smolin's in particular, have elicited thoughtful response from Perry himself. *See supra* note 103, at 139–45, 206–8.

105   *See, e.g.,* Lindbeck, *supra* note 96 at 20.

106   Paul Nelson, *Narrative and Morality: A Theological Inquiry* 75 (Pennsylvania State U. Press, 1987), quoting David Kelsey.

107   Ronald H. Thiemann, *Revelation and Theology* 94 (U. of Notre Dame Press, 1985), quoting Richard Bernstein. For a discussion of the cultural-linguistic approach to theology, *see, e.g.,* Thiemann, *id.*; Lindbeck, *supra* note 96; Nelson, *supra* note 106; Hans W. Frei, *The Eclipse of Biblical Narrative* (Yale U. Press, 1974) and *The Identity of Jesus Christ: The Hermeneutical Bases of Dogmatic Theology* (Fortress Press, 1975). This approach seems consistent with Jeffrey Stout's view that theology, if it wants to be taken seriously, must find again a "voice of its own, sufficiently distinctive to be interesting but sufficiently critical to be respected." "Review Symposium," 46 *Theology Today* 55, 71 (April 1989). Notably, however, the most important goal might not be one of academic acceptance, although there is surely some connection between academic acceptance and public attention. As Thiemann points out, the hard epistemological questions are of slight interest to the public; the effective practice of the narrative tradition is what is required for public attention. Thiemann, *supra* note 90 at 42–43.

108   *See* Stout, *supra* note 66.

109   *See infra,* p. 147.

110   Whether a state official should act as an ethical neopragmatist, doing moral bricolage, in Stout's terms, seems to us not an easy question. There may, however, be little sociological alternative. Stout himself does not seem to give a public model of bricolage as such, calling it something "individuals do." *See* James F. Gustafson, "Review Symposium," 46 *Theology Today* 55 (1989), at 70.

111   For a good account of this dilemma, *see* John O'Neill, "Property in Science and the Market," *Monist* 73, no. 4 (Oct. 1990), at 601–20.

112   *See* Mary Midgley, *Evolution as a Religion: Strange Hopes and Stranger Fears* (Methuen, 1985), at 103–4.

113   *Id.* at 143–44.

114   *Id.* at 143.

115   There is some dispute as to whether Gustafson, whose approach is emphatically theocentric, draws on a sufficiently "non-natural" view of God. *See, e.g.,* Lisa Cahill, "Consent in Time of Affliction: The Ethics of a Circumspect Theist," 13 *J. of Religious Ethics* 22–36 (1985). *See also,* Stout, *supra* note 66, at 163–88. Never-

theless, Gustafson's two-volume *Ethics* is a serious theological inquiry into the meaning of ecology.

116   *See* Gustafson, "Review Symposium," 46 *Theology Today* 55 (1989), at 71.

117   *See* Robert Casey, "What I Would Have Told the Democrats," *Wall Street Journal*, July 31, 1992, p. A14.

118   Planned Parenthood of Southeastern Pennsylvania v. Casey, 112 S.Ct. 2791 (U.S. Sup. Ct., June 29, 1992). For a characterization of *Casey* as eschewing a jurisprudence of "rules" and choosing instead a "moderate difference-splitting standard," see Kathleen Sullivan, "The Supreme Court 1991 Term—Foreword: The Justices of Rules and Standards," 106 *Harvard L. Review* 24–123 (1992).

119   448 U.S. 297 (1980).

120   Richard A. McCormick, *Health and Medicine in the Catholic Tradition: Tradition in Transition* 3 (Crossroad Press, 1985). In an earlier volume, McCormick offered an excellent review of the literature on abortion as a moral issue. *See How Brave a New World?—Dilemmas in Bioethics* 117–75 (Doubleday, 1981). Also instructive is his brief chapter, "Rules for Abortion Debate," id. at 176–88, which includes suggestions such as "Avoid the use of slogans" (id. at 178), "Represent the opposing position accurately and fairly" (id. at 179), "Admit doubts, difficulties, and weaknesses in one's own position" (id. at 181), "Distinguish morality and public policy," and "incorporate the woman's perspective, or women's perspectives" (id. at 186).

121   McCormick, *supra* note 120, at 135.

122   *Id.* at 136.

123   *Id.*

124   *Id.* at 137.

125   *Id.* at 137–38.

126   Heim, *supra* note 48.

127   The full text of the four major presentations at the National Dialogue on Abortion Perspectives is published in the January/February 1990 issue of *Church and Society* 80, no. 3. The dialogue resulted from a resolution of the 199th General Assembly of the Presbyterian Church (USA) (1987), recognizing that the "abortion question is a complex, multifaceted theological, moral, and legal problem, demanding for those struggling with it more than the polarizing slogans and win/lose confrontations to which Christian factionalism has subjected it" and hoping to promote "dialogue among the varying and diverging Christian perspectives on the abortion issue, thus creating a model of reconciliation for the church and the watching world." *Id.* at 1.

128   *See* "Presbyterians and Abortion," 108 *Christian Century* 192 (Feb. 20, 1991). Polling results are included as appendix A to the Report of the Special Committee on Problem Pregnancies and Abortion, presented to the 204th General Assembly (1992).

129   Special Committee on Problem Pregnancies and Abortion, *supra* 128.

130   *See* David Heim, "American Baptists Maximize the Middle" 105 *Christian Century* 660–62 (July 20–27, 1988).

131   *See* Willimon, *supra* note 62. An effort to amend the pro-choice position of the United Methodist Church was, however, voted down at the 1992 national meeting.

132   Quoted in R. Bellah, R. Madsen, W. Sullivan, A. Swidler, & S. Tipton, *The Good Society* (Knopf, 1991), at 201.

133   Among the signers were Governor Robert Casey of Pennsylvania, Richard Neuhaus, Mary Ann Glendon, Sidney Callahan, and Michael McConnell. For a thoughtful and sensitive discussion from the pro-life side, *see* James Kelly, "A Political Challenge to the Prolife Movement: Toward a Post-'Webster' Agenda," 117 *Commonweal* 692–96 (1990).

Afterword

1   We find ourselves in great agreement with Christopher Lasch's *The True and Only Heaven* (Norton, 1991). On the intellectual elite as "new class," and how its right- and left-wing members, despite their tendency to caricature each other, have more in common with one another than with the ostensible beneficiaries of their politics, *see* 509–29. Their common outlook, in its idealized form, writes Lasch, is "an inordinate respect for educational credentials, a refusal to accept anything on faith, a commitment to free inquiry, a tendency to question authority, a belief in tolerance as the supreme political virtue" (at 527). The downside of this "critical temper" is that it "can degenerate into a snobbish disdain for people who lack formal education and work with their hands, an unfounded confidence in the moral wisdom of experts, an equally unfounded prejudice against untutored common sense, a distrust of any expression of good intentions, a distrust of everything but science, an ingrained irreverence, a disposition (the natural outgrowth of irreverence and distrust) to see the world as something that exists only to gratify human desires."

2   *See* Dietrich Bonhoeffer, *Ethics* 146 (Macmillan, 1965). On the fundamentally Christian basis of Kant's moral philosophy, as well as his own confrontation with faith, *see* Paul Louis Lehmann, *Ethics in a Christian Context* (SCM Press, 1963), at 128, 165–89.

3   *See* Alasdair MacIntyre, *After Virtue*, (2d ed., U. of Notre Dame Press, 1984), at 34–72. For a similar account, *see* Charles Taylor, *Sources of the Self: The Making of the Modern Identity* 82–107 (Harvard U. Press, 1989). Another important book in this regard is Jeffrey Stout, *The Flight from Authority: Religion, Morality, and the Quest for Autonomy* (U. of Notre Dame Press, 1981), a rare instance of a secular philosophy book that takes theology seriously as an independent body of knowledge. *See id.* at 95–176. Notably, Stout places much emphasis on Barth, *id.* at 141–48, saying that "It would be hard to overestimate the importance of Barth's authorship, taken as a whole, in twentieth-century theology" (*id.* at 145) and that "[t]heology since Barth is a sad story." *Id.* at 147.

4   *See* MacIntyre, *supra* note 3, at 51–60.

5   *See id.* at 63–66, 70–71.

6   *See* Kelly, "Bayle's Commonwealth of Atheists Revisited," in *Religion, Morality and the Law* (ed. J. Roland Pennock & John W. Chapman, NYU Press, 1988), NOMOS XXX, at 78, 86.

7   For our own effort to talk about "responsible" capitalism, in the context of advertising and antitrust law, *see* Elizabeth Mensch & Alan Freeman, "Efficiency

and Image: Advertising as an Antitrust Issue," 1990 *Duke L.J.* 321; *see also* Amitai Etzioni, *The Moral Dimension: Toward a New Economics* (Free Press, 1988).

8   The Jewish Bible is, after all, the Christian Old Testament. The characteristically Christian injunction to "love your neighbor as yourself" appears first in the Torah, in Leviticus 19:17–18, 33–34. New England Calvinists, for example, identified themselves with the Israel of the Old Testament and, accordingly, "could as a people feel constituted by God's law." *See* Taylor, *supra* note 3, at 229–30. Jewish/Christian similarity/difference becomes even more complicated when one seeks to understand the early Christianity of, for example, the first century, A.D. The Sermon on the Mount, Matthew 5:3–7:27, which may be the oldest of Christian texts, is both a peculiarly Jewish Christian text and a peculiarly Christian Jewish text. *See generally* Hans Dieter Betz, *Essays on the Sermon on the Mount* (trans. Laurence Welborn, Fortress Press, 1985). *See also* Frank Kermode, "Matthew," in *The Literary Guide to the Bible* 387–401 (ed. Robert Alter & Frank Kermode, paperback ed., Belknap Press, 1990). On St. Paul as both Jew and Christian, *see* Alan F. Segal, *Paul the Convert: The Apostolate and Apostasy of Saul the Pharisee* (Yale U. Press, 1990).

9   It was just a small shift in orthodox Augustinian theology that led the Reformers to understand "faith, defined as a total and trustful commitment of the self to God, and in itself not a human achievement but the pure gift of God." That small shift was, however, important enough to topple the entire institutional and theological structure of the Catholic system. *See* Patrick Collinson, "The Late Medieval Church and Its Reformation (1400–1600)," in *The Oxford Illustrated History of Christianity* 233, 259 (ed. John McManners, Oxford U. Press, 1990). On the closeness of Augustinian Catholicism to radical (Roger Williams) Protestantism, *see* Garry Wills, *Under God: Religion and American Politics* (Simon & Schuster, 1990) at 349–50. On the other hand, Richard Neuhaus, who as a Lutheran minister had been an avid proponent of "civic religion," and is editor of the monthly *First Things*, became a Catholic, having decided that Luther's goals have been achieved and the Reformation should be over. *See New York Times*, Sept. 9, 1990, § 1, at 26. With respect to ethics and law, Paul Ramsey's *Nine Modern Moralists* (Prentice-Hall, 1962) is an effort to prove that neither "Catholic" essentialism/natural law/absolutism nor "Protestant" faith/immediacy/ particularity can effectively rule out the other, that both are two sides of the same ethical dilemma.

10 *See* Hall, "Commentary," in *Abortion and the Law* 224, 234 (ed. David T. Smith, Press of Western Reserve U., 1967). He expresses some incredulity, for example, that anything important might turn on "the meaning of a five-word phrase in the book of Exodus." *Id.* at 231.

11 In this retrospect, three works, dismissed at the time for their affront to orthodoxy, seem more prophetic in retrospect: Ernest Becker, *The Denial of Death* (Free Press, 1973) (cultural anthropologist criticizing orthodox Freudianism for its failure to understand religion, and, consequently, death); Jacques Ellul, *The Betrayal of the West* (trans. Matthew J. O'Connell, Seabury Press, 1978) (French Protestant criticizing Western Marxism); Frederick Henry Heinemann, *Existentialism and the Modern Predicament* (paperback ed., Harper, 1958) (criticism "from

within," with emphasis on religion and theology). *See also* MacIntyre, *supra* note 3, at 103 (reminding us of our "vulnerability and fragility"). In a similar vein, *see* Ball, "The City of Unger," 81 *Northwestern U.L. Rev.* 625 (1987) (reviewing R. Unger, *Politics* [1987]), in which he suggests that "the City of Unger has room it seems to me, only for an elite that is both intellectually and politically athletic" (*id.* at 641), that Unger's "self-transcending self travels deeper into its own space, losing contact with the limiting love of the neighbor and therefore with the possibility of transcendence" (*id.* at 661); moreover, he chides Unger for trusting "in the ultimate harmony of being and goodness in human nature," and, consequently, leaving "out of account" what the "Bible calls sin" (*id.* at 661 & n.196 (quoting Unger, *Knowledge and Politics* 247 [1975]).

12   For a good account, *see* Page Smith, *Killing the Spirit: Higher Education in America* (Viking, 1990), at 99–107 ("Although most Americans remained doggedly religious, academic fundamentalism banished from the academy any form of belief for which there was 'insufficient evidence' except the belief in the immutability and sufficiency of Science").

13   Which Karl Barth understood as well as anyone. *See* chap. 3, *supra.* One of the most astute twentieth-century philosophers of science, Michael Polanyi, affirmed both the provisionality of knowledge and the significance of presuppositions, and, like Barth, saw the resemblance, rather than opposition, between theology and science. As Polanyi describes Christian religious faith: "The indwelling of the Christian worshipper is therefore a continued attempt at breaking out, at casting off the condition of man, even while humbly acknowledging its inescapability. Such indwelling is fulfilled most completely when it increases this effort to the utmost. It resembles not the dwelling within a great theory of which we enjoy the complete understanding . . . but the heuristic upsurge which strives to break through the accepted frameworks of thought, guided by the intimations of discoveries still beyond our horizon. Christian worship sustains, as it were, an eternal, never to be consummated hunch: a heuristic vision which is accepted for the sake of its unresolvable tension. It is like an obsession with a problem known to be insoluble, which yet follows, against reason, unswervingly, the heuristic command: 'Look at the unknown!' Christianity sedulously fosters, and in a sense permanently satisfies, man's craving for mental dissatisfaction by offering him the comfort of a crucified God." *Personal Knowledge: Towards a Post-Critical Philosophy* 198–99 (Harper Torchbooks, 1964). For both science and religion, absolute truth is the illusion: "Objectivism has totally falsified our conception of truth, by exalting what we can know and prove, while covering up with ambiguous utterances all that we know and *cannot* prove, even though the latter knowledge underlies, and most ultimately set its seal to, all that we *can* prove. In trying to restrict our minds to the few things that are demonstrable, and therefore explicitly dubitable, it has overlooked the a-critical choices which determine the whole being of our minds and has rendered us incapable of acknowledging these vital choices." *Id.* at 286. Even more dramatically, we are learning today from the insights of chaos theory just how accurate was Barth's understanding of the limited character of scientific knowledge. *See generally* Heinz-Otto Peitgen, Hartmut Jürgens, & Dietmar Saupe, *Chaos and Fractals: New Frontiers of Science*

(Springer-Verlag, 1992); James Gleick, *Chaos: Making of a New Science* (Viking, 1987).

14 Dietrich Bonhoeffer, *Letters and Papers from Prison* 208–9 (SCM Press, 1953).

15 *See* Becker, *supra* note 11, at 268–81; MacIntyre, *supra* note 3, at 73–78.

16 Jonathan Edwards had a different view of the matter. He understood that it is difficult to reconcile the "expectation of worldly success and happiness, so often undone by events, with the idea of a just, loving, and all-powerful creator." For Edwards, the reality was "a God who did not regard human happiness as the be-all and end-all of creation," and the "central paradox of Christian faith" was "that the secret of happiness lay in renouncing the right to be happy." *See* Lasch, *supra* note 1, at 248 (discussing Edwards). On Edwards, *see id.* at 246–56. On "rights," *see* MacIntyre, *supra* note 3, at 68–70, 119.

17 Becker, *supra* note 11, at 282–83. Despite his criticisms of Freud, Becker does acknowledge, approvingly, the "somber pessimism" of *Civilization and Its Discontents. See id.* at 281. Similarly, Iris Murdoch notes that Freud "presents us with . . . a realistic and detailed picture of the fallen man." Iris Murdoch, *The Sovereignty of Good* (Schocken, 1971), at 51.

18 *See* Job 38–42:6.

19 *See* Lasch, *supra* note 1, at 487–92, 530.

Index

......

Elizabeth Mensch and Alan Freeman are spouses as well as colleagues at the School of Law of the State University of New York at Buffalo. They have authored numerous articles and reviews, both singly and jointly, on topics ranging from civil rights to colonial history. Over the past few years their scholarship has taken a distinctly collaborative turn. They have contributed chapters to *The Politics of Law*, *The Blackwell Encyclopedia of the American Revolution*, *The Tikkun Anthology*, and *Animal Experimentation*, and recently coedited their own two-volume anthology, *Property Law*. They are also members of the advisory committee of the *Journal of Law and Religion*. The authors live in Amherst, New York, where their household includes two children, one dog, one cat, and a small lop-eared rabbit.

Library of Congress Cataloging-in-Publication Data
Mensch, Elizabeth.
The politics of virtue : is abortion debatable? / Elizabeth Mensch and Alan Freeman.
Originally published as a special supplement, "The Politics of virtue: animals, theology, and abortion," Georgia law review 25, no. 4 (1991).
Includes index.
ISBN 0-8223-1331-6 (cloth : alk. paper).—ISBN 0-8223-1349-9 (pbk. : alk. paper)
1. Abortion—United States. 2. Abortion—Moral and ethical aspects.   I. Freeman, Alan, 1943–   .   II. Title.
HQ767.5.U5M476   1993
363.4'6—dc20   92-41302 CIP